Second Edition

Economics
Ideas and Issues
For a Sustainable World

Jerry Evensky

PEARSON

Custom
Publishing

Cover images courtesy of Getty Images.

This book is dedicated to the memory of Mr. Herbert Behrend. Mr. Behrend taught me algebra, chemistry and physics in high school, but more than that, he taught me the meaning of vision. He showed me that to study one dimension of human experience is valid only if that study is set into a vision of the many dimensions of our experience. In his classroom I learned physics in the context of its history and its relationship to the development of the arts and literature. He was truly a man of vision. I hope that I have honored his memory by communicating some measure of that vision here.

This book is and always will be a work in progress. Progress depends on rich, constructive feedback from the students and faculty who use it. If you use this book and have comments, suggestions, or corrections to offer, please send them to me at jevensky@syr.edu.

In order to ensure that your feedback gets processed correctly, please put the word *text*, and <u>only</u> the word *text*, on the subject line of your email. Thank you in advance for any feedback you offer.

Jerry Evensky

Printed in the United States of America

10 9 8 7 6 5 4 3 2

ISBN 0-536-51353-8 (paper)
ISBN 0-536-52046-1 (cloth)

2007160848 (paper)
2007160900 (cloth)

LH/SD

Please visit our web site at *www.pearsoncustom.com*

PEARSON CUSTOM PUBLISHING
501 Boylston Street, Suite 900, Boston, MA 02116
A Pearson Education Company

TABLE OF CONTENTS

TABLE OF CONTENTS—DETAILED

1.0 INTRODUCTION

AN INTRODUCTION TO *ECONOMICS: THE IDEAS, THE ISSUES*

In the pages that follow you will find explanations and applications of a sophisticated set of economic tools for systematic analysis and critical thinking about significant ideas and issues . . . past, present, and future. The economic analysis presented here is the core of any standard text. What sets this book apart is that

- It is written in a voice that speaks to you.
- It is designed for developmental learning so that step by step you move from a simple to a very complex and very powerful framework of analysis.
- It uses examples that are historically significant and/or personally accessible.
- It integrates micro and macroeconomic analysis.
- It is informed by the history of economic thought.
- It sets the economics analysis into larger social and political contexts addressing issues like the role of social stereotyping, political power struggles, and ethics in market systems.
- It addresses the central issue of our modern economic system, sustainability, at every stage in the presentation of the analysis.

1.1 GENERAL INTRODUCTION TO OUR STUDY

1.1.1 Introduction

Our subject is economics. We'll be exploring economics somewhat like we might explore an ecosystem such as a forest. There are many individual elements to a forest—the trees, the flowers, the insects, the animals, and so on. Each of these is important and worthy of note and investigation in its own right. But the forest is not just the sum of all the elements that make it up. It is all those things . . . and it is the web of connections makes them into a single wholeness—an ecosystem we call a forest.

Economic systems are like that. There are lots of individual elements that we will need to identify and understand. But as with a forest, we can only fully appreciate and understand the *system* that is an economy by setting all its elements into the web of connections that makes the economy a single wholeness—an economic system, or an *econosystem* if you will.

My goal here is to help you understand and learn the principles of economic systems. (Hi Nina!)

1.1.2 My Goal—Understanding and Learning

I just used the terms "understand and learn". Let me explain my usage.

To understand is to follow the analysis I present—to "get it." To learn is to master that analysis—to "own it." When you "own it" you can use its logic for systematic critical thinking . . . you can think more richly for yourself.

Understanding is a prerequisite for learning. You can understand how to ride a bike by watching someone do it, but to understand is not to learn. You might understand how to ride a bike, but not be able to do it. You might follow my explanation of supply and demand, but not be able to apply it. To take what you understand and then learn it requires that you practice with it. To learn to ride a bike requires getting on and trying until you have transformed what you understand into a real feel for it so you can do it yourself. Similarly, the only way to learn the economics that follows is to make sure that you understand it—if you are not sure you do, ask your teacher questions—then when you have "got it", practice with what you understand until you "own it". If you carefully develop your understanding and then practice and play with the ideas to learn them, when you are done you will have a good grade, but more importantly you will have an excellent education. Grades are letter or number labels that reflect what you seem to have learned. An education is what you have learned.

I hope you get a good grade in this course . . . But my real goal is that in 20 years you will be reading or listening to or watching a thoughtful commentary on world events and you will think: "Gosh, I could never have followed the web of connections in these issues so clearly if it hadn't been for that econ course I took." That is what a successful education does for you.

1.1.3 On Language and Definitions

In order to make a point about my goal for you, I defined the terms "understanding" and "learning." I am quite certain you know these words, so why did I bother to define them? Because while I know that you know the words, I also know that the definitions you associate with these words may not be the ones I mean. A word can mean many things. If we do not share the same meanings, then even though you know the words I use, we will not be communicating. I defined those terms just now because I do not want to "talk" at you, I want to communicate with you.

In the pages that follow I will be defining a lot of terms. Most will be words you already know. But in many cases these words have very specific meanings in economic analysis, and you will not follow that analysis if you do not know what the words mean to an economist.

1.1.4 Economics as a Tool

Economics is a tool for thinking about the world in which we live. I want you to be able to use this tool skillfully and enjoy using it for the rest of your life. But keep in mind: Economics is just one tool. It's like a hammer in a carpenter's tool kit. A carpenter cannot build much of beauty or value with just a hammer—but she cannot build much without it either. To build, a carpenter needs a hammer, and also a saw, and a level, and a plane, and so on. She needs a complete tool kit.

Economics is like that hammer. It's an invaluable tool if you want to build a rich understanding of the human condition, of how societies work and how they evolve. But it's just one tool, and alone it's not very productive. If you want to get the most out of economic analysis, you will need to use it in concert with political and social theory, You will need to practice using these tools together by applying them to history and/or anthropology and/or current events. If you develop a full social science tool kit and hone your ability to use those tools together to study the human condition past, present, and future; you'll have a tool kit that will enrich the rest of your life.

1.1.5 The Limits of Economics

We will be developing a model to represent the economic system. The model we will develop is not an absolute Truth that economists have passed down from generation to generation. It is the current dominate view that has emerged from several hundred years of debate, and that debate continues. Along the way, as I present this model, I will try to point out sources of debate about its structure and the policy implications of its logic. If you master the current state of economic thinking and understand the points of debate, you can appreciate the model's strengths, recognize its potential weaknesses, and observe or participate thoughtfully in the debates of today and the development of model for tomorrow.

At the end of this study you won't have all the answers. There is no answer key as to how the world works at the back of the book. What I hope you will have is a tool that will help you ask insightful questions, and that will help you to develop systematic, thoughtful answers to those questions.

We begin our study by defining the subject of economics. Then I'll describe the method we'll use to study this subject.

1.2 THE SUBJECT OF ECONOMICS

1.2.1 "The Road Not Taken" by Robert Frost

Before you read on, write down what you would have chosen to do with this time if you were not here reading this text. Be realistic; don't put down "Sitting on the beach in Cancun." Put down what you reasonably think is the choice you gave up (having dinner, doing your laundry, watching TV, studying bio . . .) to be doing this.

OK, now let's start economics.

A great place to begin is with Robert Frost:

The Road Not Taken
by
Robert Frost

Two roads diverged in a yellow wood,
And sorry I could not travel both
And be one traveler, long I stood
And looked down one as far as I could
To where it bent in the undergrowth;

Then took the other, as just as fair,
And having perhaps the better claim,
Because it was grassy and wanted wear;
Though as for that the passing there
Had worn them really about the same,

And both that morning equally lay
In leaves no step had trodden black.
Oh, I kept the first for another day!
Yet knowing how way leads on to way,
I doubted if I should ever come back.

I shall be telling this with a sigh
Somewhere ages and ages hence:
Two roads diverged in a wood, and I—
I took the one less traveled by,
And that has made all the difference.

1.2.2 On Scarcity

Economics is about how humans function individually and collectively in the "ordinary business of life" (Alfred Marshall, *Principles of Economics*, 1890). In "The Road Not Taken," Frost focuses on the issue that according to economists lies at the heart of human experience: We have to make choices, and making choices is a challenge.

"Two roads diverged in a yellow wood, and sorry I could not travel both and be one traveler, long I stood . . ." We cannot be one traveler and travel both, to choose one direction in life is to give up another. Why can't we do it all? Because our resources, our money and/or our time, are scarce. The study of economic life begins from the fact that we all face scarcity and thus we must each make choices.

1.2.3 Scarce Money

Consider your own life. You have limited funds; you cannot buy everything you desire. When you do buy something, you spend that money and it's gone. Whenever you spend money on one thing, you are giving up the opportunity to spend that limited resource, that money, on something else.

Now let's meet the very first term in the language of economics you will be learning. Economists call the *best* forgone opportunity you give up when you make any choice the *opportunity cost* of the choice you have made. It is the cost of choosing.

A little while ago I asked you to think about what you would have chosen to do with this time if you were not here reading this economics book. That "best available option you gave up" is your opportunity cost of doing this—it's the price of choosing this.

Every choice you make in a world of limited resources has an opportunity cost. That is why making choices is a challenge.

1.2.4 Scarce Time

But what if you were rich? I mean *really* rich! What if you had billions of dollars? Would you still have to make choices? It seems like billions of dollars would be enough to buy anything you could possibly desire. Let's assume it is. Let us assume you have all the money you could ever want. Then you have escaped the challenge of choice—right? Wrong! To enjoy all that you want requires not only money, it requires time.

Even if you had all the money you could ever hope to spend, your time is limited—very limited . . . and, unlike money, it cannot be stored up and saved for another day. As each moment of your life goes by, it is a moment spent and gone forever. You can capture these moments in pictures, but they are just images of times past. Each moment is in the next moment only a memory. If you are lucky you will live a long and happy life, but inevitably and inexorably time goes by.

You may be able to prolong your life with money, but by 80 or 90, or almost certainly by 100, your time resources will be exhausted, your life will be over. The lesson here is that time is a scarce resource for each of us, so all of us, from the richest to the poorest, face the challenge of choice.

OK, so scarcity applies to individuals, but how about to society as a whole? Does society face a challenge of choice? Yes.

Society faces a scarcity issue that is in some sense the opposite of that confronting each of us as an individual. For you and me, the natural resources of the earth are so great that relative to our desires they are virtually infinite. Time is the resource that is inevitably scarce for each of us as an individual. In contrast humankind could conceivably continue to exist beyond any time horizon we can imagine. So for humankind, time is not necessarily scarce. Humankind, however, includes several billions of us now and our numbers are growing rapidly. Relative to the needs and desires of all of us put together, the resources of the earth are scarce.

As I write this, billions of people around the globe—in China, in Russia, in Nigeria, in countless countries—are striving to achieve the standard of living that most United States families take for granted. If every family in China used resources to the degree each family in the United States does today, is that a sustainable prospect? Given our current model for production and consumption, does the earth have the resources to satisfy all those desires? Does the environment have the capacity to absorb all the waste from that level of global consumption? If the answer to either of these is "no", how will humanity adapt to this rising tide of effective demand? How will we address the challenge of choice?

Scarcity and its consequence, opportunity cost, set the scene for our study. A theme that will weave its way through our study is the relationship between scarcity and sustainability. We will examine the issue of sustainability at every step in our analysis, from its microeconomic importance in individual lifestyle choices to the macroeconomic debate about globalization of the market system and the sustainability of such a global prospect.

1.3 A PREVIEW OF THE STUDY

1.3.1 Microeconomics

The first topic we will explore is individual choice. How, according to economists, do we decide between chocolate and vanilla, between going to college and joining the army, between two roads that diverge in a yellow wood? We will model that choice process.

With an economic model of individual choice in place, we will explore the economic theory of interdependent choice. In an interdependent world, our choices affect one another—I depend on lots of other people for what I consider the necessities of life (farmers, police, plumbers, and so on) and for the luxuries I can afford (the airline workers who take me on vacation). Those workers in turn send their children to people like me for an education. I desire what they produce, they desire what I produce. But more often than not, even as we serve one another's wants, we never actually meet one another. So how do we know what to do for one another? How is it possible for all of our individual choices about producing and consuming to work out in a coherent way that allows us to efficiently and effectively serve one another's needs and desires? We will see that under the right conditions, markets can coordinate our choices very effectively and efficiently.

Using lots of real world examples, we will examine how individual markets work, under what conditions markets coordinate choices perfectly efficiently, how a system of markets functions as a general system, and what forces distort that system undermining its efficiency.

Markets are a lot like the computer I am using right now. This computer has amazing functionality, but it is vulnerable to electrical surges or viruses and it does not care whether what it is doing is moral or not (terrorists use these things). So too markets. They are vulnerable to distortions caused by circumstances or by purposeful manipulation; and like a computer they are amoral, so it is possible for a perfectly efficient market to exist and result in what some participants might consider an unjust outcome

These issues of potential injustice and/or inefficiency bring us to the question of the government's role in the microeconomy. If markets can be distorted and/or if market outcomes can be unjust, is government part of the solution for "fixing" these problems or is government itself part of the problem? I can't answer this question for you. It's a philosophical question that depends on the assumptions you make about markets, government, and justice. What I will try to do is lay out the assumptions that underlie each side in the debate about government's role in the economy so that you can make a thoughtful judgment for yourself.

The analysis economists do at the level of the individual and of individuals interacting through markets is called microeconomic theory. "Micro" comes from the Greek word *mikros*, meaning "little" or "small." As the name implies, microeconomics looks through a microscope at individuals and how they interact as they seek to resolve the challenges of choice they face in an interdependent world.

You will be developing a powerful tool for understanding individual choice and the market system. The best place to practice with that tool is in the world that surrounds you. So, as our microeconomic analysis unfolds you should explore how what you are learning relates to the world that surrounds you, the world "out the window".

We will begin our study at the microeconomic level, then with our micro foundation in place we'll study the system at the macroeconomic level.

1.3.2 Macroeconomics

"Macro" comes from the Greek word *makros*, meaning "large." Macroeconomics examines a nation's or the world's economic condition as a whole. As with micro, we will build a model to represent the macro economy. Then with this model in place we will explore the issues of macroeconomics: Issues of national production, unemployment, inflation, globalization and sustainability. In terms of the forest and trees analogy: Micro is the study of the trees, the other elements of the forest, and of the web of connections that weaves them together into an ecosystem. Macro, on the other hand, is a study of that system, the forest, as a wholeness.

As with the microeconomy, under the right conditions the macroeconomy can work very well, but absent those conditions the macroeconomy can break down. The classic case of macroeconomic breakdown is the Great Depression. The Depression is a case we will examine in some detail.

Because the macroeconomy is simply the aggregate (added up) result of all the microeconomic activity, we will see that "the right conditions" for macroeconomic health are those that insure microeconomic efficiency. If everything is working well at the micro level, then by definition the macro system is going to be healthy. Thus the resilience of the macroeconomy, its ability to respond to shocks, depends on the right conditions existing for the micro market system to adjust efficiently. It follows that when we turn to the debate about the role of government in the macro economy, we will see that whether one sees government management of the macroeconomy is a good idea depends on one's assumptions about the dependability of the microeconomic system.

As our macroeconomic analysis unfolds you should tune in to the news of national and world events. You will be developing a powerful tool for understanding the economic dimension of those events more richly, and the best place to practice with that tool is in today's news.

Our study will close with a word on why I can only offer you a tool for systematic analysis of important questions and not "answers." Economists cannot decide and agree once and for all on how the world works because it is impossible to have perfect tests of the theory. We will see how economists go about testing their theories and some of the problems inherent in this process that make perfect tests impossible.

That is our subject, now a word on our method.

1.4 OUR METHOD FOR DEVELOPING THE MODEL

1.4.1 Joseph Schumpeter on Model Building

The model presented here is the one that mainstream economists consider the best available representation of how the economy works, a model often referred to as Neoclassical Theory. We are going to master that model by building it from the ground up. So in order to understand our method, it is helpful to appreciate how models are built.

According to Joseph Schumpeter, one of the great early 20th century economists, model building begins with a vision. He called this vision a "preanalytic cognitive act." In other words model building begins in one's mind's eye. This mind's eye view, this vision of how things work, is a synthesis of all the raw materials one brings to the project. These raw materials come from "looking out the window" and from the work of others who have preceded you. No one starts from scratch.

From this vision comes the analytic effort. Analysis is that part of the scientific process during which the vision is formalized. "The first step [in analysis, quoting Schumpeter,] is to verbalize the vision or to conceptualize it in such a way that its elements take their places with names attached to them that facilitate recognition and manipulation, in a more or less orderly schema or picture." (Joseph Schumpeter, *History of Economic Analysis*, Oxford University Press, New York. 1954, p. 42) In other words, it is during this first stage of analysis that the scientist defines her terms and arranges them so that they begin to tell a story.

1.4.2 The Role of Assumptions in the Process of Model Building

In order to make this modeling enterprise manageable the scientist makes assumptions.

The world is an incredibly intricate web of connections. Since no scientist studies the whole order of the universe simultaneously, all scientists are required to isolate that piece of the web they want to study in detail. The traditional technique for accomplishing this is to assume a specific, fixed set of conditions that prevail in the surrounding environment. Assumptions allow the scientist to abstract from the complications of changes in those surrounding conditions. While studying the universe as a single whole is the most realistic way to do analysis, that is impossible. Assumptions are made in order to simplify the problem, and thus they make analysis manageable.

1.4.3 Developing the Model

As a scientist works out the details of her model according to her original vision and examines its implications against the available evidence, it is inevitable that flaws will become obvious. She addresses these by making adjustments in her assumptions, her definitions, or her story line. Once the scientist feels the model is mature she tries to get it into the marketplace of ideas by presenting it to colleagues at a conference or through a scholarly publication.

If the marketplace is functioning in an unbiased manner, the scientist's model will be examined on its merits. Some scholars will trace the logic of the presentation for flaws. Others will examine whether the empirical evidence is indeed consistent with the model. There are two basic sources of problems with a model: Ideological bias and lack of care in construction.

1.4.4 Assessing Models: Where to Look for Flaws

According to Schumpeter all models embody ideology because, to quote him, "vision is ideological almost by definition." (Schumpeter, 42) When our mind's eye reviews the world as we take it in through our senses, it distorts what our eyes have seen. The shape of this distortion in our mind's eye is our ideology. As a result of this distortion, we all see the world through biased eyes. Thus, while we should not be so suspicious that we throw away valuable insights of others because we are too cynical, we should always examine theories with a constructively skeptical eye.

Problems enter a model as terms are defined and arranged, and assumptions are introduced. Vague definitions and/or sloppy specification of assumptions may simply represent sloppy work. They can also reflect conscious or unconscious ideological bias at work.

Malleable definitions or assumptions make it possible to interpret the model such that it is always consistent with empirical tests. This makes it impossible to reject the model. Sometimes assumptions can do this virtually invisibly because assumptions are often taken for granted, and thus their implications are not critically examined. A model built on such a movable foundation may have staying power, but it has very little value.

With that in mind, you should be a skeptical but not cynical consumer of the model I present. In particular, keep your eye on the assumptions we make. The ultimate strength of the model depends on the sturdiness of its foundation, and the assumptions form that foundation.

1.4.5 The Role of Assumptions in My Method

Assumptions play a central role in my method here. I am going to present the model by building it. I will start with a very simple, even simplistic, version of the analysis and then add complexity by relaxing assumptions. Let me explain.

As I noted before, *assumptions* are systematic abstractions from reality. By making assumptions we can define the conditions of the world we want to study, and do analysis within those given conditions. That allows us to hold some of the complexity of the real world at bay. For example, when I start talking about individual choice I am initially going to assume that there is only one person in the world, Robinson Crusoe, and that Crusoe lives in a place like the Garden of Eden—a world with no scarcity, no future to take into consideration, and no risk or uncertainty to worry about. That is clearly not a very realistic world, but I can assume anything I want.

Assumptions are legitimate so long as you are up front about them so that people can see what you are assuming as you make your case.

1.4.6 Strong versus Weak Assumptions

Assumptions come in different strengths. A *strong assumption* abstracts significantly from what is considered to be reality. My Robinson Crusoe/Garden of Eden assumption is a very strong assumption. In effect a strong assumption holds a lot of reality at bay. It has to be strong to do that, ergo the name "strong assumption". Assumptions are termed *weak assumptions* when they are considered more realistic. For example, if the assumption is that the sun will come up tomorrow, that is a pretty weak assumption. It is termed "weak" because it does not have to hold so much of reality at bay. Since strong assumptions abstract from a great deal of reality, a model constructed on strong assumptions is less credible than one built on weak assumptions. In an irony of language, the weaker the assumptions the stronger the model's foundation.

Keep in mind, whether an assumption is strong or weak depends on your perception of reality. We can probably agree that the Robinson Crusoe/Garden of Eden assumption is a strong assumption. But in many cases the strength or weakness of an assumption is a point of strenuous debate. For example, the strength or weakness of the assumption that markets work well lies at the heart of the debate among economists about the role of government in the market system. Those who think it is a strong assumption tend to see a role for government in fixing the problems of markets. Those who see it as a weak assumption tend to see government intervention in the market system as unnecessary and even counterproductive.

1.4.7 Building the Model by Relaxing Assumptions

Remember the steps in model building. You begin with assumptions that identify the given conditions in the world. Next you define terms so that you have a careful language for describing and analyzing that world. Your model takes shape as you arrange those terms into a story that represents your vision of how that world works.

Our first task here is to model the decision rule that individuals follow when making choices. To do that we will start with the strong assumption of Robinson Crusoe in the Garden of Eden. Holding lots of complexity at bay with that very strong assumption gives us a very simple world within which to work. But while starting with strong assumptions makes the start easy, it also makes it unrealistic. If we stopped there, it would be a pretty trivial exercise.

We are not going to stop there. We are going to build up the complexity and thus the realism of the model by *relaxing assumptions*. To relax an assumption is to move from a stronger to a weaker assumption, to move from what is perceived to be a less to a more realistic set of given conditions. So, for example, after beginning in the Robinson Crusoe/Garden of Eden world, we are going to relax the assumption of no scarcity and expand the complexity of our model of individual choice to encompass the consequences of scarcity. Then we will relax the no future assumption, then the no risk and uncertainty, then the no interdependence. At each step we will be allowing more complexity into the model.

1.4.8 More Complexity Requires More Vocabulary

More complexity means more to talk about, more to describe. So each time we relax an assumption we will have to define more terms to deal with the growing complexity. Each new set of terms will have to be woven into our model so that even as the scope and, therefore, the complexity of the world the model represents expands, it continues to do so in a coherent, efficient, and informative way.

I designed this story of economics around this process of relaxing assumptions because it allows us to build what is a very complex model step by step in your mind—carefully adding each new piece so that the scope of the model expands systematically. If you stick with the program, follow the story, and practice with the ideas as they come . . . at the end of the process you will have a very sophisticated mastery of the principles of economics . . . an essential tool for systematic analysis of and critical thinking about the issues of our world past, present, and future.

1.4.9 On The All-Purpose Assumption: Ceteris Paribus

Clearly, assumptions play a central role in model building. As the model is developed I will try to be explicit about what I am assuming, but sometimes I will just say, "*ceteris paribus.*" *Ceteris paribus* means "other things being equal." It is a convenient way of saying, "There may be complicating factors that I haven't specifically assumed away, so whatever they are . . . I'm assuming them away."

1.4.10 The Value of Our Model Depends in Large Part on Our Maintained Assumptions

Some of our assumptions will not ever be relaxed, they will be maintained for the entire course of the story—taken as a constant in the state of the world. The model we build will be a superstructure that rests on a foundation made by those maintained assumptions. As I noted before, it is an odd twist of language but it is true that models are only as strong as their assumptions are weak. If those maintained assumptions are strong assumptions, then it raises questions about the value of the entire construct—the model. So as we review the assumptions, especially the maintained assumptions, you should reflect on how strong or weak you think those assumptions are.

Now let's begin by laying out our assumptions, defining some terms, and arranging them into a model of individual choice.

2.0 MODELING INDIVIDUAL CHOICE

2.1 MODELING INDIVIDUAL CHOICE— INTRODUCTION

"I cast my eyes to the stranded vessel, when the breach and froth of the sea being so big, I could hardly see it, it lay so far off, and considered, Lord! how was it possible I could get on shore?"

Daniel Defoe
The Life and Adventures of Robinson Crusoe, 1719.

There he was, ashore and alone in a world into which fate had cast him. How was Crusoe to decide what to do? Indeed, how does any human being decide what to do? In this chapter we will examine the economist's answer to this question. We will develop a model of individual choice.

We begin with Robinson Crusoe because doing so allows us to abstract from a complication we face in our own world: Crusoe is alone; we are not. His choices are entirely independent of any other human being; ours are not. To simplify matters even more, we are going to initially assume that Crusoe is in a place like the Garden of Eden—a place with no scarcity. In fact he was not, and neither are we.

By relaxing assumptions we'll develop our model of individual choice into a rich representation of how individuals go about making choices independent of others. Once we have that model in place we'll be in a better position to understand the more complex reality of interdependent choice. Thus we begin here with Crusoe, but soon we'll be leaving him behind.

2.2 MODELING INDIVIDUAL CHOICE— OUR ASSUMPTIONS AND DEFINITIONS

2.2.1 Assumptions

Setting Crusoe in a Garden of Eden, we make several strong assumptions that we will relax shortly:

1. No scarcity—Crusoe can have as much as he wants of anything he wants.
2. No production is necessary—Crusoe doesn't have to make anything for himself; it all comes like manna from heaven.
3. No future—Crusoe has no sense of time passing.
4. No risk or uncertainty—All of Crusoe's choices work out just as he expects.

These assumptions set the scene, but we need to make more assumptions and we need to define some terms before we can model even this very simple case.

2.2.2 Definitions

First, if we are going to model individual choice we need to make an assumption about motives. What drives our choices?

We are going to make and maintain the assumption that the objective of all choices made by every individual is to maximize utility. We define *utility* as satisfaction. I get utility or satisfaction from ice cream, from music, from a smile on my kid's face. Your sources of utility are surely different from mine. Whatever the sources, our assumption is that we each seek to maximize our utility.

A term closely related to utility is *consume*. Consumption is the act of deriving utility. Consumption is often associated with using things up, such as consuming an ice cream cone. In the sense in which we use it here, however, consumption does not invariably imply "using up." You can consume a work of art or Niagara Falls, and it will still be there for the next person to consume.

Since we consume things that provide us with utility and since we like utility, we identify the things we consume with flattering names like *goods or services*. Both goods and services are things that provide utility when consumed. The distinction is that goods can be stored (like food), while services cannot (like a haircut).

2.2.3 More Assumptions

Given the assumptions and terms we have developed so far, we can say that individuals consume goods and services in order to maximize utility. All well and good, but if we are going to model the logic of choice to achieve utility maximization, we need to assume that there is in fact a logic that guides this process. We ensure such a logic by adopting the assumptions that

- Everyone knows her own preference ordering
- Everyone is rational

A person who knows her preference ordering is able to rank available choices in order of the utility they offer; she knows what she prefers. A person is rational if there is an internal, consistent logic that guides her choice process. So a rational person, given her preference ordering, makes logical, internally consistent choices that maximize her utility.

Keep in mind: That does not mean she will appear rational to you or me. She may do things that we think are nuts, but our opinion is not the standard of rational here. The standard is internal to the individual. Is there a consistent internal logic guiding her choices even if it is not obvious to those of us looking on? We are going to assume that for everyone there is.

These assumptions are the foundation of economic modeling. You should reflect on whether you think these are weak or strong assumptions.

2.2.4 Reviewing Our Assumptions

Now let's take a moment to review our assumptions.

TABLE 2.2.1 ASSUMPTIONS

MAINTAINED	TO BE RELAXED
Individual's Objective Is to Maximize Utility	No Scarcity
Individuals Know Their Own Preference Ordering	No Production Necessary
Individuals Are Rational	No Future
	No Risk or Uncertainty
	No Interdependence

Given these assumptions, we can collect and arrange the terms we have specified into the following statement: "Rational individuals consume goods and services in order to maximize their utility." But this is only a general description of the process; it does not model how choices are made. With one more assumption, however, we can begin to develop a model of individual choice.

2.3 DIMINISHING MARGINAL UTILITY

2.3.1 Introduction

We are going to assume and maintain the assumption that, *ceteris paribus*, the utility you or I or anyone derives from the consumption of a good or service diminishes with each successive unit consumed.

Consider this experience: You love m&ms and you're famished. Suddenly you find a huge bag of m&ms. You gasp: "Oh joy! I'm saved!" and you begin to eat. The first m&m is a joy. The utility it gives you is huge. The second is almost as good, but not quite as satisfying as the first, so it brings slightly less utility. On and on you go consuming m&ms . . . So, when would you stop? Your body "tells" you to stop by sending you a signal.

With each successive m&m you get less and less satisfaction, less utility. At some point you reach an m&m that gives you no more (zero) utility. At that point, with no satisfaction from that last m&m, your body says "stop".

Let's review this process because it is central to the logic of our model of choice: In our example, as you consume you get a certain amount of satisfaction from each successive m&m you eat. With each successive m&m you consume, you ask yourself: "Did that give me any satisfaction, any utility?" If it did, you eat the next one because it holds the promise of more utility. When you get to an m&m that gives you no utility, you stop eating because there is no prospect of more utility from the next m&m.

Economists refer to this kind of decision making as choice at the *margin*. In a succession of units the marginal unit is the specific unit you are focusing on, the one under consideration. In our m&m example the marginal unit is the one under consideration as you ask yourself: "Do I want this one?"

Each unit in the succession of m&ms you consume is at some point the marginal m&m, and each of these has a unique effect on you. Each gave you a specific amount of satisfaction, of utility. This specific effect of an individual unit is called the *marginal utility* of that particular unit.

This example represents a general principal of economics. In economic modeling the process of choosing takes place at the margin: "Do I want one more m&m?" or "Do I want to play a minute longer?" or "Do I want another gulp of water?" Since marginal choice involves making choices about individual units in a succession of units, the smaller the units the more finely tuned your choices can be.

Clearly, big units of choice give us less decision flexibility than small units of choice. The smaller the units, the more finely tuned our decisions can be: Spending time in seconds allows more fine tuning than spending time in hour blocks. We assume, therefore, that all goods and services, and, when we get there, all inputs used in production, are divisible into infinitesimally small units. This is a strong assumption because in fact the only thing we consume/spend in life that is truly divisible into infinitesimally small units is time. But we are going to assume perfect divisibility because it allows us to build a model based on finely tuned marginal decision making: Finely tuned decisions about "Do I want one more?" Indeed, the theory we are studying is often referred to as *marginal analysis*.

2.3.2 Marginal and Total Utility

Now let's return to our assumption that the utility we derive from the consumption of each successive unit of a good or service diminishes with each successive unit consumed. We will refer to it as the assumption of *diminishing marginal utility*. To practice with the concept, consider this story of diminishing marginal utility.

TABLE 2.3.1   JESSE'S AND ABBY'S MARGINAL UTILITY SCHEDULES

Jesse's Marginal Utility Schedule			Abby's Marginal Utility Schedule		
m&m	MU	TU	m&m	MU	TU
0	0	0	0	0	0
1st m&m	999	999	1st m&m	540	540
2nd m&m	997	1996	2nd m&m	538	1078
3rd m&m	994	2990	3rd m&m	534	1612
4th m&m	990	3980	4th m&m	528	2140
5th m&m	980	4960	5th m&m	521	2661
6th m&m	975	5935	6th m&m	512	3173
7th m&m	955	6890	7th m&m	498	3671
8th m&m	920	7810	8th m&m	484	4155
9th m&m	870	8680	9th m&m	469	4624
10th m&m	800	9480	10th m&m	450	5074
11th m&m	710	10190	11th m&m	425	5499
12th m&m	600	10790	12th m&m	395	5894
13th m&m	470	11260	13th m&m	360	6254
14th m&m	320	11580	14th m&m	320	6574
. . .			. . .		
49th m&m	-7	11833	49th m&m	7	8352
			50th m&m	1	8353
			51st m&m	0	8353
			52nd m&m	-1	8352
			53rd m&m	-2	8350

As you can see from Table 2.3.1, Abby and Jesse really enjoy m&ms. Now suppose they have not had any in a quite while and then they come upon a huge pile of m&ms with a sign on it saying: "Free, take all you'd like." Joyfully they begin to consume. These schedules show the number of utils each of them gets from each successive m&m consumed. In other words, these are their respective *marginal utility* (*MU*) schedules.

Note: A *util* is an abstraction. It is a measure of a unit of utility. Strictly speaking, these should be called Abby utils and Jesse utils, because what this satisfaction feels like to each of them may be different. No one but Abby really knows how much satisfaction each successive m&m gives her, and so too with Jesse. If one of them tries to tweak the other by saying "Na-nu-na-nu-naaaaa-na, I'm getting more utils out of this pig out session than you are." The ensuing argument is truly a pointless exercise . . . Unless of course there's pleasure in tweaking your sibling—which does seem to be the case.

Notice that for the first 10 m&ms consumed, while the utility Abby and Jesse each derive from the consumption of successive m&ms is falling . . . the marginal utility is falling . . . the total utility each derives from consuming m&ms is rising. This is true because the positive marginal utility of each of these first 10 m&ms adds to their total utility, albeit by successively smaller amounts.

Marginal utility is the unique, individual effect of each unit consumed: How much did this one satisfy me? The total utility is the sum of all these marginal effects: How much satisfaction have I gotten from eating all these m&ms? So long as the marginal utility is positive, no matter how small, it adds its positive effect to the total. What happens to the margin and total if one keeps consuming? To answer this look at Abby's marginal utility schedule.

Toward the end of Abby's schedule we see that the 50th m&m would give her one additional unit of utility, the 51st m&m would give her zero additional utility, the 52nd m&m would reduce her utility by one unit, the 53rd m&m would reduce her utility by two units, and so on. In other words if Abby were to eat more than 50 m&ms, the marginal utility of the m&ms goes to zero and then becomes increasingly negative.

Both Abby and Jesse are making their decisions to consume at the margin, constantly asking themselves: Do I want one more? Given our assumptions, at what point would Abby stop consuming m&ms? She would eat the 50th because the 49th gave her utility and she would want more. She would eat the 51st because the 50th gave her utility and she would want more. But the 51st did not give her any additional utility, so why have more? She would stop at 51. If she was forced to eat the 52nd m&m, she would wish she had not because it would actually lower her utility.

We can represent marginal utility (MU) and total utility (TU) schedules graphically as shown in Figure 2.3.1. (Note: the scales on the vertical axes for the total and marginal graphs are different.)

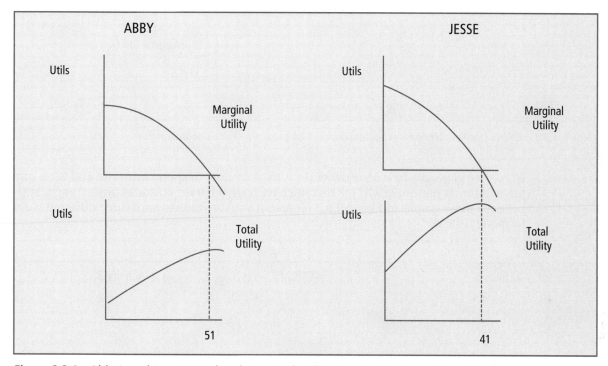

Figure 2.3.1   Abby's and Jesse's Total and Marginal Utility Graphs. Starting at the 1st m&m

Let's assume for a moment that Jesse's and Abby's utils are the same and that the axes on their MU graphs are the same so we can directly compare their MU lines. The shapes of their MU lines are different. What does that mean? Jesse's starts higher and falls off pretty quickly to zero. Abby's on the other hand doesn't start off quite as high but it has a more gentle drop as it steadily goes to zero. These lines reflect the fact that Jesse and Abby have different attitudes toward m&ms.

We can see the difference in their attitudes by the shape of their respective MU lines. Since his initial MU is higher, Jesse gets the most satisfaction from digging into the bag at the outset. But since her MU falls off more slowly Abby's satisfaction is sustained most consistently. So, who will eat the most? Abby, because Jesse reaches zero MU before Abby does.

2.3.3 Marginal Utility with Multiple Choices

So we see that a marginal utility line represents how much utility a person derives from each successive unit of consumption. Take, for instance, playing. You can choose how much you want to play. Each unit of play offers the opportunity for more satisfaction. Figure 2.3.2 shows how much utility you can derive from each successive unit of playing.

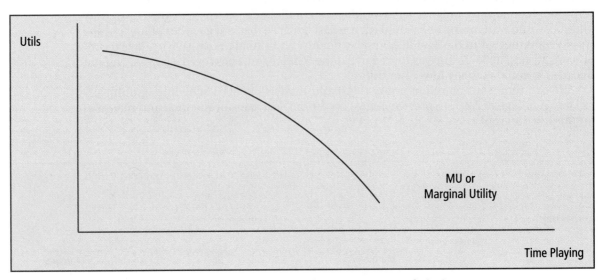

Figure 2.3.2 Utility derived from each successive unit of playing, or MU of playing

In fact we generally face an array of options as to how to spend our time and each one has a different pattern of MU returns since we have different attitudes toward each. Suppose the three graphs in Figure 2.3.3 represent your attitude toward three different ways to spend time.

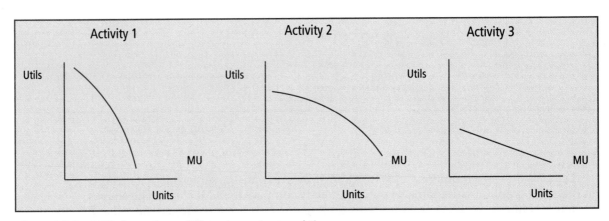

Figure 2.3.3 MU's from three different way to spend time

We will assume same scales on similar axes, so we can compare across graphs. Since it is all about you, these utils do mean the same thing in each graph—they are your utils. So what do the shapes of these different MU lines reflect about the differences in your attitude toward each activity?

Activity 1 is something you really like to do at first, but you do not care to do it for a long time. You like Activity 2 less than Activity 1 at the outset, but Activity 2 sustains its appeal longer. However, as you do Activity 2 the satisfaction falls off ever more rapidly. Activity 3 is not a big priority. You probably would not do it if you did not have much time. But it sustains some pleasure for a pretty long time.

These three graphs represent your attitudes toward Activities 1, 2, and 3 *now*. The graphs might be different at another time because our attitudes change over time, and clearly someone else's graphs would be different because we all have different attitudes about what gives us satisfaction.

One of the great strengths of the model of individual choice we are developing here is that as attitudes (represented by these lines' shapes) change either from person to person or for a given person from time to time, the analysis adapts to reflect that. It is a very powerful model in large part because it is tailored to each of us and it is capable of adapting with our changing attitudes.

2.4 CONSTRUCTING A DECISION RULE

2.4.1 The Initial Decision Rule

Now we can pull together all of the current pieces of our model and identify a decision rule for choice under the strong set of assumptions laid out above. Given those assumptions a rational individual will maximize utility by consuming a good or service up to the point at which the marginal utility equals zero (e.g., Abby and Jesse consumed the m&ms until $MU_{m\&m} = 0$).

In mathematical terms, this general decision rule appears as follows: For any good or service

$$\textbf{Consume until MU} = \textbf{0}$$

If there is no scarcity and there are "n" different things to consume where n is some large number, an individual will follow that same rule in consuming all things from 1 to n:

$$\textbf{Consume until}$$
$$\textbf{MU}_1 = \textbf{0}$$
$$\textbf{and MU}_2 = \textbf{0}$$
$$\textbf{and MU}_3 = \textbf{0}$$
$$\textbf{...}$$
$$\textbf{and so on to}$$
$$\textbf{...}$$
$$\textbf{MU}_n = \textbf{0}$$

We can write this more efficiently as

$$\textbf{MU}_1 = \textbf{MU}_2 = \textbf{MU}_3 = \ldots = \textbf{MU}_n = \textbf{0 for all n goods and services.}$$

This then is the decision rule an individual will follow if she lives like a Robinson Crusoe in the Garden of Eden. She will consume each thing up to the point at which it offers no more utility at the margin. This will allow her to get all the utility that the world has to offer her. She will *satiate* herself in all dimensions of consumption, which means she reaches a *bliss point*.

What would happen to her total utility if she consumed less of anything? It would go down because she would not be consuming all the units that offer a positive MU.

What would happen to her total utility if she consumed more of anything? It would go down because she would be pushing into the negative MU range.

Only by following this decision rule can she maximize her utility. Since we have assumed that she knows her preference ordering, that she is rational, and that she does indeed want to maximize her utility, this then is the rule she will follow.

2.4.2 Reflecting on this Initial Decision Rule

We just established our first, rudimentary decision rule. Let's pause and make an important point about this process. We are modeling the decision rule we all follow to maximize utility given our assumption about the nature of human nature. This is not to suggest, however, that we each keep little tables of marginal utility in our head and consciously make calculations unit by unit at the margin as we choose. Indeed, most of the time the choices we make seem to take little or no thought.

What we are doing here is in effect unscrewing the top of our heads and looking down at the computer that runs our choice system to see how it works. It does not matter that most people never actually reflect on how they choose between chocolate and vanilla or between two roads that diverge in a yellow wood. To the degree that our assumptions are valid, our model accurately describes the rule we all follow for making choices.

Is this initial version of our decision rule very realistic? No. As I tried to demonstrate at the beginning of our story:

- We all do face scarcity.
- Things do not come to us like manna from heaven.
- The future does matter in our choices.
- Decisions do not always work out just the way we plan.

So why do we bother to develop such an unrealistic decision rule?

We start here because it provides a first approximation of reality. We have modeled how people make choices under the very strong (unrealistic) set of assumptions. From this point of departure, step by step, we will relax assumptions and build in the complexities of scarcity, production, the future, and risk and uncertainty. When we are done I think you will see that we have developed a very rich, pretty realistic model of individual choice.

2.5 RELAXING OUR "NO SCARCITY" ASSUMPTION: EXPANDING OUR DECISION RULE TO REFLECT THIS NEW COMPLEXITY

2.5.1 Introduction to the Decision Rule Under Scarcity

Now let's add a layer of realism by relaxing the no scarcity assumption—allowing time to be scarce. We will focus on time because it's a perfectly divisible resource.

As a point of departure, let's rewrite the decision rule under no scarcity to reflect our focus on spending time, or as economists refer to it: *Time allocation*. The rule from above

$$MU_1 = MU_2 = MU_3 = \ldots = MU_n = 0$$

becomes

$$\frac{MU1}{UnitofTime} = \frac{MU2}{UnitofTime} = \frac{MU3}{UnitofTime} = \ldots = \frac{MUn}{UnitofTime} = 0$$

Since you face no scarcity you will spend time on each activity until the marginal utility per unit of time spent offers no more (i.e., zero) utility.

But what if you do not have the time to do as much as you desire of every available option? What does this dose of reality do to our decision rule?

2.5.2 Your Decision Rule Under Scarcity—A Case

Suppose your set of opportunities includes two options, study and play, represented on the marginal utility graphs in Figure 2.5.1, and that your have 10 units of time to spend. I'll refer to hours of time just because it sounds reasonable, but clearly you can break down the units into milliseconds.

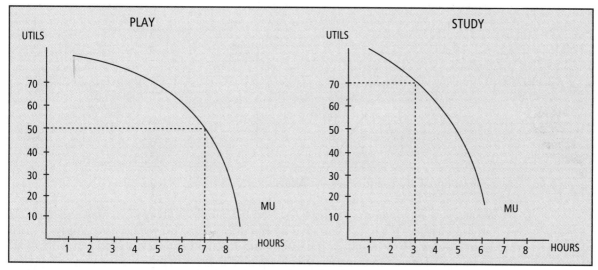

Figure 2.5.1 Marginal Utility of Study and Play—An Initial Possible Allocation

First question: Given what you see in Figure 2.5.1 do you have enough time resources to reach a bliss point? No. Ten hours would not satiate you in either activity, so it certainly will not be enough to do it for both. You would need more than 14 hours (> 8 for play and > 6 for study) to do that. So, given that you do not have the time to reach a bliss point, how do you spend (allocate) your time between the two opportunities when your time resources are scarce relative to your desires? What decision rule do you follow in order to maximize your utility, given scarcity?

Figure 2.5.1 shows a possible time allocation of your ten hours. Does this allocation maximize your utility, or is there a better way to allocate ten hours of time between Study and Play in order to optimize? By *optimize*, I mean to reach the best outcome. In this consumption case the *optimal allocation* is the one that maximizes your utility.

Figure 2.5.1 shows you allocating three hours to study and seven hours to play. In that case the marginal utility from the last hour of study (70) is greater than that from the last hour of play (50). At the margin, study seems to be paying greater dividends. So what to do? Does it make sense to shift some time toward the higher marginal return? Let's try it.

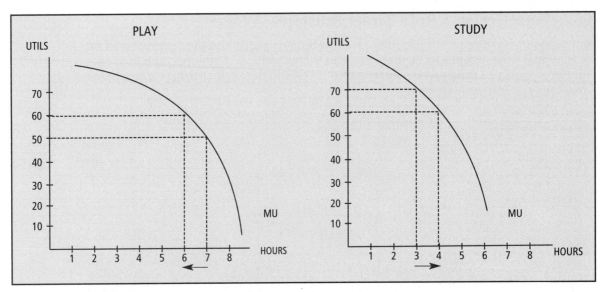

Figure 2.5.2 Marginal Utility of Study and Play—An Adjustment

Suppose, as shown in the Figure 2.5.2, you take an hour away from play and spend it on studying instead. If you do, you give up the utility that you would have enjoyed from that hour of play. How much is that? Remember each unit of time generates its own, unique marginal effect. In this case, giving up the 7th hour of play means you give up the 50 utils you would have enjoyed if you had kept playing for the 7th hour.

You are going to study another hour instead. So what does that extra hour of study do for your utility? Reallocating an hour from play to study means that now you'll have a 4th hour of study. That 4th hour of study has a marginal utility of 60 utils.

So are you better off to reallocate toward the opportunity with the higher marginal utility, in this case from play to study? You give up 50 utils from play to gain 60 utils from study. The net effect is a gain of 10 utils. Your total utility is increased by the move, and total utility is the name of the game, so yes . . . it is a good move.

Now what? You are spending 6 hours playing and 4 hours studying. The marginal utility for the 6th hour of playing is 60 utils and the marginal utility for the 4th hour of studying is 60 utils. Is there any further benefit to changing your allocation of time? If you take away an hour of study to play more, you are back where you started which was not as good. If you take away another hour of play to study more, you will loose 60 utils and gain what? Look at the graph. Another hour of study is going to give you less than 60 utils benefit, so this is not a good idea.

The general decision rule for choice under scarcity that we can take from this exercise is this: So long as there is a difference in marginal utilities across options there is an opportunity to do better. You can achieve greater total utility by reallocating from an option that is offering less utility at the margin to one that is offering more. Each time you do this, the relative advantage will diminish, but so long as the margins are unequal this kind of move pays off. When the margins are finally equal there is no more advantage to reallocating, this is the best you can do. So, we can say that utility is maximized when the marginal utilities for units of time spent are equalized, or in terms of an equation, the general decision rule for utility maximization is:

$$\frac{MU_1}{UnitofTime} = \frac{MU_2}{UnitofTime} = \frac{MU_3}{UnitofTime} = \ldots = \frac{MU_n}{UnitofTime}$$

In the no scarcity case the balance would be:

$$\frac{MU_1}{UnitofTime} = \frac{MU_2}{UnitofTime} = \frac{MU_3}{UnitofTime} = \ldots = \frac{MU_n}{UnitofTime} = 0$$

In our study/play example above which reflected scarcity the balance is

$$\frac{MU_{Play}}{UnitofTime} = \frac{MU_{Study}}{UnitofTime} = 60$$

Of course the numbers on the study/play example above are made up. They reflect attitudes toward study and play that I built into these marginal utility lines. Your real attitudes and thus the shape of your actual marginal utility lines would surely be different, and so your optimal allocation would be different.

Our decision rule now describes how, given our assumptions, individuals solve what economists refer to as a *constrained optimization problem*: How do people maximize utility in the face of a scarcity? *We balance at the margin,* setting:

$$\frac{MU_1}{Unit} = \frac{MU_2}{Unit} = \frac{MU_3}{Unit} = \ldots = \frac{MU_n}{Unit}$$

2.6 RELAXING OUR "NO PRODUCTION NECESSARY" ASSUMPTION: EXPANDING OUR DECISION RULE TO REFLECT THIS NEW COMPLEXITY

2.6.1 Introduction

Up until now we have assumed that all things come to us like manna from heaven, already produced and ready to consume. But that is clearly not very realistic. Even in a lush world full of good things to eat growing all around us, we would have to take time to collect our food. Even in that world there is time spent on production. Clearly in our more complex world of goods and services, lots of time is spent producing things.

Production takes resources. What is ultimately scarce in the world is not products, what is scarce is the resources necessary to make those products. Bringing production into our model brings us to the roots of scarcity. We face scarcity because our resource endowment is finite.

A society's *endowment* includes the natural and human resources from which all goods and services must be produced. Society's endowment can expand: New resource discoveries expand the endowment. Society's endowment can also contract as resources are used up or ruined or in some other way destroyed. In other words a society's endowment is finite, but it is not fixed. Since it is finite, there is scarcity.

Given our resource endowment, we produce in order to consume and we consume with the goal of maximizing utility. Relaxing the No Production Necessary assumption, we now expand the scope of our model to analyze the ultimate challenge we face in the real world of a finite endowment: How do we get the most utility out of our resources?

Let's start with a statement about production that embodies a number of new terms we will need:

> Factors of production are allocated to and then combined in processes of production that apply techniques chosen from available technology in order to produce goods and services.

2.6.2 On Factors

The *factors of production* are the basic inputs we use to produce. They include natural resources, labor, and capital. The natural resources, labor, and capital available to our society make up our society's resource endowment.

Natural resources are all those things that come to us from in, on, or around the earth.

Labor is the natural power humans have to exert themselves. It is a raw concept of human productive capacity. Natural resources and labor, as we define them, are humankind's natural endowment.

Capital is different. We define capital as "a produced means of production." Capital does not exist in nature; we have to produce it if we want to use it for production. For example, Robinson Crusoe can hunt by chasing deer and catching them barehanded, in which case he would be using pure labor. But he can increase his productivity by taking time to produce a spear which he can then use to hunt. The spear is capital. It is a produced means of production. We take the time to produce capital on the expectation that it will increase our productivity and thus benefit us as producers and in turn as consumers.

Be careful to note that when I talk about capital here I mean *production capital*. Later, in macro, I will use the term capital to refer to financial capital, like money. This is a classic case of the fact that terms can have many meanings. As I noted at the outset of our study, using the same terms does not guarantee that we are speaking the same language. Let's be sure we're speaking the same language.

We distinguish two kinds of production capital: physical and human. *Physical capital* is embodied in a tool that makes us more productive: like the spear, or like a hammer, or a computer, or a machine and so on. . . . *Human capital* is embodied in ourselves and makes us more productive. For example, an education is something we produce in ourselves. If your education makes you more productive, it is human capital embodied in you. Similarly, being healthy can make you more productive, so spending time or other resources taking care of your health can be a form of human capital production.

If you dig ditches with your hands, which factors will you be using in your work? Clearly labor—your natural power to exert yourself, and not much else.

If you go to work as a violinist for the symphony, which kinds of factors will you be using? Labor—your natural power to exert yourself, physical capital—someone made your violin, and human capital—you spent a lot of time learning how to make music with the instrument. If you go to work as a rocket scientist at NASA designing the space station on a computer, which kinds of factors will you be using? Labor—your natural power to exert yourself, physical capital—someone made your computer, and human capital—you spent a lot of time learning how to make things work in space.

Now back to our statement for more terms: Factors of production are allocated to and then combined in processes of production that apply techniques chosen from the available technology.

2.6.3 Allocations, Techniques, and Technology

When factors are *allocated* that means we decide how we are going to use them. We met this concept before when we discussed allocating time.

Once factors are allocated they are combined in a *process of production*. This means using the factors together to actually make a good or service, or capital. A rocket scientist might combine her labor, her human capital in the form of an education, and physical capital in the form of a computer to produce a space station design. The process of production is that period when these factors are set into motion together and production takes place. Virtually all such processes require that several factors be combined in order to make the good or service.

So, factors of production are allocated to and then combined in processes of production that apply techniques chosen from available technology.

The *techniques* are all the possible ways to produce something. For example, a ditch can be dug by hand, with a shovel, or with a backhoe. Each one of these is a technique. The set of available techniques is the technology available. *Technology* is like the book of blueprints for production processes, and techniques are the pages of that book.

2.6.4 Capital-Intensive versus Labor-Intensive Techniques

Let's note some language that is used to distinguish among types of techniques. We call techniques that use relatively more labor than capital *labor-intensive techniques*. We call techniques that use more capital relative to labor *capital-intensive techniques*. So, digging with a shovel is labor intensive relative to digging with a backhoe which is more capital intensive. Later we will see that when technology offers a choice of techniques, the choice between more labor intensive or more capital intensive techniques is based on the relative costs of labor and capital. In the world today where shovels and backhoes are both in the available technology, we find that in places where capital is expensive relative to labor, ditches are dug with lots of labor and shovels; while in other places where labor is expensive relative to capital, ditches are dug with a little labor and a lot of capital: a backhoe and significant human capital (the person has to be trained in running the backhoe).

Now we have defined all the terms embodied in the statement about production: Factors of production are allocated to and then combined in processes of production that apply techniques chosen from available technology in order to produce goods and services. But we still need to define a few more terms and specify two assumptions before we can expand the scope of our model to reflect the fact that we need to produce in order to consume.

2.6.5 Scale of Production

One concept we will need is *scale of production*. Scale refers to the size of the process of production. Changing scale means increasing all the factor inputs in the same proportion to expand production. So, doubling the scale of production would be a doubling of all the inputs. *Returns to scale* is the degree to which a change in the scale of production changes the level of output. Generally we refer to decreasing or constant or increasing returns to scale. Decreasing returns to scale refers to the case in which as the scale of production is increased the output expands proportionally less. For example, if you double all inputs and output does not double, then you have decreasing returns to scale. Under constant returns the output grows in exactly the same proportion as the scale of inputs grows. So, for example, if you double all inputs the output doubles. Increasing returns to scale means that as the scale of production is increased the output expands proportionally more.

2.6.6 Marginal Productivity

Within a given scale of production there is some flexibility in how much of each factor gets used. For example, a given automobile assembly plant is fixed in size, but the number of workers on the assembly line in that plant can vary.

If we assume a fixed scale of production in all factors except one and add successive units of that one factor input, we refer to the additional output that comes with each successive additional unit of that input as the *marginal product* (*MP*) of that input. So for example, holding all other inputs constant, if auto workers are added to the line of the auto assembly plant, the additional output that comes from each successive worker put on the line is the marginal product (MP) of that worker.

A standard assumption of economic theory that we will make and maintain is that marginal productivity eventually diminishes. This *eventually diminishing marginal productivity* assumption means that, holding all other inputs constant, as one input increases, initially the successive units of that input may exhibit increasing marginal productivity (each adding successively more and more to output), but eventually and inevitably each successive unit of that input begins to exhibit decreasing marginal productivity (each adding successively less and less to output).

Consider the case of our auto assembly line. The very first worker at the line is hardly productive at all—one person in a great big plant cannot get much done. Adding a second person would certainly more than double the output, if for no other reason than they can divide up the line and save time running around. More than doubling the output by adding the second person means that the second person has a marginal productivity that is greater than the first person. It is not inconceivable that this increasing marginal productivity might continue for the third and fourth and fifth person. But clearly at some point the marginal product from successive workers will begin to diminish. Once all the big advantages of adding labor are exhausted, each successive worker may expand production, but by less and less.

So should the objective of production be to identify the point at which the marginal productivity of an input is highest and stop there?

NO. The point of production is not the marginal product, it is the utility derived from the product. In a world of scarcity the ultimate question in production is: How do we get the most utility from our factors as we allocate them across our production options? Simply maximizing marginal productivity is not the answer. In order to maximize the utility we can get from our resources, we need to know how much utility we will get at the margin from each available allocation of the resource.

In order to determine how much marginal utility a particular allocation of successive units of a factor will give us, we need to combine information about the marginal productivity of that factor allocation with information about the marginal utility of the product that comes from that allocation. Together this information can be used to determine the utility derived from each successive unit of input allocated to producing a particular output. Since we value the marginal product of a particular allocation to the degree that it gives us utility, we will call this utility derived from the marginal product of a particular allocation the Value from the marginal product (V).

2.6.7 Value from the Marginal Product—V

For each process of production to which a factor can be allocated (for example: making bread or a shirt or whatever) there is a marginal productivity schedule. For the output from these various processes of production (bread, shirts, or whatever) there is a marginal utility schedule. With this information on the marginal productivity of a factor input and the marginal utility of its output we can determine the Value from the marginal product (V) of that factor for each successive unit of its potential allocations. Let's do a simple hypothetical case from Robinson Crusoe's world.

2.6.8 Developing a Value Marginal Product, V, Schedule

Table 2.6.1 shows the marginal productivity of Crusoe in hunting rabbits.

TABLE 2.6.1
CRUSOE'S RABBIT HUNTING
MARGINAL PRODUCT SCHEDULE
(product of successive hours hunting rabbits)

LABOR HOUR	MP (# of Rabbits)
1st	1
2nd	2
3rd	3
4th	2
5th	1
6th	0
7th	0
8th	0
9th	0

Table 2.6.2 shows the marginal utility Crusoe derives from consuming rabbits.

TABLE 2.6.2
CRUSOE'S RABBIT
MARGINAL UTILITY SCHEDULE
(utility from successive rabbits consumed)

RABBIT	MU (in utils)
1st	100
2nd	90
3rd	80
4th	70
5th	60
6th	50
7th	40
8th	30
9th	20

We calculate the Value from marginal product (V) for each hour of hunting rabbits as follows (See Table 2.6.3):

In the first hour of hunting Crusoe gets his 1st rabbit, and the marginal utility of the first rabbit is 100, so the Value from the marginal product (V) of that first hour spent hunting is 100.

In the second hour of hunting he gets his 2nd and his 3rd rabbit. The marginal utility of the 2nd rabbit is 90 and the marginal utility of the 3rd rabbit is 80, so the Value from the marginal product (V) of that second hour of hunting is (90+80) or 170.

In the third hour he gets his 4th, 5th, and 6th rabbits, and the marginal utilities of these, respectively, are 70, 60, and 50. So the Value from the marginal product (V) of the third hour of hunting is (70+60+50) or 180.

In the fourth hour he gets his 7th and 8th rabbits, and the MUs of these are 40 and 30, respectively, so the Value from the marginal product (V) of the fourth hour is (40+30) or 70.

In the fifth hour he gets his 9th rabbit, and the MU of this rabbit is 20, so the Value from the marginal product (V) of the fifth hour of hunting is 20.

In the sixth hour Crusoe is exhausted and all the slow rabbits near his hut are dead, so he gets nothing. Thus the Value from the marginal product (V) of the sixth hour of hunting is zero.

Table 2.6.3 shows Crusoe's Value marginal product (V) from spending time hunting rabbits.

TABLE 2.6.3   CALCULATING
VALUE MARGINAL PRODUCT OF RABBIT HUNTING

LABOR HOUR	# RABBITS CAUGHT IN EACH SUCCESSIVE HOUR (MP) AND THE MARGINAL UTILITY (MU) OF EACH RABBIT	VALUE MARGINAL PRODUCT the sum of the utility from that hour of hunting	TOTAL UTILITY
1st	1st @ 100	100	100
2nd	2nd @ 90 + 3rd @ 80	170	270
3rd	4th @ 70 + 5th @ 60 + 6th @ 50	180	450
4th	7th @ 40 + 8th @ 30	70	520
5th	9th @ 20	20	540
6th	MP = 0, none caught	0	540

The Value marginal product (V) combines two pieces of information: Crusoe's marginal productivity schedule and his marginal utility schedule. Combining these, the V represents how much utility Crusoe gets from successive units of a factor allocated to a particular process of production, in this case successive units of time allocated to hunting rabbits.

2.6.9 Why Value marginal product (V) Always Falls

The first thing to notice about the Value marginal product schedule is that as Crusoe allocates more and more labor to hunting, the Value marginal product (V) eventually begins to fall. This is inevitable because V is determined by the marginal product (MP), which may increase briefly but inevitably begins to fall, and by the marginal utility (MU) from successive units produced which falls from the very first unit. Since for any possible allocation of labor the MP will eventually fall and the MU will fall from the first unit produced, the Value from the marginal product (V) for all possible allocations of his labor will fall. If Crusoe knew the marginal product (MP) for each possible allocation of his labor (e.g., hunt, fish, pick berries, pump water) and the marginal utility (MU) derived from the units of output, at the outset of each day he could calculate the Value marginal product schedule for each possible allocation of his labor. With this information Crusoe is in a position to determine the optimal allocation of his labor.

2.6.10 Value marginal product and Optimization—A Case

Suppose Crusoe wakes up in the morning, makes his calculations, and gets the results shown in Table 2.6.4.

TABLE 2.6.4 CRUSOE'S VALUE MARGINAL PRODUCT (V) SCHEDULES FOR ALL ACTIVITIES (TOTAL UTILITY IN PARENTHESES)

LABOR (hrs)	V hunting	V fishing	V picking berries	V pumping water
1st	100 (100)	50 (50)	50 (50)	180 (180)
2nd	170 (270)	60 (110)	70 (120)	70 (250)
3rd	180 (450)	180 (290)	40 (160)	5 (255)
4th	70 (520)	170 (460)	10 (170)	0 (255)
5th	20 (540)	70 (530)	5 (175)	0 (255)
6th	0 (540)	5 (535)	0 (175)	0 (255)
7th	0 (540)	0 (535)	0 (175)	0 (255)
8th	0 (540)	0 (535)	0 (175)	0 (255)

Assuming these are the only ways Crusoe can use his labor, this represents his set of opportunities for labor time allocation. He also knows that he faces a time constraint. All of these activities must be done during the 13 hours of daylight, because the bears come out at night. Given his time constraint a bliss point isn't achievable. His problem then is: How does he allocate 13 hours of labor among these competing uses in order to maximize his utility? What decision rule would he follow?

As in the simpler marginal utility case of play and study above, the optimal allocation is reached when there is no opportunity that offers any advantage at the margin. If there were, there'd be good reason to reallocate. As we saw in that simpler case, this optimization condition is met when the margins (in this case the Vs) are equal. Thus, in this case the decision rule Crusoe would follow is to set

$$\frac{V_1}{Unit\,of\,Time} = \frac{V_2}{Unit\,of\,Time} = \frac{V_3}{Unit\,of\,Time} = \ldots = \frac{V_n}{Unit\,of\,Time}$$

Given his time constraint of 13 hours, he would allocate 4 hours to hunting, 5 hours to fishing, 2 hours to picking berries, and 2 hours to pumping water. Doing so would bring the value marginal products into balance at 70.

$$\frac{V_{hunt}}{Unit\,of\,Time} = \frac{V_{fish}}{Unit\,of\,Time} = \frac{V_{pick}}{Unit\,of\,Time} = \frac{V_{pump}}{Unit\,of\,Time} = 70$$

The overall total utility he would generate by this optimal allocation is 1,420 utils. No other allocation of 13 hours would generate as much utility. Try it. You'll see.

We are back to the concept of balance at the margins. One might say that according to economic theory, a good life is a life of good balance.

Obviously this is a contrived example, but the principle applies generally. As we allocate our resources we optimize by balancing at the margin.

2.6.11 Value marginal product and Optimization—The General Decision Rule

We have relaxed several assumptions and now we have the following model for a decision rule governing individual choice. Across all "n" possible allocations of factors, set:

$$V_1 = V_2 = V_3 = \ldots = V_n$$

where V includes information about both the productivity (MP) and the preferences (MU) of the individual.

Our model now encompasses the fact that we need to produce in order to consume, and the fact that since we have finite endowments we have to allocate our scarce resources based on their productivity (MP schedules) and our preferences (MU schedules) in order to maximize our utility. Our decision rule not only describes how someone maximizes her utility given a finite resource endowment, her current preferences, and her productivity; it allows us to predict how she will respond to particular changes in her set of resource constraints, her preferences (MU schedules), and/or productivity (MP schedules).

2.6.12 Changing Constraints and Optimization

For example, consider the following change in Crusoe's constraints: Suppose winter comes and the days are shorter. Now he can only be out seven hours and there are no berries to pick (assume that the MP and MU schedules for the other goods remain the same). Will Crusoe's behavior change? His constraints have changed. He has less time and no berries to pick, so the solution to his constrained optimization problem will have to change. Look back at his Value marginal product (V) schedule (Table 2.6.4), eliminate the option of picking berries, and consider a seven hour time constraint. How will Crusoe allocate his time now? You should be able to convince yourself that he would spend three hours hunting, three hours fishing, and one hour pumping water. At this allocation the Vs are equalized at 180.

2.6.13 Conclusion on the Value marginal product Decision Rule

Let's take a moment to reflect. We are in effect unscrewing the top of your head and looking down in there to see how you make choices. It does not matter whether you do this consciously, the point is that if our assumptions are realistic this model accurately and efficiently describes how you do make choices given that there is scarcity.

Are our assumptions strong or weak? To answer that we have to ask: Does the model seem realistic? It is supposed to be about all of us: about me, your mom, the folks who work in the cafeteria, the President, . . . everybody. But most immediately and intimately for you, it is about you. The best test of its realism is its relevance to you and your life. Ask yourself: "Do I consciously or unconsciously allocate my time as the decision rule describes?"

To the degree that the model seems realistic, it is interesting in and of itself if you find human nature interesting. But above and beyond any pure "academic" interest, to the degree it accurately and efficiently describes how individuals make choices and how individuals respond to changes in constraints and/or opportunities, it is a very powerful tool for developing and implementing public and/or private policies.

If you can set some of the constraints and opportunities people face you can significantly affect and to some degree manage their choices. The rewards and punishments of parents and/or teachers, the advertising and pricing strategies of businesses, the taxes and regulations of governments, the shaping of media information—these are generally designed to manage human behavior. A model of the decision rule people follow is an essential tool for understanding how policies like these work and for planning thoughtful policy.

Our decision rule is not nearly complete. We still have to build in the reality that there is a future and that there are risks and uncertainties in life. Now let's turn to the future.

2.7 RELAXING OUR "NO FUTURE" ASSUMPTION: ADJUSTING OUR DECISION RULE TO REFLECT THIS NEW COMPLEXITY

2.7.1 Setting the Scene

Suppose the following course of events unfolds: You are sitting here reading and suddenly a friend interrupts you, turns on a radio, and says "Listen to this!" A special announcement from the mayor comes on. She says:

> I've got some bad news, and some good news, and some bad news. The bad news is that there's been a slight error in Russia. Given the fact that they're not paying the employees that run their nuclear missile sites very well, those employees are not paying as much attention as they should . . . Well, you know how these things go, it's really sad and they're very sorry, but they inadvertently fired a couple of missiles at the U.S.. That's the bad news.
>
> The good news is that they were able to remotely destroy all but one of the missiles, so there's only one still on its way. There is this pesky problem that Northern Europe is now covered with nuclear radiation, but hey, these things happen . . . Anyway, that's the good news.
>
> There is, however, one more little piece of bad news: The one missile that's still coming is, lo and behold—hey, don't we always have the luck—headed right here and no one can stop it.

OK, that's the news flash. Let's assume you have a test on this chapter tomorrow. My question is this: Would you stay here and finish reading the chapter? I'll return to your answer shortly. Now on with our story.

2.7.2 The Future and Choice

Thus far we have analyzed choices as if we live in a bubble of time and the future does not matter in our choices. When we talk about having a future our choices become more complex because they are *intertemporal,* that is, they have consequences across time. When you make choices in life you are choosing not just for the moment, you are choosing from options that create consequences, and thus flows of utility, across time. Remember where I started this story:

> Two roads diverged in a yellow wood,
> And sorry I could not travel both
> And be one traveler, long I stood . . .

You are constantly doing this in life. Whether it is small decisions like "What do I want for breakfast?" or big decisions like "Where do I want to go to college?," you are constantly faced with diverging paths and you cannot choose both. When you look down those paths you try to imagine: "Where will this path take me? What does that path hold for me?"

Most of the utilities from the choices you make, especially from the big choices, are going to be realized as a flow of satisfactions that go deep into your future . . . and yet you have to evaluate them *now*. As you stand and look ahead, you have to choose between those two roads that diverge in the yellow wood *now*.

All decisions in life have intertemporal consequences. The challenge is that you have to decide *now*.

Consider, for example, buying a car. You expect a car to generate utility for at least a couple of years to come. Should you buy it? Maybe not. You could use the money in lots of other ways that might give you utility sooner, or longer, or. . . .

Each option represents a package of utility spread over time, and the packages are different. In order to make a choice, you must be able to compare all of the available packages and you must make that comparison now, in the present, because all choices are made in the "now," in the "present." So you have to take the future flow of utilities from each available choice and somehow telescope it back into the present so that you can directly compare the benefits and costs of the choices . . . now.

2.7.3 Discounting the Future

In this case, as always when we start relaxing assumptions and expanding the scope of our model, we need more terms to deal with this new complexity: intertemporal choice. Our first new term is "discount." In our language we are going to use the term *discount* to mean 'to diminish value'. For example, if someone promises to help you move your things to a new apartment, you value that promise. But if later you hear from a friend you trust that the person who promised to help you is not at all dependable, you discount that promise—you diminish its value.

With respect to time economists assume that, *ceteris paribus*, people discount the future. This means that the further into the future a utility is going to be realized, the less it is worth to us now. Suppose, for example, that I promise (and assume I'm trustworthy) to give you either $100 at 5pm tomorrow or $100 exactly one year from 5pm tomorrow. *Ceteris paribus*, i.e., assuming all else in your life is constant so the choice abstracts from differing circumstances and is simply about when you prefer to have $100: Which would you choose?

If you think "Give me the money now!" you are consistent with the assumption of economists and you are like the hundreds of students in class to whom I have posed this choice. About 99.9% of them prefer to have the money now. Based on my informal survey, therefore, the assumption that people discount the future is a weak assumption. *Ceteris paribus*, people want their utility sooner not later.

2.7.4 Discount Rates

Economists assume everyone discounts the future, but that does not mean everyone discounts the future the same. Quite to the contrary, economists understand that everyone perceives the future differently. To make this point, let me adjust the offer I just made. The choice is now between $100 at 5pm tomorrow or some larger amount exactly one year from 5pm tomorrow. The question: What would be the lowest amount I would have to offer you to entice you to wait a year for the money? Think of an amount . . .

Whatever you decided would be the minimum amount you feel you would have to be offered to entice you to forgo $100 now and wait a year for the money. Your attitude toward the future is such that I would have to pay you a waiting premium in order to get you to wait. The size of the premium you just demanded can be thought of as a percentage increase in return you require for waiting. For example if you thought, "I'd forgo the $100 now to wait for $150," then your waiting premium is 50%.

In microeconomics we call the waiting premium you require your *discount rate*. It is because you discount the future that I have to pay you to wait, and your discount rate is a measure of the rate at which you discount the future which in turn represents that degree to which you would have to be compensated for waiting.

The level of your discount rate reflects your willingness to wait. *Ceteris paribus*, people with high discount rates are less willing to wait for their utility than people with low discount rates, because the future is worth less to those with higher discount rates.

It is very important to understand that there is no "right" discount rate. A person's discount rate is just a reflection of that person's attitude toward waiting . . . toward the future. Everyone has her own discount rate. Indeed, not only do we each have our own discount rate, but our personal discount rate can change as our situation changes.

2.7.5 Changing Discount Rates

Remember the question I posed earlier about the bomb coming and would you continue to read given that you have a test on this tomorrow? Suddenly with the mayor's announcement your situation has changed. There is no future now that the bomb is coming. You sat down to work on economics because you have a test, because you want to do well, because you want to graduate, because you want an education for your future. After the bomb announcement would you finish what you set out to do? Probably not. If you suddenly learn that in a few moments you'll be annihilated, your attitude toward the future changes dramatically. You would probably discount the future entirely. When your discount rate changes, your choices change. If, heaven forbid, the bomb was coming, you would quickly abandon my words for more immediate utility, like maybe the company of loved ones.

2.7.6 Discount Rates and Social Frames

Discount rates are personal, they are contextual, and to some degree they are socially developed. Our attitudes toward time and waiting evolve as we grow up. That evolution is a function of our experiences and our socialization. Little kids (and some big kids) have notoriously high discount rates. Waiting is torture for little kids. Telling a little kid who is waiting for an ice cream cone that "You'll just have to wait 5 minutes" is like telling her "We've started milking the cow and someday it'll be ice cream." For little kids 5 minutes is forever. And if she doesn't dissolve into tears at the prospect of such an unbearably long delay, then after about 30 seconds and at successive 30 second interval, the kid will invariably ask "Is 5 minutes up yet?" Little kids can make 5 minutes feel like forever when they are asked to wait.

As kids grow up they are encouraged to be patient. My mom always told me that "Good things come to those who wait." It is not an easy lesson, and not one that all folks buy into. But most do, so adults are generally more willing to wait than kids.

This is one of those places where you can explicitly see how the tools of social science depend on one another in order for the analysis to be rich. Discount rates are central to economic theory and in turn economic policy, but to understand discount rates and how they are determined one must reach into social theory. Attitudes toward time seem to vary across cultures, and also within cultures across time, so the model helps us understand why choices are different across cultures and across time.

2.7.7 Present Value

The discount rate is central to individual choice because all decisions in life have, to some degree, intertemporal consequences. The challenge is, you have to decide now. Somehow you have to take the future and telescope it back into the present so that you can directly compare the benefits and costs of the various choices.

> Two roads diverged in a yellow wood,
> And sorry I could not travel both
> And be one traveler, long I stood . . .

As I stand there I contemplate: "What can I see from here? Where does each path go? What can I expect to find along each? How much utility will I get along each way? What is that flow of utility worth to me now?"

With my discount rate I can take those future flows of utility and measure their *present value*. I can use the rate at which I discount the future to calculate the value that any future flow of utilities holds for me now. The present value is the value of those future utilities all telescoped back into a single value now. With the present value I can directly compare my intertemporal choices now, and make a rational choice.

The point is not that we each pause at every divide in the road of life, consciously survey the pattern of utility flows each path has to offer, and then with a specific discount rate in mind pull out a calculator and determine the present value of each path. The point is that if our assumptions are realistic, then this is a reasonable description of what we are doing—more often subconsciously, but sometimes very consciously. So what does building in this new dimension, the future, do to our decision rule?

2.7.8 An Intertemporal Decision Rule

Before we relaxed our "No Future" assumption, our decision rule was, set:

$$V_1 = V_2 = V_3 = \ldots = V_n$$

where the Vs reflect our productivity and preferences with respect to these n different choices.

Now we have to take into account that these choices generate flows of future utilities and that we need to compare and assess and make our factor allocation choice now. Because of this our decision rule has to change.

It becomes: Across "n" possible allocations of factors, at the margin we allocate our factors such that:

$$PV_1 = PV_2 = PV_3 = \ldots = PV_n$$

The V still reflects our productivity and preferences, and now we add the P to make it PV—*present* value. Present value (PV) reflects the fact that the future streams of utility that the alternative allocations of our resources generate must be discounted back into the present so that we can directly compare their relative values *now*. Let's look at an example of this logic at work.

2.7.9 Saving, Investing, and Intertemporal Choice

Consider the decisions people make to save and invest. To save is to forgo using resources for immediate utility. To invest is to use saved resources in order to increase future productivity in the hopes of increasing future utility. *Ceteris paribus*, and individual's decision to save and invest depend significantly on her discount rate. *Ceteris paribus*, who would you expect to do more saving and investing, someone with a high discount rate or someone with a low discount rate?

Someone with a high discount rate sees very little present value in future utilities. Like the little kid, but maybe for different reasons, waiting is very difficult. Unless the payoff from an investment is very high, she is very unlikely to make it. At the extreme, someone who totally discounts the future would never make an investment, because future benefits have a zero present value for her.

In contrast, someone with a low discount rate is, *ceteris paribus*, more likely to save and invest if the investment increases future utility, because that future utility is worth the wait. For the person with the low discount rate, waiting is not so high a price to pay.

2.7.10 Saving, Investing, and Intertemporal Choice—Should I go to College?—A Case

Consider for example the decision as to whether to invest in a college education. Suppose the "now" is when the graduating high school senior is making that decision. We will assume she faces two roads ahead—college or a job. Each is the opportunity cost of choosing the other. Let's imagine what she expects to find down each road:

1.   College. What can she expect down that road?

Going to college is four years of great costs. There are the obvious financial costs like tuition, books, other supplies, and living expenses. There are also the psychic costs like sweating out many hours studying for exams or writing papers.

College also offers benefits. There are the day-to-day joys of the new experiences and friends. There is the real and rich possibility that she will enjoy what she is learning. There is the long-term flow of utilities from the pleasure of appreciating the world more richly and getting a good job with a bright future because she is qualified for and ready to do jobs that offer significant advancement over time. Note the term "over time" here—that is the issue at hand. Many of the big payoffs to college are in the future.

2.   A job. What can she expect down that road?

Getting a job now has costs. There are still living expenses and the time one has to be on the job.

But it also has benefits. She might like the job. She will have a salary she can spend on herself from Day 1. She will leave work at 5 and won't work many, if any, weekends, so she will have her evenings and weekends to use as she pleases rather than struggling to keep up with all the schoolwork that never seems to end.

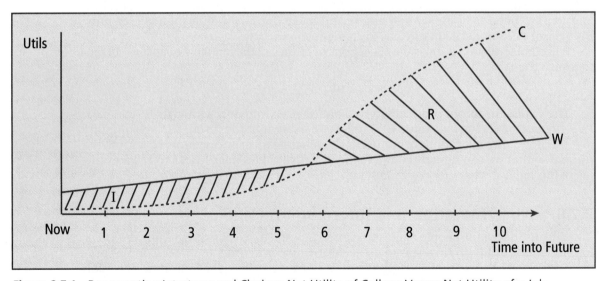

Figure 2.7.1   Representing Intertemporal Choices: Net Utility of College Versus Net Utility of a Job

Let's assume that we can represent the net flows of utility from these two options graphically as in Figure 2.7.1.

The horizontal axis is time into the future and the vertical axis is utils. The C line represents the net flow of utility if she goes to college. The W line represents the net flow of utility if she goes directly to work. Net utility here means the positive utility (the benefits) minus the negative utility (the costs).

As it is drawn the graph represents working as offering more net utility during the first four years. That reflects the assumption that work offers a real salary and much less stress, as compared to college, which offers many joys but also costs a lot in financial and psychic terms.

Beyond the first four years, working keeps its advantage for a while. Assuming the best case for working she would have pay raises by then so she would be doing pretty well, while on the college path she would be just starting out at the bottom and having to prove herself.

However, at some point around six years out the net utility from the college path rises above that from going straight to work. Beyond that the W path rises slowly, while the C path rises much more significantly. The assumption I am making is that college opens lots of opportunities for long-term advancement.

OK, there's the choice. So how does she choose?

Let's look at it as a judgment on whether to invest in a college education. The area between the two lines when W is higher is the opportunity cost of going to college. It represents the net utility she must give up if she chooses to go to college. We will call that the investment cost, and label it "I."

The area between the two lines when C is higher represents the net utility gain from going to college. We will call this the return from the investment in college and label it "R."

So again, how does she choose? She uses her discount rate to calculate the present value of the cost of the investment (I) and of the return on the investment (R). *Ceteris paribus*, if the present value of the return is higher than the present value of the cost, she goes. If not, she takes the job.

The cost of the investment is right up front, so the cost is not discounted very much. On the other hand the return is pretty far out there; it does not even begin until the 6th year out. There is a lot of waiting for the return so the discount rate has a significant impact on the present value of the return. Clearly, the higher the discount rate, the less likely she is to choose college.

2.7.11 Saving, Investing, and Intertemporal Choice—The Case of College Demographics

So now think about this: Why are undergraduate college classrooms like the one I teach in populated almost entirely by folks aged 18 to their mid 20s? Where are all the geezers? Why aren't they there? Quite a few, like my parents, have never been to college. Why aren't they coming now that they are retired and have the time? As with most complex issues there is not a single right story for all cases, but here is one that is consistent with our model.

For folks who are retired and doing OK financially the opportunity cost of going to college as a matriculated student is very high. They give up a pretty quiet existence for the stresses and sweat of exams and papers and grades. Furthermore, they would have to lower their standard of living to pay for college. And for what? The return to college as an investment is down the line. In my scenario above it only begins to kick in six years after you start, then it grows to something significant over many years. But retired folks do not have many years to wait. As we learned at the very beginning of our course, the one thing we all have in common is a finite allocation of time—a limit on life. Retired folks are much closer to that limit than 20-year-olds, so retired folks discount the future much more highly. Given the high opportunity cost and the high discount rate, you see very few retired folks as matriculated students in college. You do see some, however, and this reflects the fact that while our model represents general tendencies, we are each unique in our preferences and our perceptions of time, so we each make our own unique decisions.

I should note that there are a lot of retired folks who, like my parents, take college courses. In most cases, however, they do not do it as an investment activity, they do it as a consumption activity. They don't do it for the future utility they hope to enjoy someday, they do it for the pure joy of learning. Representative of this is the huge number of people who participate in a program called Elderhostel. Quoting from the Elderhostel homepage: Elderhostel "is a not-for-profit organization dedicated to providing extraordinary learning adventures for people 55 and over. Whether you want to stay close to home or venture around the world, you will find programs that meet your interests, activity level, budget, schedule and lifestyle." (as of this writing: *http://www.elderhostel.org/*)

2.7.12 Conclusion on Intertemporal Choice with a Note on Sustainability

One of the issues that enters the analysis of choice when we bring time into that analysis is the question of sustainability.

Sustainability is a question of time. In particular it is the question: How long can I/we maintain a choice? If the answer is "forever" then sustainability is not a constraint on a choice. If, however, there is a sustainability limit, whether it is a constraint depends on the location of that limit relative one's time horizon, and that in turn depends on one's discount rate.

If the sustainability limit lies beyond that point in time when the future is totally discounted, then the limit is not a constraint on choice because it is beyond one's time horizon. If, on the other hand, the sustainability limit lies within one's time horizon, i.e., the limit is reached before total discounting occurs, then that limit becomes a constraint one will take into account when making a choice. As with all other information processing in decision making, in this case too we factor in sustainability based on our perceptions of sustainability, and these perceptions may or may not be consistent with reality.

In some cases a choice is totally driven by the perceived sustainability limit. Consider, for example, a track person who runs the 200 meters. She wants to achieve the highest average sustainable speed that totally exhausts her resources. She does not want to "run out of gas" too soon, but she doesn't want anything left over either. She wants to "leave it all on the track." In this case, she is very careful to factor in the sustainability issue as she makes her choices.

Now let's compare this behavior at the track with her behavior as a consumer. If she perceives that there is no chance that global resources will run out in her lifetime, she may consume with no concern about the future sustainability of global production.

But, what if she has children? She may derive utility from positive prospects for her children's future. This would extend her time horizon. And then there are her possible grandchildren to consider, and her great grandchildren, and her great-great grandchildren, and so on. Does the prospect of endless generations of progeny mean she would be concerned about the sustainability for endless future generations? No. Given a positive discount rate, the weight of her concern about sustainability will diminish toward zero as the time gets more distant.

The point here is that based on our model it is hard to imagine a choice system that would motivate individuals to forgo very much of their current consumption for the sake of distant generations. So, if humans today discount the future and use resources accordingly, does the model predict a very gloomy long term human prospect as humankind inevitably reaches the limit of sustainability?

Not necessarily. In the chapters that follow we will see that regarding this question the mainstream of economic thought splits into two very different channels of analysis, each of which suggests a more hopeful human prospect. Let's briefly preview these positions:

The environmentalist ("green") channel of analysis argues that with appropriate realignment of incentives, e.g., increasing taxes on carbon based fuels to discourage their use and to encourage conservation, humankind can adjust from the current model of production and consumption that has emerged in the last century to a more sustainable model.

The alternative channel of analysis makes the case that sustainability is not actually a "binding constraint" (one that invariably limits us) because market incentives combined with human creativity invariably push back the boundaries of sustainability. The folks that believe this consider expressions of concern about sustainability to be naïve "The sky is falling!" gloom and doom. They argue that policies for a "green" future are in fact foolish and even perverse because such policies unnecessarily limit the current possibilities of enhanced material wellbeing for ourselves and for those around the world today who legitimately strive to join us in our opulence.

To which, those concerned about sustainability for future generations respond: The planet cannot sustain the current pattern of production and consumption, much less an expanded version of this pattern as millions more consumers from China and India and other developing countries join the party. They assert that this "not to worry, it'll all be OK because incentives through markets will solve these problems" view is naive.

We will revisit this sustainability debate often in the chapters that follow. I introduce it here because I want you to see that the concepts we are developing at this early stage, e.g., the discount rate, provide a foundation for understanding and participating in the great policy debates of your generation—in this case the global debate about sustainability.

For now, let's return to individual choice. We have just relaxed our "No Future" assumption and expanded our vocabulary to include discounting, discount rates, and present value. Now our decision rule can represent choice much more richly. Across "n" possible allocations of factors, at the margin we allocate our factors such that:

$$PV_1 = PV_2 = \ldots = PV_n$$

But there is one more dimension of choice that is significant, and our model must account for if it is to be considered realistic. It must reflect the fact that decisions do not always turn out as planned—that there are risks and uncertainties in life.

2.8 RELAXING OUR "NO RISK AND UNCERTAINTY" ASSUMPTION: ADJUSTING OUR DECISION RULE TO REFLECT THIS NEW COMPLEXITY

2.8.1 Introduction to Risk and Uncertainty

Both risk and uncertainty relate to whether the future is going to unfold the way you plan. They each reflect the fact that it never unfolds exactly as you plan. So, both relate to the reality that the paths in the future are not clear. Remember the poem.

> Two roads diverged in a yellow wood,
> And sorry I could not travel both
> And be one traveler, long I stood
> And looked down one as far as I could
> To where it bent in the undergrowth . . .

Much about the future is beyond our sight, around the bend in the undergrowth. In some cases we have some sense of what might unfold. But there is much out there that we have never imagined and that will in fact unfold. This distinction between what we have some sense about and what we have never imagined is what distinguishes risk from uncertainty.

Risks are those things that might affect our plans for better or worse and about which we have some sense of the probability that they will happen. *Uncertainties* are those things that might affect our plans for better or worse, but that we have not even imagined so we cannot assign them a probability. For example, if somebody says to you, "Hey, I'm going do something really cool this weekend; why don't you come with me?" Your initial reaction might be: "Cool, so what is it?" If she says: "Have you ever parachuted?"—There would likely be a long pause as you reflect on that thought: Jumping out of an airplane, parachute, long drop . . . and then you start processing the "Will it open?" question. There is always the possibility that it won't—the probability of failure is not zero, it is between 1 and 100 percent. So you assign a probability to it. In your own mind you have some notion as to whether you think "Sure, it'll open" versus "Given my luck . . ." So in your mind you give it a 1%, or a 25%, or in my case I know it is a 90% probability of failure.

Since you can and do assign a probability to the various risks you can imagine in life, risk is a significant factor in distinguishing among choices. Different choices have different *perceived* risks associated with them. As you choose among different options you do not simply assess the present values of the choices at hand. You factor in the probability for each choice that it will work out the way you plan, you factor in your perception of risk associated with the choice.

2.8.2 Building Risk into our Decision Rule

Expanding our model of choice to include this risk dimension expands the scope of our decision rule beyond the present value (PV) to the *expected* present value (EPV). The "E" reflects how much I actually *expect* to enjoy this utility given my perception of the risk involved: The higher the perceived risk, the lower the expectation.

Thus our decision rule becomes: Across n possible allocations of factors, at the margin we allocate our factors such that

$$EPV_1 = EPV_2 = \ldots = EPV_n$$

Now we have a very rich decision rule.

The V (value) captures our individual productivity and preferences at the margin,

the P (present) reflects the fact that the future stream of utility that the choice generates is discounted back into the present based on our individual discount rate, and

the E (expected) represents our adjustment for our perception of the risk associated with that choice.

2.8.3 Risk and Choice—A Case

Consider the parachuting case. If my friend gives me the option of going parachuting or going to a movie, I know in my heart that, *ceteris paribus*, the present value of parachuting is much higher than the present value of a movie. I mean sitting in a theater eating popcorn and watching flickering images pales in comparison to the rush of hurtling toward the earth, feeling the thump of the chute opening, and then floating over a meadow listening to only the wind. So

$$PV_{parachuting} > PV_{movie}$$

Clearly the choice is to jump—right? ——— Not a chance! I may know in my heart that, *ceteris paribus*, the present value of parachuting is big time better than the present value of a movie, but my head knows that in this case *ceteris* is not *paribus*—all other things are not in fact equal. My head says to me: "You jump, you die!" or in other words that risk of parachuting is huge compared to sitting in a movie, so once the risk adjustment is included my view of the options they look like this:

$$EPV_{parachuting} < EPV_{movie}$$

Obviously not everyone feels as pessimistic as I do about parachuting, so others make different choices. You can see that differing perceptions of risk can have significant impact on the choices we make.

2.8.4 Uncertainty and Choice—A Case

In contrast, uncertainties have no impact on our choices. Having not imagined the prospect we do not associate it with any particular choice and cannot assign it a probability. Anything that you can imagine as a possibility is located among the array of choices and can be assigned a probability. So once you imagine something, you take it into account and it becomes a risk. Let me give you an example.

Every now and then I go down to New York City. When I'm there, I am one of those classic country bumpkin tourist types. I walk along the canyons of buildings gawking at the architecture, the people, the displays in the windows. On one trip down I was sitting in the City reading the *New York Times* and I read a little article about this accident that had happened the day before. It read in part: "A man walking down East 23rd Street was critically injured . . . when an air-conditioner slipped from the window of a building, plunged seven stories and struck him on the head." Apparently a maintenance person was working on the window when the air-conditioner slipped out. This sad story gave me pause. I had never considered the possibility that anything would fall on me as I walked down the streets of New York City. Until the moment I read that story, from my perspective falling objects in the City were among the uncertainties in my life: Things that could happen to affect my plans, but not anything I had ever taken into account in making my plans. Having read the story, I now took it into account. Indeed, the next day as I walked around the City I was hyper conscious of the risks of falling objects. More than once I scanned the windows above for loose air-conditioners, dangling flowerpots, and the like.

When I read that article about the air-conditioner I thought "That's horrible." At first I responded by adjusting my behavior significantly . . . looking up for danger. But the more I walked down the City's streets the more I started to think "Now come on, what are the odds . . ." Clearly the probability that it will happen to me is not zero, but it is very low. Once I convinced myself of that, my scanning of the skies stopped. We all determine our perceptions of the probabilities of various risks by our own experience and by learning from others.

2.8.5 Risk and Learning—A Case

A very important point here is that our perceptions of risk, like our perceptions of time, are in large part a learned behavior. Again you can see this most vividly in kids.

In a house we had when my daughter was very young there was a closet door that made a big "BAM!" sound when it slammed. For a long time she never walked by that door without giving it a good slam and basking in the "BAM!" Then one day when she was about 3, she did that but she was just a little too slow to pull her hand away.—"BAM!"—Waaaaaaaaaaaaaa! She slammed her thumb in the door. For weeks after that she would not get near that door. She seemed to be convinced that the door was out to get her. She went from no perception of risk—slamming a thumb in a door was for her an uncertainty, she had not contemplated the possibility of that outcome; to a perception that the risk was huge. Over time she came to terms with the door, and she didn't avoid it anymore. Classic kid learning. Classic learning at all ages.

2.8.6 Risk as Perception—A Case

Our perceptions of risk significantly affect our choices, and those perceptions come from experience and socialization. It is important to emphasize the word *perceptions*. Even as we learn about risks, all we usually learn are perceptions of risk. Rarely do we know the actual risk, the actual probabilities, involved in a choice. For example, I have asked my class the following question many times: "Suppose you had unprotected sex with someone who goes to school here at Syracuse University, but whom you did not previously know. What do you think the probability is that you would contract HIV?"

The answers I get from my students are widely distributed from 1 to 99 percent. There is no common sense on this probability. And in any case the common sense is often more common than accurate. Clearly most of my students have very little real, accurate information as to the risk of unsafe sex. And yet, just as surely, some of them are having unsafe sex. It's like playing Russian roulette without knowing how many bullets are in the gun.

Ceteris paribus, which students would be most likely to have unsafe sex, those who think the probability is very low or those who think the probability is very high?

All things being equal, the expected present value of unsafe sex is higher for those who perceive the risk as lower, so those who see little risk are more likely to engage in unsafe sex. That is one of the reasons people are more likely to have unsafe sex when they are under the influence of a drug such as alcohol. Drugs affect your perception of risk, often diminishing or obscuring those perceptions.

2.8.7 Risk, Perception, and the Media—A Policy Case

By identifying the factors that affect choices our model allows us to understand how choices are made. If our model is correct, which depends on our assumptions, we can predict that any of the following will change that person's pattern of choices:

> Changing a person's perception of her productivity in and/or preference for an allocation (V), or
>
> Changing her discount rate (P), or
>
> Changing her perception of risk (E)

To the degree that perceptions can be managed, management (manipulation?) of perceptions can be a tool for policy.

For example, a number of years ago the John Jay College of Criminal Justice in New York City produced a videotape for use in police cadet training. In the video the cadets see a former police officer telling the tale of his descent into crime. He used the power of his badge to extort money and drugs from criminals. In the tape the former officer breaks down and cries about how what seemed so tempting and easy at the outset has now ruined his life. The tape has been described as gut-wrenching. In the terms of our model, what is the purpose of the videotape?

There are several possible ways to answer this, but there is one central element that should be in any answer: Clearly those who made the videotape hope to raise the perceived risk of this choice so that anyone who might otherwise be tempted by this path would be discouraged from doing so by hearing about this person's experience. The film virtually screams: The risk of getting caught is real and the consequence is dramatic.

Is this "government propaganda"? That depends on what "propaganda" means to you. Whatever you call it, clearly governments do use the media to shape citizens behavior. During World War II the U.S government plastered the country with posters of Rosie the Riveter. These were part of a concerted advertising campaign designed to change women's perceptions of work so that they would join the labor force when labor power on the home front was desperately needed.

Just as governments can use such perception management to train police cadets to be more honest or to persuade women to go to work, government or business interests or any interest with the resources to reach mass audiences through the media can use the same technique to promote its objectives.

Governments sometimes use risk perception management to justify the sacrifice of liberty in the name of security. For example, it is not uncommon for a government to focus the public's attention on a perceived enemy within, protestors who pose a threat to public order (this was the justification for police spying on civil rights activists during the civil rights movement) or terrorists who would harm the public, to justify spying on citizens. In North Korea this constant hyping of the enemy without justifies the police state. The result is no liberty, and citizens have no choice. In a democratic society this balance between the risk of harm to individuals and the risk of harm to the very liberty that makes a nation a democratic society is a delicate balance. Clearly the measure in this balance must begin with the questions: Is the risk a clear and present danger? How significant is it? And, what is the price of more government policing in terms of that which we value most as a nation: Our liberties? In the U.S. during World War II innocent Japanese-Americans were interred without due process. This was justified by exploiting perceptions of risk based on racial stereotypes. This case represents a tragic loss of balance in a democratic society.

Businesses use risk perception management when they run ads that imply that if you don't use their toothpaste, you will never get a date. In some cases businesses manage risk perception by hiding or suppressing information about the risks associated with their products, because full information about risks would depress sales.

Interest groups use risk perception management by funding ads that frame a Congressional bill or a candidate for office as a blessing for your future or a threat to your well-being, so that you will actively support/oppose the bill or the candidate.

Clearly the media serves a central role in the development of social perceptions, and perceptions play a central role in our model of choice, so we can see from the model why the media are so powerful.

2.8.8 Perceptions, Choice, and Advertising

The use of the videotape in cadet training is just a variation on what advertising does. Advertising is designed to affect or effect our perceptions and in turn our choices. In some cases ads are designed to make products seem more attractive by increasing our sense that this is the path to utility: Lots of people on our TV screens dance and sing and enjoy beautiful company as they drink Pepsi or Coke. In other cases ads are designed to increase our discount rate so we won't wait to buy with tag lines like: "Be the first in your block . . . ," or "Hurry on down to . . ."

The media in general is a significant factor in shaping our perceptions and thus in determining our choices. When the images of the media make incredibly skinny women seem like the standard of beauty, some girls become anorexic in pursuit of the expected present value that such an image seems to hold for them. This is all the more likely if they have a very high discount rate and a very low perception of the risk.

Many teens do indeed have very high discount rates and many who hear about the possible destructive consequences of a choice (anorexia, drinking and driving, unprotected sex, . . .) think: "Yeah, but it won't happen to me."

2.8.9 Gender Perceptions and Choice—A Case

Similarly, the power of socially developed perceptions of gender roles can be understood given our model. The following case explores this issue. Read each part and reflect on the question I pose. Then read my reflection on the question and ask yourself: "Is my response similar to his? If not, how is mine different?" You may respond differently and still be "getting it." The issues embodied in this case are complex and there are many ways to interpret them, but you should at least be able to see how I used the logic given my assumptions. Think about how our responses differ. Discuss any differences with others. Can you make a thoughtful, systematic case for your responses? The ultimate question you must ask yourself is: "Am I applying the concepts thoughtfully, using the terms correctly and appropriately?" This case is meant to give you some practice with the rich and complex model we have developed. If you play with it and discuss it, you will be on your way to learning what you understand and making a good education for yourself.

2.8.10 Taking on the System: Mary Goldburt Siegel

The Situation (based on a *New York Times* obituary):

On January 24, 1991, Mary Goldburt Siegel died. She was 94. Mrs. Siegel was a 1917 graduate of New York University Law School. When Mrs. Siegel started her law career, she was a woman in a man's world. Unwelcome in the legal world's "good old boy" club, her life was a constant struggle to gain access to opportunities that men could take for granted.

Mrs. Siegel's first attempt to find a job was unsuccessful. In order to gain experience she had to accept volunteer work in the office of one of her law school classmates. She moved from there to a job that paid her $4 a week. This rate was only slightly higher than what she would have earned if she had not even completed high school. It was four to eight times less than the rate paid to men in similar positions. This "opportunity" gave her "pay," but the responsibilities that came with this position were largely limited to running errands, so she left this paid position for another non-paid position that allowed her to get real legal experience.

Recounting her first courtroom appearance as a lawyer, she said, "When my case was called and I walked over to the appropriate table, the bailiff rushed over to direct me to where he said I belonged—the spectator's bench." She went on to describe the moment when the judge called the lawyers forward: "As I walked toward him, I was reproached by the judge, who virtually sneered when he repeated that he wanted to confer with the legal representatives, not an office stenographer."

My question is this:

Why did Mrs. Siegel choose this career path? Clearly she was swimming against a very strong tide of ignorance and animosity. There were other paths a woman of the 1920s could have chosen that would have allowed her to enjoy a higher salary and much more respect from her colleagues, for example, nursing or elementary school teaching. Why take on this obstacle course? Use the language of economics to analyze her choice.

My response:

I obviously have no idea what was in Mrs. Siegel's mind. But if our model is reasonable, one possible story of her choice goes like this:

Mrs. Siegel's choice suggests that she valued a career in the law very, very highly. We know this because she must have been aware that there would be many obstacles and they might be so high that she might not be able to overcome them. In economic terms, she chose a very high-risk option. A choice that carries a high risk must also carry an offsetting high return—a high Present Value (PV). Otherwise, one would move to a less risky choice that carries a relatively good return.

We can also imagine that Mrs. Siegel must have anticipated enjoying utility generated by the psychic (as opposed to the monetary) benefits of being a lawyer (e.g., the intellectual fascination of the work and/or the pleasure of helping those who needed legal assistance), because she must have anticipated from the perspective of 1914 when she entered law school that the monetary reward would be diminished by the fact that she was a woman.

Finally, we can also speculate that Mrs. Siegel had a relatively low discount rate. She must have known that any benefits she might hope to enjoy would not begin flowing until after the many years it would take to get her career started. Only with a low discount rate could her Present Value (PV) be high.

Understanding all this helps us understand the accelerating shift of women into traditionally men's jobs since the 1960s. As barriers break down more and more women find the risk diminished, the waiting and thus the present value enhanced, and therefore these hitherto daunting options more attractive. Indeed, Mrs. Seigel may have been motivated by the utility she felt as a trailblazer. If her discount rate was in fact fairly low and if her assessment of the benefit stream included the opportunities her effort might create ("might" because there is the risk it would not work) for future generations of women; that would have a significant positive impact on the present value of this choice, thus providing more motivation to make it.

Now consider another case:

2.8.11 Fooling the System: Billy Tipton

The Situation (based on a *New York Times* obituary):

In 1988, at 74 years old, Billy Tipton died of a bleeding ulcer. Tipton was born December 29, 1914, in Oklahoma City and raised in Kansas City, MO. He began his career as a jazz musician in the 1950s and pursued that vocation for the rest of his life. Tipton married Kitty Oakes in 1960. They separated in 1978. Tipton was survived by three adopted sons. He also left behind a dramatic surprise.

Upon his death Tipton's friends and family discovered that Tipton was a woman. One of Tipton's sons responded to this revelation with the words: "I am lost." Tipton's former wife said, "No one knew." His wife went on to note that "He gave up everything" to pursue his career as a musician, observing that "[t]here were certain rules and regulations in those days if you were going to be a musician." This is a true story.

My question is this:

Why did Billy Tipton go to such lengths to hide her identity as a woman? Consider the effort it must have entailed to spend everyday of one's life in the male world of musicians, including road trips with "the boys," hiding her gender. As with Mrs. Siegel, Billy Tipton had more conventional options available. Why choose such an unconventional path? Use the language of economics to analyze her choice.

My response:

As with Mrs. Siegel, I have no idea what was in Billy Tipton's mind. But if our model is reasonable one possible story of her choice goes like this:

Billy Tipton's choice was, as was Mrs. Siegel's (and everyone else's according to our theory), based on her assessment of the expected present value of that choice compared to the opportunity cost. She wanted to be a jazz musician. She may have been convinced that she would never realize that dream as a woman. Or maybe she had a very high discount rate and was convinced that it would be a very long wait to realize that dream if she "took on" the system as a woman, in which case a dream deferred is a dream denied. The only solution was to "become" a man, accepting all the risks and difficulties that strategy entailed. When the decision to actually do that was made, the present value of the future stream of benefits was apparently so high that, even in light of the obviously huge risk incurred by such a choice, it was better than the opportunity cost—to choose a life considered appropriate for a woman in the 1950s or to take on the system as a woman.

At this point one implication of our model seems clear. Given the central role of perceptions and expectations in individuals' choices, if a society wants to benefit fully from the human potential of all of its citizens, regardless of gender or race or religion or any other distinguishing characteristic, it must equalize real and perceived opportunities and risks.

2.8.12 On Role Models

From this case we can see: If our model is reasonable then role models matter! They matter because they frame a child's mind with respect to *preferences, discount rate,* and *risk.* Let's look at each in turn:

Preferences: If you never see a person of your gender or race in the role of (for example) a lawyer, then it is hard to imagine yourself in that role. If you cannot imagine being in that role, that career choice may not be among the options you consider—it won't be in your preference ordering.

Discount Rate: Many career paths require human capital investments, and an investment means waiting. If your role models have a very high discount rate—if they model immediate gratification—then *ceteris paribus* it is more likely you will too. Thus it is less likely that you will consider career paths that require the waiting that goes with making human capital investments.

Risk: Even if you can imagine being in a given role, like a lawyer, an absence of role models sends a signal that the probability that someone like you is going to make it along that path is low. Low probability = high risk, high risk means, *ceteris paribus*, a reduced likelihood that you'll make that choice.

2.8.13 Social Constructions and Individual Choices

All these role model factors contribute to a socially constructed perception of reality, a way of seeing the world that frames our choices. This is not to suggest that we are socially determined beings with no responsibility for our individual choices. We are social beings, but while society shapes the frame of our lives each of us has a unique biography that makes us a unique being. Within the social frame into which we are born we make choices that shape our lives and in turn reshape our world. That power that we have to affect our world makes us responsible for our choices. Indeed, Adam Smith, the father of modern economic thought made personal responsibility the central element in his story of constructive liberal society. He believed that the success of a liberal society depended on the development of responsible citizens who shared and adhered to a common set of civic values—especially justice. We will return to this subject at the end of our study.

Microeconomic theory helps us to understand the process of choosing given our social frames. It serves us best when we use it alongside social theory as a tool in a social science tool kit. Understanding how frames are socially constructed is an important complement to understanding how choices are made within a given frame.

2.8.14 Perceptions, Individual Choices, and the Challenge of Policy

Developing this economic model highlights how complex the web of connections that shapes our world is, and thus how complicated it is to make policy even with a good model. Take for example policies aimed at stopping drug use.

Let's say the government really worked hard to cut down on heroin use and it got very good at interdicting heroin and/or catching folks with it—raising the risk significantly. That probably would reduce the amount of heroin people use, but it might not solve the drug problem.

Our equation

$$EPV_1 = EPV_{heroin} = \ldots = EPV_n$$

is an interactive equation. If heroin becomes more risky, there are other choices. If a government policy raises the risk of heroin, it may not move people into more constructive choices, it may simply move them to another, less risky kind of perverse behavior. There are lots of alternative choices from 1 to n in our equation, including crack cocaine.

Or consider a campus case. If a university's anti-drinking program successfully raises the risk of getting caught with alcohol on campus, some students might decide, "Well, there are other mind-bending options." Presumably not what the policy was supposed to accomplish.

Our equation not only shows the decision rule people follow, it highlights the interactions among our choices as preferences and perceptions change. This is where economics really gets fascinating, because this brings to the fore the *web of connections* that makes our world complex and that drives the interactions among all choices. One of the themes that I will repeat again and again as our analysis unfolds is that, when it comes to policy: "Anybody who says it's simple is either simple minded or thinks you are." Policy is not simple . . . because the world is not simple . . . it's complex. But, that's what makes it fascinating!

At this point we have seen that individual human beings are complex. We are a very complex web of preferences, perceptions, and values. When you tweak us in one dimension of our being there is no telling how the effect is going to unfold across our choices. By highlighting the interactive character of peoples' choices, our decision rule highlights the complexity of individual choice. And we will soon see that in a complex world of many interdependent people interacting in markets, the web of connections and, thus, the complexity of the system grows exponentially.

2.8.15 Perceptions of Risk and Sustainability Policy

In the context of our analysis of the affect of time on our choices we examined the debate about sustainability: Does the earth have the capacity for us to continue to increase the standard of living many enjoy in the developed nations and at the same time expand that well-being to the rest of humanity? Is global economic growth sustainable if that growth is based the current model of production and consumption?

As we have seen: Some say "No! The earth cannot sustain continued growth under the current production/consumption model. We need a new model and government must be instrumental in developing that new model." Others argue: "Thanks to human creativity and market agility sustainability is not a binding constraint, and policies that address this non-issue are perverse because they artificially constrain our prospects."

At the heart of this debate are conflicting assessments (perceptions) of the risk involved in continuing to pursue the current model of economic growth. Those who see an ominous prospect if there is no change in the model of economic growth base their argument on what they believe is a high probability that this path will lead to deadly degradation of the planet. For example, the Intergovernmental Panel on Climate Change (IPCC for short. The IPCC won the 2007 Nobel Peace Prize.) presents a probabilistic case that global warming is a problem, and asserts that the probability of very significant problems from the current model of growth is unacceptably high.

Those who argue that this sustainability panic is a tempest in a teapot also argue probabilistically. They make their case by asserting that markets have demonstrated an ability to guide humankind's constructive adaptations to changing conditions. Markets can do this for us because changing conditions lead to changing market incentives, and people respond to these incentives in ways that serve society. There is, therefore, a high probability that if resources like clean air and/or clear water become scarce, their value will rise and unfettered markets will in turn ensure the provision these commodities. More generally, if climate change does occur entrepreneurs will meet our changing needs as they respond to the new market opportunities that the evolving climate presents. Change is never a threat in a market system, it is invariably an opportunity.

In these polar terms both sides cannot be correct, and the consequences of a mistake are significant. In one case we limit the current material possibilities for humankind. In the other we diminish or even destroy the human prospect. Whose probabilities are correct? That is for you to decide.

This is a debate worthy of your consideration for it is about the world of your future. Our model can inform your thinking about the issues . . . all the more so as we develop it further in the chapters that follow.

2.9 CONCLUDING OUR ANALYSIS OF INDEPENDENT INDIVIDUAL CHOICE

So far we have been assuming that individual choice is independent of all other human beings . . . that choice takes place as if we are each a Robinson Crusoe. In making his decisions, Crusoe does not have to depend on anyone except himself. This means that all of his decisions are perfectly coordinated. When he decides to produce, it is automatically coordinated with a decision to consume. Obviously, there is no point in producing something unless he plans to consume it. Similarly, if he decides to invest time in building a bow and some arrows or in planting seeds, his investment decision is automatically coordinated with a decision to save time or seeds for those investments. Crusoe's decisions to save and invest or to produce and consume are always perfectly coordinated because they are made simultaneously in his own mind.

This does not mean that Crusoe's decisions always lead to results he desires. He might decide to save corn for seed and find it wasted because no rain comes. He might build a tool that proves to be useless. Being alone does not make Crusoe immune from the problems of risk and uncertainty. Just because his production and consumption or savings and investment intentions are consistent, that does not mean they will work out as intended.

But one thing Crusoe has going for him is that since his decisions to produce and consume or to save and invest are made simultaneously in his own head, they are perfectly coordinated. It is this coordination issue that really distinguishes the simple, isolated world of Crusoe from the complex world of interdependence in which we actually live. We will see shortly that when people are making interdependent decisions to save and invest or to produce and consume, the coordination of all those individual decisions is a huge challenge that must be addressed if a society is to be successful. Absent some form of coordination mechanism, society would break down.

3.0 Interdependent Choice and Market Coordination

3.1.1 The Division of Labor—Benefits and Costs

Is it inevitable that simple economies give rise to complex economies? There are animals that live Robinson Crusoe-type existences even though they are not isolated from others of their species. Why do humans live in complex societies rather than in isolation? Why is it that human society has become progressively more complex over time? Why do we give up the autonomy of total independence for the vulnerability of interdependence? Here are several related possible reasons.

First of all, there is the possibility that we are instinctively social animals. Adam Smith wrote in his book *The Theory of Moral Sentiments* (first published in 1759) that humans "can only subsist in society." According to Smith we are interdependent by our very nature.

But not only is interdependence natural, it is inevitable. It's inevitable because there are many of us, and the resources of the earth are finite. Thus we inevitably find ourselves trying to live off the same set of resources. So the need to determine who will get to use which of our resources, either through conflict or cooperation, makes us interdependent.

And finally, whether interdependence is natural or inevitable, while there are costs there are also benefits from interdependence, benefits that make it an attractive social arrangement. One benefit comes from the connection between social complexity and social productivity. Adam Smith begins his famous work on economics, *The Wealth of Nations* (first published in 1776), with the following words (*An Inquiry into the Nature and Causes of the Wealth of Nations.* Edited in two vol. by W.B. Todd; Vol. 2 of *The Glasgow Edition of the Works and Correspondence of Adam Smith.* General editing by D.D. Raphael and Andrew Skinner. 1976. Oxford: Clarendon Press):

> The greatest improvement in the productive powers of labour, and the greater part of the skill, dexterity, and judgment with which it is any where directed, or applied, seem to have been the effects of the division of labour. (*WN*, 13)

What Smith is referring to here is individuals dividing up the labor across trades as well as within trades; the former is often referred to as *specialization.* In his classic example of the increased productivity that comes from the division of labor within a trade, Smith cites pin making. He writes that there are "eighteen distinct operations" involved in making a pin. According to his estimates, if one person tries to do them all she would be lucky to produce 20 pins in a day. If, however, the operations are divided among ten persons, they could "make among them upwards of forty-eight thousand pins in a day." (*WN*, 15) As for the productivity benefits of the division of labor across trades, Smith cites the advantages of dividing labor so that some people specialize in farming while others specialize in manufacturing.

Smith recognizes that the division of labor comes with potential costs. He specifically expresses concern that if it is too finely divided a person "whose whole life is spent in performing a few simple operations . . . naturally loses . . . the habit of such [mental] exertion, and generally becomes as stupid and ignorant as it is possible for a human creature to become." (*WN*, 782) But he believed that this problem of the division of labor could be solved, especially by education, and that the benefits were many.

3.1.2 The Division of Labor—Reason for Its Productivity

Smith cites three reasons for the increased productivity from the *division of labor*. First, there is what he refers to as "the increase of dexterity in every particular workman." By this Smith means that when you focus on a particular task you get better at it. As the saying goes: "Practice makes perfect." Second, Smith notes that the division of labor saves "time which is commonly lost in passing from one species of work to another." In other words, if you do everything for yourself, much of your time is spent moving from activity to activity and then getting into gear. Finally, Smith believes that when you specialize and get to know your job very well, you are much more likely to be inventive about doing it better and/or faster. For these three reasons, he argues, the division of labor increases productivity.

To show how complex the division of labor had become as of 1776, Adam Smith plays with our imagination. He writes:

> Observe the accommodation of the most common artificer or day-labourer in a civilized and thriving country, and you will perceive that the number of people of whose industry a part, though but a small part, has been employed in procuring him this accommodation, exceeds all computation. The woollen coat, for example, which covers the day-labourer, as coarse and rough as it may appear, is the produce of the joint labour of a great multitude of workmen. The shepherd, the sorter of the wool, the wool-comber or carder, the dyer, the scribbler, the spinner, the weaver, the fuller, the dresser, with many others, must all join their different arts in order to complete even this homely production. How many merchants and carriers, besides, must have been employed in transporting the materials from some of those workmen to others who often live in a very distant part of the country! How much commerce and navigation in particular, how many ship-builders, sailors, sail-makers, rope-makers, must have been employed in order to bring together the different drugs made use of by the dyer, which often come from the remotest corners of the world! What a variety of labour too is necessary in order to produce the tools of the meanest of those workmen! To say nothing of such complicated machines as the ship of the sailor, the mill of the fuller, or even the loom of the weaver, let us consider only what a variety of labour is requisite in order to form the very simple machine, the shears with which the shepherd clips the wool. The miner, the builder of the furnace for smelting the ore, the feller of the timber, the burner of the charcoal to be made use of in the smelting-house, the brick-maker, the brick-layer, the workmen who attend the furnace, the mill-wright, the forger, the smith, must all of them join their different arts in order to produce them. (*WN*, 22-3)

This was from 1776—a much simpler era. Consider the complexity of our own time. Pick a garment that you have on and do as Smith did. Imagine all the hands that went into producing it. Your list will probably only scratch the surface, but the exercise should give you a feeling for the complexity of our world.

If there was no division of labor could you possibly live at the level of material well-being that you enjoy now? The answer is clearly no. Thanks to the division of labor you live at a level of material well-being that is far beyond that enjoyed by many people today and most of humankind in the past. But while the division of labor makes us more productive, greater productivity alone is not enough to make us better off. To see why consider the simple case in which there are three roles in society: shelter-builders, food-gatherers, and clothes-makers.

3.1.3 Surpluses, Exchange, and Gains from Trade

If we envision the aggregate or total social product as a pie, the division of labor makes the size of that pie bigger at the end of the day because by dividing up the labor we have more huts, more food, and more clothes than we would have had if we had each tried to produce everything for ourselves. But, if at the end of the day all that each person has is what she produced, the division of labor leads to a skewed result. What each person has is not a market basket of what she needs: some food, some shelter, some clothes. She only has what she specialized in making: just food, or just shelter, or just clothing. Each person has a *surplus*—much more than she needs—of the one thing she produced, and none of the other things she needs. So if the division of labor is going to be beneficial, there has to be a mechanism to coordinate the exchange of these surpluses so that each person ends up with a useful combination of all things, not just a lot of one thing.

An effective coordination mechanism for the exchange of surpluses makes possible what economists refer to as the *gains from trade*. This term was first used to describe the benefits of international trade among nations, but it describes the benefits of the division of labor at the micro level as well.

A simple example can demonstrate how the gains from trade work.

3.1.4 Absolute Advantage and Gains From Trade

Table 3.1.1 shows how productive you and I are for each hour we spend producing wheat or cloth.

TABLE 3.1.1 ABSOLUTE ADVANTAGE		
	WHEAT IN BUSHELS	**CLOTH IN YARDS**
me	10	7
you	6	10

I am better at producing wheat. You are better at producing cloth. We each have what economists refer to as an *absolute advantage*—each of us is absolutely better at something. If instead of dividing up the labor, we both work one hour at wheat production and one hour at cloth production, how much total wheat and cloth do we produce? In my hour of cloth production I can make 7 yards. In your hour you can make 10 yards, so our total production is 17 yards. In my hour of wheat production I can make 10 bushels. In your hour you can make 6 bushels, so our total production is 16 bushels.

Now suppose that instead we decide to divide up the labor, specializing in the productive activity at which we have our respective absolute advantages. Since I can produce 10 bushels of wheat in an hour and you can product 10 yards of cloth in an hour, by specializing I can produce 20 bushels of wheat in those two hours and you can produce 20 yards of cloth. Between us we therefore increase our net wheat production by 4 bushels and our net cloth production by 3 yards. But now I am holding all the wheat and you are holding all the cloth, so we trade. The exact outcome of the trade is not clear, but it can clearly benefit both of us. So long as we both benefit from these gains from trade we will both continue to participate in the division of labor and exchange of surpluses.

3.1.5 Comparative Advantage and Gains From Trade

Now suppose you are better than I am at both kinds of production. Would there still be mutual benefits from dividing up the labor and exchanging surpluses? Are there still gains from trade? Yes. David Ricardo demonstrated in his *Principles of Political Economy and Taxation* (published in 1817) that specialization and exchange of surpluses can be mutually beneficial even if one of the parties is absolutely better at doing everything. In this case, the benefit derives from each party specializing in what is referred to as her respective *comparative advantage*.

Let's assume you have an absolute advantage over me in the production of both wheat and cloth, as represented by Table 3.1.2.

TABLE 3.1.2 COMPARATIVE ADVANTAGE		
	WHEAT IN BUSHELS	**CLOTH IN YARDS**
me	4	1
you	12	2

Since any hour spent on one activity is one less hour that can be spent on the other activity, your opportunity cost of producing 2 yards of cloth is 12 bushels of wheat. In other words, each yard of cloth "costs" 6 bushels of wheat in terms of forgone production. For me, however, the opportunity cost of producing 1 yard of cloth is 4 bushels of wheat—that is, each yard "costs" 4 bushels. So while you are absolutely better at producing both products, the opportunity cost of producing cloth is greater for you than it is for me. In that case it is relatively or comparatively cheaper for me to produce cloth than it is for you to do so. In the language of economics we say that an individual (or country) has a comparative advantage when she (or it) can produce a good at a lower opportunity cost. As long as such comparative advantages exist, trade is beneficial. The division of labor will emerge and continue to develop as long as the gains from the trade of the surpluses it generates are beneficial to the parties involved.

3.1.6 Division of Labor is Limited by the Extent of the Market

As Adam Smith understood and made clear, the limitation on the division of labor is *the extent of the market*. After all, it is pointless to specialize if there is not enough of a demand to warrant the specialty. For instance, in New York City you will find people who make their living as taxi drivers, as couriers, and as professional baseball players. None of these professions could be justified in a village of 600 people in upstate New York or in a little bayou town in Louisiana.

But no matter how small or big the market, in order to enjoy the gains from trade that flow from the division of labor there must be a mechanism for exchanging surpluses. There are a number of alternative mechanisms possible. History offers examples of each.

3.1.7 Tradition as a Mechanism for Exchanging Surpluses

One of the oldest forms of coordination is based on tradition. In a *traditional system* the patterns of the division of labor are based on social definition of place (e.g., based on gender) and these patterns are passed down from generation to generation. If you are a boy and your father tilled the earth, you will till the earth. If he worked in a guild, you will work in that guild. If you are a girl and your mother took care of the home, you will take care of the home. If she served an aristocrat, you will be a servant to an aristocrat. As a coordination mechanism tradition works well because interdependent decisions to produce and consume and to save and invest are based on predictable patterns that have been clearly established over long periods of time.

Ironically, this predictability of tradition is one of its great limitations. There is no room for creativity, no room for new ways of doing things in a traditional society. Indeed, new ways are suspect and often considered dangerous, so traditional societies are materially stagnant. The standard of living is constant from generation to generation.

The one great strength of a traditional system is its internal stability. But that strength is also the source of its greatest weakness. Its internal stability derives from its rigid structure. A rigid structure cracks easily when exposed to external stresses. Historically, traditional societies have generally broken down very quickly when exposed to more dynamic systems.

3.1.8 Command as a Mechanism for Exchanging Surpluses

Another coordination system that has a long history is a centralized system or a *command economy*. In such a system a central authority, for example a dictator, determines what is produced and consumed and what is saved and invested. The good news about a command economy is that as in the Robinson Crusoe case, to the degree that decisions to produce and consume and to save and invest are made by one person those decisions are very well coordinated. Further, if the dictator is benevolent those decisions reflect her view of what is best for the people. And if her benevolence includes justice, the result is a system that may be just.

There is, however, bad news too. First, while the dictator may be benevolent, she is not omniscient. Her decisions must be made according to her own impressions of what the people desire, not on the basis of their actual preferences. So the system does not necessarily produce what people want or need.

The quality of production in a command economy is also limited by the knowledge and creativity of those in command. Even brilliant leaders cannot know all there is to know about every process of production, nor can they be creative in all dimensions of that production . . . so the production processes are inevitably inefficient and slow to change. Further, in a command system people are told what to do and how much they will get for their efforts, so there is very little incentive for them to work hard or carefully or imaginatively. Thus while the command economy may be internally consistent and decisions may be made with the best of intentions, they will inevitably be inefficient. As for the justice of such a system, benevolent dictators are a very rare phenomenon and no one lives forever, so there is little chance that such enlightened leadership would last very long.

3.1.9 The Liberal System of Free Markets as a Mechanism for Exchanging Surpluses

The third coordination system alternative is a relatively new experiment for humankind—only a few hundred years old. It is called a *liberal system of free markets*. This is the system of coordination that we are going to focus on here. As we will see shortly, under the ideal conditions that ensure perfectly free competition a market system can be incredibly efficient. It responds quickly to people's preferences, and it is extremely agile—it adjusts quickly to changes in conditions including changes in preferences. The beauty of a liberal society under ideal conditions is that

1. People are free to make their own choices based on their own preferences,
2. The efficiency of the markets ensures that people get the most utility out of the share of the social endowment they own, and
3. The agility of the market system allows it to respond creatively to changing conditions and evolve in constructive ways.

We will also see that free markets are amoral. At their best all markets do is efficiently coordinate the choices of those individuals who are free and autonomous. The markets do not care if every individual is actually free and autonomous, or if anyone is impoverished or enslaved or exterminated.

3.1.10 The Liberal System of Free Markets, and Justice

A perfectly functioning free market system does not create justice, it requires it. Adam Smith, the father of modern liberal economic thought, understood this very well. He wrote about justice in his first book (*The Theory of Moral Sentiments*) before he wrote about free market economics in his second book (*The Wealth of Nations*), because he recognized that the success of markets rests on establishing justice as a foundation. "Justice [Smith wrote] . . . is the main pillar that upholds the whole edifice [of society]. If it is removed, the great immense fabric of human society must in a moment crumble into atoms." (Adam Smith. *The Theory of Moral Sentiments.* Edited by D.D. Raphael and A.L. Macfie of *The Glasgow Edition of the Works and Correspondence of Adam Smith.* General editing by D.D. Raphael and Andrew Skinner. 1976. Oxford: Clarendon Press. (Hereafter *TMS*), p. 86)

So the issue of justice is not simply an academic question in a liberal, free market system. Just as traditional and command economies have sources of weakness—so, too, this system. The long-term sustainability of a liberal society depends on the constructive participation of its citizens. If the rules of fair play are not clear and commonly shared by all citizens regardless of their gender, race, religion, national origin, or any other difference that can distinguish and demarcate us; and/or if a significant number of citizens feel the system is unjust, the sustainability of the system is inevitably undermined.

Again we meet this issue of sustainability. It has many dimensions. In this case we will find that the sustainability of a liberal system of free people and free markets depends on the justice of that system.

3.1.11 On Distributive and Commutative Justice

We will see that the challenge of establishing a just and therefore sustainable liberal system has two dimensions:

> *Distributive justice*: Ensuring that the outcome of what Adam Smith referred to as "the race for wealth" is fair?

and

> *Commutative justice*: Defining and enforcing our common rights as citizens in a liberal society, including property rights, such that the conditions in the race for wealth and the conditions surrounding that race are fair?

At the close of our analysis we will return to these issues of justice and the sustainability of liberal society.

3.1.12 The Magic of Markets

The premise of a liberal, free market system is that each individual owns a share of the social endowment (e.g., her labor and possibly some capital and natural resources) as her private property: This concept of property ownership is essential, because it establishes her right to use her resources as she sees fit and to have them protected from theft.

Given her property rights, she can use her resources in isolation, she can work cooperatively, she can participate in the market system, or she can pursue some combination of these options.

If she chooses to participate in the market system, she allocates her share of the social endowment (her labor and any capital or natural resources she owns) to a particular process of production and in return she is compensated with a share of the value her allocation helped produce. She can then use this compensation to exchange for an array of products being produced by others. All of these exchanges—her resources exchanged for compensation from the production to which she contributed, her compensation exchanged for products made by others—are coordinated by markets. To the degree markets do this efficiently and effectively, she and all the other participants enjoy gains from trade.

The magic of the market system is this: Under the ideal condition, perfect competition, the gains from trade are greatest for everyone. This is so because each individual's own interest drives her to work as hard as possible to serve the preferences of others. This incentive exists because the more the market values what she produces, the more her compensation will ultimately exchange for in the market. She can only survive to the degree that she serves the market's values with her production at least as efficiently as her competitors. She only gets ahead to the degree that she serves the market's values with her production more effectively than her competitors. So under perfect competition, we each work hard to serve ourselves by working hard to serve one another, and only best efforts move us ahead.

In what follows we will explore:

- How a generic market works,
- How a general system of markets works under ideal conditions,
- How and why the system can break down,
- Why a perfectly efficient market system may not necessarily be just, and
- What, if any, role there is for government in a market system.

We will see that under the ideal conditions of perfect competition a market system is not only an efficient mechanism for coordinating the use of current resources, it is also a dynamic developer of efficiency because it encourages creativity in using resources to better satisfy the evolving preferences of the participants. Before we turn to our analysis of markets, however, we need to introduce the concept of money. Money is used to facilitate exchange in any complex market system.

3.2 THE ROLE OF MONEY IN MARKETS

3.2.1 On Money Capital

Let me begin with a distinction that is very important because the language can get tricky. Some people refer to money as capital. Certainly if you have read the newspaper you have seen articles about capital flowing into this country or out of that country, or about an entrepreneur looking for the capital necessary to make a new investment. In these cases the term capital refers to money. Earlier we defined capital as "a produced means of production," and that is NOT money. So let's clarify this concept of capital.

When I introduced capital as a produced means of production, I identified it as *production capital*. It is something that is produced and then applied in further production. Our examples included machines and an education. When we talk about money we are talking about a different concept of capital.

Money is *financial capital*. It finances the exchanges that make production possible (buying and selling factors) and purposeful (buying and selling products), but money is not used in the process of production itself. Be sure to keep this distinction in mind. When you hear the word capital ask yourself, "Which concept of capital are we talking about here?"

Now with that distinction in place let's see why money emerged as part of an exchange system, and how money has evolved.

3.2.2 From Barter to Money Exchange—The Function of Money

In what Adam Smith referred to as the "rude state" when the division of labor and exchange of surpluses begins, exchange is initially through barter. *Barter* is an exchange of equivalents: A share of my surplus wheat for a share of your surplus meat. Clearly, shares must be of roughly equivalent value if we are going to agree to the exchange. In small societies with traditional systems barter is functional because everyone can interact with everyone else pretty easily, and the exchanges are in constant patterns that everyone knows by tradition. But as exchange becomes more complex, barter becomes an impediment to the process.

Barter requires matching. If you have surplus wheat and desire cloth, you have to find someone who has surplus cloth and desires wheat. Failing this, you have to arrange a multi-person trade; your wheat for person 2's meat, then person 2's meat for person 3's cloth. Since you need an array of goods, you would have to repeat this process for each item you seek. As the exchange system gets more complex, the challenges and costs of barter increase dramatically.

This growing inefficiency in barter (the exchange of equivalents) gives rise to the emergence of a *general equivalent*—one particular commodity that is generally accepted in barter for any other commodity. Gold is the commodity that historically took on this role most widely.

When gold became a standard general equivalent, units of gold became an acceptable measure of the exchange value, the price, of any good or service. A coat, for instance, was worth a certain number of units (grains) of the general equivalent, gold. Since gold does not deteriorate, it also became a useful way to store value between exchanges. Thus gold became a multipurpose commodity. It was always valued for its ornamental beauty, but it also took on the following roles:

- a medium of exchange—others accepted gold for any good or service,
- a unit of account—it allowed people to measure the value of their holdings,
- a store of value—people could hold value in the form of gold.

We define any item that serves these three roles as *money*.

3.2.3 Characteristics of Good Money

The reason gold emerged as the standard form of money is that it has characteristics that make it work well as money. It is, except for periods of plunder or discovery, fairly fixed in supply. Anything that grows on trees would not make very useful money. Why? The quantity of anything that you can grow on trees, like leaves, can expand endlessly. So the number of leaves you would need to pay for things would increase constantly. This means that any leaves you saved and stored would be worth less and less as the leaf-based prices rose. Furthermore, these rapidly changing prices would make accounting a nightmare.

Gold also has the advantages of being fairly portable, continuously divisible, and storable. Why are these important characteristics if a commodity is to be used effectively as money?

Portability is handy because money is used in trade. As trade becomes more complex it takes place over longer and longer distances, so being able to carry your money around is very important. Since even an ounce of gold is worth a great deal, a large value of gold can be carried very easily, making transactions across long distances easy.

Continuously divisible is important because it allows you to finely tune how much you spend so that you can make your choices at the margin—do I want one more? A dairy cow would not make good money. Half a dairy cow is not half as valuable as a whole dairy cow. Gold is divisible into dust.

Easy-to-store matters because money is supposed to be a way to store value. You do not want your wealth to lose value while it is stored, so you would not want to use strawberries as money. They would rot in your "bank". If a commodity is going to be useful as money it has to be storable for a long time. Gold can be stored forever.

3.2.4 Commodity and Fiat Money

Initially the things people used for money were commodities. They functioned as money, but they also had value in and of themselves. Gold is a classic example. It can be used as money, but it's also used for jewelry and other things. This kind of money is called *commodity money*. There is very little commodity money in use today. Today we use *fiat money*.

A dollar bill is a classic example of fiat money. It says on the top "Federal Reserve Note, The United States of America". It is "signed" by the Treasurer of the United States and the Secretary of the Treasury to show that it is official. It says on the front that "This note is legal tender for all debts, public and *private*." (Emphasis added) In effect the United States government is telling you that by law you have to take this in an exchange even if it is a private exchange. So it is money by government *fiat*. It has absolutely no inherent commodity value.

Governments have taken control of issuing fiat money because there is significant power in controlling the printing of money. But, the usefulness of fiat money as money depends entirely on the willingness of people to accept it as such. As long as people believe the government is stable and as long its money serves well as a unit of account, medium of exchange, and store of value, people will use it.

If a government's days seem numbered, people abandon its money. As people began to doubt that the Confederate States of America would survive, people tried to exchange their Confederate money for other forms like gold.

If a government mismanages its fiat money and prints it as if it was growing on trees, this flood of money would mean more money buying the same amount of commodities so the prices of everything would rise. If this general rise in prices gets totally out of hand, a situation called a *hyperinflation*, no one wants to hold or use that money any more. Dependable money is an essential element in a complex world of market exchange.

Now with our model of individual choice as a foundation, let's see how a market actually coordinates exchange among autonomous individuals.

3.3 HOW A MARKET WORKS

3.3.1 Introduction

During the 17th and 18th centuries as experiments in liberal systems were in their infancy, most people understood order as something to be imposed on a society by tradition or by a king. Even today, for many people the concept of a society with no central control conjures up images of chaos. In an incredible leap of vision Adam Smith imagined how a system with no one in charge could work constructively. Smith's *Wealth of Nations*—published in the year the American colonies declared their independence and began a new experiment in liberal society—describes his vision of how humankind has evolved toward the liberal experiment and how an ideal liberal order would realize the greatest possible wealth for the nation. In Smith's vision of an ideal constructive liberal society there is liberty *and* justice for all. Smith believed that under those conditions markets would generate a constructive, efficient, spontaneous order. He believed that moving along the path from the best case of liberal society in 1776, his own Great Britain, toward the ideal required a progressive maturation of civic ethics. But what Smith is most famous for is his presentation of the principle that markets can coordinate the choices of autonomous individuals in a socially constructive way. Let's see how they do that.

3.3.2 Markets as Dynamic Feedback Systems

Markets work on the same principal as your body. If your body is healthy it functions as a *dynamic feedback system*. It constantly and quickly sends signals that help you assess your behavior and adjust it to be more constructive. Under ideal conditions of perfect competition, markets do the same thing.

If you touch a hot stove, you get a quick, strong signal that says, "No, idiot! This is not a good place for your hand!" and you respond real quickly—you change that behavior. When you find a nice place to sit and watch a sunset, your body says, as my son Jesse likes to say: "Ahhhhhhhhhhhhhhhhhhh yes, this is the life!" You respond by settling in to enjoy the show. A constant flow of signals from your body allows you to continuously assess and adjust your behavior so that it can be most constructive.

Under the ideal conditions of perfect competition markets do the same. The markets send a constant flow of signals to all who participate, all adjust their behaviors to the signals, these new behaviors generate new signals. Through this dynamic feedback system of signaling, behavior adjustments, new signals, and so on, the market system moves all individuals to decisions that are personally optimal (i.e., utility maximizing) and at the same time well coordinated with the choices of all others. Thus it makes interdependent resource allocation of independent individuals efficient. The amazing thing about a market system—the magic of markets—is that under ideal conditions it does this beautifully with nobody in charge. To see how the market system's signaling process works, we begin by examining how a single generic market works.

3.3.3 The Market Picture

Here in Figure 3.3.1 is a generic *market picture*.

We're going to see a lot of this picture, so let's be careful to understand what it represents.

Figure 3.3.1 A Generic Market Picture

One of the issues in market exchange is "How much?" On the horizontal axis we measure quantity or how much. We represent quantity with a capital Q.

When things are exchanged in a market, they are going to be exchanged for a price measured in money. If we are going to represent exchange we need a graph that shows the possible prices of exchange. The vertical axis represents the price scale with a lower case p.

So, in our generic market picture, the "p" on the vertical axis measures price and the "Q" on the horizontal axis measures quantity.

In every market we will have suppliers—those who come to sell, and demanders—those who come to buy. Let's see how we represent those two participants in our market picture.

3.3.4 Representing the Participants—The Supply and Demand Lines

The supply line in our market picture represents the attitudes of suppliers—how much or what quantity Q are they willing to bring to the market at each possible price p. For reasons we will explore in detail shortly, *ceteris paribus,* the suppliers' attitude is—raise the price and we will bring more to the market, so the supply line slopes up.

The demand line represents the attitude of demanders—how much or what quantity Q do they intend to buy at a given price p. For reasons we will explore in detail shortly, *ceteris paribus*, the demanders' attitude is—lower the price and we will buy more from the market, so the demand line slopes down.

As I have noted before, it is very important as we build this model to ensure that we are using the same language—that a given term means the same thing to both of us. In the case of supply and demand there is some vocabulary I need to clarify. In order to do this it is helpful to represent the information embodied in the supply and demand lines in an alternative form—in functional form, or in other words, as an equation.

3.3.5 Functional Form

Functional form is a way of describing a causal relationship between two variables. For example, all other things being equal, your grade in a class depends on the amount of effort you put into the class. In functional form we can represent this relationship as

$$G = f(E)$$

This equation says that, *ceteris paribus*, your grade in a class (G) is a function (*f*) of, or in other words depends on, your effort in the class (E). The function "*f*" stands for how G depends on E. My experience suggests that G is positively related to E—the better your effort the better your grade. So in this case the *f* represents a positive relationship between G and E.

In the case of demand we can write

$$Q^D = D(p)$$

This says that the quantity demanded, Q^D, is a function D of the price, p. The D stands for the relationship between Q^D and p. *Ceteris paribus*, the D stands for a negative relationship—that is, *ceteris paribus*, the quantity demanded falls as price rises.

Now let's be sure our terms are clear.

3.3.6 The Terms of the Demand Relationship

The *quantity demanded*, Q^D, is a specific number like 4 or 86 or 6,534. The price, p, is also a specific number like 25 cents, or $5, or $9,000. The *demand*, D, is *not* a number. It is a function that represents the current attitude of demanders: How much will they want at a given price. That attitude encompasses a lot of price/quantity combinations. So for example, D can be represented as a schedule of prices and quantities that looks like Table 3.3.1.

At price = $1, given the attitude of demanders embodied in this particular schedule, the quantity they would like to buy is 10. At price = $2 the quantity demanded is 9, and so on down to price = $9 where the quantity demanded is 2.

TABLE 3.3.1

p	Q^D
1	10
2	9
3	8
4	7
5	6
6	5
7	4
8	3
9	2

This schedule can be plotted on a graph and represented as a demand line as in Figure 3.3.2. At price = $1 the quantity demanded is 10, at price = $2 the quantity demanded is 9, at price = $3 the quantity demanded is 8, at price = $4 the quantity demanded is 7. What is the Q^D when the price is $1? Look at the graph. . . .

At the price = $1, the schedule tells us that the quantity demanded is 10, so the point on the demand line that represents this is where p = $1 and Q = 10.

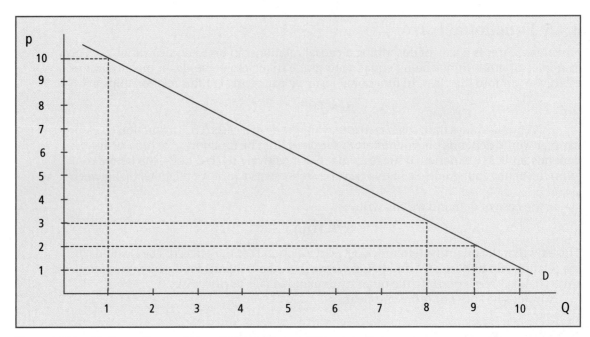

Figure 3.3.2 Ploting a Demand Line, D, from Demand Schedule Data

Connecting these points we have a demand line that represents the attitude embodied in the demand schedule. Be careful with the distinction between demand and quantity demanded. Demand is a function. It reflects the attitude of demanders and is represented by the demand line. Quantity demanded refers to a specific number. A change in price moves us along the demand line to a new quantity demanded. A change in the item's price *does not* change the demander's basic attitude toward that item, so it does not affect the demand line. But what happens to demand if demanders' attitudes do change? How do we represent that?

3.3.7 Attitude Shifts and Shifting Demand

A change in attitude is represented by a demand schedule as shown in Table 3.2.2. We see that at any given price the quantity demanded is greater. At price = $1 the quantity demanded increased from 10 to 14. At price = $2 the quantity demanded increased from 9 to 13. At price = $3 the quantity demanded increased from 8 to 12, and so on down to price = $9 where the quantity demanded increased from 2 to 6.

Table 3.3.2

p	$Q^{D\text{-OLD}}$	$Q^{D\text{-new}}$
1	10	14
2	9	13
3	8	12
4	7	11
5	6	10
6	5	9
7	4	8
8	3	7
9	2	6

If the demand schedule and the demand line are just two alternative ways of representing the same attitude, how do we represent this attitude change on the graph? Attitude changes shift the demand line as shown in Figure 3.3.3.

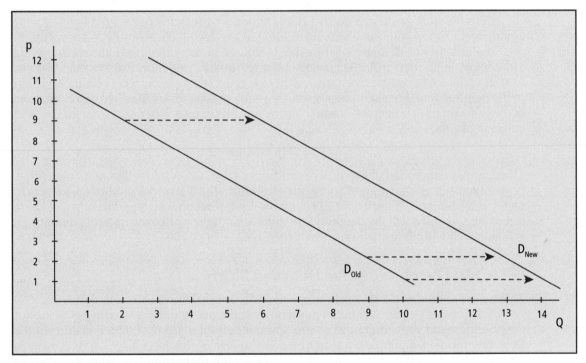

Figure 3.3.3   Representing a Shift in Demand, D

For each given price we move the point to the right to represent the fact that at that price a greater quantity is now demanded. At price = $1 the point moves from Q = 10 to Q = 14. At price = $2 the point moves from Q = 9 to Q = 13. For each price $3, $4, $5, $6, $7, $8 the point shifts accordingly all the way down to price = $9 where now the quantity demanded is 6. In effect, this change in attitude is represented on our demand graph as a shift in the entire line from its original position to a new position that reflects demanders' new attitude toward the item.

Any given demand line represents the attitude of demanders under the given set of conditions. If a change in conditions causes a change in demanders' attitudes, the demand line will shift.

3.3.8 Functional Form for Demand and Shift Variables

Suppose for example, an item suddenly gets very popular—like a hot new CD. In that case there will be a greater quantity demanded at any given price. This change in attitude shifts the demand line, D, to the right—as in Figure 3.3.3. The fact that new conditions change attitudes and shift demand can be built into the functional form we use to represent the demand line. Instead of writing the demand relationship as simply

$$Q^D = D\ (p)$$

we can write

$$Q^D = D\ (p\ |\ \textbf{shift variables})$$

The vertical line stands for "given." To understand this concept of the given shift variables consider this a non-economic example. Remember our case of

$$G = f(E)$$

The relationship between your grade and your effort does not exist in a vacuum. One thing that can clearly affect the relationship is your health. We can reflect this by rewriting the functional form as:

$$G = f(E\ |\ \textbf{your health})$$

This says your grade in a course is a function of your effort given the level of your health. A change in your health status can affect this overall effort/grade relationship.

Similarly, in our demand relationship a change in the variables that determine the attitudes of demanders will affect the overall price/quantity relationship. We refer to these as shift variables because any change in them is reflected in our market picture as a shift in the demand line. For example, we will see in the market for products like CDs that one of the shift variables is peoples' "tastes." So the product market functional form for demand will look like this

$$Q^D = D\ (p\ |\ \textbf{tastes, ...})$$

The quantity demanded of a good in a product market, Q^D, is a function of its own price, p, given consumers' tastes and some other variables I will introduce shortly. Changes in tastes shift demand. If, as in our CD example, tastes become stronger for a good, then, *ceteris paribus*, how will the demand line shift? At any given price the quantity demanded is higher so it will sift just as shown in Figure 3.3.3.

3.3.9 My Terminology for Demand Shifts

This is a good time to clarify some language I will use to describe shifts in demand.

I will generally refer to shifts in demand as shifts out or back, or to the right or left. I describe demand shifts this way because I find it helpful to think of demand shifts in the following terms: Do people want to buy more or less of this item at any given price. In effect I orient myself by using the price axis as my reference, and I envision movements of the demand line as closer to the price axis (at any given price quantity demanded is less) or farther away from the price axis (at any given price quantity demanded is more). Given this conception of the shift in attitudes, when I describe movements of demand I generally use the terms left and right or out and back.

3.3.10 The Supply Line

All the tools I have just introduced to represent the demand relationship exist for the supply relationship as well.

The supply function looks like this:

$$Q^S = S\ (p\ |\ \textbf{shift variables})$$

This equation says that the quantity supplied, Q^S, is a function, S, of the price given the current state of the shift variables. As we will see when we dig into supply, these shift variables are different from those for demand because, not surprisingly, the considerations that shape the attitudes of the suppliers are different from those that shape the attitudes of demanders.

This relationship between quantity supplied and price can be represented by a supply schedule as shown in Table 3.3.3. (We will see why it's a positive relationship, that is—why a price rise causes quantity supplied to rise, soon. For now we will just assume it is true.)

TABLE 3.3.3

p	Q^S
1	1
2	3
3	5
4	7
5	9
6	11
7	13
8	15
9	17

This table camp be represented a supply line as shown in Figure 3.3.4.

Supply refers to an attitude represented by the whole supply line. Quantity supplied refers to a specific number. At price = $1 the quantity supplied is 1, at price = $3 the quantity supplied is 5, at price = $9 the quantity supplied is 17. A change in price moves us along the supply line to a new quantity supplied.

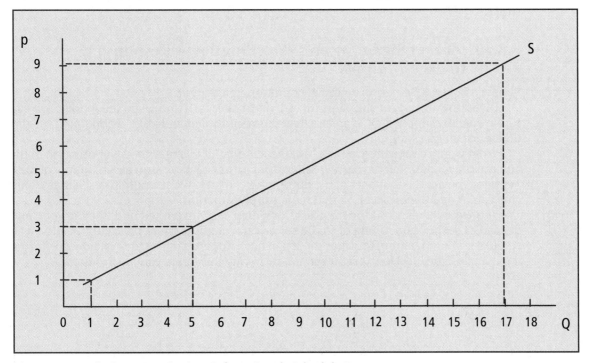

Figure 3.3.4 Ploting a Supply Line, S, from Supply Schedule Data

Any given supply line represents the attitude of suppliers under the given set of conditions. If a change in conditions causes a change in suppliers' attitudes, the supply line will shift. As we will see the attitudes of suppliers are shaped by variables that determine the cost of production or, in other words, the costs suppliers have to cover to bring their item to the market.

3.3.11 My Terminology for Supply Shifts

Now a note on how I will describe supply shifts. I find it helpful is to use the quantity axis as the frame of reference and think of the supply line as shifting up or down. This is useful because the supply line reflects the cost of production and one can ask oneself, "has the change in the shift variable made it more or less expensive to supply this item?" If it becomes more expensive for suppliers to bring an item to market then the price they will charge will be higher at any given quantity. In this case the supply line shifts up. On the other hand, if it becomes less expensive for suppliers to bring an item to market then in a competitive market (we're assuming perfect competition here) the price they will charge will be lower at any given quantity. In this case the supply line shifts down.

You can use other stories to describe the shifts in Supply and Demand. Whatever your method, the crucial issue when discussing supply or demand shifts is to orient yourself by one axis or the other so that you can interpret a shift as:

- larger or smaller quantity at any given price—shifts out or back, or
- higher or lower price at any given quantity—shifts up or down.

3.3.12 Market Signaling and Coordination—Introduction

Now that we have the language of markets in place, let's see how a market actually works its magic—how, with no traditional roles to dictate our relationships and with nobody in charge to tell us all what to do, the decisions of literally billions of people who more often than not don't know one another and have no direct interest in one another can be guided by the *invisible hand* of the market to a well coordinated outcome. It is that potential in markets that makes them so powerful and so fascinating. Let's walk through how that works.

3.3.13 Market Signaling and Coordination—Response to Excess Supply

Suppose Figure 3.3.5 shows an initial condition in a market.

Given the attitude of suppliers (S) and demanders (D) and given the market price at P_1, the quantity supplied, Q^S, is greater than the quantity demanded, Q^D. Economists call this difference an *excess supply*.

What would it actually look like "out the window" if this really was the situation in the automobile market; if at the current market price there really was an excess supply of cars? Suppose you are the manager of the automobile factory. What would you see that would clue you in that the market is in an excess supply situation?

You would look out at the *inventory* lot where cars are parked until they're sold, and instead of seeing cars rolling off to be sold, you would see them piling up unsold—you would see your inventory growing. So, if you have this growing inventory, how do you get it moving off the lot? How do you get people to buy these cars you are producing?

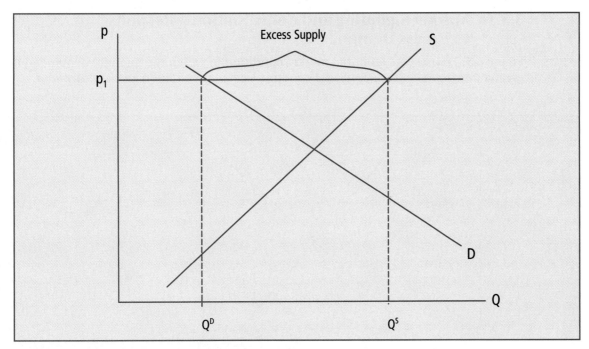

Figure 3.3.5 Initial Market Condition - Excess Supply

If you want to move your product, you lower your price. Clearly you like a high price, but if you can't sell the cars at the high price you have no choice but to lower the price. We see in Figure 3.3.6 that as the price goes down, the quantity demanded increases and the quantity supplied decreases. What happens to the excess supply? It gets smaller. Now let's take another case.

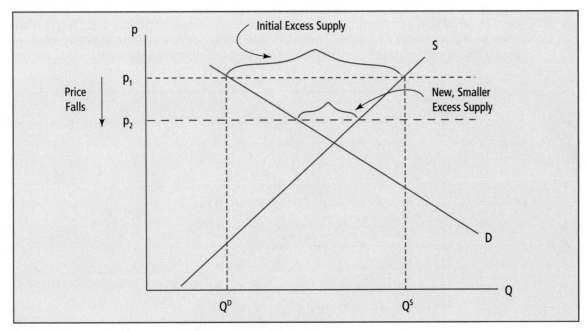

Figure 3.3.6 Falling Price Making Excess Supply Smaller

3.3.14 Market Signaling and Coordination—Response to Excess Demand

Figure 3.3.7 represents an initial market condition in which the quantity demanded is greater than the quantity supplied. Economists call this condition an *excess demand*.

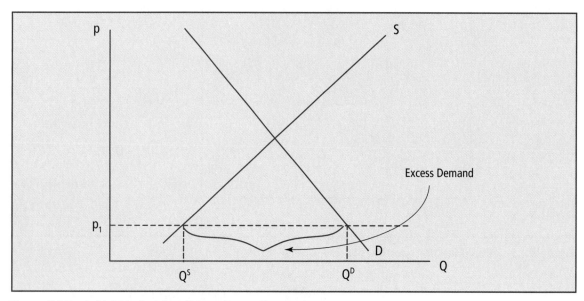

Figure 3.3.7   Initial Market Condition - Excess Demand

What would an excess demand look like in the real world?

This would look like a lot of folks clamoring for a hot item when there is not enough for everyone who wants to buy. In a perfectly competitive market people would start bidding up the price. Someone yells "I'll pay $5," someone else yells "I'll give you 10," and so on. The point is, if at the going price there is an excess demand people say, "Hey, I really want it—I'll pay more." Clearly demanders love a low price, but if the quantity supplied at that low price is not sufficient to meet the quantity demanded, the demanders have no

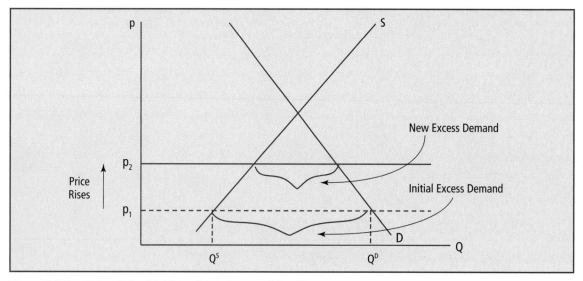

Figure 3.3.8   Rising Price Making Excess Demand Smaller

choice but to bid a higher price. As the price goes up, the quantity demanded decreases and the quantity supplied increases. What happens to the excess supply? It gets smaller as shown in Figure 3.3.8.

3.3.15 Market Signaling and Adjustment to Equilibrium

Where does this price adjustment process stop? In the case of an excess demand the price will continue to adjust upward as long as there is an excess demand. It will stop when the excess demand is gone. That happens at the point where supply and demand intersect in Figure 3.3.9 at the **e**.

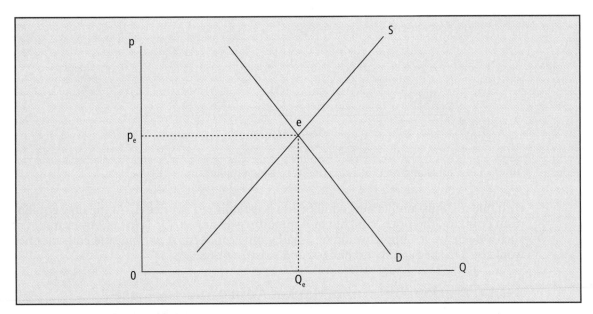

Figure 3.3.9 Market Equilibrium

At this price, p_e, the quantity demanded exactly equals the quantity supplied. There is no excess supply or excess demand. The market is in balance, or as economists refer to it, the market is in *equilibrium*. The price p_e is referred to as the equilibrium price (that's what the subscript "e" tells us). It is the price at which the intentions of suppliers and demanders are in balance. If nothing about the conditions surrounding this market changes, that is as long as the supply and demand shift variables do not change, the market will remain in an equilibrium position.

Whenever there is an excess supply or an excess demand in a market, the market is said to be in a disequilibrium condition—it is out of balance. But disequilibrium is not a stable condition in a perfectly competitive market. If there is an excess demand the price will rise, reducing the excess demand until the market price reaches p_e and the market is in equilibrium. If there is an excess supply the price will fall, reducing the excess supply until the market price reaches p_e and the market is in equilibrium. In equilibrium the market is stable.

Now let's look at some cases of changing conditions in a market and adjustments to a new equilibrium so we can see how markets respond to new conditions.

3.3.16 Market Shifts and Market Adjustments—Case 1

Suppose that for some reason supply moves from S_0 to S_1 as shown in Figure 3.3.10.

Before the Supply shift, p_0 was an equilibrium price, but after the shift at p_0 there is an excess demand. This excess demand will cause a price adjustment upward. The price will

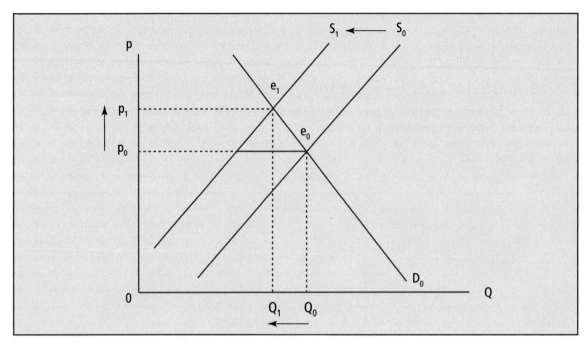

Figure 3.3.10 Fall in Supply and Market Adjustment to New Equilibrium

continue to adjust until a new equilibrium is established at price p_1. At the new equilibrium point, e_1, the price is higher and quantity exchanged, Q_1, is lower. An example of such a decrease in supply would be a bad grain crop. *Ceteris paribus*, the consequence would be a fall in quantity exchanged and a rise in price.

3.3.17 Market Shifts and Market Adjustments—Case 2

Suppose supply moves from S_0 to S_2 as shown in Figure 3.3.11.

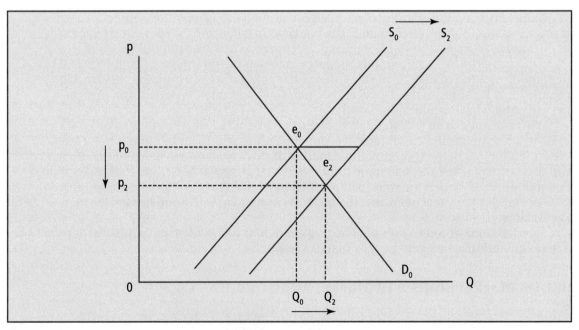

Figure 3.3.11 Rise in Supply and Market Adjustment to New Equilibrium

At price p_0 there is now an excess supply, so p_0 is no longer an equilibrium price. The excess supply at price p_0 will cause a price adjustment downward. The price will continue to adjust until a new equilibrium is established at price p_2. At the new equilibrium point, e_2, the price is lower and the quantity exchanged, Q_2, is higher. An example of such an increase in supply would be a bumper grain crop. *Ceteris paribus*, the consequence would be a rise in the quantity exchanged and a fall in price.

3.3.18 Market Shifts and Market Adjustments—Case 3

Suppose demand rises from D_0 to D_3 as shown in Figure 3.3.12.

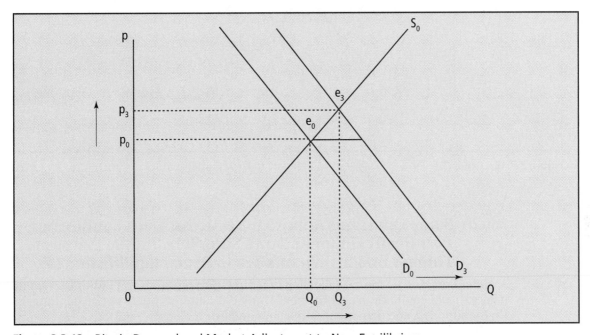

Figure 3.3.12   Rise in Demand and Market Adjustment to New Equilibrium

At price p_0 there is now an excess demand, so p_0 is no longer an equilibrium price. The excess demand at initial price p_0 will cause a price adjustment upward. The price will continue to adjust until a new equilibrium is established at price p_3. At the new equilibrium point, e_3, the price is higher and the quantity exchanged, Q_3, is higher. An example of such an increase in demand would be a music group that gets hot. *Ceteris paribus*, the consequence would be a rise in quantity exchanged (of tickets or CDs) and a rise in price.

3.3.19 Market Shifts and Market Adjustments—Case 4

Suppose demand falls from D_0 to D_4 as shown in Figure 3.3.13.

At price p_0 there is now an excess supply, so p_0 is no longer an equilibrium price. The excess supply at initial price p_0 will cause a price adjustment downward. The price will continue to adjust until a new equilibrium is established at price p_4. At the new equilibrium point, e_4, the price is lower and the quantity exchanged, Q_4, is lower. An example of such a fall in demand would be a music group that falls out of fashion. *Ceteris paribus*, the consequence would be a fall in quantity exchanged (of tickets or CDs) and a fall in price.

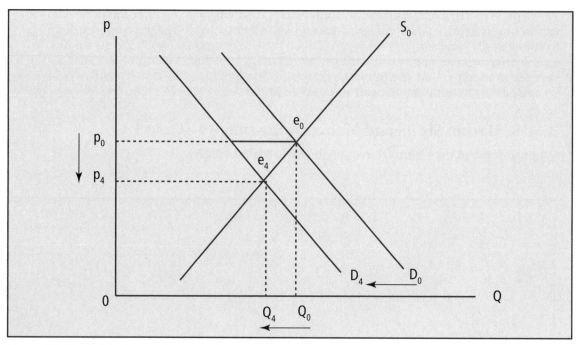

Figure 3.3.13 Fall in Demand and Market Adjustment to New Equilibrium

3.3.20 Some Questions About This Process: Does Equilibrium Ever Really Happen? Don't Suppliers Put the Prices on Things? Do Participants Try to Reach Equilibrium?

A student once asked me the following rich three-part question and I want to respond to it here: "Does equilibrium ever happen? Don't the suppliers put the price on things? and Do the suppliers and demanders strive for equilibrium?"

"Does equilibrium ever happen?" Strictly speaking—no. As we will see shortly when we talk about how an individual market is woven into a general market system, all markets in the system are interconnected. Given this web of connections, so long as any one market in the system is adjusting in some sense they are all still adjusting. As a practical matter, however, because the outside forces acting on particular markets can be pretty weak, it is fair to say that for at least a while some markets can be viewed as in equilibrium.

At the level of theory it is most important to understand that under perfectly competitive conditions markets are moving toward equilibrium than to argue about whether they reach it. Establishing tendencies of markets is what is necessary in order to understand how a world of markets works. At the level of practice it is most important to understand that when we look at a particular market and the forces that affect its equilibrium condition, we had better keep in mind that it functions as part of a general system, not in isolation.

"Don't the suppliers put the price on things?" Yes, they do often put on the price stickers, but in a perfectly competitive market they do not set the price. In a perfectly competitive market they simply put on the best price the market will bear, and they are constantly adjusting the price (putting on new stickers) to reflect changing market conditions over which they have no control—no power.

"Do the suppliers and demanders strive for equilibrium?" No. It is important to understand that suppliers and demanders do not care about the market or equilibrium as such. They are all just trying, or so we have assumed, to maximize their utility. The demanders do not necessarily care about or know the suppliers or one another. Similarly, the suppliers do not necessarily care about or know the demanders or one another. Everyone comes to the market with her own utility in mind, and who else is there or how it all works or where it settles is of no consequence so long as it serves their objective. To do this, they respond to price signals.

3.3.21 The Signal on Which the Entire Market System Depends: The Price

The thing that allows a market to coordinate the autonomous choices of all of the individuals involved is that everyone involved has one signal in common to which they are simultaneously responding: the price. Under perfect competition everybody gets to see the undistorted price signal and everybody is free to respond to it as they choose.

Market systems work because in the process of responding to the price, people's intentions are brought in to balance. If there is an excess supply the price falls and as it does people adjust their individual choices until the market is in balance. If there is an excess demand the price rises and as it does people adjust their individual choices until the market is in balance.

People are not responding to each other. They are responding to the price. As long as everybody gets to respond freely, the price signal will bring all the individual intentions of the millions or billions of participants into balance by adjusting from any disequilibrium condition toward equilibrium. The market system is a price-signaling based system.

3.3.22 Problems When Prices Can't Adjust, the Promise of an Efficient System When They Can

In the old Soviet Union the government dictated most prices. Under an administered price system there is no price signal adjustment to an excess supply or an excess demand, so there is no market response. Not surprisingly what one saw in the old Soviet Union was long lines in which people stood for hours waiting for things that were in short supply. In effect these things were rationed by time, waiting in line, rather than by price. One also saw lots of waste because with no price signals to bring quantity supplied into balance with quantity demanded, resources were often allocated to make more of some things than anyone wanted.

The beauty of the market system is that under perfect competition when there are no distortions in the price-signaling process, the individual markets will constantly move toward equilibrium, and the whole of the market system will be constantly tending toward what economists refer to as a General Competitive Equilibrium—an efficient equilibrium of the whole system. Now let's move from the analysis of how individual markets work to an analysis of how a general system of markets works.

3.4 THE GENERAL MARKET SYSTEM

3.4.1 Introduction

The division of labor brings tremendous benefits in the form of increased productivity, but it also increases the complexity of society. As this complexity grows we are progressively more interdependent, and this complex interdependence makes us vulnerable to "the system." Robinson Crusoe's fate depended on luck, nature, and his own decisions. In a complex society our fate depends on these three factors, but it also depends on the decisions of others and on the quality of the coordinating system—the markets. The greater the complexity, the more dependent we are on one another and on the health of the market system.

It is precisely this fine weave of interdependence and the role of markets as coordinators that makes microeconomics so interesting, so important, and so complex. We have seen how a generic market works. Now our story moves into the general market system.

3.4.2 Circular Flow: The Two Kinds of Players

We can represent the general system with a *circular flow diagram* as in Figure 3.4.1. It represents the players in the system, the markets in which these players interact, and the flows that move through system.

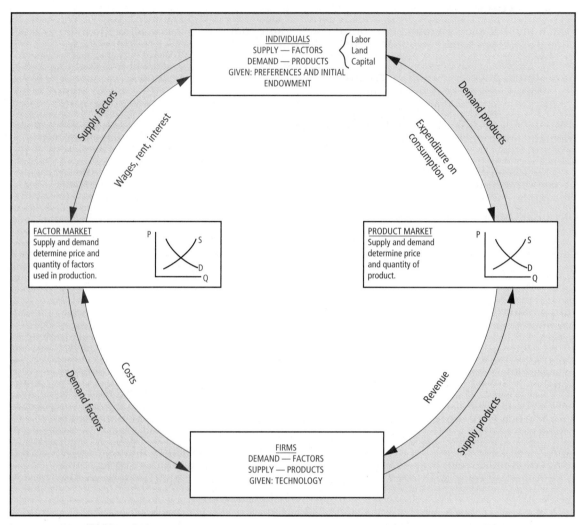

Figure 3.4.1 Circular Flow

There are two primary kinds of players in our general system story: *individuals* and *firms*.

You and I and all the other individuals in the market system own shares of the social endowment. From these shares we supply the all basic factors of production to the market system: labor, natural resources, and production capital. We are also the ultimate demanders of products. The system exists to facilitate the maximization of our individual utilities by providing us with the goods and services we desire given our preferences.

The other player is the firms. The firms are an artificial construct since they are ultimately owned by individuals, but they do serve a distinct instrumental role in the system. The firms demand the factors and, given the available technology, they use the factors to produce the goods and services people desire.

3.4.3 Circular Flow: The Two Basic Kinds of Markets

These two basic players interact in two basic kinds of markets. There are literally millions of markets, but for our purposes they can be divided into two basic kinds: *factor markets* and *product markets.*

In the factor markets the individuals are the suppliers. They bring their natural resources, labor, and production capital to the market to sell. So for example you may have been, may be, or almost certainly will be a participant in the factor market because you have had, have, or will have a job. When you have a job you are selling your labor and whatever human capital you have accumulated, so you are participating in the factor market.

While the individuals are the suppliers in the factor market, the firms are the demanders. The firms buy the factors, like your labor and human capital, and given the technology, the firms apply the factors they buy in a process of production to make products.

This brings us to the product market. In the product market, the firms are the suppliers. They bring the goods and services they have produced to the product market for sale. The individuals are the demanders in the product market. They come to the market to see what the firms have to offer and to decide what they want to buy.

3.4.4 The Flow of Real Things

So there is a circular flow of real things: Individuals supply factors to the factor market, firms demand those factors. Firms take those factors and make the products that they supply in the product market. Individuals demand those products. It all exists for the sake of individual utility maximization with firms playing a role as the catalyst of production. In some sense it is a process with no beginning and no end, because the circuit must be in continuous motion if the well-being of the individuals is to be continuously sustained.

3.4.5 The Flow of Money

There is another circuit going on at the same time in the opposite direction that facilitates the flow of factors and products. That's the money flow. When individuals sell their factors they earn wages, rent, and interest—they earn an income. They take their income and they spend it in the product market to buy food, clothing, shelter, entertainment, and so on. These are their expenditures. These expenditures become the revenue of the firms, and these revenues are the means the firms have to cover the costs of production—buying the factors of production in the factor market. These costs become the wages, rent, and interest of the individuals—and so the money circuit begins again. This money flow facilitates or, if you will, lubricates, the real flow of factors and products.

3.4.6 The Web of Connections that is the General System

There are millions and millions of individual markets in the full market system. There are thousands even millions of factor markets—markets for plumbers and teachers and salespeople and rocket scientists, markets for farm land and factory sites, and markets for stamping machines and backhoes, and on and on and on. There are certainly millions of product markets—just think of all the products you see in the stores.

The circular flow diagram represents the fact that these markets are all connected. In fact, however, the market system is not a simple circular connection. It is an incredibly complex multidimensional *web of connections* that makes the whole market system into a *general system* of markets. One of the great philosophical leaps of liberal thought was Adam Smith's recognition that under the right conditions this general system of markets works incredibly well—with an elegant efficiency.

3.4.7 General Competitive Equilibrium

The term economists use to identify the condition the general system tends toward under ideal conditions, *perfect competition*, is a *General Competitive Equilibrium*. "General" refers to the fact that it includes the whole market system. "Equilibrium" refers to the fact that the entire system is in balance, all the markets are simultaneously in balance. "Competitive" refers to the fact that this balance is *optimal* or, in other words, the best case, because it's been achieved under ideal, perfectly competitive conditions.

3.4.8 General Competitive Equilibrium as a Special Case of the Possible General Equilibria

A General Competitive Equilibrium is not the only outcome possible for the general system. Indeed, there are many possible General Equilibria—many possible outcomes toward which the economy can be moving. A General Competitive Equilibrium is that unique case in which the outcome is perfectly efficient. All the other possible General Equilibria are less efficient because in all those other cases there are distortions that lead to inefficiencies.

3.4.9 Exploring the General Competitive Equilibrium Case— Introduction

We will refer to the conditions that make a General Competitive Equilibrium possible as our *nice assumptions*. They are "nice" because they make the system efficient. They are "assumptions," because for now we are going to take them as a given so that we can see how the general system works when it is working ideally. Once we see how a general market system works ideally, we will relax our nice assumptions and examine

- What kinds of distortions make the system inefficient and even cause it to break down, and
- What, if any, role is there for government in a market system.

But for now we will model a world in which the nice assumptions do hold so that we can understand how, under these ideal conditions, markets can be almost magically efficient. Much of the world, including Russia and China, has been experimenting with market systems because they want to capture the magic—the efficiency. If you understand what conditions make markets work well, why they work so well under those conditions, and what kinds of distortions mess up the system, then you will be in a much better position to understand the successes and/or failures of those experiments as well as the successes or failures of this 200+ year liberal experiment in the West.

3.4.10 Our Nice Assumptions—Introduction

Our *nice assumptions* are the ideal market conditions that ensure perfect competition. There are two nice assumptions.

1. *No market power.* This means that any advantage in the market is transitory. It can be eliminated by competition. This assumption allows us to abstract from any advantages that give an individual control in a market. Under our no market power assumption everyone faces the same set of opportunities and obstacles in the race for wealth. Thus it assumes those rules of commutative justice that assure that the race is run fairly:

   a. Everyone has equal access to information.
   b. Everyone has equal access to markets.

2. *No market failure.* This assumption allows us to abstract from the possibility that markets won't do the job they are supposed to do. Remember, in a market system the markets coordinate the interdependent choices of autonomous individuals. If choices are

interdependent and no market forms to coordinate them, or if a market forms but does not do its job well, that's a problem. No Market Failure means that:

a. Markets form quickly when needed to coordinate choices.
b. Markets function smoothly and quickly to coordinate choices.

3.4.11 No Market Power—Equal Access to Information

In order to understand the "no market power" assumption let's look at each of its elements in turn.

"Equal access to information" means everyone has an equal opportunity to access information. It does not mean that everyone has all information or that everyone has the same information.

Information is not costless. It takes time and often money to collect information. As we make our choices in life one choice we constantly make is: "Do I want to spend more resources acquiring information? How much is more information worth?" Equal access to information simply means that any information that is available to one person is available to all other people at roughly the same price.

What would a violation of this assumption look like? Have you ever heard of a "good ol' boy network"? This term describes networks within which people share valuable information, but only with the "good ol' boys"— the insiders of the network. So for example, if a new job opens up in a company and the word goes out through the "good ol' boy" network, the only people with access to that information are those connected to that network. Clearly, any such network of information exchange creates significant advantages in the market and, thus, market power.

Inside information that one has and exploits for oneself is another example of a violation of equal access to information. If you have inside information about a corporate move that you know is going to affect the price of that corporation's stock, you can make a killing in the market by using that information to beat the market. Again, unequal access to information creates significant power and, thus, advantage in the market.

3.4.12 No Market Power—Equal Access to Markets

"Equal access to markets" means that everyone has an equal opportunity to pursue all options in the market. Think about this case. In the 1940s and 1950s in New Orleans where I grew up the first level headings of the job-listing section of the Sunday newspaper were not as they are today work categories like professional, medical, food service, and so on. Back then, the first level heading of job listings was divided into two categories. Want to guess what they were?

They were: "Help Wanted—Male" and "Help Wanted—Female"

If you were a woman you might read a listing that said "Apprentice plumber wanted, starting pay $5/hour. Will train. For information call TW1-0708." But there was no point in picking up the phone. That listing was under the male column and you weren't eligible. So if you were a single white woman with a kid, you might like the thought of "$5.00/hour. That sounds great." but your options read like: "Waitress wanted. Must be able to work flexible hours. $1.00/hour + tips. Call UN6-5782."

And imbedded in the structure of those job listings was another power structure— race based preferences. An actual ad from the June 21, 1948 *Times-Picayune* reads

> WAITRESSES
> YOUNG ladies, white only, experience not
> necessary. Apply Worner's Drug Store.
> 706 Canal St.

Then four spots down the page one finds:

> Pantry Girl (colored), capable and experienced. Hours 12 noon to 9 p. m., 6 days a week. Meals and uniform furnished. . . .

In the "Help Wanted—Male" section there are ads that read:

> WHITE UPHOLSTERER
>
> $5\frac{1}{2}$ days a week. Time and half for over 40 hours. Apply in person . . .

and

> COLORED PORTER
>
> If you are not lazy and want to work at a steady job with good pay, answer this ad. Pelican Bar, 301 S. Rampart. St.

In those days all the available jobs were listed. Abstracting from the market power created by "separate but equal" schools and assuming all could read—everyone had equal access to information. Anyone who wanted to buy a Sunday newspaper could see all the available options. But knowing the options is not enough to ensure a fair race. For the race to be fair, you have to have equal access to participate. In those days in New Orleans and in many other places before and since, equal access to markets was/is a strong assumption.

3.4.13 Our No Market Power Assumption, Commutative Justice, Efficiency, and Equity

Equal access to information and equal access to the market are standards of commutative justice that go hand in hand to help ensure a fair race. In a fair race the thing that distinguishes the winner is the effort the winner makes.

Power changes all that. For example, if some of the participants arrive at a track meet to find that the times and places of the events are not available, they are eliminated from the competition. If some of those participants do locate the race but find upon their arrival that their lane has hurdles every 10 meters while their competitors face 100 meters of open track, the race is no real contest.

Any distortions that reduce the keenness of the competition not only affect who wins, they affect how the race is run. Those who face the obstacles may not even compete. If they do, those with the advantage need not exert themselves fully to win. The quality of performances will be lower than they would have been under perfect competition.

In races that simply means slower times. In the market economy the loss of the human talent and energy of those who do not compete and the lack of keenness in competition that reduces the effort of those who do compete mean that the system does not benefit from the best efforts of all who do and/or would like to participate. In economic terms this means that the efficiency of the system is reduced, so if we think of the full social product as represented by a pie, the size of the social pie is smaller than it could be. Equity is also affected because in the economic system winning has a payoff. Those with power can enjoy more winnings with less effort—a larger piece of a smaller pie.

3.4.14 A Classic Case of Market Power: South African Apartheid

Consider the following blurb that appeared in the news in July of 1983:

> JOHANNESBURG, South Africa: Lize Venter is 4 weeks old and nobody knows who her parents are. In a society where the races are separated by law, that means the government will decide if she's black, white, or of mixed race—and set the course of her life. . .
>
> The decision on her race will determine who can adopt her, where she goes to school, what neighborhood she may live in, who she can marry, whether she can vote, where she can eat—what she can hope for in life.
>
> This is decreed by the Population Registration Act of 1950, adopted by the governing National Party two years after it took control of the white minority government.

Lize Venter's access to the full set of options in society's opportunity set, and therefore her future share in the distribution of society's product, was determined by where she was placed in the social and political pecking order. For most children the decision is clear at birth—determined by gender, race, and other indices. While it is not impossible to overcome disadvantage or to waste advantage, on average the relative advantages participants bring to a competition determine the outcome.

The efficiency implications of the market power created by apartheid are clear. In the old South Africa the white minority enjoyed a very large share of an artificially small social pie. The pie was artificially small because the limitations on access to information (e.g., lack of quality schooling) and access to the market (e.g., discrimination in job opportunities) kept blacks and mixed race South Africans from contributing their energy, talents, and creative imagination to the markets. At the same time it kept whites in the market from being pushed by potential competitors to be their best. Lack of competition eliminates the punishment for inefficiency: Doing badly in the race.

3.4.15 Commutative Justice and Stability in Liberal Society

South African apartheid is a classic and extreme case of a point I noted earlier: The absence of commutative justice creates a fundamental weakness in a society that is trying to run on liberal economic, free market principles. Now we can see why. The rules of commutative justice ensure that the race is fair. In the absence of such rules, perverse incentives exist. People can "win" by using resources to create advantages based on power, rather than by competing to be most productive for themselves or for the market. Winning at the power game creates more resources to sustain that power position. But when the race is for power, competition becomes destructive rather than constructive.

Our nice assumption of no market power holds the issues of destructive competition at bay for now. To what degree destructive competition is a real problem depends on how weak or strong the no market power assumption actually is. For now we are simply going to assume that there is no market power. Later we will relax that assumption and examine the issue of market power more closely.

3.4.16 No Market Failure

Our second "nice assumption" is *No Market Failure*, that:

    a. Markets form quickly when needed to coordinate choices, and
    b. Markets function smoothly and quickly to coordinate choices.

What would a violation of this assumption look like? Suppose a factory that produces chemicals is built upwind from your neighborhood. In the process of the factory's production it not only produces chemicals, it also produces lots of particulate waste.

Hey, no problem, all that waste can be costlessly disposed of by letting it float off as smoke from the factory's smokestacks. Costless for the factory owner, maybe—but potentially unhealthy for you, your family, and your neighbors who live downwind from the plant. This smoke makes you and your neighbors interdependent with the owners of the factory. Their choice to run their factory this way is affecting your choice to live in a healthy neighborhood environment. According to our model, when choices are interdependent like this a market needs to form to coordinate them. But in this case it won't.

Your interdependence with the factory owners occurs because you both want to use a resource which neither one of you "owns"—the air. The factory owners want to use it as a disposal space and you want to use it as a source of clean air. As we will see, this is a classic example of a market failure. To the degree such failures occur, markets do not do their job when we need them. The consequence, as with market power, is that it reduces the efficiency of the system and it affects the equity. To what degree market failure is a problem in our economy depends on how weak or strong our nice assumption of no market failure really is. For now we are simply going to assume no market failure and thus hold any of the problems that market failure creates at bay. Later we will relax the assumption and examine its implications more fully.

3.4.17 Pareto Optimality

Our nice assumptions ensure the conditions that result in a perfectly competitive *General Competitive Equilibrium* and thus perfect efficiency. The term economists use to describe this most efficient condition is *Pareto optimality*. It is named for an Italian economist named Vilfredo Pareto (1848–1923) who first defined this standard: An economy is in a *Pareto optimal* condition when there is no way to make one person better off without making someone else worse off.

Think about it. In material terms, the way you make someone better off is to give her more of the social pie. There are only two ways to do that. You either take the extra piece you are going to give her from someone else, which makes someone else worse off; or you make the pie bigger. If there is any way to squeeze a little bit more production out of the economy, that is, if there are any inefficiencies that can be eliminated to make more from the resources we have, then the pie can get bigger and someone can do better at no one else's expense. Pareto optimality is the case in which we are using our resources so perfectly efficiently that for the given resource base making the pie bigger is no longer possible. There is no slack left in the economy, so the only way to make someone better off is to do so by taking something from someone else. Ergo Pareto's definition of perfect efficiency: An economy is in a Pareto optimal condition when you can't make anyone better off without making someone else worse off.

Our current focus is on this efficiency issue. We want to see how, under our nice assumptions, a market system reaches a *Pareto Optimal General Competitive Equilibrium*. In order to hold at bay the complexity of equity issues raised by the distribution of the social endowment among individuals, we will assume that the race for wealth begins with each person holding a given share of that social endowment as her property to use as she likes. Once we get a rich model of the perfectly competitive market system developed we will relax this assumption and explore the issues related to endowment distribution and distributive justice.

We begin our analysis of how the market system works under our nice assumptions in the product market.

4.0 PRODUCT MARKET DEMAND UNDER PERFECT COMPETITION

4.1 INTRODUCTION

Figure 4.1.1 shows our market picture.

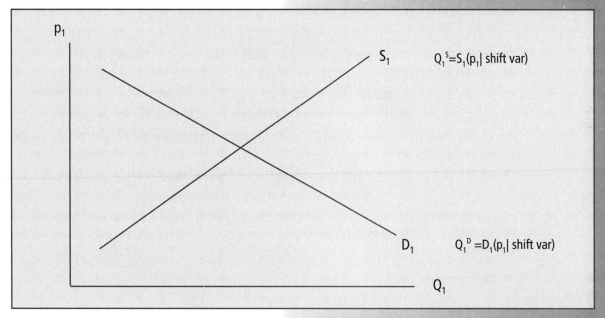

Figure 4.1.1 Product Picture Market for Good #1

This represents a product market, so Q_1 is a quantity of a good or service (we'll call it Good #1) and p_1 is the price of that good. The demand line D represents the attitude of demanders in this market and S represents the attitudes of the suppliers. Next to the supply and demand line labels you see the functional form of the relationship that line represents.

The Demand relationship is:

$$Q_1^D = D\,(p_1 \mid \textbf{shift variables})$$

The Supply relationship is

$$Q_1^S = S\,(p_1 \mid \textbf{shift variables})$$

We will look at the Demand and the Supply relationships in turn.

4.2 PRODUCT DEMAND

4.2.1 Introduction

We will start with Demand and explore:

1. Why does product demand D slope down?
2. What determines the responsiveness of Q_1^D to p_1?
3. What are the shift variables of the product demand relationship D, and how does Demand (D) respond to changes in these shift variables?

Once we have covered demand, we will examine similar issues with respect to supply. Finally we will put supply (S) and demand (D) together to see how the dynamics of the product market assure efficiency under our nice assumptions.

4.2.2 Why the Product Demand Line Slopes Down: Setting the Scene

In order to understand why the demand line slopes down we'll start with the simplest version of the individual decision rule we developed. We could use the full rule, but it is not necessary to make our point.

We determined that in order to maximize utility you allocate your resources over "n" products such that the utility you derive is equal at the margin. When you allocate your time your decision rule looks like this:

$$\frac{MU1}{Unit\,of\,Time} = \frac{MU2}{Unit\,of\,Time} = \ldots = \frac{MUn}{Unit\,of\,Time}$$

Now in the product market you're allocating your money instead of your time, so your decision rule becomes:

$$\frac{MU1}{Dollar} = \frac{MU2}{Dollar} = \ldots = \frac{MUn}{Dollar}$$

Or in other words, you set the marginal utility per dollar spent equal across all possible choices. But in a market system these different choices (Good #1, Good #2, . . . , Good #n) have different prices ($p_1, p_2, \ldots p_n$), so the marginal utility per dollar derived from the last unit of each depends on the price of each. To reflect this effect of different prices the decision rule becomes, set:

$$\frac{MU1}{p1} = \frac{MU2}{p2} = \ldots = \frac{MUn}{pn}$$

Where $\dfrac{MU1}{p1}$ stands for your marginal utility per dollar from Good #1 that costs p_1, and so on.

This adjusted decision rule still says that you maximize your utility by maintaining your balance—setting the marginal utility per dollar equal across all choices. All we have done to our equation is adjust for the fact that in reality different goods have different prices.

4.2.3 Making the Case for a Downward-Sloping Product Demand Line

Given this adjustment of the decision rule to reflect the fact that different goods have different prices, let's go back to the first product market question we want to explore: Why does the product demand line slope down? Or in other words, *ceteris paribus*, as price of Good #1 rises why does the quantity of Good #1 demanded fall? To see why let's trace the course of events as p_1 rises.

Suppose, *ceteris paribus*, the price of Good #1 does go up. Suddenly, before you can adjust your behavior to this new reality, you are out of balance. The price you pay—the denominator, p_1 - goes up. But you are still consuming the same amount, so your marginal utility—the numerator, MU_1 - stays the same. As a result the value of $\dfrac{MU1}{p1}$ goes down. Your now consuming such that

$$\frac{MU1}{p1} < \frac{MU2}{p2} = \ldots = \frac{MUn}{pn}$$

You are out of balance, and out of balance means you are not maximizing your utility. In order to get back to maximum utility you need to adjust your behavior. *Ceteris paribus*, focusing on Good #1, what has to happen to $\dfrac{MU1}{p1}$ in order to bring you back into balance? *Ceteris paribus*, you need to increase $\dfrac{MU1}{p1}$.

Mathematically, $\dfrac{MU1}{p1}$ increases if either p_1 goes down or if MU_1 goes up. Which one can you affect? You cannot lower p_1 because under our nice assumptions the market sets the price and you just respond to it—price is not your choice. Under perfect competition you are, as economists put it, a *price taker*. You can, however, change MU_1 because marginal utility is a function of how much you choose to consume. So how do you have to change your consumption of Q_1 in order increase $\dfrac{MU1}{p1}$ and bring yourself back into balance? Decreasing the quantity you demand of Good #1 will increase the MU_1 of the last unit you actually consume. As you decrease your quantity demanded, Q_1, the MU_1 will rise until at some point you will be back in balance.

4.2.4 Reviewing the Reason for Product Demand Sloping Down

Now let's walk through the logic from start to finish. A rise in p_1 puts you out of balance with respect to your utility maximizing decision rule. *Ceteris paribus*, by decreasing the quantity, Q_1, you demand, you can bring yourself back into balance. Since we assume you want to maximize utility and balance is the way to do that, when the price of that good, p_1, rises you will respond by reducing your quantity demanded, Q_1.

The logic is symmetric. A fall in p_1 puts you out of balance with respect to your utility maximizing decision rule. *Ceteris paribus*, by increasing the quantity of Q_1 you demand, you can bring yourself back into balance. When the price, p_1, of that good falls you will increase your quantity demanded, Q_1.

This relationship between p_1 and Q_1 is precisely what the downward sloping demand line, D_1, represents. The quantity demanded is inversely related to price: As p_1 rises Q_1 falls, and as p_1 falls Q_1 rises. Now we do not have to take the shape of D_1 on faith. We have derived it from something (our decision rule) that we carefully constructed earlier. OK, but what about the responsiveness of the quantity demanded to a change in price? If the price, p_1, does change, what factors determine how significantly the quantity demanded, Q_1, will respond? This brings us to the issue of own price elasticity of demand.

4.2.5 Own Price Elasticity of Demand—The Concept

Own price elasticity of demand (from now I'll simply refer to own price elasticity) is a measure of the responsiveness of the quantity demanded of a good, Q_1, to a change in its own price, p_1. When the quantity demanded of a good responds very significantly to change in its own price, we say that the demand for that good is elastic. *Elastic* means responsive. If the quantity demanded of a good does not respond very significantly to change in its own price, we say that the demand for that good is inelastic. *Inelastic* means not very responsive.

4.2.6 Comparing Elastic and Inelastic Cases

Let's look at two product market graphs in Figure 4.2.1.

D_1 represents attitudes toward Good #1 and D_2 represents attitudes toward Good #2. We are going to assume that the axes on these two graphs are identical, so even though you see no numbers you know the scales on both graphs are exactly the same.

Both demand lines reflect what we just established about demand: Each slopes down. But there is more information here. Since we are assuming that the axes are measured exactly the same way, the difference in the slopes of these two demand lines reflects a difference in attitudes toward these two goods.

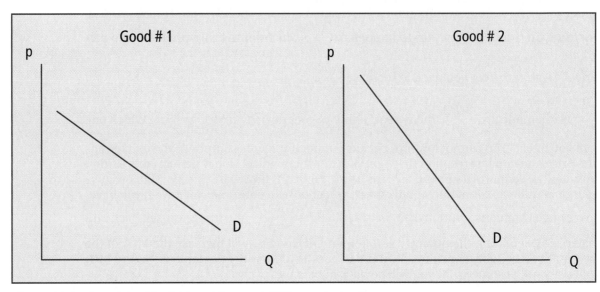

Figure 4.2.1 Own Price Elasticities of Demand–Different Attitudes

Suppose the price of these two goods goes up by the same amount, from p to p'. Since the vertical axes have the same scales, we can represent both the initial and new price by lines at p and p' respectively that extend across both graphs. Figure 4.2.2 represents what happens to the quantity demanded in each case.

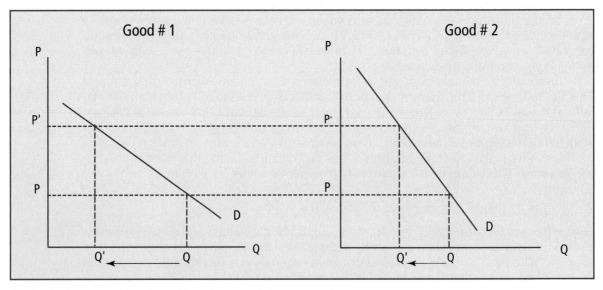

Figure 4.2.2 Own Price Elasticities of Demand–Comparing Responses

In both cases the quantity demanded fell. That is a given because, as we demonstrated, quantity demanded is inversely related to price. But what about the amount the quantity fell? Since both quantity axes are measured on the same scale, we can say that given an identical price rise the quantity of Good #1 fell by more than the quantity of Good #2. So which one was more responsive?

Good #1 was more responsive. If that's the case, in the language of economics, which good has the more elastic demand? If Good #1 responded more to an identical price rise, then economists say that Good #1 has the more elastic demand.

4.2.7 Elasticity—Its Importance for Policy

Own price elasticity is a big deal in policy—a BIG deal. Own price elasticity is one of several kinds of elasticity economists study. Among all the professional economists, I would guess that the majority make their living working with databases in order to estimate elasticities—responsiveness to changes in conditions. They want to figure this out as precisely as possible because to the degree they can accurately estimate how people will respond to a change . . . to that degree they can predict the effect of such changes. If for example you are the director of marketing for McDonalds and you are considering a price rise on your burgers, you really want as much information as you can assemble on how people are likely to respond to that price rise.

4.2.8 Elasticity—A Private Policy Case

With that in mind, McDonalds is constantly collecting information. When you walk into a McDonalds and they take your order, they don't put it into an old fashioned cash register. It goes into a computer. Those McDonalds computers accumulate tons of data on purchase patterns. If the marketing folks at McDonalds want to estimate the own price elasticity of demand for their product they can develop a database for the analysis by trying out a price change in a test market—a market that, based on previous data analysis, seems representative of their larger national market. So maybe they go to Peoria, Illinois, and try a new price. By comparing the data on quantity demanded before the price rise to data on quantity demanded after the price rise, and assuming nothing else relevant and dramatic is happening in that market (i.e., assuming the shift variables are pretty constant), they can calculate the own price elasticity of demand for their hamburgers.

What are they hoping for? Presumably they would like to find that if they raise their price their sales will not fall significantly. In other words, they hope the demand for their burgers is relatively inelastic. If the price rise plays well in Peoria, then they can feel pretty good about implementing it nationwide.

4.2.9 Elasticity—A Public Policy Case

Governments do similar things. If you are a city planner and you are proposing a reduction in bus fares in order to encourage people to use public transportation rather than private cars, you want as much information as you can assemble on how people are likely to respond to this bus fare price change.

Or suppose that to encourage people to carpool so fewer cars are used to commute, you propose carpool lanes on an expressway—lanes that are only open to cars with multiple riders. What you are doing in effect is offering a lower time cost for commuting in the hope that commuters will substitute the carpool arrangement for the privacy and flexibility of their own cars. This is an elasticity issue with respect to the time cost of travel, and the sensitivity with respect to this time cost will depend on individuals' perceptions of the quality of carpooling as a substitute for their personal cars.

4.2.10 Own Price Elasticity of Demand—By Degrees

The extreme cases of own price elasticity of demand look like Figure 4.2.3—perfectly elastic, or Figure 4.2.4—perfectly inelastic.

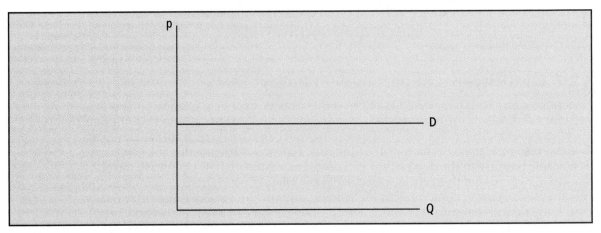

Figure 4.2.3 Perfectly Elastic Demand

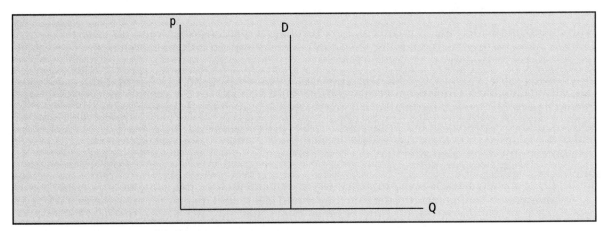

Figure 4.2.4 Perfectly Inelastic Demand

If you were going to sell a product, which of these own price elasticity of demand cases would you wish your product to have? If you were going to be selling a product you would like the demand to be perfectly inelastic because that would allow you to raise the price without losing any quantity demanded.

4.2.11 Own Price Elasticity of Demand—Necessities versus Luxuries

Think of a product that you believe might have a very inelastic if not a perfectly inelastic own price elasticity of demand. . . . With your pick in mind, let's examine the conditions that determine a good's own price elasticity of demand.

First there is the degree to which a good is a necessity or a luxury. *Ceteris paribus*, which do you think would exhibit a more inelastic demand, a necessity or a luxury?

Think about this: Imagine that there is a good that you need to live. Without it you die. *Ceteris paribus*, is your quantity demanded going to be affected very much by the price? Probably not. These kinds of goods are the ones for which price does not matter. No matter how high the price goes you have to have it, so to the extent your wealth allows you pay to get it. The classic examples of this kind of good are in the realm of health care.

Suppose, God forbid, you are on a life support system. The good news is that your brain is still fully functional and you have a real chance of getting better if you can hold on for a few more weeks. The bad news is that the administrator of your health insurance plan comes to your family and says, "We have some bad news. You've reached your maximum benefits for the year, so from here on you'll need to pay for the care yourself." This is a *very expensive* treatment. Your family could easily use up its life savings and have to sell all its assets (like your house) just to run the system for a few weeks—all for a hope that you'll get better based on probabilities. Your family says, "We'll do what we need to do. We'll pay whatever it takes."

If you have to have it to live, then as the expression goes "price is no object." You pay whatever you need to pay. In this case, demand is perfectly inelastic. Graphically, if price really is no object and you just need one of the item, like just one dose of a lifesaving drug, then *ceteris paribus* your individual demand line would be a vertical line at the $Q^D = 1$. On the vertical axis the line would reach as high as your ability to pay. It represents the idea that you would pay any price for one unit up to the limits of your ability to pay.

So, one of the factors that affects own price elasticity of demand is the degree to which an item is a necessity or a luxury. *Ceteris paribus*, the more an item is a necessity the more inelastic its demand will be. But, *ceteris* is not always *paribus*, and so while the necessity or luxury of a good is a factor in determining the degree of a good's elasticity, it is just one factor.

4.2.12 Own Price Elasticity of Demand—Other Determining Factors

Another important factor is the number and quality of available substitutes. Consider the life-saving drug I just described. Suppose Life-o-save is the drug and it is indeed a lifesaver, but there is also Gottamakeit which is another drug that does the same job just as well. In that case, as the price of Life-o-save goes up you can switch to Gottamakeit. The more of such high quality substitutes there are, the more flexible your choice set and the easier it is to switch away from a particular good as its own price goes up. Clearly a substitute is less attractive if it is lower quality. So this substitution effect depends not only on the availability but also the quality of the substitutes. The number and quality of substitutes is therefore a very significant factor in determining the own price elasticity of demand for a particular good.

Consider another example: Many commuters choose to use their private cars to get to work, and even stick with the cars if gasoline prices jump up. But if those gasoline prices stay up and if public transportation becomes perceived as a good substitute for using private cars, then the demand for car transportation would become more elastic. This example brings us to another factor in determining own price elasticity that is closely related to the number and quality of substitutes. The time frame matters too.

Assuming no market power when a price jumps up in a market that has an initially inelastic demand, this creates an opportunity in the market and encourages entrepreneurs to get involved. Thus over time more and better substitutes enter the market. Take for example the gasoline case. When the oil crises of the 1970s caused gasoline prices to shoot up, the initial reaction of consumers was to cut back a bit on travel. But since the patterns of their lives and thus much of their travel (to work, to school, etc.) was necessary, for the most part they just paid the higher price. The own price elasticity of demand for gasoline was initially very inelastic. But over time as the gasoline prices stayed up, people began to reduce their gasoline consumption. That was possible in part because more gasoline-efficient cars came onto the market. In the 1980s and 1990s the relative price of gasoline went down, so consumers moved back to more gas-guzzling kinds of vehicles.

And finally, one more factor that affects own price elasticity is the price of the good relative to a person's wealth and income. If the price of those little bubble gum balls you buy from those little round machines goes from one cent to two cents, that change will not affect the quantity demanded of an adult who makes a middle class income. The price is so low relative to her income that a 100% increase in price is nevertheless of no consequence. If, however, you're a 10-year-old kid on a 10-cents-a-week allowance, that one-cent increase may seem like a big deal and may indeed cause a change in your consumption. Alternatively, if the price of a car doubles, for most of us that would significantly affect our attitude toward buying that car, but not Bill Gates. If your wealth is measured in the many billions of dollars, almost everything has a very low price relative to your wealth and income, so even big percentage changes in price are not going to affect your attitude. *Ceteris paribus*, the lower the price relative to someone's wealth and income, the less responsive that person will be to a change in price—or in other words the more inelastic the demand will be.

To summarize, these are the factors that determine own price elasticity of demand:

- Necessity *v.* Luxury
- Number and Quality of Available Substitutes
- Time Frame
- Price Relative to Wealth and Income

No one of these factors is the determinant; together they determine the own price elasticity for any particular good or service. It is a complicated story about a complicated real world.

As I mentioned before, many economists spend their lives trying to measure elasticities. Let's look at the measure economists use to represent own price elasticity of demand.

4.2.13 Own Price Elasticity of Demand—Measuring It

We will use a Greek epsilon (ϵ) to stand for own price elasticity. This is the equation economists use to represent the measure of own price elasticity.

$$\epsilon = \left| \frac{\text{% } \textbf{\textit{QuantityChange}}}{\text{% } \textbf{\textit{OwnPriceChange}}} \right|$$

Since along a given demand line price moves inversely to quantity, we know this fraction is always negative. The absolute value sign (the two vertical lines around the fraction) eliminates a negative sign and thus spares us the hassle of having to carry around the negative sign.

The equation uses percentage change rather than absolute change because percentages give a more accurate sense of the degree of change than an absolute measure does. To see why consider the following case: A change in price from $1 to $2 is the same in absolute terms as a change in price from $1,000,001 to $1,000,002. Clearly, however, the change from $1 to $2 is a much larger degree of change (100%) than the change from $1,000,001 to $1,000,002 (a tiny fraction of 1%). Since percentage change reflects the degree of change more accurately, it is a better measure for elasticity which is about the degree of responsiveness.

ϵ is the measure of own price elasticity, but what does the number mean? Let's look at some cases. Suppose $\epsilon > 1$. In that case the numerator is larger than the denominator, so the percentage quantity change (Q_1) is larger than the percentage own price change (P_1). In that case a price change is causing an even greater degree of change in the quantity. That is a pretty responsive demand. So, $\epsilon > 1$ represents an elastic demand.

If $\epsilon < 1$ then the percentage quantity change is smaller than the percentage own price change. In that case quantity is not very responsive to an own price change. If $\epsilon < 1$ the demand is referred to as inelastic. Earlier we saw an example of a perfectly inelastic demand—the "you have to have it to live, and there's no time to waste and no substitutes" case. What would the elasticity measure be in that perfectly inelastic case? As own price changes the quantity demanded remains constant. If you need one dose of the "have to have it" drug, no matter what the price is you want one: no more, no less. So no matter what the percentage change in price is, the percentage change in quantity is zero, and therefore the $\varepsilon = 0$.

Between $\varepsilon > 1$ and $\varepsilon < 1$ there is obviously the $\varepsilon = 1$ case. That is called unitary elasticity. In that case the percentage change in price and the percentage change in quantity are equal.

4.2.14 Own Price Elasticity of Demand and Total Revenue

Now let's play with this own price elasticity concept. Consider the following case: Suppose you are selling tickets to a concert and all your costs (the bands, the stadium, the security, . . .) are already contracted so they are fixed. You were initially going to charge $50 per ticket, but one of your brilliant friends says, "Hey, this is a great lineup you've got; you can get more for those tickets!" So you start cogitating about raising the price. Should the concept "own price elasticity" matter to you as you cogitate? If yes, why?

It certainly should. You better have some sense of how strongly the market will respond to your price increase before you try it. Remember, unless your demand is perfectly inelastic, which is unlikely, the higher the price the fewer tickets you will sell. The total revenue you will make depends on the price you charge *and* the number of tickets you sell.

Total revenue = Price * Quantity

Since your costs are set, the size of your profit (or maybe your loss) will depend entirely on how much total revenue you bring in. If your demand is inelastic, as you raise your price the quantity demanded will fall by a smaller percentage than the price rises, so your total revenue will rise. You're a winner! If on the other hand your demand is elastic, as you raise your price the quantity demanded will fall by a larger percentage than the price rises. In that case your total revenue will fall, and you lose!

Your brilliant friend is right on one point; you can charge more for the tickets. There might be folks who would pay $1,000 for a ticket to the concert you are putting on. But if your friend had taken this course she would know that her logic about raising prices has its limits. If you jack up the price to $1,000 and still sell 900 tickets—that is a lot of total revenue: $900,000. But you would be better off if at $50 each you can sell 20,000 tickets and make a total revenue of $1,000,000. When you are making your pricing decision, you better take own price elasticity into account. And if you raise your price you better pray you are right that the demand is inelastic.

This own price elasticity issue is extremely important to any firm or, for that matter, any kind of organization that is making pricing decisions. Many large firms turn to economists rather than prayer as they consider price moves. They hire economists to estimate the own price elasticity of the demand for their product so they can evaluate the consequences of a price change. If the economist's calculations of elasticity are correct, the firm can avoid pricing mistakes.

4.2.15 Own Price Elasticity of Demand and Advertising

Obviously, firms prefer that the products they sell have a very low own price elasticity of demand. They do not want their customers to be too price sensitive. If an individual firm can make its demand inelastic it has some choice over the price it sets and it can try to move to the best price given its cost structure. One way firms can try to affect the own price elasticity for their product is through advertising. If the firm can convince you that its competitor's product is not a good substitute for its product, then you will be less price sensitive with respect to its product. In the past Coke tried to convince people that it's the "real thing." Pepsi has warned you that you are a geezer if you're not in the Pepsi generation. To the degree that a firm can create brand loyalty it can make the demand for its product more inelastic. Another way firms can protect their own market and keep the demand for their product inelastic is to keep substitutes out of the market. If you can keep your competition from entering the market and/or from getting known in the market, that is good for your firm.

But under the perfectly competitive conditions we are currently assuming the individual firms are not able to distinguish their products or keep competitors away, so as we will see shortly in perfectly competitive markets the individual suppliers face a perfectly elastic demand line.

4.2.16 Own Price Elasticity of Demand and Public Policy—A Case

Suppose you were a public policy planner and your job was to reduce drug crime in New York City. You decide that the best policy is a powerful interdiction program to reduce the amount of drugs in the city. Seems sensible enough. . . .

Now let's suppose your interdiction program was very successful. After six months the supply of drugs in the city is down significantly. But low and behold, crime is up! What went wrong? Fewer drugs mean fewer drug crimes right? Not necessarily. What did you forget to consider?: The demand side of the market.

Given that drugs are addictive and that there are no good substitutes for these drugs, the demand is very inelastic. If demand is inelastic and you have significantly reduced the supply, what is going to happen to the total revenue of the drug dealers that are still on the street? It is going to go up: Given the very inelastic nature of demand for an addictive drug, as the quantity goes down the price will go up dramatically. Since price will be rising faster than quantity is falling, the effect will be more money spent on drugs. If drug crime is generated by addicts desperately trying to find the cash for drugs, then ironically, there will be more crime after your policy "success" because the addicts will need more money to buy the now much-more-expensive drugs.

Does that mean the policy is a bad idea? Not necessarily because the market is a dynamic environment. The current market is made up of all the current addicts who are going to exhibit the inelastic demand we just described. But the suppliers are also constantly seeking new customers. These folks are not addicted yet so their demand will be much more elastic and as a consequence the large price rise might discourage these potential customers from buying. Thus the intertemporal effect of your policy may be to raise crime in the short run as current addicts bid for the now-more-scarce drugs, but to lower crime in the long run as fewer people try this much-more-expensive experiment.

Whatever one thinks of interdiction as a drug policy, our analysis makes one thing clear: Any policy that is going to be successful against drugs must deal with not only the supply side of the market but also the demand side.

Whether you are making public policy on drugs or on commuting, or making private policy on the price of hamburgers, you often do not know in advance what kind of demand line you are dealing with. But at least if you understand our model you will appreciate that there are variations in own price elasticities of demand and that if you are implementing policy these elasticities can often matter a lot to the success of your policy. That is really what the model does for us. It does not tell us answers to policy questions, it equips us to think systematically about the questions we are exploring so that we don't come up with silly answers based on trivial thinking.

And even if you are not going to be the one making policy, you will be voting for those that do. So as a citizen if you are going to make informed choices you need a systematic approach to critical thinking. A thoughtful model like ours provides that.

4.2.17 Own Price Elasticity of Demand and Public Policy— Taxes and Markets

Now let's look at an example of the importance of own price elasticity on public policy. In particular, let's see how own price elasticity relates to tax policy in markets. Consider the following case:

In Figure 4.2.5 there are two graphs representing different demand possibilities (different attitudes) in the market for a given good. The axes in both graphs are the same, the initial supply lines in both graphs are the same, and the initial equilibrium price and

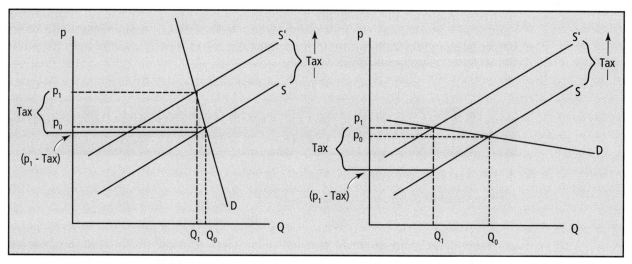

Figure 4.2.5 Elasticity and Tax Incidence

quantity in both graphs are the same. The only difference is the own price elasticity of demand: The demand for this good is inelastic on the left and elastic on the right.

Now suppose a tax is imposed in this market. We will assume that the tax is added to the cost of providing the item, which adds to the cost of supply, raising the supply line.

In the very inelastic case on the left, as the supply line goes up the price goes up with it. You can see that the increase in price covers almost all of the tax. In this case, while the tax appears to be on the producer, in fact the tax is almost entirely passed on to the consumer. The effective price the supplier will receive (the market price minus the tax) is almost the same amount as before, and the tax is paid almost entirely by the consumer.

In the very elastic case on the right, as the supply line goes up the price does not go up with it. In this case the price did not rise nearly as much as the full tax imposed. That is because when the demand is very elastic the supplier cannot pass much of the tax along. An attempt to raise the price to pass on the tax results in a much lower quantity demanded rather than higher price. So in this case the *tax burden*, the actual weight of the tax, falls primarily on the supplier. The small increase in price above the old price represents the little share of the tax burden carried by the consumers. The effective price the supplier will receive (the market price minus the tax) is now significantly below the initial price received by the supplier. The burden is mostly on the supplier.

Tax incidence is all about who really pays the tax, who really bears the burden. The importance of all this for policy is clear. If you are going to impose a tax you want to have some sense as to how the market is going to respond to the tax and who is going to ultimately bear the burden. If you want to the consumer to bear the burden, tax goods for which the demand is inelastic. If you want the supplier to pay the tax, tax goods for which the demand is elastic.

The case also highlights how tax policy can be used for different purposes.

If you want to discourage the consumption of a good, a tax will work if the demand is elastic. This is clear from the right picture in Figure 4.2.5.

If you want to generate revenue, a tax works better on inelastic goods. That is the case because you add the tax and people are willing to pay it (albeit not happily).

In some cases, if the market is segmented, you might be able to both generate revenue and affect behavior. Take the case of tobacco for example. Tobacco is an addictive drug. If you raise the tax on tobacco you can generate a lot of revenue from smokers who are addicted because their demand looks like the left picture in Figure 4.2.5. But you might also succeed in discouraging new consumers because the demand of the non-addicted is presumably more like that in the right picture in Figure 4.2.5.

Here, as before, the model directs your thinking by giving you a sense of the web of connections you should consider as you try to trace out the consequences of your policy before you implement it. A thoughtful model is a much better basis for policy than no framework for systematic thinking at all.

4.3 EXPANDING THE DEMAND RELATIONSHIP— IDENTIFYING THE SHIFT VARIABLES

4.3.1 Introduction

We have explored the product demand relationship

$$Q_1^D = D(p_1 \mid \text{shift variables})$$

as if the shift variables are always constant. Now it is time to identify the shift variables and see how they move the relationship. Our full product demand relationship is written

$$Q_1^D = D(p_1 \mid p_r, I, T)$$

where

- p_r stands for the prices of any related goods,
- I stands for income, and
- T stands for tastes

4.3.2 Tastes as a Shift Variable

Let's take the tastes variable, T, first since it is the easiest to understand. If your taste for a product changes that is by definition a change in your attitude toward a product. If your tastes changed toward that product, if for example you now like the CDs of a music group much more, that means that at any given price your quantity demanded for that product is greater. Graphically a shift of tastes toward a product can be represented as shown in Figure 4.3.1.

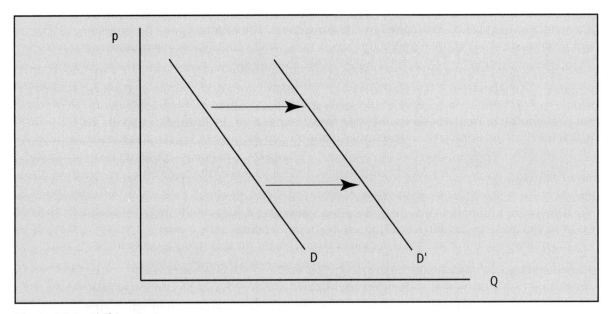

Figure 4.3.1 Shifting Tastes

If at every price your quantity demanded is higher, then the result of this change in tastes is a shift in your demand to the right. If your tastes move away from a product, your demand shifts left.

Tastes can be powerful movers in markets. When a music group gets hot the price of tickets to their concerts can go up very quickly, and if they suddenly fall out of favor those ticket prices can go down just as quickly. But tastes are not the only variable that can shift demand. Another is the price of related goods, p_r.

4.3.3 Price of Related Goods as a Shift Variable

Let's take our classic case of McDonalds. Suppose the price of hamburgers at McDonalds goes up. *Ceteris paribus*, we know this means that unless that demand is perfectly inelastic, the quantity of hamburgers sold at McDonalds goes down. But that will not be the end of the story. More often than not people buy hamburgers along with fries and a drink. If this is true, then a rise in the price of hamburgers doesn't only affect the quantity of burgers demanded, it also affects the quantity of fries and the quantity of drinks demanded. This effect of a change in price in one good on the quantity demanded of another good is called a *cross price effect*. In this case the initial change was a rise in the price of hamburgers that caused a fall in the quantity demanded of hamburgers. Now we are assuming that hamburgers and french fries are consumed together. Economists call items that are consumed together *complements*. Since hamburgers and french fries are complements, the price rise that causes fewer hamburgers to be purchased causes in turn a fall in the demand for fries, which means that at the going price the quantity of fries demanded is lower. We can trace the effect as follows:

$$\uparrow p_{hbg} \rightarrow \downarrow Q_{hbg} \rightarrow \downarrow D_{ff} \rightarrow \downarrow Q_{ff}$$

This cross price effect is represented by a concept called the *cross price elasticity of demand*. Cross price elasticity is measured by

$$\varepsilon_{1 \times 2} = \frac{\%QuantityChangeofGood2}{\%PriceChangeofGood1}$$

As with own price elasticity we use the percentage change because it gives a more accurate sense of the degree of change. In this case, however, there is no absolute value sign. That is because unlike the own price elasticity case in which the sign is always negative, in this case the sign may be negative or positive. Indeed, in the case of cross price elasticity it is the sign that interests us.

4.3.4 Cross Price Elasticity of Complements

To see why let's go back to our hamburgers and fries at McDonalds example. Remember the sequence of events: A rise in the price of hamburgers caused a fall in the quantity demanded of hamburgers. This in turn causes a fall in the demand for fries, which means that at the going price the quantity of fries demanded is lower. In this scenario the change in p_{hbg} is positive and the change in Q_{ff} is negative. So in terms of our cross price elasticity measure

$$\varepsilon_{(hbg) \times (ff)} = \frac{\%QuantityChangeofGood"ff"-is-negative}{\%PriceChangeofGood"hbg"-is-positive} \text{ so this is} < 0$$

The cross price elasticity of any two goods that are consumed together, as I have assumed is the case for hamburgers and french fries, is negative. As the price of one goes up you consume less of that one and in turn want less of the other, so the ultimate effect on the quantity demanded of the other is negative. Goods with a negative cross price elasticity of demand are consumed together, and so economists call such goods *complements*.

4.3.5 Cross Price Elasticity of Substitutes

If the cross price elasticity of demand is positive it must be the case that as the price of Good 1 goes up and thus the quantity demanded of Good 1 goes down, the effect is to demand more of Good 2 and thus have a larger quantity demanded of Good 2 at the current price of Good 2. In effect, you are substituting Good 2 for the now more expensive Good 1 . . . just as you might substitute Burger King hamburgers for McDonalds hamburgers if the price at McDonalds goes up. A positive cross price elasticity of demand

$$\varepsilon_{1 \times 2} = \frac{\%QuantityChangeofGood2 - is - positive}{\%PriceChangeofGood1 - is - positive} \text{ so this is} > 0$$

is the case of *substitutes* and the size of the cross price tells how easily people substitute one for the other. If the sign is positive, but the value of ε_{1x2} is very small, then the goods are substitutes but it takes a big price increase in one to cause a significant substitution to the other. So in general economists are interested in the sign of the cross price—to determine the nature of the relationship, and the size of the cross price—to determine the degree of the effect.

4.3.6 Cross Price Elasticity and the Market System as a Web of Connections

The market system is a web of connections. Cross price elasticity measures the direction and strength of the threads that connect all the product markets in that web. In the market system as in a spider's web, if you tweak it anywhere it affects the web everywhere. Obviously the impact is most significant at points closer to the point of the tweak. The demand for hamburgers at the McDonalds down the street from you is much more significantly affected by the price charged at the Burger King in the same neighborhood than by the price of tea in China, but both ultimately have some effect. Cross price elasticity brings into direct focus the reality of the market system as a complex web of connections, and it also brings into focus the complexity of markets when one is trying to do policy—private or public.

When doing policy you better remember that the market system is a general system. If you only focus on one piece of the action—for example focusing on own price effects and ignoring cross price effects—you are going to miss some very important connections that will have a significant bearing on how your policy unfolds. Ignoring such connections can make for very foolish policy. The value of developing a model is that it provides you with a systematic way of thinking. It does not tell you answers, but to the degree that the model reflects reality, or, in other words, to the degree that the model's assumptions are realistic, a model can be helpful in guiding your thinking systematically so you know what questions to ask.

4.3.7 Cross Price Elasticity and Private Policy

When McDonalds considers a price change for its burgers, it has to consider not only the own price effect, but also cross price effects—and these are related. Remember, a significant determinant of own price elasticity is the number and quality of good substitutes. If McDonalds goes to Peoria and test markets a price increase, its measure of own price elasticity gives it some sense of the cross price elasticity with other products. If it finds that the own price elasticity is high—that might suggest that another product is being substituted. If McDonalds can identify the competition, it can try to reduce the cross price elasticity with this substitute by an advertising campaign that tries to affect consumers' sense that the two items are indeed substitutes. But folks in marketing at McDonalds have more to worry about than the competition. They also have to worry about the effect of a burger price increase on their other products. If the cross price elasticity between their burgers and their own fries and drinks is very high, then a price increase on burgers will reduce sales of fries and drinks significantly.

4.3.8 Cross Price Elasticity and Public Policy

Congratulations! Based on your excellent education in this course you have been chosen to solve a very serious problem of modern society: highway deaths due to impaired driving.

Now you're on it: You begin thinking to yourself: "Let's see, how can we discourage impaired driving? Of course! Raise the price of alcohol with a big tax increase. Then people will consume less. But, ah ha!" you say, "I'm no fool. I know I need to determine the own price elasticity of alcohol. If it's inelastic then I'll need a Plan B. If it's elastic, I'm golden! A simple, targeted tax and lives are saved. It'll be a laser-guided policy missile that saves lives. Am I good or what!"

So you do a study and, lo and behold, alcohol has an elastic demand. "Let's get moving—there are lives to be saved. There's a Presidential medal to be received at the White House. There's fame and fortune ahead." So you implement your tax and, just as predicted by your study, alcohol consumption declines. But alas, highway deaths do not go down. It was all so simple and obvious. . . . What might have gone wrong?

The initial problem with your thought process was thinking of highway deaths as caused by drunk driving rather than impaired driving. There are plenty of ways to become impaired. Alcohol is the most easily available and legal way, but other drugs (like marijuana) impair a driver just as much.

The scenario I just presented is consistent with a world in which marijuana is considered a good substitute for alcohol. Given such a good substitute, a rise in the price of alcohol would result in a significant fall in quantity demanded—so alcohol would exhibit a high own price elasticity. But given that the substitute also impairs one's ability to drive, even as alcohol consumption falls with the new tax the number of deaths on the highway from impaired drivers would not fall. All that would change is the nature of the impairment.

When you did your study and found that alcohol has an elastic demand, you should have asked yourself: Why is it so elastic? That question would have guided you into the complex web of connections. You would have thought, "Hmmmm, more elastic can imply good substitutes are available. Is that what's going on here?" Good models equip you to ask thoughtful questions about "What's going on here?"

4.3.9 Cross Price Elasticity and Policy

Once again, the moral of the story is that when it comes to policy, be it public or private, anyone who says it's simple is either simple-minded or thinks you are. The world is a web of complex connections. Problems in a complex world are complex. Solutions to problems of a complex world are rarely obvious, never perfect, and sometimes complex. When you tweak a web, you cannot know the consequences of that tweak unless you trace the threads that make up the web.

A good model is based on explicit and reasonable assumptions and offers a systematic approach to critical thinking about policy in a woven world.

4.3.10 Cross Price Elasticity and Shifting Demand Lines

Now let's represent the connections among markets graphically. Figure 4.3.2 shows the hamburger, french fries, and pizza markets.

Suppose for some reason the supply line in the hamburger market shifts up. This would result in a higher price and lower quantity demanded for hamburgers.

In the picture of the french fry market, a rise in the price of hamburgers, a complement, causes french fry demand to shift left. At any given price, people want fewer french fries because now with the hamburger price rise they're eating fewer hamburgers.

In the pizza market picture, if pizza is a substitute for hamburgers, a rise in the price of hamburgers causes pizza demand to shift right. At any given price, people want more pizza because now with the hamburger price rise they're eating more pizza.

In general we can say that changes in prices of related goods, p_r, shift a product's demand line so we include the p_r among the shift variables.

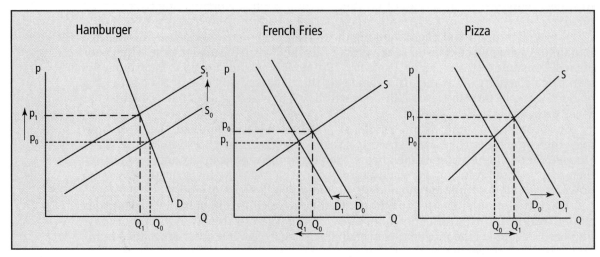

Figure 4.3.2 Connecting Markets by Cross Price Effects

4.3.11 Cross Price Elasticity and Shifting Demand Lines— Practice

In order to practice with this cross price you should try to graph cases of market interactions that you see out the window.

4.3.12 Income Elasticity

The shift variables of product market demand are price of related goods, income, and tastes. We have looked at price of related goods and tastes, now let's consider income. *Ceteris paribus*, as your income goes up you will normally consume more of a given good, and as your income goes down you will normally consume less. In terms of our market picture, that means that normally, if income goes up you consume more at any given price so the demand line shifts right and if income goes down you consume less at any given price so the demand line shifts left. Since economists expect this to be the normal case, goods that exhibit this relationship between income and demand are referred to as *normal goods*. Obviously, as the term "normal" implies, most goods are normal goods. If your income goes up you buy more clothes or nicer clothes, or more or nicer food, or more or nicer cars, and so on . . . keep in mind to buy nicer is to expand your demand for the product by quality rather than quantity.

In contrast, if as your income goes up your demand goes down, or if as your income goes down your demand goes up, such goods are called *inferior goods*. These are goods that you would choose not to consume if you could afford not to. For example generic brands might be considered an inferior good by some folks. If they could afford to they would buy the name brand, but if their income is low they buy generic. If and when their income goes up they would switch to the name brand. Note the words "might consider" in this example. What is a normal or inferior good is based on the perception of the individual. What is inferior to some, might be precisely what others desire.

4.3.13 Representing Income Elasticity

The measure for the response of a good's demand to a change in income is called *income elasticity of demand* and it is represented by the equation:

$$\varepsilon_I = \frac{\%QuantityChange}{\%IncomeChange}$$

As in the case of cross price elasticity, there is no absolute value sign here because it is the sign and size of the income elasticity that is of interest. Since for a normal good quantity demanded at any given price rises with income, the sign of income elasticity for a normal good is positive. Inferior goods exhibit a falling quantity demanded as income rises, so the sign for inferior goods is negative.

4.3.14 Income Elasticity—One Person's Inferior Good Is Another Person's Ambrosia

Goods are not inherently normal or inferior. Attitudes are personal perceptions. The market's perspective on what is a normal or an inferior good is based on the aggregation of the attitudes of all the participants in the market. For example:

When I was a 12-year-old kid we used to pig out on burgers from the "Belly Bomber," an alias since I don't want to be sued for calling their product inferior. Belly Bomber burgers were small (barely larger than the pickle that came on top), greasy, and cheap (like 10 cents/burger). Not exactly gourmet eating, but hey, I was on a 12-year-old budget. Later when I became an affluent teen, I left Belly Bombers behind for a delicious delicacy called a #2 without the onions at Bud's Broiler. In my preference ordering, Belly Bombers are an inferior good, and Bud's Broiler burgers are a normal good.

The key words here are "in my preference ordering." Whether a good is inferior or normal to an individual depends on her own personal preference ordering. Much to my amazement, I did know folks who preferred a bag of Belly Bombers to a juicy Bud's. As the classic expression goes *De Gustibus Non Est Disputandum*, which is Latin for "there's no accounting for tastes."

This discussion on differences among individuals in product markets brings us to an important point. The full demand in a product market is just the sum of the effects of the all the demands of the individuals who are participating in that market.

4.3.15 From Individual to Market Demand

The sum of all individuals' demands for a given good or service is the market demand for that good or service. In other words, at any given price, the market quantity demanded is the sum of the individuals' quantities demanded at that price.

Consider Figure 4.3.3. At the top we see three pictures that represent three different persons' demand lines for candy bars. At any given price, the market quantity demanded is the sum of the three individuals' quantities demanded at that price. The picture at the bottom shows the market demand if these are the only three persons in the market.

In this example at a $1 price for candy bars we find that individual #1 has a quantity demanded of 3 bars, individual #2 has a quantity demanded of 4 bars, and individual #3 has a quantity demanded of 5 bars. Summing these up, we see that the market quantity demanded at a $1 price is 3+4+5 or 12 candy bars. At a $5 price, individuals 1, 2, and 3 have as quantities demanded 1, 2, and 1 bar, respectively. Therefore the market quantity demanded for candy bars at a $5 price is 4 bars. By repeating this summing of the individuals' quantities demanded over all prices we derive the market demand line.

Since the market demand line is simply the sum of the individuals' demands, changes in individuals' demands due to changes in tastes, income, or prices of related goods can cause a shift in the market demand. Whether the market demand moves depends on the net effect of all the individual changes. If attitudes move in the same direction, the market demand will move in that direction.

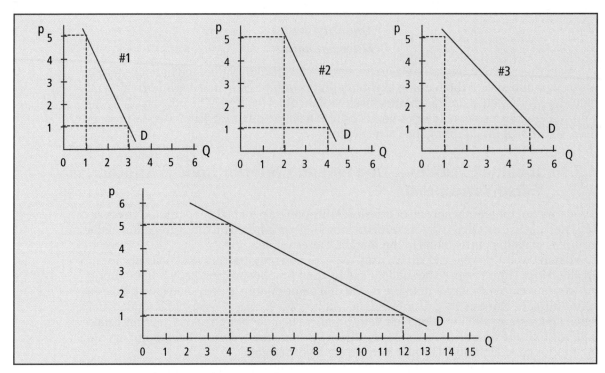

Figure 4.3.3 From Individual to Market Demand

4.3.16 Entry & Exit and Shifts in Product Market Demand

At the level of the market there is one more shift variable besides attitude changes of those in the market. There is also entry of individuals into or exit of individuals from the market. A classic case in point is the impact of the baby boom on demand for diapers in the late 1940s and early 1950s, for primary and secondary education in the early 1960s, for college education in the late 1960s and early 1970s, and so on. You can bet that there will be a surge in demand for dentures, medical care (the elderly use a disproportionate share of medical resources), nursing homes, coffins, and the like when the "boomers" reach their 70s and 80s in the second and third decade of the 21st century.

Clearly this demographic case has huge policy implications. Private enterprises are already planning and investing with the future needs of the boomers in mind. Public policy makers should also be planning now for the impact of the boomers on public services: What will be provided? How will services be paid for? These folks (including me) are in the prime of life as I write, but soon enough we will be geezers and we will want and vote for those public services. What will be the impact of this demographic demand on you?

The boomers are a big example of a general reality in markets: Demographics matter. Public and private analysts follow demographics because they know that as the size of groups in the population changes, those changes mean expansion and contraction of the market demand for goods and services that are used primarily by particular groups. But, demographics are just an example of a larger market phenomenon, entry and exit in markets.

Entry and exit can be volatile, affecting conditions in a market very quickly, so I is a potential source of rapid changes in market conditions.

4.3.17 Conclusion on Product Demand

Product market demand originates in the behavior of individuals with limited resources following our utility maximization decision rule: Across "n" possible allocations of resources, we allocate our resources such that

$$EPV_1 = EPV_2 = \ldots = EPV_n$$

From this decision rule we determined that quantity demanded falls as price rises or rises as price falls—in other words, that the demand line slopes down.

We then examined the characteristics of a given level of demand—what it represents, its responsiveness, and the conditions that determine the level of demand (tastes, income, and price of related goods). Finally, we saw how all these individual demands constitute the foundation of market demand. Now to complete our analysis of the product market picture we turn to an analysis of supply.

5.0 Product Market Supply

5.1 Product Supply

5.1.1 Why the Product Supply Line Slopes Up: Setting the Scene

Alfred Marshall wrote the book on microeconomic theory. His *Principles of Economics* published in 1890 laid out the framework that we now use for modern micro theory. One of Marshall's many major insights lay in his analysis of the supply side in the product market. Marshall's earliest predecessors in modern economic analysis, following the work of David Ricardo who published his *Principles of Political Economy* in 1817, believed that the product supply line was perfectly elastic, a horizontal line. Ricardo argued that cost of production determined the price suppliers put on their product, and that in most market cases the cost of producing any item was constant. A perfectly horizontal supply line reflects this view. No matter where the demand is, the price is determined by the level of production costs as reflected in the level of the supply line.

In the 1870s three economists (William Stanley Jevons, Carl Menger, and Leon Walras) argued, independently of one another, that Ricardo had it all wrong. They viewed level of supply as fixed by the quantity available in the market. That implies a vertical supply line at the given level of quantity supplied. In this case the market price is determined by where the demand line intersects the supply line. In effect they reverse the logic from Ricardo's "supply determines price" and made the case that "demand determines price."

5.1.2 Why the Product Supply Line Slopes Up: Marshall's Analysis

In 1890 Marshall offered a more complete analysis that included both Ricardo and the Jevons/Menger/Walras cases as special cases of a larger set of possible market conditions. Marshall defined Ricardo's case as the *long run* condition—defining the long run as the period it took for the entire scale of production to be adjusted. If returns to scale are constant then in the long run cost of production would be constant and the long run supply line would indeed be horizontal. Marshall defined the Jevons/Menger/Walras case as the *market period* condition—defining the market period as the immediate condition when there is a fixed amount of an item actually available in the market. If the amount of product in the market is a given, then the supply line would indeed be vertical.

Having defined the long run and the market period, Marshall went on to argue that the most reasonable frame for analyzing market activity is in an intermediate case between these two extremes—a case he called the *short run*. In the short run the scale of production is fixed, but some factor inputs are variable. This means output can be expanded by applying more of the variable factor. But as we learned earlier, if all other factors are constant the marginal product of that variable factor falls. We will see in a moment that this means that the supply line is not always, as Ricardo suggested, horizontal, meaning supply determines price; or as Jevons/Menger/Walras suggested, vertical, meaning demand determines price. Marshall believed that the most common case is an upward sloping supply line. In Marshall's analysis it is not supply *or* demand that determines price, it is the interaction of supply conditions *and* demand conditions that determines price. As Marshall wrote in his *Principles*:

> We might as reasonably dispute whether it is the upper or the under blade of a pair of scissors that cuts a piece of paper, as whether value is governed by utility [(demand)] or cost of production [(supply)]. It is true that when one blade is held still, and the cutting is effected by moving the other, we may say with careless brevity that the cutting is done by the second; but the statement is not strictly accurate . . .

Modern economics has adopted Marshall's more complete analysis and his representation of the short run upward sloping supply line as the most important case for market analysis. So let's see why diminishing marginal productivity in the short run makes the supply line slope up.

5.1.3 Why the Product Supply Line Slopes Up: From Marginal Product to Marginal Cost

Remember what diminishing marginal productivity means: Holding all other factors constant as you increase one input, the output from each successive unit of that input may increase initially but eventually the productivity of marginal units of an input will decline. We can represent diminishing marginal productivity graphically as shown in Figure 5.1.1.

This has important implications for what it costs per successive unit of output, or what we will refer to as the marginal cost of production.

To see why consider the following: Let's say the input is labor, so we are talking about successive units of labor. Let's assume that the labor is being paid at a constant rate—say $20/hour. As the marginal product of that labor rises then falls while the worker is being paid a constant rate per hour, what is going to happen to the cost per successive unit of output? In other words, if the marginal product of labor looks like Figure 5.1.1, what will the output's marginal cost curve look like?

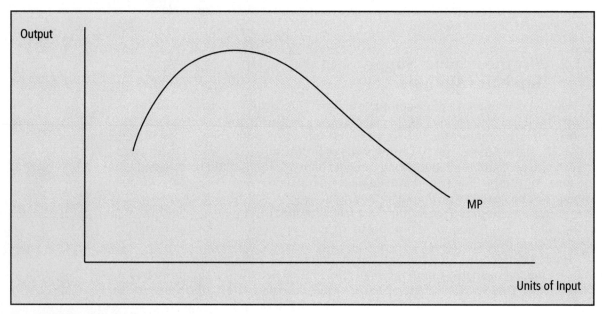

Figure 5.1.1 Marginal Productivity

5.1.4 Why the Product Supply Line Slopes Up: Deriving the Marginal Cost Curve

To answer this question let's walk through a simple case. Suppose the labor is producing candy bars. Successive units of labor produce more candy bars at first, but eventually they produce less. Table 5.1.1 is a marginal product (MP) table showing candy bar output for each successive unit of labor input.

TABLE 5.1.1 MARGINAL PRODUCT IN CANDY BARS

Unit of Labor	MP for Labor in Candy Bars
1st	25
2nd	100
3rd	200
4th	180
5th	160
6th	140
7th	120
8th	110
9th	100
10th	90

These numbers are consistent with the shape of the marginal product line (MP) in Figure 5.1.1—MP rises, then falls. Now, let's assume that labor is paid $20/hour. With the MP schedule and the wage we can calculate the marginal cost of successive units of candy bars. This is shown in Table 5.1.2.

TABLE 5.1.2 FROM MARGINAL PRODUCT TO MARGINAL COST

Labor at $20/hour	MP of Labor in Candy Bars	MC/unit of candy in cents (rounded off)
1st	25	.80
2nd	100	.20
3rd	200	.10
4th	180	.11
5th	160	.13
6th	140	.14
7th	120	.17
8th	110	.18
9th	100	.20
10th	90	.22

Based on this we see that when we pay constant input price and the marginal product of that input rises and then falls, this means that the marginal cost of the output will fall and then rise. Graphically, given our assumptions, a generic marginal cost curve (labeled MC) looks like Figure 5.1.2.

We can understand the relationship between the marginal product and marginal cost curves as follows: If you pay workers $20/hour and they are making more and more stuff per hour, then the cost for successive units of that stuff is going to go down, down, down. When they are most productive, the cost per unit is lowest. Beyond that point they begin

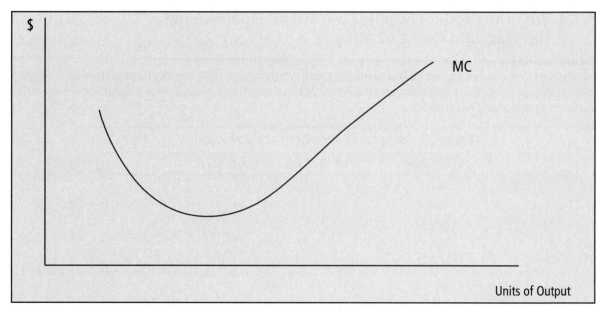

Figure 5.1.2 Marginal Cost

to get less productive at the margin, and the output is going to get more and more expensive to produce. So we see that the MC curve looks like Figure 5.1.2 because of our assumption of eventually diminishing marginal productivity.

5.1.5 Why the Product Supply Line Slopes Up: From MC to the Supply Line

This relationship between marginal product and marginal cost is important because for an individual firm the upward sloping segment of the MC curve *is* the firm's supply line. Think about it from the firm's point of view: It is easy for a firm to expand production when marginal costs are falling; the real question a firm faces is "How far do we want to

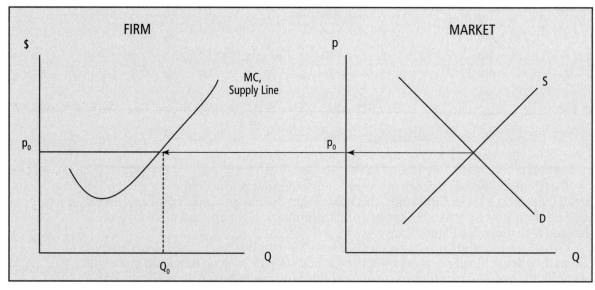

Figure 5.1.3 Price Signal and a Firm's Response

expand production as MC rises?" The firm determines how much it will supply by following its MC curve.

When the firm gets the market signal—the price—that signal says in effect: "We're willing to pay this much; how many will you produce?"

As shown in Figure 5.1.3, the firm will look at that market price, it will look at its marginal cost curve, and it will say, "Well, at that price we can cover the marginal cost of successive units up to this much output. If you want more you have to pay more, because the marginal cost of units beyond that is higher than the price you offer." If the market price rises, the firm looks at its MC curve and in effect says, "OK, that'll cover a higher MC, so we're willing to produce this much more."

The firm determines its output by moving along the upward sloping section of the MC curve, so this section of the MC curve is the firm's supply line.

5.1.6 Supply, MC, and Normal Returns

It is very important to note that when a firm considers the costs it incurs, those costs include all that the firm has to pay other people *and* the return the owner of the firm has to pay herself.

Consider the gift shop that my sister owned for many years. She had to pay a lot for the rent on her space in the mall . . . the electricity, the phone, the water . . . the gift paper and mailing paper and bags . . . salaries for all the employees . . . insurance . . . gifts she sold . . . and on and on and on. There were a lot of costs to running her business. All these costs are represented in her marginal curve. . . . And when she finished writing checks to all of those other people she had to pay to run her business, she wasn't finished with the basic cost of running a business. She also had to be able to pay herself. We have a term in economics, and it is going to be very important for our analysis, that describes what she had to pay herself to stay in business. It is called a *normal return*.

A normal return can come in the form of money, or to some degree it may also come in the form of psychic satisfaction. But whatever its form, it is that amount that just covers the opportunity cost of using your resources (your labor, human capital, financial capital, or whatever else of your own that you put into your business) in someone else's enterprise instead of your own.

5.1.7 Normal Returns

The opportunity cost of owning a business is the value of the best available option you forgo in order to be in business. So, to stay in business you have to make enough in your enterprise to cover all the costs you have to pay others and to at least cover that opportunity cost. If you cannot cover all that, then the alternative is better and it is not worth staying in business. When all the bills are paid, there has got to be enough left to make it worth staying in business—to beat the opportunity cost. That is what the normal return is.

For everyone cash matters a lot—but there is more to it than cash. There is also the personal satisfaction of running one's own business well. There is the sense of independence in working for yourself. There is the pride in ownership of a firm others point to with respect. Whatever the source of the utility, a normal return is enough of it to beat the opportunity cost.

Since the normal return is an essential part of a firm's costs, the marginal cost curve of every firm has this normal return built right into it. When a firm is just covering the costs embodied in the marginal cost curve there is no "gravy", but there is enough to stay in business.

5.1.8 Cost Structure and Individual Firm's Supply Shift Variables

The marginal cost curve shows how the cost of a unit of output changes with each successive unit produced. It is one way to represent an individual firm's *cost structure*. This cost structure is based on

- the prices of inputs into production
- level of technology, and
- the environment of production

These variables determine the level of costs that underlie the cost structure. If one of these changes, it changes the level of the cost structure and shifts the MC curve. Since the MC curve of a firm is its supply line, these are the shift variables for the firm's supply line. Using the same functional form tool we used with demand, we can write the functional form of the supply relationship as:

$$Q_1^S = S_1 (p_1 \mid p_I, \text{Tech., Env.})$$

Where

- p_I stands for the prices of inputs,
- Tech. stands for the level of technology, and
- Env. stands for the environment of production

5.1.9 Cost Structure and Individual Firm's Supply Shift Variables—Case of Input Prices (p_I)

If the price of an input, p_I, goes up, then, *ceteris paribus*, the whole cost structure of the firm goes up. With higher input prices it costs more to produce any given quantity. On our graph a rise in an input price, p_I, causes the supply line to shift up as in Figure 5.1.4.

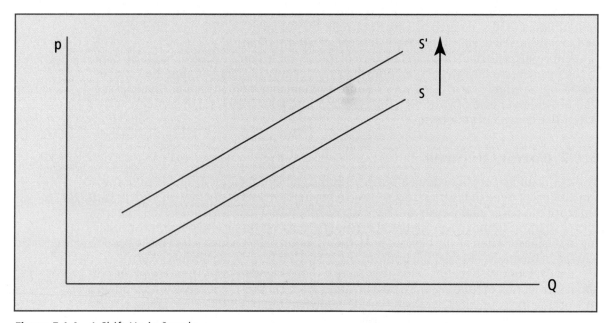

Figure 5.1.4 A Shift Up in Supply

Note: In what follows I'll refer to shift 'up' or 'down' in supply because on the supply side I think in terms of cost structure going up or down and in turn causing supply, S, to go up or down.

Suppose for example that the cost of fabric went up for a firm producing clothes. That would look like the case in Figure 5.1.4. If this happened, *ceteris paribus*, would the firm hope that the demand for its clothes was elastic or inelastic? Inelastic, because in that case it would be able to pass on the higher costs without losing much in the way of sales or revenue.

Suppose the cost of oil went down for a gasoline company. In that case the supply line shifts down. If this happened, *ceteris paribus*, would this firm hope that the demand for its gasoline was elastic or inelastic?: Elastic, because the company would love to expand sales quickly as the price fell.

5.1.10 Cost Structure and Individual Firm's Supply Shift Variables—Case of Technology

Suppose a new, improved technique of production is developed, so the available technology is now better. Obviously there is a cost to implementing this technology, but once it is in place what will happen to the cost structure of the firm and, in turn, the supply line if it adopts this new improved technology? An improvement in the technology used by a firm will lower its production cost structure and thus shift the supply line down.

5.1.11 Cost Structure and Individual Firm's Supply Shift Variables—Case of Environment of Production

The classic case of environment of production can be found in agriculture. Suppose the weather was miserable for apples and the orchards produce a terrible crop. The output per unit of cost is way down on account of the bad environmental conditions. What would happen to the supply line? Any decline in the environment of production for a firm will raise its production cost structure and thus shift the supply line up. *Ceteris paribus*, is this good for the orchard owners? This cannot be answered until we know the demand conditions, because it depends on the elasticity of demand. If demand is elastic the rise in price will not be enough to offset the more significant decline in quantity demanded, so the total revenue of the orchards will fall. If demand is inelastic the rise in price will more than offset the decline in quantity demanded, so the total revenue of the orchards will rise. But keep in mind that weather does not affect all producers the same. One grower's disaster can be a boon for another whose crop now faces less competition.

5.1.12 From Individual to Market Supply

The sum of all individual firms' supplies for a given good or service is the market supply for that good or service. In other words, at any given price, the market quantity supplied is the sum of the individual firms' quantities supplied at that price.

Consider Figure 5.1.5. At the top we see three pictures that represent three different firms' supply lines for candy bars. At any given price, the market quantity supplied is the sum of the three firms' quantities supplied at that price. The picture at the bottom shows the market supply if these are the only three firms in the market.

At any given price, the market quantity supplied is the sum of the three individuals' quantities supplied at that price. In this example at a $1 price for candy bars we find that firm #1 has a quantity supplied of 1 bar, firm #2 has a quantity supplied of 1 bar, and firm #3 has a quantity supplied of 1 bar. Summing these up, we see that the market quantity supplied at a $1 price is 1+1+1 or 3 candy bars. At a $5 price, firms 1, 2, and 3 have as quantities supplied 4, 4, and 4 respectively. Therefore the market quantity supplied for candy bars at a $5 price is 12 bars. By repeating this summing of the individual firms' quantities supplied over all prices we derive the market supply line.

Since the market supply line is simply the sum of the individual firms' supplies, changes in firms' supplies due to changes in input prices, technology, or environment of production can cause a shift in the market supply. Whether the market supply moves depends on the net effect of all the individual changes.

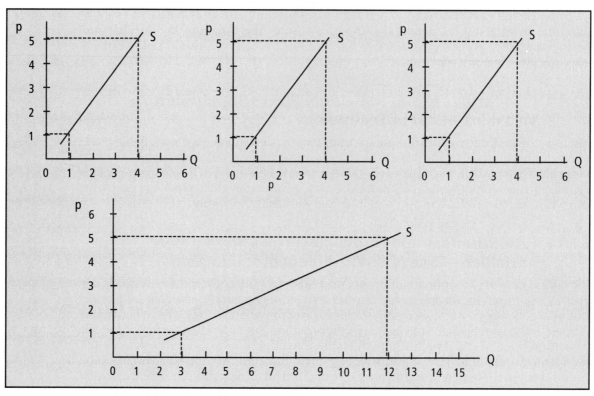

Figure 5.1.5 From Individual to Market Supply

5.1.13 Entry & Exit, and Shifts in Market Supply

At the level of the market there is one more shift variable in addition to the variables that can affect the cost structures of individual firms: The entry or firms into or exit of firms from the market. *Ceteris paribus*, the entry of new firms shifts the market supply line to the right since there will be more quantity supplied in the market at any given price. Conversely, *ceteris paribus*, the exit of existing firms from the market shifts the market supply line to the left since there will be less quantity supplied in the market at any given price.

5.1.14 The Firm in the Market—Firms as Price Takers Under the Perfect Competition of Our Nice Assumptions

We have seen that under our nice assumptions that ensure perfect competition, the market sets the price and each individual and each firm simply responds to that price. Firms and individuals are *price takers*. Graphically, the relationship among individuals, firms, and the market can be represented as shown in Figure 5.1.6.

The market pictured in the middle determines the price. Given that the vertical price axes have the same scale we can trace that price over from the market to the graph representing the generic firm and the generic individual.

The firm can sell as much as it likes at that going market price, so from the perspective of the firm the demand line it faces is perfectly elastic at the level of the price set in the market. What quantity will the firm choose to supply?

Think about it: The price line from the market is the firm's demand line. The MC curve is the firm's supply line. The firm can cover the cost of each successive unit it produces up

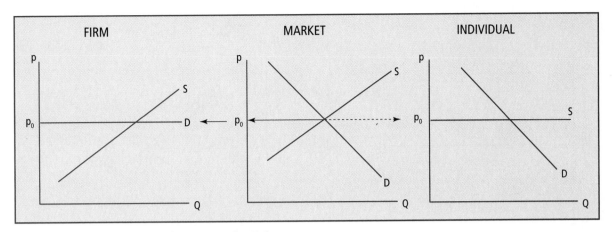

Figure 5.1.6   Individuals and Firms as Price Takers

to the point where the price equals marginal cost, or where its supply and demand lines intersect. The quantity at this point, which we identify by going down from there to the horizontal axis, is the quantity the generic firm will choose to supply. This is represented in Figure 5.1.7.

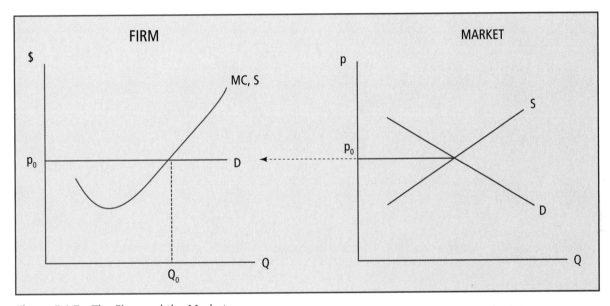

Figure 5.1.7   The Firm and the Market

Now suppose there is entry of new firms into the market. If this shift in supply occurred in the market, what would happen to the quantity the generic firm would supply?

In Figure 5.1.8 you can see that, *ceteris paribus*, as the market supply expands, the price falls. As this happens the intersection between the price and the MC lines in the firm graph slides down to the left. When the market price stops falling the firm will be at a new position with a lower quantity supplied.

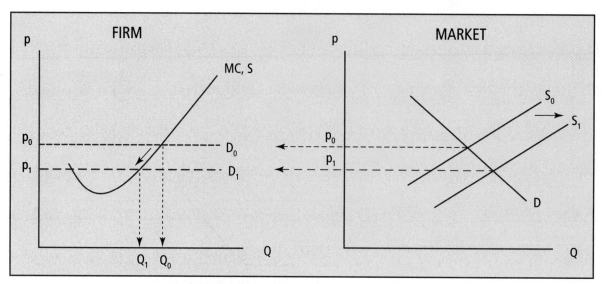

Figure 5.1.8 The Firm in a Changing Market—As New Firms Enter

Just as with the demanders, the suppliers in the product market are constantly responding to the price signal. Under our nice assumptions that ensure perfect competition, all this individual behavior leads to an incredibly efficient outcome. Let's see why.

6.0 REPRESENTING THE POWER OF THE INVISIBLE HAND

6.1 THE MAGIC OF MARKETS—PRODUCT MARKET EFFICIENCY UNDER OUR NICE ASSUMPTIONS

6.1.1 Introduction

In the last 20 years many nations of the world have joined the global experiment in markets. They have done so because there is a conviction among many that markets can do magic. In particular, many believe that the invisible hand of markets can guide nations to realize greater wealth by making their systems of production more efficient.

This conviction does have a theoretical basis. With one more tool we will have all the equipment necessary to demonstrate the potential magic of markets. We will see that the perfect competition that exists given our nice assumptions forces firms in product markets to choose the most efficient (lowest cost) technique of production. Furthermore, we will see that perfect competition encourages constructive creativity by firms because it rewards those that are dynamic developers of ever greater efficiency.

The one additional tool we need for this demonstration is the concept of average cost.

6.1.2 Marginal and Average—Introduction

Marginal cost is one way to represent a firm's cost structure; *average cost (AC)* is another. Let's be clear about the distinction. Marginal cost identifies how much each specific unit costs as it is produced; it represents the unique cost of each successive unit. The average cost is an undifferentiated measure of cost per unit to produce a certain number of units of a product. It is measured by dividing total cost of production by total number produced.

Look at Table 6.1.1. It shows how marginal cost, MC, and average cost, AC, are changing as successive units are produced.

TABLE 6.1.1 MARGINAL AND AVERAGE COST

Unit of Output	MC	AC (rounded)	Calculating AC: Total Cost for that # (Sum of MC)/ # of units
1st	100	100	100/1
2nd	90	95	190/2
3rd	80	90	270/3
4th	70	85	340/4
5th	80	84	420/5
6th	90	85	510/6
7th	100	87	610/7
8th	110	90	720/8
9th	120	93	840/9
10th	130	97	970/10

The marginal cost of the first unit is 100. To calculate the average cost we divide the total costs for all the production by the number of units produced. In the case of the first unit the total cost is just the 100 that the first unit cost and the total number of units is just 1, so the Average Cost is 100/1 or 100. For the first unit the margin equals the average.

The marginal cost of the second unit is 90. That is how much it cost to produce that particular unit. The total cost after two units is the sum of the marginal costs of the first two units produced, so it is 100 + 90, or 190. Dividing this total cost by the number of units, 2, gives the average cost after two units, 95.

And so it goes down the table. The marginal cost represents the actual cost of a specific additional unit. The average cost represents an undifferentiated measure of how much units cost for the given number produced.

6.1.3 Marginal and Average—The Relationship Between Them

The margin moves faster than the average. For example in Table 6.1.1, the margin goes 100, 90, 80, 70 while the average goes 100, 95, 90, 85. This lag of the average behind the margin is due to the way the average is calculated. In this falling margin case the average calculation does not drop as fast because it includes the effects of the higher margins before.

Now think about how changes at the margin affect the average. Suppose you play in the Women's Professional Soccer League and over the last five seasons you have *averaged* 27 goals a season. Then this season you score 35 goals. How is that change in your productivity at the margin, your goals this particular season, going to affect your career average goals scored per season?

It is going to raise your career average.

More personally and hopefully, suppose your GPA this semester ends up higher than your overall GPA has been up until this semester. What is this semester's performance going to do to your overall GPA? It is going to raise it.

The margin always pulls the average along with it. Whenever the margin is above the average it pulls the average up. Conversely, if the margin is below the average it pulls the average down. Even when the margin is rising if it is below the average it will pull the average down. Look at the data in Table 6.1.1. As the margin goes from 70 to 80, the average goes from 85 to 84. Even though the margin went up, the average fell. This is so because while the margin is rising at that point, it is still below the average so it pulls it down. Once the margin goes above the average, the average starts to rise because then the margin is pulling the average up. In our example as the margin goes from 90 to 100 to 110, the average goes from 85 to 87 to 90.

6.1.4 Marginal and Average Cost Curves—Their Relationship

Now let's look back at the MC line for our generic firm. It starts down and then swoops up. If we add an AC line to this cost structure picture what would it look like? AC would start right with the MC line at the first unit. Average cost would follow the marginal cost down, but because AC does not fall as fast as MC, the AC would be above the MC. Even when the MC turns up the AC would continue to go down as long as the MC is below it.

As marginal cost rises it would eventually reach and cut above the average cost. At the point at which the MC cuts above the AC it starts to pull the AC up. So what can we say about the point along the AC line at which the MC cuts across the AC?

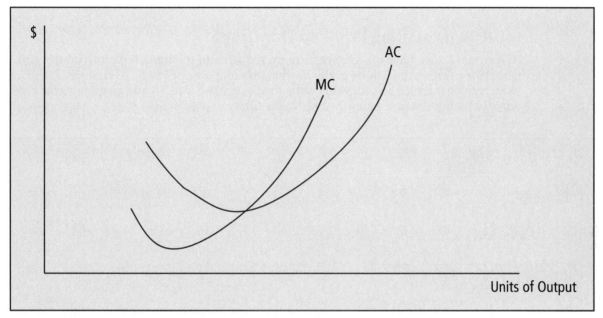

Figure 6.1.1 Marginal Cost cuts Average Cost at the *Minimum Point* along AC curve

As shown in Figure 6.1.1, *the marginal cost curve, MC, intersects and cuts across the average cost curve, AC, at the bottom or minimum point along the AC curve.* It does so because the margin always pulls the average in its direction. When the marginal cost is below average cost, AC falls. Where the marginal cost cuts above the average cost the AC begins to rise. So the marginal cost cuts the average cost at that point where AC stops going down and starts going up. Again: the MC cuts the AC at the minimum average cost point. This bears repeating because the relationship between the marginal and average costs is a very important tool for telling our efficiency story.

6.1.5 Total Revenue, Total Cost, and the Case of Profit

Now that we have all our product market tools in place we can represent the condition of a generic firm in the product market. In particular, we can identify whether the firm is making a profit, suffering a loss, or breaking even. We will call it a profit when the total revenue of the firm is greater than the total costs, a loss (or a negative profit) when total costs are higher, and breaking even when total costs equal total revenue.

The *total revenue* of a firm, TR, is the amount of money it takes in from the sale of its product. Total revenue is measured by price times quantity:

$$\textbf{TR} = \textbf{p} \times \textbf{Q}$$

For example, if a firm sells 5 cars at $20,000/car, its total revenue is $100,000.

The *total cost* of a firm, TC, is the amount of money the firm spends in the process of producing. Total cost is measured by average cost times quantity:

$$TC = AC \times Q$$

For example, if a firm produces 5 cars at an average cost of $17,000, its total cost is $85,000. We will use a Greek letter pie, Π, to stand for profit.

$$\Pi = TR - TC$$

In the case of this firm producing the 5 cars, total revenue minus total cost is $100,000 – $85,000 so this firm is making a profit of $15,000. Let's see how we represent this kind of situation with our graphs.

6.1.6 Representing Profit on Our Graph

In Figure 6.1.2 we have our generic firm on the left and the market picture on the right. Given the current conditions in the market, the market price is p_1. At that market price (which given our nice assumptions is the firm's demand line, D) and given the firm's MC curve (which is the firm's supply line, S), the firm will produce Q_1.

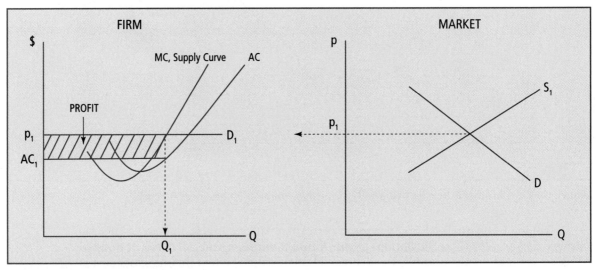

Figure 6.1.2 The Firm and the Market—Identifying Profit

On our graph p is measured vertically so we can think of it as a height, and Q is measured horizontally so we can think of it as a width. Height multiplied by width is an area on a graph, so in the framework of our graph we can represent the total revenue, TR = $p_1 \times Q_1$, by the area of this rectangle on which price, p_1, is the height, and quantity, Q_1, is the width.

What is the average cost (AC) at Q_1 units of production? To determine that we go from Q_1 up to the AC line, and then over to the vertical axis. We see that the average cost when the firm is producing Q_1 is AC_1. In this case we can represent the total cost, TC = $AC_1 \times Q_1$, by the area of a rectangle on which AC_1 is the height and Q_1 is the width.

Look at the total revenue and the total cost rectangles we have just identified. Which is bigger? The total revenue is bigger. Is this firm making a profit or a loss? Since total revenue is greater than total cost, the firm is making a profit. How big is the profit? The area of the rectangle $(p_1 - AC_1) \times Q$, identified by hash-marks, measures the firm's profit: $\Pi = TR - TC$

6.1.7 The Market's Response to Profits

Like many of our terms, profit may be defined differently in other contexts. As always, the important thing for our purposes is that we share a common understanding of what it means here. In our model, a positive profit is realized when total revenue is greater than total cost. As such, it is "gravy". All firms want a profit, but no firm needs a profit. Why?

Remember, our definition of costs includes a normal return for the owner of the firm. So as long as a firm is covering costs, it is making enough to make staying in business worthwhile. It is covering its opportunity cost. Anything above a normal return is gravy: Very nice, but not necessary. So in our model *profit* is gravy, but it is also a very important signal in the market system.

Profits signal that a particular market is a very nice place to be. Under our nice assumptions everyone has equal access to information and equal access to the markets, so as competitors learn about this sweet market that offers a profit they join the market. As each new competitor enters the market the market supply shifts out and the price falls. As long as profits exist, more competitors come to get a piece of the action. As the market price falls with each new entrant, the profits of the firms in the market get squeezed. Ultimately competition will force the price down to the point at which only the costs are covered. The profit is gone. New entries stop.

Figure 6.1.3 represents this dynamic. At the initial market supply, S_1, the market price, p_1, generates a profit (as in Figure 6.1.2 on page 108) for every firm in the market. (Note: All the firms have the same cost structure because under our nice assumptions everyone knows and uses the best available production process.) As firms enter the market Supply (S) shifts out and price (p) falls. Firms continue to enter until supply reaches S_2 and price has fallen to p_2. At that price, each firm in the market will produce Q_2 at average cost AC_2. But now for every firm p = AC so TR = TC. Firms are covering all of their costs, including their normal returns—so they can stay in business as long as they like, but there is no longer any profit.

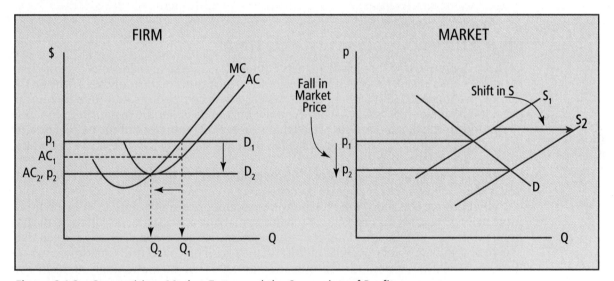

Figure 6.1.3 Competition, Market Entry, and the Squeezing of Profits

6.1.8 Profit, Market Signaling, and the Invisible Hand

Profit is a powerful yet ephemeral signal. By signaling that a market is a good place to be it attracts resources in pursuit of it, and yet it extinguishes itself in the process. Under perfectly competitive conditions firms seek profit, but they end up earning only a normal return that covers the interest and wage return on the capital and labor the owners put into the enterprise. Similarly, losses send firms fleeing from markets in pursuit of better opportunities elsewhere until all losses are gone. The net effect of these resource flows in or out of markets is that under perfect competition normal returns are the norm. Adam Smith described this dynamic of perfectly competitive markets and how it eliminates advantages (profits) or disadvantages (losses) very nicely more than 200 years ago in *The Wealth of Nations*:

> The whole of the advantages and disadvantages of the different employments of labour and stock must, in the same neighbourhood, be either perfectly equal or continually tending to equality [(i.e., ultimately everyone will just make the same return: a normal return)]. If in the same neighbourhood, there was any employment evidently either more or less advantageous than the rest [(i.e. making a profit or a loss respectively)], so many people would crowd into it in the one case, and so many would desert it in the other, that its advantages would soon return to the level of other employments. This at least would be the case in a society where things were left to follow their natural course, where there was perfect liberty, and where every man was perfectly free both to chuse what occupation he thought proper, and to change it as often as he thought proper. Every man's interest would prompt him to seek the advantageous, and to shun the disadvantageous employment. (*WN*, 116)

and Smith writes later in *The Wealth of Nations* that:

> by directing that industry in such a manner as its produce may be of the greatest value, he intends only his own gain, and he is in this, as in many other cases, led by an invisible hand to promote an end which was no part of his intention. . . . By pursuing his own interest he frequently promotes that of the society . . . (*WN*, 456)

This is almost certainly the most famous passage in the most famous book ever written about economics. It highlights that in pursuit of our self-interest we will, under our nice assumptions, promote the wealth of the nation. To see how this self-interested behavior serves society, let's look again at our firm/market picture: Figure 6.1.3.

6.1.9 Efficiency and the Invisible Hand

We have demonstrated that profit attracts competitors. These new entrants expand market supply. This lowers the price. As the price falls, the profits of the individual firms in the market get squeezed. But so long as profits exist new competitors continue to enter in pursuit of some of this "gravy". This dynamic only ends when the expansion of market supply lowers the market price to a level that squeezes all profits out of the market. In that case, p = AC. Graphically that happens when the price intersects the MC curve just where the MC cuts the AC curve.

This is a very special point along the average cost curve. What is so special about it? . . . *It is the bottom of the average cost curve.*

What can we say about the efficiency of production at this point? . . . It is the minimum average cost point. That's hugely significant. Look at what the market dynamic has done when our nice assumptions hold and competition is perfect. Nobody is in charge, everyone is pursuing her own self-interest. In pursuit of profits all firms are driven to produce at a level that realizes the minimum average cost. That is the absolutely *most efficient level of production*. This is a central part of the story of the magic of markets. Under our nice assumptions, the dynamic of a perfectly competitive market forces every firm to charge the lowest price consistent with making a living—a normal return, and to produce in the *most efficient* way.

6.1.10 Competition, Speed, Agility, Getting Ahead, and Survival— the Market Dynamic Under Perfect Competition

Another dynamic of the market magic is that success and even simple survival are only possible for the quick and the agile. To see why, picture this dynamic in our firm/market picture:

Suppose one firm in a market comes up with a more efficient technique of production than the one everyone else is using. In terms of our firm picture this would mean that this firm has a lower cost structure (the cost lines shift down because at any given quantity, Q, the marginal and average costs are lower).

If the firms using the old technique (with the old cost structure) are breaking even at the market price, then the lower cost firm will be making a profit at that price. Since under our nice assumptions all players have equal access to information and equal access to the market, the other firms will see this profit, figure out the lower cost production technique, and switch techniques to share in the profit. But inevitably these profits will attract new competitors. Price will begin to fall. If any of the participating higher-cost firms do not adjust to the more efficient production technique they will eventually be too inefficient to survive. Competition from more efficient firms drives down the price and drives the slow footed out of business. Under our nice assumptions market systems reward speed and agility. If you can't keep up, you can't survive.

6.2 MARKETS, PERFECT COMPETITION, CREATIVITY, AND MATERIAL PROGRESS

6.2.1 Introduction

We have seen that under our nice assumptions that ensure perfect competition, all firms in a market will be driven toward the most efficient level of production with the most efficient technique—or they will be driven out of business. But there is more to the efficiency story. There is another dynamic that over the long run is even more significant: Market systems encourage creativity and inventiveness because they reward it.

6.2.2 Building a Better Mousetrap

To see where the incentive for creativity comes from in markets let's reflect on our picture of the generic firm and the market. Recall that under perfect competition the firm is forced to produce at the bottom of its average cost curve so it is just breaking even: No profit, no loss, just a normal return. Its competitors are forced to use the same technique as well, so their pictures are identical and they are also making a normal return.

All these firms can live like this forever. A normal return is enough to make this business worthwhile since it beats the best available alternative—the opportunity cost of being in this business.

But if you are one who thinks divergently, sees new possibilities, and is willing to take the risk of trying new things—if you are an entrepreneur and you are in this market—what can you do to do better? How can you get ahead in life? How do you get a profit out of this market? You can do it by lowering your cost structure.

How do you do that? You have to come up with an innovation that makes you more efficient than your competitors. An obvious source of such an innovation is improved technology—developing a more efficient technique. If you can come up with innovations that lower your cost structure, then while everyone else is breaking even, you are making a profit until they figure out what you have done.

6.2.3 Creating a New Market Niche: Inventing the Mousetrap

Another way to beat the market is to identify or create a new market niche. Before mousetraps there were cats. Now I have three cats and they do a very nice job of catching mice. But they do most of their best work outside of the house catching mice . . . and birds and rabbits and all sorts of small animals in our neighborhood. Unfortunately this is not only wreaking havoc with the ecological balance of the neighborhood, more often than not these cats take pride in their work and bring their captives home. Note the term *captives*. They bring these critters home alive, and let them go. Ever try to catch an adult blue jay as it flies around your living room?

Anyway, mousetraps obviously have some major advantages in the eyes of many in the market, because a lot of them are sold. The first person to market one had the market to herself—a big advantage that produces a big profit if, as in this case, the market decides it likes the product. When the market begins to imitate your product, build a better one and you can beat the market again. This is classic: Build a better mousetrap and the world will beat a path to your door.

6.2.4 The Market Dynamic

When you bring your new mousetrap or your better mousetrap to the market, what are your competitors going to do? They are going to mimic you. ("Imitation is the sincerest form of flattery.") As they figure out what you are doing they will come up with their own new mousetrap or new production techniques. Then the market price will fall and your profit will begin to disappear. So what is your incentive as they catch up with you? What do you always want to be doing? You want to come up with yet a better idea.

This is really the beauty of markets. Not only do they drive people to do what is currently efficient, they encourage creativity and inventiveness by rewarding it. So people are constantly thinking of new products, better versions of old products, or ever more efficient ways of producing products. Under our nice assumptions, markets are incredibly powerful engines for material progress, and this can benefit all of us. Creativity can serve everybody. It serves those with a large share of society's endowment a lot more than it serves those with a small share, but all are better off if we each get the most from our resources.

6.2.5 The Magic of Markets

A picture is a powerful way of representing an idea, and that is what we have just done. With words and graphs we have painted a picture in your mind's eye of one of the most powerful ideas in modern history; a picture first fully painted in Adam Smith's *Inquiry into the Nature and Causes of the Wealth of Nations* in 1776.

Smith understood that the magic of markets lies in their potential for efficiency and creativity. It is this magic that underlies the modern love affair with markets.

Under our nice assumptions, perfect competition in markets makes every firm move to the most efficient available technology and to produce at the most efficient level. Even more amazing, markets bring out the creativity, the entrepreneurial imagination of people to always do it better. If you join this competition, even as you are striving to do it better, you are being chased by the people who are trying to keep up and get ahead of you. You are pressed by this competition to do even better yet, to be even more imaginative in responding to the market. In this case the nation gets the most from its resources and thus achieves the greatest wealth for the nation. This is the power of Adam Smith's invisible hand.

But as Smith understood very well, while the invisible hand can bring efficiency under the nice assumptions, it does not necessarily assure a just distribution of the product among the individuals in society. Remember, markets are amoral. They just coordinate individuals' choices given:

- the distribution of the social endowment among individuals,
- individuals' preferences, and
- the state of technology.

Now we want to see how the distribution is determined in the best market case, that is, under our nice assumptions. For that we turn to the factor markets.

7.0 THE FACTOR MARKET

7.1 THE FACTOR MARKET—INTRODUCTION

7.1.1 The Factor Market—Introduction

Let's begin by looking at our general system again as represented by the circular flow picture.

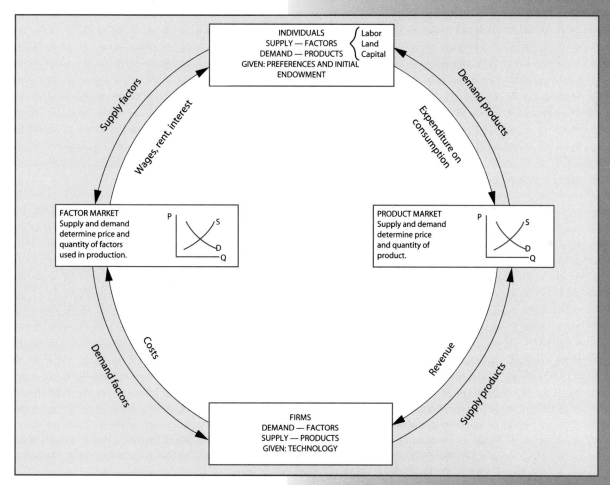

Figure 7.1.1 Circular Flow

Thus far we have focused on the product market side of this system. We have seen that in the product market firms supply products that individuals demand them. The forces of supply and demand establish the prices and quantities exchanged of all goods and services.

In the factor market individuals come with a share of the social endowment in the form of factors they own that they can supply like labor, capital, and natural resources. Firms demand these factors. Here again, the forces of supply and demand establish the prices and quantities exchanged. But in this case it is prices and quantities of factors. The prices that firms pay for the factors determine the income of the people who bring the factors to market. So the distribution of income is determined in the factor market.

7.1.2 The Factor Market Adjustment Process Under Our Nice Assumptions

Our factor market picture, Figure 7.1.2, looks like the product market picture.

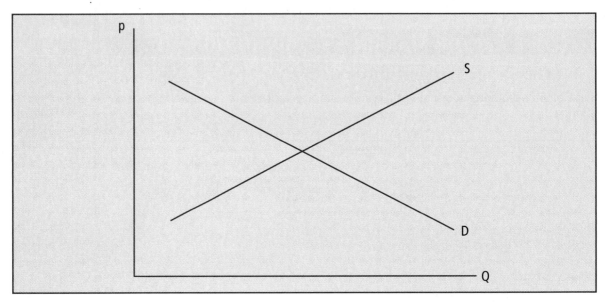

Figure 7.1.2 Factor Market Picture

Quantity is on the horizontal axis and price is on the vertical axis, although the prices in factor markets do not always come with the word "price" attached to them. For example, the price of labor is more often than not called the wage, but it is still a price. The price of land is generally referred to as rent, but it is still a price. The price of using someone's machine is sometimes called rent or interest, but again it is still a price.

Under our nice assumptions, the process of adjustment to equilibrium in a factor market is just like in a product market. If there is an excess supply of a factor, the price of that factor will begin to fall and will continue to do so until the market has reached equilibrium.

Consider, for example, a labor market. (I'm going to use labor markets as my basic example because it's the one most of us can relate to most directly.) The wage is the price paid for labor. Actually, in most cases, a wage is a price paid for a package of labor and human capital embodied in an individual. The vast majority of labor markets (like those for carpenters, lawyers, rocket scientists, forklift operators, teachers . . .) require some degree of human capital along with pure labor.

Now let's suppose that there is an excess supply in a labor market. What would that look like in real human terms? What would an economist have to see in order to assert that a labor market has an excess supply?

An excess supply means that the quantity supplied is greater than the quantity demanded. In a labor market that implies that there are more people looking for jobs in that market than there are jobs available. So, at least in that market, there would be some unemployment.

Under our nice assumptions what kind of dynamic would be set off in a labor market that has an excess supply? The wage would begin to fall as workers bid for jobs by offering to work for less. This bidding and the falling wage would continue until the excess supply is eliminated. At that point that labor market has reached equilibrium.

How would a labor market respond to an excess demand? The wage would begin to rise as employers bid for workers. This bidding and the rising wage would continue until the excess demand is eliminated. Again, at that point the labor market has reached equilibrium.

Under our nice assumptions, the market dynamic is the same whether it is a market for products or a market for factors. As in product markets, the decisions of suppliers and demanders in factor markets are independently determined but are coordinated by the market adjusting on a price signal.

Now let's look at the conditions that determine factor supply and factor demand in turn, beginning with the supply line.

7.2 FACTOR MARKET SUPPLY

7.2.1 Factor Market Supply—Its Upward Slope

On our graph of the factor market the supply line slopes up. This implies that the quantity of a factor supplied and the price of that factor are positively related. Pay more, and more of the factor will be supplied. Why is this so?

It has to do with the relationship between quantity of a factor supplied and opportunity cost. Every resource has alternative uses. To use a resource in a particular market means forgoing the opportunity to use it in some other way. The best forgone opportunity is the opportunity cost.

Take for example the market for nurses. When a nurse is determining how much time he is willing to work at any given wage, he must calculate the opportunity cost of the time at work. He could be at the beach or working at another kind of job or at home getting his housework done. His individual supply line slopes up because as he spends more time at work he digs more and more deeply into his other opportunities, giving up those that are successively more and more dear. The opportunity cost rises, and if he is going to be enticed to work more hours, the wage must go up to beat that rising opportunity cost. The upward-sloping factor supply line reflects this: You want more of my factor? Then you have to pay me more.

In the real world, as opposed to this hypothetical world, factor supply is not a nice, smooth upward-sloping line—but you can at least see the general positive relationship between price and quantity of factor supplied in the stepwise structure of wage scales that offer time-and-a-half for overtime and double wages for extreme overtime. The principle is there. It is clearer in some markets than others, in part because in some markets it is distorted by the market power that we have assumed away for now.

7.2.2 Factor Market Supply—The Shift Variables

An individual's level of factor supply, the position of an individual's factor supply line on the graph, depends on that individual's wealth, preferences, and alternative opportunities. In our functional form we can represent the factor supply relationship as follows

$$Q_f^S = S\,(p_f \mid W, \text{Pref., Alt.})$$

Where Q_f^S is the quantity of the factor supplied, S is the positive functional relationship, p_f is the price of the factor. The shift variables are W for wealth, Pref. for preferences, and Alt. for alternative opportunities. A change in any one of these shift variables can change the level of supply, shifting the factor supply line.

7.2.3 Factor Market Supply Shifts

Suppose you won the lottery. Congratulations! Given this dramatic increase in your wealth you might choose to work less no matter what the wage. If at any given wage your quantity supplied is lower, this appears graphically as a shift to the left in your labor supply as shown in Figure 7.2.1. A drastic income decrease might have the opposite effect.

Similarly, a change in preferences can cause such shifts in factor supply. If you suddenly decided that leisure time with your family is much more important than it ever seemed before (maybe you had a brush with death and realized how much you value that sharing), then your labor supply line, S, would shift left. You would offer less time to the market at any given wage. Conversely, if your kid is going to be in college soon and you need more income, S may shift right.

And finally, a change in your opportunity set can shift your labor supply. Suppose you have a new child at home. You might decide that the opportunity to be with your new child is one you do not want to miss, so you decide to work less. Obviously your ability to do so depends significantly on whether you can afford to work less. If your wife has a good job, then maybe you can afford to.

As you can see, these shift variables—in this case alternative opportunities and wealth—are not entirely independent. This should not be surprising. The web of connections is complex, and few things are truly beyond its reach.

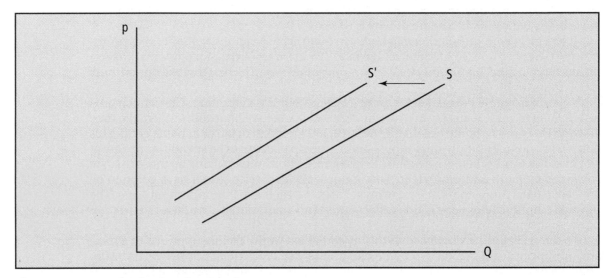

Figure 7.2.1 A Reduction in Labor Supply

7.2.4 From Individual to Market Supply

As with product supply, the factor market supply line is the sum of all the individual supply lines. Thus any shifts in individual factor supply lines that are not mutually offsetting will shift the market supply line. The factor market supply line will also shift in response to entry and exit. In order to understand the forces that determine entry and exit, let's return to the labor market.

7.2.5 Entry and Exit in the Overall Labor Market

If we consider the labor market in total—that is, as the overall market for people who work, entry and exit from the labor market has to do with people choosing to begin participating in or to stop participating in the labor market. The variables we have identified that shift an individual's factor supply line (wealth, preferences, and alternative opportunities) can, if they change significantly enough, move people in or out of the labor market.

If you win the lottery and it is a really big prize, you might not just cut back on your work—you might quit working all together. If you suddenly decide you prefer to think deep thoughts and write great novels, you might quit your job. If you have a new kid at home you might decide to stay home full time.

7.2.6 Labor Force Participation Analysis—An Example

Analyzing people's labor force participation is a big field in economics, and it is complicated. Just for a bit of the flavor, let's consider the new kid case. A decision about how to care for a new kid depends on the relative values one places on the two options. The higher one's market wage and/or the more one values having a career for personal satisfaction and role modeling reasons, the greater the opportunity cost of leaving the market. Focusing on the wage dimension, *ceteris paribus*, we would expect high-wage people to hire a babysitter or use child care and low-wage people to quit paid work and take care of their own child. However, *ceteris* is never *paribus* in the real world; there are also wealth and income issues. Those with wealth or with a good income source that is independent of their market work (e.g., investments or a spouse's income) have a lower opportunity cost of quitting work than someone with no wealth or non-wage income. This suggests that poorer people are less likely to quit their jobs in order to stay home with a child. If a poor parent has to work to survive, she or he must find affordable child care—which may or may not be quality child care. The decision of any given individual to enter or leave the labor force will depend on the interaction of all these issues.

7.2.7 Entry and Exit from Specific Labor Markets—Labor Market Mobility

When we think of "the labor market" not in its wholeness, but rather in terms of individual labor markets like plumbers, police officers, or doctors, then entry and exit does not necessarily imply entering or leaving the labor force. It also includes leaving one kind of labor market for another: For example leaving nursing to become a financial planner.

In order to analyze the dynamics of this kind of movement, let's return to the market for nurses. The current equilibrium wage for nurses must include an interest component. After all, if there was not a sufficient return to the educational investment necessary to become a nurse, no one would make that investment in their human capital.

Now suppose the demand for nurses shifts out for some reason. *Ceteris paribus*, the pay will go up. If the original pay scale offered a normal return, this market now seems advantageous. Given our nice assumptions, there will be new entrants attracted by this excellent opportunity. This flow into the market will continue, shifting supply out, until the pay goes back to a level that simply offers a normal return and all advantage is gone. So people move into nursing when it seems like the best available option. Conversely, people leave the nursing market due to death, retirement, or the discovery of better alternatives elsewhere.

Under what conditions would someone give up a career as a nurse for another option? It is a big decision to do so. Those folks who have made the human capital investment necessary to become a nurse cannot get back the time and money they spent on that training. Those are *sunk costs*—costs paid for choices made. The sunk costs of choices past are best left in the past. If the path down which those investments led is no longer the most satisfying, it makes no sense to follow that path simply because you sank resources into it. Current choices are about the future. Choices are most constructive if the decision is based on the lessons of the past and on future costs and future benefits.

The choice a current nurse faces is whether to continue to use the skills he has developed as a nurse, or to leave that investment behind and go on to an alternative occupation or activity. He might choose to give up the field he trained for and try an alternative if his expectations about pay and psychic returns to nursing were not fully realized. Or even if those expectations about nursing were realized, he may leave the field if an unexpected, preferred attainable alternative becomes available. Choices are based on lessons past, but they are all about the future.

7.2.8 Factor Market Supply and the Web of Connections

If the rewards of nursing are low relative to that for comparable occupations (occupations that have similar requirements in terms of human capital investment, personal responsibility, and so on . . .), then, given our nice assumptions, we would find individuals leaving nursing and seeking opportunities in those alternative, comparable occupations that offer greater rewards. This exit from nursing and entry into those comparable occupations decreases the supply and raises the pay in nursing while at the same time increasing supply and lowering pay in the comparable occupations. This dynamic would cease when the rewards for nursing and the comparable occupations are roughly equivalent. At that point there would be no further advantage to changing jobs. So, under our nice assumptions, comparable occupations would have comparable wages.

As in the product market, so, too, in the factor market, when there is equal access to information and equal access to markets, people and their resources will flow to their best advantage. As a result all advantages will diminish and all participants will enjoy the sustainable benefits of a normal return. This flow among markets creates a web of connections in the system of markets that makes all a part of a single general system.

7.3 FACTOR MARKET DEMAND

7.3.1 Factor Market Demand—Its Downward Slope

Now let's consider the demand side of the factor market.

The only reason firms demand factors is for the purpose of making something to sell in product market. Since firms live and die by the marketability of their products, the firm is constantly adjusting its output to product market demand conditions. Because the demand for factors used in production depends on the demand for the output that those factors are used to produce, economists refer to factor demand as a *derived demand*.

To understand why factor demand slopes down, or in other words why price is inversely related to quantity demanded, consider two things we already know. First, the firm faces eventually diminishing marginal productivity as it uses more and more of a factor. And secondly, given our nice assumptions, the firm is a price taker: The prices of its factors and of its product are set by the market. Since the price per unit of the product is constant but the product of each successive unit of a factor used is falling, the value of the marginal product (VMP) of the factor—(output price) x (factor marginal product)—is falling.

In Table 7.3.1 we see that the VMP starts up, but because the marginal product inevitably begins to fall so too does the value of the marginal product.

TABLE 7.3.1	PRICE BASED VALUE OF MARGINAL PRODUCT (VMP)		
Unit of Input	**Factor MP**	**Price of Product**	**Factor VMP**
1st	25	$10	$250
2nd	100	$10	$1000
3rd	200	$10	$2000
4th	180	$10	$1800
5th	160	$10	$1600
6th	140	$10	$1400
7th	120	$10	$1200
8th	110	$10	$1100
9th	100	$10	$1000
10th	90	$10	$900

Clearly, if the value of the product from each successive unit of a factor input (VMP) falls, the amount that successive units of that factor are worth to the firm also falls. Thus the firm will only hire more units of that factor if the price of the factor goes down. This is why the demand line for factors slopes down.

7.3.2 Factor Market Demand—The Shift Variables

The conditions that determine the level of demand for a factor are:

- the price of the product the factor is producing,
- the technology available, and
- the relative prices of other factors.

In our functional form we can represent the factor demand relationship as follows:

$$Q_f^D = D\ (p_f\,|\,p_p,\ \text{Tech.},\ p_{of})$$

Where Q_f^D is the quantity of the factor demanded, D is the negative functional relationship, p_f is the price of the factor. The shift variables are: p_p for price of the product the factor is producing, Tech. for the available technology, and p_{of} for the prices of other factors. A change in any one of these shift variables can change the level of demand, shifting the factor demand line. Let's look at each of these shift variables in turn.

7.3.3 The Shift Variables—Price of the Product

In order to appreciate the effect of the price of the product on factor demand, let's reflect on the firm's product market. A firm's product supply line shows that, *ceteris paribus*, the higher the price for their product the more the firm is willing to produce. *Ceteris paribus*, if an increase in product demand causes the price of the product to go up, the firm produces more. In order to produce more the firm must demand more of the factors that go into its production. So, *ceteris paribus*, a rise in product price will shift the derived factor demand to the right.

Again we see the web of connections at work. In this case the conditions in the product market are woven closely together with the conditions in the factor market.

7.3.4 The Shift Variables—Technology and the Prices of Other Factors

The other two shift variables for factor demand are technology and prices of other factors. In most cases the technological book of blueprints a firm has at its disposal includes several different techniques for producing its product. Since the firm has a choice among these techniques, it will choose the one that minimizes the cost for the level of production it intends. If labor is very expensive and capital is relatively cheap, the choice will be a technique that uses more capital and economizes on labor. This is called a *capital-intensive technique*. If the labor is cheap and the capital is expensive, the choice will be a technique that uses more labor and economizes on capital, a *labor-intensive technique*.

If technology does include several techniques then it allows for the possibility of input substitution. *Input substitution* means moving from a more capital-intensive to a more labor-intensive technique or vice versa. If input substitution possibilities do exist then the demand for any particular factor will be affected by any change in the price of other factors. The responsiveness of this substitution effect to a change in the relative prices of capital and labor is measured by *the elasticity of input substitution*: the more elastic, the more responsive. The higher the elasticity of input substitution, the more easily and therefore the more quickly the substitution of one factor for another can be made as relative factor prices change.

7.3.5 Relative Factor Prices, Input Choice, and Input Substitution: Ditch Digging

For example, as described earlier, there are at least two techniques for digging a ditch. You can use a shovel (pretty labor intensive) or you can use a backhoe (pretty capital intensive). If labor is very cheap and capital is very expensive, which technique would you expect to see in use?

If labor is cheap relative to capital, you would expect to see the more labor-intensive technique in use. And indeed if you look around the globe, in nations where labor is cheap and capital is dear such tasks are often done by very labor-intensive techniques, while in places like the United States you will often see the same job being done with a backhoe.

If in a nation where labor is initially cheap opportunities for workers expand and wages rise, the choice of techniques will eventually switch from labor-intensive to capital-intensive. Since capital-intensive techniques make the value of the marginal product of the labor greater, that means higher wages for the worker. If this occurs in an economy that is expanding and thus creating more job opportunities, so long as workers have opportunities to develop the human capital necessary to work with these new techniques, this movement to capital-intensive production can be good for workers.

Here again we see the web of connections at work. In this case, because of input substitution possibilities, the conditions in one factor market are woven closely together with the conditions in other factor markets. Or at least this will be the case when individuals have equal access to information and equal access to markets so that resources can always flow to their best advantage.

7.3.6 Asking for a Raise—What's the Best Position to be in? I

Suppose you are a worker and you are going to ask for a higher wage. What would you hope is the case with respect to the elasticity of input substitution for your labor and human capital? Would you like that elasticity of input substitution to be high or low?

If you have a high elasticity of input substitution and you ask for a raise, your employer might say: "Well, you know what? We can get a machine to do this. You were cheap labor before and we liked you then, now you're getting pretty pricey. Relatively speaking we'll be better off with a machine if you're going to cost that much. Bye!" So as a worker you always hope your elasticity of input substitution is low.

7.3.7 Asking for a Raise—What's the Best Position to be in? II

OK, let's try another one. Same scenario: You are a worker and you are asking for a raise. But now let's assume you have a low elasticity of input substitution. So you are thinking: "OK, this is good! They can't replace me with a machine. I'm going to get this raise and they're just going to have to deal with it." If you ask for a raise, what else had you better worry about given that the demand for your labor and human capital is a derived demand? As you think about your response consider these questions: Why did the firm hire you in the first place? From the firm's point of view, given the technique of production, what determines how much of your labor and human capital it wants to buy?

The firm hired you and uses your resources because it needs those resources to produce a product. But it can only use your resources so long as it can sell that product. If you ask for and get a higher wage, you are raising the firm's cost structure. We learned before that raising the firm's cost structure by increasing the price of inputs shifts the firm's product supply line up. If the product supply line shifts up, what is going to happen to the quantity demanded in the product market? It will go down. How much it goes down depends on the own price elasticity of demand for the product. What own price elasticity of demand case is best for you?: An inelastic or an elastic own price elasticity of demand for the product you make.

If the product demand is elastic, the shift up in the supply line caused by your higher wage will result in a significant drop in quantity demanded. In that case you might have a somewhat higher wage, but you will also have a whole lot fewer hours of work, or you might even be laid off. If, on the other hand, the product demand is inelastic, the shift up in the supply line caused by our wage increase will result in only a slight drop in quantity demanded. So you will have a higher wage and not lose many of your hours. That is clearly the best case for you.

8.0 GENERAL COMPETITIVE EQUILIBRIUM (GCE)

8.1 GENERAL EQUILIBRIUM THEORY

8.1.1 Introduction

We have been looking at elements of a market system, the product markets and the factor markets, to see how they function. Along the way I have tried to consistently emphasize that all of these markets are tied together by a web of connections that makes each a part of a general system. Now let's look again at that system as a whole. Analysis at this level is referred to as general equilibrium theory.

8.1.2 General Equilibrium Theory – The Concept

As I explained earlier, the modern analysis of market equilibrium prices and quantities determined by the interaction of supply and demand dates from Alfred Marshall's *Principles of Economics* published in 1890. But Marshall's analysis of markets has since been imbedded in a larger frame, *General Equilibrium Theory*, the analysis of markets as part of a web of connections, as part of a system. General equilibrium theory was first explored theoretically by Leon Walras in the latter part of the 19th century, but it did not become a central element of modern economic analysis until the middle of the 20th century.

In general equilibrium theory all markets are part of a *simultaneous system*—a system in which all elements function as part of a larger whole, like an ecosystem. Let's review some of the threads that weave markets into this web of a general system:

- Product markets are connected to one another
  - through cross price elasticities because all products have substitutes or complements

- Factor markets are connected to one another
  - through elasticities of input substitution because most inputs have substitution possibilities

- Product and factor markets are connected to one another
  - through the product supply line, because it is cost structures in production, and thus factor prices and technology, that determine the shape and level of product supply,
  - through product demand line, because the money with which people demand goods and services in the product markets comes from the incomes they make by selling their resources in factor markets, and
  - through the factor demand line, because that demand is derived from product market sales

8.1.3 General Equilibrium Versus Partial Equilibrium Analysis

The only givens in general equilibrium theory are

- society's current resource endowment
- the distribution of the shares of the social endowment among individuals,
- individuals' tastes, and
- the current technology.

From these givens, through the workings of the general system, the prices and quantities in all the factor and product markets are determined. But, these prices and quantities in individual markets are only determined when the entire system resolves itself. As long as any market is still adjusting, then at least theoretically, all markets are still adjusting.

I hope that now you can see why at the beginning of this story I referred to the economic system as an econosystem. It is analogous to an ecosystem—integrated in its nature, all elements interacting and interdependent with one another. General equilibrium theory is essential for representing this vision of the market system.

But as a practical matter, the web of the general system is far too complex to deal with in any detail. It is often, therefore, much more fruitful to study markets independently. This kind of analysis, called *partial equilibrium analysis*, examines equilibrium conditions in, and the dynamics of, individual markets. While general equilibrium theory is essential for representing the vision of modern theory, partial equilibrium analysis is an essential tool for policy analysis.

8.2 GENERAL COMPETITIVE EQUILIBRIUM (GCE)

8.2.1 GCE and Efficiency

Under our nice assumptions, when the general system has reached an equilibrium it is Pareto optimal. That unique Pareto optimal general equilibrium condition is called a general competitive equilibrium. We have seen why our nice assumptions lead to such a nice efficient outcome: Under perfect competition all advantages are competed away. As Adam Smith put it:

> If in the same neighbourhood, there was any employment evidently either more or less advantageous than the rest, so many people would crowd into it in the one case, and so many would desert it in the other, that its advantages would soon return to the level of other employments. [our normal return] (*WN*, 116)

Since superior efficiency is itself an advantage, given our nice assumptions any efficient techniques will be learned and adopted by others. Anyone who does not make the effort to be as efficient as her competitors will be driven from the market. The only way to get ahead is to become more efficient. So not only does a perfectly competitive market system reach Pareto optimality, it constantly enhances the level of efficiency achieved at the Pareto optimal condition. It is this potential for dynamic efficiency that people have in mind when they speak of the magic of markets or the power of the invisible hand.

8.2.2 GCE and Distributive Justice

But as I noted before, while markets can be efficient, there is nothing inherent in the market process that makes the distribution of the product among the individuals in society "just."

Distributive justice is an ethical concept. In order to decide if a distribution is just, we must first answer for ourselves the question: What is a just distribution? There is no theoretical or scientific basis for answering that question. As an economist I cannot tell you what a "just" or "ethical" distribution is. That value judgment is not within the scope of economic analysis. I have my own personal sense of justice, and I presume you have yours. We can discuss and maybe debate our respective values, but these are values, not scientific concepts.

Still, our model is helpful with respect to issues of justice. Given your values the model can help you work for justice for it can tell you much about the distributive outcome that markets will generate from a given distribution for the initial social endowment. If our nice assumptions hold, the distributive outcome of the market process will directly reflect the distribution of society's endowments of natural resources, labor, and capital among individuals. To see this let's use pie graphs. Figure 8.2.1 represents the full size of the social endowment (of the left) and of the social product (on the right). Under our nice assumptions the social product pie will be as large as it can be because the system is most efficient, it is Pareto optimal.

If the social endowment is divided among persons A, B, C, and D as shown in Figure 8.2.1, then in a perfectly competitive market system the distribution of product will be roughly the same. I say "roughly" because variations will occur due to different preferences (e.g., some people may not choose to spend as much time on market activity as others), chance (remember choices are based on probabilities associated with risk), luck (choices are also affected by uncertainties), and so on.

The elegant efficiency created by our nice assumptions ensures us that each person will get the most possible utility out of her share of the social endowment. But if like person C, you start with a relatively small share of that endowment, you are going to end up with a relatively small share of the product. To be sure, efficiency is good for you. It ensures that you will do as well as possible given your share of the endowment. But given a small share, your standard of living may not be very good.

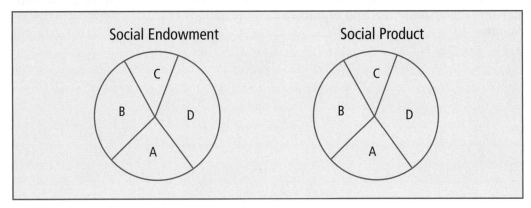

Figure 8.2.1 Distribution of Society's Endowment and Distribution of Society's Product

8.2.3 GCE: Changing Distributive Outcomes Without Destroying Efficiency

If you believe that the current distributive outcome is unjust, how can you change it without destroying the efficiency of the system? Kenneth Arrow answers that question in a talk titled "General Competitive Equilibrium: Purpose, Analytical Techniques, Collective Choice" that he gave at the ceremony at which he received the 1972 Nobel Prize for Economics. In that lecture he said:

> General Competitive Equilibrium above all teaches the extent to which a social allocation of resources can be achieved by independent private decisions coordinated through the market. We are assured indeed that not only can an allocation be achieved, but the result will be Pareto efficient. But, as has been stressed, there is nothing in the process which guarantees that the distribution

be just. Indeed, the theory teaches us that the final allocation will depend on the distribution of initial supplies and of ownership of firms. If we want to rely on the virtues of the market but also to achieve a more just distribution, the theory suggests the strategy of changing the initial endowments rather than interfering with the allocation process at some later stage.

Thus even under assumptions most favorable to decentralization of decision making [our nice assumptions] there is an irreducible need for a social or collective choice on distribution.

This need for social choice cited by Arrow raises some fundamental questions for society: What social decision-making structures should be used? Who should have a voice in these decisions? What weight should be given to the various voices? And more fundamentally, is Arrow right? Should we be making any collective choices on distribution at all?

8.2.4 GCE and Commutative Justice

These questions of process bring to the fore another dimension of justice, commutative justice, that I introduced when we first covered the nice assumptions. The rules of commutative justice help ensure that there is no market power, that the race is fair. In the absence of such rules, perverse incentives exist. People can "win" by using resources to create advantages based on power, rather than by competing to be most productive for the market. Winning at the power game creates more resources to sustain that power position. But when the race is for power the competition becomes destructive rather than constructive.

Until now we have held this destructive force at bay by our nice assumption of no market power. Now it is time to move on. We want our model to be as rich and realistic as possible. In order to reach that goal we now expand the scope of our model by relaxing our nice assumptions and exploring the implications of market power and market failure.

9.0 MARKET POWER, MARKET FAILURE, AND GENERAL EQUILIBRIUM

9.1 INTRODUCTION TO MARKET POWER AND MARKET FAILURE

The Pareto optimal general competitive equilibrium that the market system achieves under our nice assumptions is a special case of all the possible equilibria the system can resolve itself into. Relaxing our nice assumptions and allowing for the possibility of market power and market failure expands the scope of our analysis to include all those other possible general equilibria. We will see that due to the distortions caused by market power and/or market failure, all of these other general equilibria are less than Pareto optimal and have different distributions. First we explore market power.

At the top of Figure 9.2.1 there are two pie graphs representing a distribution of social endowment and the resulting distribution of product under our nice assumptions. As we have learned, the "pie" will be as large as possible and the distribution of the product will be based on the distribution of the endowment. Now let's change

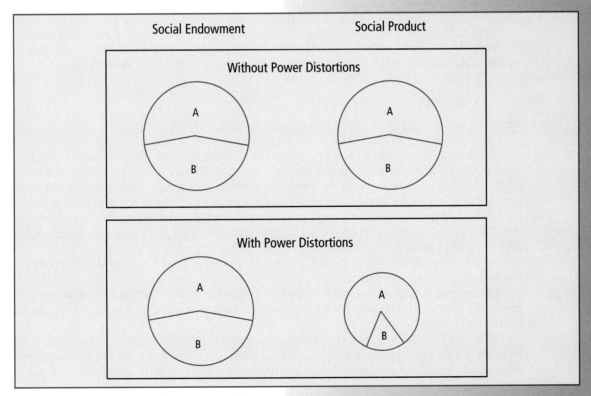

Figure 9.2.1 Distribution of Society's Endowment and Distribution of Society's Product-With and Without Power Distortions

the situation and give "A" market power. This leads to a new outcome represented by the new pie graphs at the bottom of Figure 9.2.1. Notice two things: "A" gets a much larger share of the social product than before—this is the payoff to power, and the overall size of the pie is smaller than before. To see why, we have to analyze market power.

9.2 MARKET POWER

9.2.1 Introduction

Exercising market power is not a productive activity. It is simply a process of exploiting an advantage that gives an individual some control in the market. The more power, the more control. For those who have it, power is a wonderful thing. Power makes it possible for them to enjoy a larger share of the distribution. But even as power brings benefits to those who enjoy it, it imposes costs on those who do not. These costs come in two forms:

First of all, since the larger distributive share enjoyed by those with power does not come from any productive contribution on their part, it must come at the expense of others—a larger piece for the powerful means a smaller piece for others. Secondly, for reasons we will see shortly, power distorts micro-market activity and thus makes the system less efficient, so the pie is smaller. In sum, those on the wrong side of the power structure get a smaller piece of a smaller pie.

9.2.2 Monopoly and Monopsony

At its extreme market power takes the form of *monopoly* or *monopsony*. Monopoly is the power that comes from being the only seller in a market. Monopsony is the power that comes from being the only buyer. In the case of monopoly the supplier does not face the perfectly elastic demand line of perfect competition; she is not a price taker. Instead, as the only seller she faces the market demand and can choose the price/quantity combination that is most advantageous given her cost structure.

Similarly a monopsonist does not face a perfectly elastic supply line of perfect competition; she is not a price taker either. She faces the market supply line and can choose the price/quantity combination that is most advantageous.

There are two sources of market power. It can come from natural advantages or it can be created by human action. We will refer to the former as *naturally occurring market power* and the latter as *artificially created market power*. Let's look at each in turn.

9.2.3 Naturally Occurring Market Power

Naturally occurring power comes, as the name implies, from nature.

Consider this example of naturally occurring market power. Have you ever seen the ads in which an incredibly beautiful person is draped across the front of a car or is placed right in the middle of the TV screen in order to get your attention? I've applied for those kinds of jobs—you know, to be the beautiful person on the car or on the screen. I don't know why, but I never get the job. For whatever reason, the ad folks don't consider me beautiful, and that's not something I can do much about. With all the plastic surgery and the fitness coach and everything else, nothing has changed their opinion. Apparently I just have not "got it"—you know, the "look." I don't have that natural endowment of beauty. My mom thinks I'm beautiful, but the ad folks don't see it. So the models make the bucks and I toil here in academe.

Let me give you another example. I tried out for the PGA. Watch out Tiger. When I got to tryouts they said: "OK, let's do nine holes and see how it goes." I shot a 65! Then on the 2nd hole. . . .

What do Tiger Woods and those beautiful models have that I don't? The models are by society's current standard more beautiful than I am. Tiger can do the unimaginable with a club. Beauty and athletic touch are naturally occurring gifts, and such gifts can be a source of incredible market power. You have probably heard the expression "face value"? Well a beautiful face can indeed have immense value in the market.

Consider another example. A March 3, 1999, *New York Times* article described how the demand for babies by infertile couples had created a market for egg donors. This is not really such a radical idea. There has long been a market for sperm donors. The article cited an ad for such a donor. The ad said that a desirable egg donor should be beautiful (please send pictures), about 5'6" tall, athletic, and have at least 1400 on her SATs (please submit documentation). The person chosen would be paid $50,000 for the donation. That is big return on a natural endowment.

9.2.4 Naturally Occurring Market Power and the Size of the Market

I do not think natural gifts are a rare commodity. My philosophy of teaching is based on the assumption that everyone has natural gifts. If fully nurtured we can all perform to an excellent level at most things and we will each stand out in those dimensions in which we are gifted. Part of getting the most out of life is discovering, nurturing, and enjoying your gifts. But only some natural gifts pay off in the market.

Tiger Woods makes a ton of money playing golf. The greatest Tiddlywinks player of all time is probably not living high off the hog on her earnings. Does that mean Tiger is more gifted than the greatest Tiddlywinks player of all time? No. Tiger's gifts are just different. They served him well in golf, but they might not in a Tiddlywinks tournament. (Michael Jordon was a fantastic basketball player, but was not so hot at baseball.) The significance of the difference between Tiger's gifts and the Tiddlywinks champion's gifts lies in the different marketability of each. Tiger's gift for golf is very dearly valued by the market. A gift for Tiddlywinks is not. Imagine a huge TV audience hanging on every shot of their favorite Tiddlywinks player . . . you can't. See what I mean?

9.2.5 Naturally Occurring Market Power in the Labor Market

With our factor market tools we can understand why Tiger Wood's gifts are so valuable. Remember our factor market concepts of derived demand and input substitution? Tiger makes a ton of money because he is in a labor market with a huge derived demand and very limited possibilities for input substitution. Golf fans pay dearly for tickets to tourneys and turn on millions of TVs to watch Tiger play. That is millions of eyes for advertisers. This in turn creates huge derived demand for gifted play that draws these fans, so the derived demand for Tiger's play and his endorsements is huge. Furthermore, there was no substitute for Tiger. In golf, he is one of a kind.

A factor market with a quantity of one (there was one Tiger), very low substitution possibilities so the elasticity of input substitution is very small, and a huge derived demand is the best possible case for a worker. It generates immense market power.

Tiger enjoys an advantage that will not be competed away until age diminishes his talent or another phenom comes along. The source of his advantage is not some violation of the principles of commutative justice. He is not cheating anyone. Even with equal access to information and equal access to the market, no one can compete with Tiger. His advantage derives from nature.

Does Tiger have to work hard for all the money he makes? Absolutely! Natural gifts with no substitution possibilities and a huge derived demand make market power possible, but they are no guarantee of a big payoff. Tiger could have squandered his gift. He didn't. He works extremely hard, he stays totally focused, and he is willing to learn—so he takes full advantage of his gift. There may well be golfers more gifted than Tiger who have squandered their gifts. We don't know about them because, like an uncut diamond, they never sparkled. A natural gift is an opportunity to exploit an advantage in the market; but to make it work for you, you have to work at developing that gift.

9.2.6 Economies of Scale and Natural Market Power

Another natural source of market power is *economies of scale.*

Remember, when we introduced production into our model we made a distinction between expanding production by increasing

- one factor holding all other inputs constant (the case that gives diminishing marginal productivity)

and

- expanding the scale of production by proportional increases in all inputs.

In this latter case, if the productivity goes up as the scale increases, economists call it *increasing returns to scale.* Increasing returns means production is more efficient at a larger scale. Such *scale economies* derive from the nature of the production processes, so they are natural economies.

If production for a market has scale economies, then the first firm into the market can build up scale and drive down the cost of production. Once that first firm is producing efficiently at a very large scale, it is difficult for any other firm to break into the market. In order to be as efficient as the first firm and thus compete successfully, a second firm would have to start up at the very large scale. Given the huge cost of such undertaking, that is difficult and often impossible. So scale economies create a very big *barrier to entry.* In this case the nature of production gives the first firm in a lot of market power.

Many economists believe that scale economies are becoming a more significant factor in economies as the extent of the market grows both nationally and internationally. It is argued that competing in such a large market requires a large scale to make it cost effective. So, for example, Wal-Mart has scale advantages because it can advertise on national television and can negotiate low cost volume discounts from suppliers, while a smaller competitor cannot do either.

I mentioned my sister's gift shop earlier. She was very successful for many years. Then when her lease came up for renewal the manager of the mall said he did not want her "mom and pop" operation in the mall. He wanted large chain stores because given the scale of their business, national or even international, they had the resources to advertise and that advertising served the interest of the mall. So . . . after 45 years the store that my mom started and my sister developed closed. It was not big enough to survive.

Huge operations like Wal-Mart can exercise power based on their immense scale—dictating terms to suppliers and workers. Clearly there are many huge corporate operations in the global economy. Are they exploiting scale to create market power advantages? This is an important question. If they are, while that market power serves them well it does a disservice to society. Everyday low prices are good . . . but: At what price are they low?

As always, our analysis does not answer this question. But, its systematic analysis reminds us to ask this question and its tools give us the means to develop an answer.

9.2.7 Erosion of Natural Advantages

Natural gifts of individuals like Tiger Woods do not last forever. As noted above, bodies get old. Even for the greats, as they get older their ability to dominate slips away.

Natural advantages from scale economies can erode as well. New technologies often emerge that undermine the advantage of the first firm in. Clearly, if this seems like a threat the firm with the advantage has an incentive to do what it can to maintain its advantage. As its natural advantage slips away, it might try to use the resources it has accumulated from its natural advantage to develop an artificial advantage. It might, for example, buy up the potential competitor before the threat becomes deadly. So now let's explore that possibility.

9.2.8 Artificially Created Market Power

If a firm's natural economies of scale are threatened by an emerging firm's new technology, the old, big player might choose to use the resources it has accumulated to buy up the new firm and its patents on the new technology. If it can control the new technology, its power is preserved.

Patents do not come from nature, they come from governments. They are artificially created power. Their purpose is to give an inventor the incentive to be creative by promising a period of power in the market by protecting the rights to use her invention.

The period between invention, patent, and market return can be long and very risky. Inventors are human like the rest of us. They think in terms of the expected present value (EPV) logic we learned before and patents are marketable commodities. Given the risk and waiting considerations and the scale economies that can exist in product development, an inventor may well choose to sell her patent to a big firm for big dollars now, rather than wait for it to be developed for the market. Buying up patents is a strategy through which a big firm can protect its market power—using its resources to gain control over the new technologies that might compete with it.

9.2.9 Rent-Maintenance

In the case just cited, resources are being allocated for the purpose of sustaining a market advantage. This is referred to in the economic literature as a *rent maintenance* activity. The use of the term "rent" here harkens back to Adam Smith's assertion in the *Wealth of Nations* that "landlords, like all other men, love to reap where they never sowed, and demand a rent even for its [(the land's)] natural produce." (*WN*, 67) As Smith uses the term here, rent is not a return to any productive contribution, it is a return to the landlords' power over the naturally fertile land. Following this usage, *rent is a return to control based on power* and rent maintenance is an effort to sustain a return to power—to sustain a rent.

Rent maintenance activity can take many forms. Suppose firms in a particular industry are concerned about new laws being considered in Congress that would open up their market to more competition. Maybe Congress is considering lowering tariffs (taxes on imports) that currently make the similar products from foreign competitors more expensive and thus less competitive. Those firms might consider it a wise investment to make significant contributions to the key players in this political decision-making process, so this tariff protection stays in place. If money can buy access to those Senators or Members of the House who will be involved as the tariff decisions are made, it would be money well spent.

Is it possible that the millions and millions of dollars contributed to political campaigns flows from such motives? The concept of rent-maintenance certainly suggests that the motive for such spending is strong. . . . But such contributions are not only made to protect power. Sometimes they are made in the hope of developing market power.

9.2.10 Rent-Seeking

Suppose the firms in a particular market found foreign competition to be very difficult. It certainly would be nice if Congress and the President would pass a law imposing a tariff on the products of the foreign competitors, thereby making them less competitive. The case for such new laws is often made by lobbyists, and some would suggest that the lubricant that gains access for a lobbyist is the campaign money.

From the point of view of the firms seeking protection, contributions to campaigns and the salaries of lobbyists are simply an investment. In the example just cited, if the investment pays off, it does so in the form of a new tariff that reduces foreign competition. Less competition means more market power and a bigger return in the market. This kind of activity, seeking market power, is called *rent-seeking* activity. It is an effort to achieve an artificially created advantage that will pay off.

9.2.11 Politics, Rent, and Adam Smith's Critique of the Mercantile System

In the *Wealth of Nations* Adam Smith cited rent-seeking and rent-maintenance in the political domain (he didn't use these terms) as the most dangerous threat to the integrity of what was then a new experiment in liberal society—the British political system that he valued dearly. Smith denounced those merchants who were advocating a "mercantile system" of policies in Parliament. They claimed their policies were for the public good, but Smith clearly saw them as rent-seeking and rent-maintenance efforts, efforts to distort trade for their own economic gain—for the rents. He wrote of these mercantile interests:

> It cannot be very difficult to determine who have been the contrivers of this whole mercantile system; not the consumers, we may believe, whose interest has been entirely neglected; but the producers whose interest has been so carefully attended to; and among this latter class our merchants and manufacturers have been by far the principal architects. (*WN*, 661)

On their method Smith writes that

> like an overgrown standing army, they have become formidable to the government, and upon many occasions intimidate the legislature. The member of parliament who supports every proposal for strengthening this monopoly [(their market power)], is sure to acquire not only the reputation of understanding trade, but great popularity and influence with an order of men whose numbers and wealth render them of great importance. If he opposes them, on the contrary, and still more if he has authority enough to be able to thwart them, neither the most acknowledged probity, nor the highest rank, nor the greatest publick services can protect him from the most infamous abuse and detraction, from personal insults, nor sometimes from real danger, arising from the insolent outrage of furious and disappointed monopolists. (*WN*, 471)

Have, since 1776, we moved on from this gross manipulation of the political system by monied interests . . . or could this be written about the role of those interests in the modern political world? It is a question worth pondering. The economic analysis we are developing here can make that pondering systematic.

9.2.12 Market Power and Social Institutions— Shaping Perceptions

Clearly, artificial market power can be created by political institutions. It can also be created by social institutions. The process of socialization we all go through as we grow up shapes our personal perceptions. As we learned early on in this analysis, people make choices based on perceptions. Markets are driven by choices. Thus by influencing our perceptions, socialization can have powerful market implications.

For example, socialization can develop systematically different perceptions of gender *and* by gender. Let's assume you are a little "white" girl growing up in the U.S. in the 1950s. You are in a world that constantly says to you through all that you see and read and hear that the appropriate roles for girls and boys and for blacks and whites are different. We will focus on the gender dimension here, but along the way think in parallel terms about the racial dimension.

In your world girls take care of the home, boys work. This gender demarcation is reinforced in subtle but incessant ways through the children's books you read, the movies you see, and the role models you watch.

Women who can afford to generally stay home if they have kids because the magazines say that working women with kids are neglecting their kids. The women you do see working are nurses or grade school teachers or secretaries or waitresses—jobs that seemed appropriate for women because they involve nurturing or detail or home-related skills. The men all go to work to be the doctors and the lawyers and the plumbers and the carpenters and the assembly-line workers.

9.2.13 Market Power and Social Institutions—Perceptions and Choices

This 1950s world shapes your perception of yourself and others' perceptions of who you should be. If you think about getting a job, the probability is that your thoughts turn to those "women's sphere" jobs like nursing or elementary school teaching or secretarial work and so on. If somehow you develop different ideas and dream of becoming a doctor or pursuing some other men's sphere job, that does not mean you will follow that dream.

Those people who control access to these men's sphere opportunities you desire, the admission committee at the medical school or the person doing the hiring at the factory, probably do not share your view that you belong there. Thus the odds of success are low. This makes the expected present value of such nontraditional choices very low. A low expected present value reduces the likelihood that you will make that choice. Remember what Mary Goldburt Siegel and Billy Tipton had to endure to become a lawyer and jazz musician respectively. The choices they made were not common among the women of their day precisely because of the immense obstacles that discouraged so many.

Socialized perceptions, your own or those in the market, can constrain your range of choices and effectively limit your access to the market. In so doing they violate our fair race assumptions just as powerfully as any law that says "This Job Is NOT Open to Women." Indeed, social institutions can be a more powerful constraint than political institutions because the constraints of social institutions are often taken as the natural order of things. As such they are not seen as constraints—they are natural. Thus the very real constraints they create are virtually invisible and thus are more subtle than laws that exist on paper.

Whatever one may personally think about gender roles and whether such roles are "good," the analysis makes it clear that social institutions that limit choices by constraining one's perceptions of the possibilities one can choose from do limit competition in the market. In a world of such perceptions, the effect should be evident in the market. Let's assume my representation of the 1950s is valid and see what that case would mean for the relative pay scales of men and women in the labor market.

9.2.14 Socialization, Market Power, and Gender Pay Equity— Setting the Scene

The two market pictures in Figure 9.2.2 represent two different jobs that have similar human capital requirements, responsibility, difficulty, and so on. So from an operational point of view these two jobs are comparable. The one labeled WS, is a traditionally women's sphere job. The other, labeled MS, is a traditionally men's sphere job. As a reference point let's begin by representing the case of no market power. Then we will introduce power to see how it affects markets.

Now suppose that, as shown here, the MS market currently has a higher wage. What kind of adjustment will occur between these two markets?

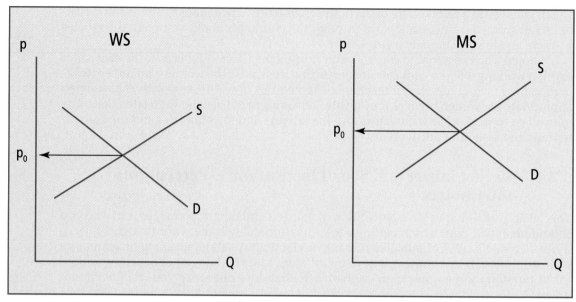

Figure 9.2.2 Market Pictures: Two Comparable Jobs, No Market Power

Since these are comparable jobs, the higher wage in the MS market represents an advantage. In pursuit of that advantage women workers would leave the WS market for the MS market. As shown in Figure 9.2.3, the supply in WS would decrease and the supply in the MS market would increase as people leave the disadvantageous market for the advantageous one.

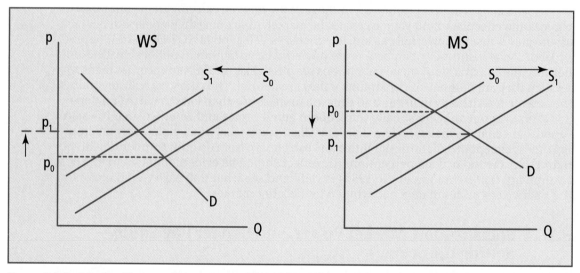

Figure 9.2.3 Market Pictures: Two Comparable Jobs, No Market Power – Adjustment

Under our nice assumptions, which of these comparable markets has a higher wage when all of the adjustments are complete? Since from the workers' point of view these two labor markets are comparable in all respects, any relative advantages are eliminated and thus all adjustments end when the wages in the two markets are the same.

9.2.15 Market Power and Gender Pay Equity—The Case

Now let's relax our nice assumptions and assume instead that there are a small number of WS markets and that these are the only socially acceptable labor market opportunities available to women. This means that all women are in effect crowded into these few WS markets. On the other hand, the many MS markets offer lots of alternative job opportunities for men.

In the world of our nice assumptions the wages in the comparable WS and MS labor markets are equal. What happens to the relative wages in these two markets in this alternative state of the world when we introduce market power?

If women are crowded into and trapped in a limited set of WS labor markets the supply in those markets is artificially expanded. This lowers the wages there. At the same time, the absence of women as competitors in the MS markets artificially contracts the supply in those markets. This raises the wages there. So the net effect of a social construction that channels women into a limited set of markets is an artificially low wage for women as they compete with each other in a very limited sphere, and an artificially high wage for men since they do not face the competition of women. In such a world, if a WS job and an MS job are indeed comparable, we would nevertheless expect to find lower wages in the WS job.

9.2.16 The Equity and Efficiency Implications of Market Power

Whatever the source of power, whether it is economic or political or social institutions, market power does alter the distribution to the benefit of those who enjoy the power. Thus it clearly affects the equity of the system. Whether this effect is just or unjust depends on something we cannot determine here: What is the right standard of distributive justice? This is an ethical question, not an economic question.

The efficiency implications of market power are, however, clear. Remember, we saw that in a perfectly competitive market the rule enforced by the competition is: "Be efficient or die!" And furthermore, the only way to get ahead even for a little while is to develop creative new ways to be more efficient.

In contrast, if a market player faces less than perfect competition she is not forced to be so efficient. This is true because in the absence of perfect competition some inefficiency does not automatically imply elimination from the market. Furthermore, when one enjoys power the pressure to be creative in the development of new efficiencies or new market products is much less. Power can keep one ahead for a while, so there is less need to worry so much about increasing efficiency or finding new angles to stay ahead in the market.

The inefficiency of market power is all the more pronounced if the power is base on rent-seeking or rent-maintenance. In that case, not only does the market loose the keen incentives of competition, but in addition resources that would be allocated to productive ends are instead being spent on the unproductive pursuit or maintenance of power (e.g., as we'll see below—buying guns to keep people in their place).

Because of these inefficiencies, a general equilibrium that is reached in a world with market power will not be a Pareto optimum.

9.2.17 Market Power, A National Case Study: South African Apartheid

A classic 20th century case of a nation designed around market power is South Africa in the years of apartheid. Remember Lize Venter? She was the little girl who was born into this world of apartheid as an orphan. Since no one knew who her parents were she had to be labeled: white, mixed race, or black. A label was necessary in order to determine which opportunity set she would get within the power structure.

Under the system of apartheid, while the vast majority of South Africans were black, the vast majority of the wealth was enjoyed by the white minority. The institutional structure of society ensured that distribution by limiting the opportunities blacks had.

For example, controlling access to education was an essential element in sustaining the white power advantage. Since black schools were poor the majority black population brought poor human capital skills to the market. This forced the individuals in this largest segment of the community to compete with one another for a small set of low-skill jobs.

In contrast, the minority white population had the opportunity to acquire a high level of human capital. With these skills they were able to compete for society's high-skilled jobs. And, they faced reduced competition because those who were discriminated against were not able to join in that competition. So what are the economic consequences?

9.2.18 Market Power and Distributive Outcomes in Labor Markets Under Apartheid

Figure 9.2.4 shows two labor market graphs labeled LS for low skilled and HS for high skilled. The equilibrium shown in each is based on the assumption of no market power. Under perfect competition the HS job receives a higher wage to compensate for the greater human capital investment, *ceteris paribus*.

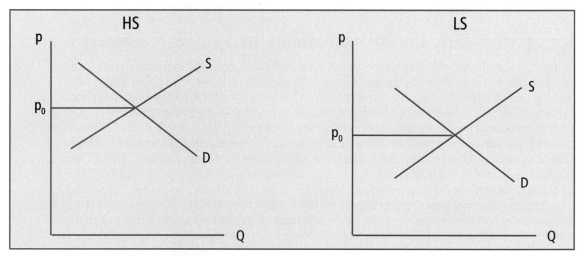

Figure 9.2.4   Market Pictures: High-Skill vs. Low-Skill Jobs without Market Power

Now let's introduce power, in particular the power of apartheid which funneled the entire majority black population into the LS sector. In Figure 9.2.5 we see how this affects the labor market graphs.

Because many individuals who would have chosen to compete in the high-skill job market were forced into the lowskill market, supply in the low-skill market was artificially

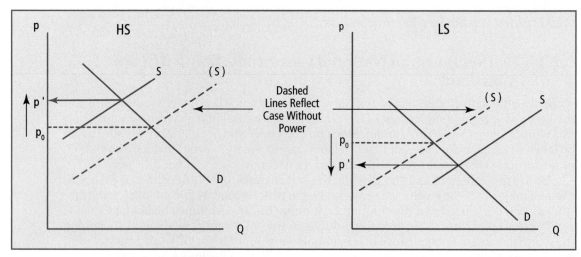

Figure 9.2.5   Market Pictures: High-Skill vs. Low-Skill Jobs with Market Power

expanded. At the same time, since blacks were not empowered to compete in the high-skilled market, supply in the high-skill market was artificially contracted. As a consequence, given demand conditions, the wages for low-skilled black workers were artificially depressed and wages for highskilled white workers were artificially raised.

9.2.19 Apartheid—The Tools of Control

The limits on educational opportunity were only one element in the regime of apartheid. Others included limited mobility for blacks (they had to carry passes) and limited access to markets. All limits were designed to ensure the advantages for whites that allowed the white community to enjoy the vast majority of the nation's wealth. All of these limits were "legal" because they were established by law.

But laws are only as effective as the power that lies behind them. In some nations that power is derived from the consent of the governed—by social consensus. In the case of South Africa under apartheid, the power of the white community ultimately derived from its control of the police and the military. These institutions enforced the system of apartheid. Thus they were the ultimate source of the market power and distributive advantages enjoyed by the white community.

9.2.20 Apartheid—The Efficiency of the System

While the white minority community gained a lot from apartheid, as a society South Africa paid a very dear price. The left pie chart in Figure 9.2.6 represents the size and distribution of an economy's product one would expect with and without apartheid. The W stands for the white community share and the B stands for the black community share. With apartheid, since a much smaller white community divides up the larger share, on average whites do much much better than blacks.

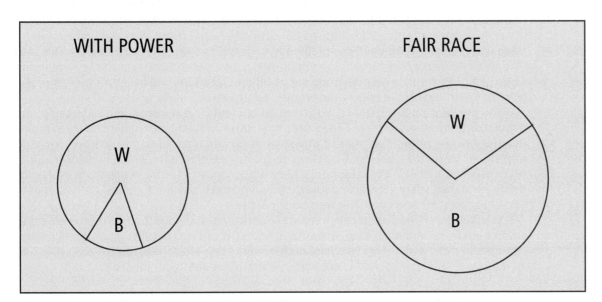

Figure 9.2.6   Distribution of South Africa's "Pie"

Now consider the counterfactual—a case that we can imagine but that did not exist. Imagine a South Africa in which all citizens, regardless of race, were fully nurtured and perfectly free to pursue their personal growth. The pie graph for such a world might look the one at the right in Figure 9.2.6. Two things immediately stand out. Absent the inefficiencies due to market power the overall size of the pie is much larger, and the share of the pie for the black community is much larger.

The overall size of the pie is larger for several reasons. First and foremost, by nurturing the members of the black community and ensuring its members equal access to information and markets, all the creativity and energy of those citizens is unleashed. The immense wealth of ability and imagination that was constrained and went untapped under apartheid joins in contributing to the social product. Furthermore, since the competition is more keen when all are allowed to compete, the abilities and imagination of all these in the white community are more fully developed.

And finally, the rent-maintenance structure of apartheid was not costless. The police and military had to be paid and equipped to enforce the system. The incessant and ever more powerful resistance it engendered in the black community made the price of enforcement ever higher. Resources spent on enforcing power are necessary if the system is to be preserved, but this allocation of resources creates no new value—just power. In the absence of apartheid those resources that were spent on maintaining the rent-generating structure could be redirected to productive enterprises thus further expanding the social pie.

9.2.21 Resistance to Apartheid and Its Demise

This point about the price of power brings us to a crucial element in the story of apartheid. A power structure that exists for the sake of a distributive benefit—a rent—is only worth maintaining so long as that benefit is larger than the cost of maintaining that structure. The resistance to apartheid by black South Africans made the price of power very high.

In a *New York Times* piece written during the days of apartheid, Desmond Tutu, Anglican Archbishop of Cape Town and winner of the 1984 Nobel Peace Prize for his work against apartheid, described the "many nonviolent ways of trying to bring change" that the black community has engaged in. These included "strikes, rent strikes, and consumer boycotts." Each of these was aimed at raising the price of power.

In the tradition of Gandhi and Martin Luther King, Bishop Tutu advocated nonviolent resistance. For this reason he bemoaned the lack of international assistance for the resistance, writing that "[i]t should come as no surprise . . . that those of us who ask desperate people to take nonviolent action are filled with despair when they learn that the U.S. and Britain have once again vetoed . . . sanctions [against South Africa] in the U.N. Security Council . . ." Bishop Tutu understood very well that international isolation increased the price of apartheid for the white community. Later, the U.S. did impose stiff sanctions.

The growing black resistance, both nonviolent and violent, meant more danger to the white community and more police, more guns, more jails, and more jailers to try to maintain the existing order. The price of power went up and up. Ultimately this ever increasing price of power led white South African leaders to negotiate a transition to black majority rule. On May 10, 1994, Nelson Mandela, the leading figure in the black South African community who had spent 27 years in South African prisons, was inaugurated as President of what Mandela referred to as The New South Africa.

Mandela faced, and his successors face, a daunting challenge. Long after the laws that enforce a rent-generating system of power are gone, the effects of that system in social perceptions and skewed shares of social endowments remain. Changing from a system of advantage to truly fair society is not simply a matter of changing the laws.

9.2.22 Market Power—Conclusion

This story of power and resistance has been repeated over and over . . . across time and across the globe. In the United States the 1956 Montgomery bus boycott, inspired by Rosa Parks and led by Martin Luther King, represents another classic example of the use of economic leverage to raise the price of oppression in a power struggle. Our rent-seeking/rent-maintenance analysis helps us understand stories of power and resistance.

I hope by now you can appreciate the role and the value of economic analysis in understanding our world. A lot of people come to an introductory economics course thinking that it is going to be all about the stock market. Well the stock market is very interesting, and it is within the realm of economics. But economics is about much, much more. It is one piece of a very large story about how we as human beings

- structure our personal lives,
- realize our dreams,
- arrange ourselves into communities, and
- how and why our communities evolve.

It is also about the forces that are at play today as modern nations continue to experiment with liberal social order. Will these experiments become, as Adam Smith envisioned and hoped: Constructive places in which we can mutually benefit one another as we each pursue our dreams; or will they degenerate into what Adam Smith feared was possible: Destructive rent-seeking societies in which there is a constant, wasteful struggle for power.

Power is one of those threads that weaves the economic dimension of society together with the social and political dimensions. It is through political and social institutions that much of the market power in societies is generated. To the degree that such power exists it distorts the flow of market activity, changing the distribution and thus the equity and reducing the efficiency of the market system. Our economic analysis of market power represents an excellent example of why the tools of an economist are essential elements of a full tool kit for understanding the human condition, past and present, and for thoughtfully moving into its future.

This brings us back to the theme of sustainability. If a liberal, free market society is to be sustainable it must combine systems of commutative and distributive justice that the citizens of the society perceive as fair. If the distribution of opportunities in society is not just or the market game is not played fairly, such a society sews seeds of discontent that if nurtured by continued injustice can ultimately lead to its destruction. Such was the case with the "old" apartheid South Africa. It claimed to be a liberal, free market society, but it was built on a power structure that insured its ultimate demise.

John Stuart Mill wrote in his *Principles of Political Economy* in 1848:

> The principle of private property has never yet had a fair trial in any country; and less so, perhaps, in this country [Britain] than in some others. The arrangements of modern Europe commenced from a distribution of property which was the result, not of just partition, or acquisition by industry, but of conquest and violence . . . [Subsequently, t]he laws of property . . . have not held the balance fairly between human beings, but have heaped impediments upon some, to give advantages to others; they have purposely fostered inequalities, and prevented all from starting the race fair. That all should indeed start on perfectly equal terms, is inconsistent with any law of private property: but if as much pains as has been taken to aggravate the inequality of chances arising from the natural working of the principle, had been taken to temper that inequality by every means not subversive of the principle itself; if the tendency of legislation had been to favour the diffusion, instead of the concentration of wealth . . . the principle of individual property would have been found to have no necessary connection with the physical and social evils which almost all Socialist writers assume to be inseparable from it. (Vol. I, pp. 267–8)

Socialist writings were and are a response to the inequities manifest in a liberal market system . . . inequities that are not, Mill argued, inherent in such a system. Rather, they emerge from power structures that, like a cancer, can grow within such a system, fed by the very rents they generate—apartheid being a classic example. Mill understood that the sustainability of liberal society depends on insuring that unbridled self-interested rent-seeking/maintenance activity does not lead to structure of market power that, like a cancer, destroys the society. The antidote to such a cancer and thus the key to sustainability of liberal society is a system commutative and distributive justice that all citizens accept as fair and to which all citizens willingly adhere. We will return to and examine this role of justice in liberal society at length at the end of our analysis.

Now we turn to another issue that complicates, but at the same time enriches, our analysis: market failure.

9.3 MARKET FAILURE

9.3.1 Introduction to Market Failure

The effectiveness of a market system depends on the principle that when autonomous individuals are interdependent and need their choices coordinated, a market will form to do the job. If a market does not form when we need it, or if a market does not work quickly and smoothly to do what needs to be done, we have a phenomenon called *market failure*. There are several kinds of market failures. One is public goods.

9.3.2 Public Goods

A *pure public good* is non-partitionable and non-excludable. Non-partitionable means a good cannot be broken into pieces like a candy bar. If you provided it, it is all or nothing at all. Non-excludable means that once you provide a good you cannot keep anyone from using it. It is there for everyone or no one.

So, is a free public park a pure public good? Is such a space inherently and inevitably non-partitionable and non-excludable? Think about it. The park is there, and it is free for the public. Sounds like a pure public good. But it is not. If the government sold the park to a private company that company could charge for entry and exclude those who do not pay to get in. It could let people into different parts of the park, or in for different periods of time. So a free public park is public and it is good, but it is not a pure public good.

Non-exclusion is not inherent in a public park. When I was growing up in New Orleans there were some very nice free "public" parks that were only open to whites. Blacks were excluded. So these parks were only good for that part of the public that the government allowed in—such a good is not a pure public good. Any good from which some people can be excluded or for which you can parcel out access differently to each user is not a pure public good.

A classic case of a pure public good is national defense from foreign armies. Think about it. National defense is provided in order to keep citizens safe within the nation's boundaries. It is non-excludable because if you are inside those boundaries you benefit from its provision. And it is very difficult to envision how national defense could be partitioned. Suppose the U.S. Army says, "OK, we're going to protect everybody in the United States . . . except . . . Jerry Evensky's house is fair game. Armies can invade his house if they want to."

In order to get to my house, the enemy has to pass through and/or over a lot of other peoples' houses, compromising their safety. If the U.S. Army is going to protect everyone else in the U.S. from some foreign army, it is stuck protecting me too. Once the military is there to defend the nation from a foreign army, everyone inside the defined defense perimeter gets defended from that army.

9.3.3 Public Goods and Free Riders

So who is going to provide a pure public good? Will free enterprise and the market do the job? In a normal market the supplier can charge for use and tailor the charge by the number of units used. But in the case of a pure public good, once it is provided we can all enjoy all of its benefits whether we pay for it or not, so no one among us has the incentive to pay. And, clearly, no private enterprise is going to provide a good or service until someone is willing to pay enough to at least cover costs including a normal return. The consequence of this is that the market fails to provide the "good" that we can all agree is good.

Pure public goods suffer from what is called a *free rider* problem. We all have an incentive to wait for someone else to pay for the good to be provided, because we all know that

that once it is provided we will all get to enjoy the full benefit without having to pay anything—we will get a free ride. Obviously everyone has the same incentive. As a result, even when we can all agree that we want and even need this good (like national defense), no market will form to provide it because either nobody or at least too few people are going to voluntarily pay for it. To the degree any good has characteristics of a pure public good, it is subject to this public good problem.

Have you ever seen a membership drive on public television? Why are they constantly there saying "Please, for heaven's sake, send money!" As the many commercial channels make clear, television is not a pure public good. The paying customers for commercial broadcast TV are the folks who pay for the commercials. They are buying "eyes" for their message and the programs are simply there to ensure that the "eyes" show up. But once it is out there a television signal is a public good. If a station like PBS does not charge for broadcast air time, it has got a problem. How does it pay for producing the signal and all that it carries since the signal is a public good? As PBS reminds us before and after every program, it depends on "members like you." If we all play free rider, the public television signal will vanish. And so too public radio.

9.3.4 Externalities

Another kind of market failure is called an externality. *Externalities* exist when property rights to resources are either not assigned or are not enforceable. To understand this externality issue let's review the role of property rights in a market economy.

One of the givens from which the market process unfolds is the distribution of the social endowment among individuals. In effect this means that property rights to the resources and products of society are assigned and that they will be enforced. We each own a share of resources and products, and our ownership is protected by law. Private property rights are essential to the system of market exchange, because we can only exchange what we own.

But for some resources in society assigning and/or enforcing property rights is problematic. And when property rights are problematic, the result can be externalities. A classic example of an externality problem has to do with air rights.

9.3.5 Externality Example—Property Rights and the Air

We generally take air for granted, but obviously it is a resource we all use every second of every day as we breathe. There are, however, other uses for air besides breathing. Lots of individuals and firms and governments use it as a disposal space for waste. For example, smokers or firms or governments often dispose of their waste smoke into the air.

If there was enough air for all of us to use it as we each choose without affecting the way others would like to use it, then there would be no problem. But . . . there isn't. And therein lies the problem of an externality.

Suppose I like to use the air to refresh my lungs. If you smoke in my class, your use of the air as a disposal space affects my use. I cannot enjoy the air as I would like to. If a firm spews chemical waste into the air near my neighborhood, its use of the air as a disposal space affects me. I cannot use the air as I would like—to keep myself and my family healthy.

It is not that the smoker and the firm are trying to make my life miserable. They are each just pursuing their private activity to maximize their well-being. From their perspective, the effect their activity has on me is just an unintended, negative consequence on a bystander. To the degree that this negative effect on me has no affect on them, they feel nothing of the effect. Feeling nothing, they do not take it into account as they determine the optimal level of their activities. The cost I bear from their activity is off of their radar screens, *external* to their considerations—thus the term externality. But while they do not feel the cost they are imposing on me, I do . . . so they are making their private decision as to how much smoke to emit without considering the full cost of their activity.

9.3.6 Externalities, Markets, and Property Rights

This is a classic problem for the market. We have learned that markets form to coordinate interdependent choices of autonomous actors. The smoker and I are autonomous actors. We are interdependent because we are both using the same resource, the air, and our uses conflict. So where is the market when we need it to help us resolve this interdependence by coordinating our choices? It's not there. Why?

. . . Because no one owns the air. We each simply use the air as if it is free...which is fine for them, because my air use does not diminish their ability to use the air as they would like. But it not so good for me because their use does diminish my air quality and thus my ability to use the air as I would like.

If property rights could be assigned and enforced, that would help solve the problem. Suppose for a moment that I own the air, that I can enforce my property right, and that you want to smoke in MY air. In that case I could send you a signal that I do not like smoke in my air. I could charge you a price for using my air as a disposal site. I have some notion in my head as to what price would compensate me for the opportunity cost of a certain level of freshness lost in my air. This determines my supply schedule. You have some notion as to how much you are willing to pay for the opportunity to dispose of your waste in my air, to have a cigarette in my space. This determines your demand schedule. Given our respective supply and demand schedules, there is a price/quantity equilibrium that brings our attitudes into balance.

It would also work if you, the smoker, were assigned the property right to the air and could enforce your property right. In this case I could offer to pay a price to have you reduce your smoking. I have some notion in my head as to what price I would be willing to pay for a certain level of freshness in YOUR air. This determines my demand schedule. You have some notion as to how much of a price you would require to provide a certain level of freshness in your air. It would have to compensate you for the opportunity cost of having more cigarettes. This determines your supply schedule. Again, given our respective supply and demand schedules, there is a price/quantity equilibrium that brings our attitudes into balance.

Both of these solutions solve the externality problem because the assignment and enforcement of property rights makes it possible for a market to form. The market price provides a signal between us that can adjust to bring our interdependent choices into equilibrium.

All too often, however, as with air, property rights are not assignable and/or enforceable. In such cases no market forms. No market means no price signal. Receiving no signal from a market, an individual may not even be aware of the unintended consequence of her action that affects bystanders. She certainly has no monetary incentive to take this external effect into account when choosing how much of this activity to do (e.g., how much to smoke).

9.3.7 Negative and Positive Externalities

The case of smoking is called a *negative externality* because the activity imposes a negative effect: An unintended *external cost* on bystanders that smokers do not have take into account when determining the level of their private activity. Air pollution, water pollution, noise pollution—"pollution" is associated with the concept of negative externality because it often involves spoiling a common resource like air or water. If a resource is held in common, then individual property rights are not assigned and the possibility of externalities arises.

It is also possible for a positive externality to occur. In the neighborhood near my campus there is a modest house with a spectacular garden. The story I have heard is that the gentleman who lives there maintains the garden for the pleasure of his wife who is housebound. I am one among many who on a lovely summer day will go out of my way to drive by and enjoy the view. This garden is not for my benefit, but I do benefit from it. My benefit is external to the considerations of the gentleman who maintains it. He does not take this *external benefit* into account when he decides how much garden to plant. But he plants, and I enjoy a positive externality.

Many externalities are clearly either positive or negative, but not all. There is a lovely, very large hill near my campus. When I was a footloose and fancy free grad student here, any evening the weather permitted I used to go up there to watch the sunset. It is a wonderful spot. Often there would be other folks up there, and sometimes their activities would affect my enjoyment of the evening.

On occasion there would be someone playing some wonderful music that really fit my mood as I watched the sunset paint the clouds in lovely colors. That was for me a positive externality. But on some nights I would go to the hill and there would be somebody up there playing something that seemed like it had come from another planet. And they would be playing it loudly enough for the folks back home, in Texas, to hear it. That was, for me, a negative externality. But what was positive or negative for me might have been just the opposite for someone else sitting up there. Whether an externality is positive or negative ultimately depends on how the individual receiving its effect perceives it.

9.3.8 Representing Externalities Graphically—Setting Up the Graph

Now we set the graphical scene for the externality analysis as shown in Figure 9.3.1A.

On the vertical axis we are measuring in dollars because that is our metric of costs and benefits. On the horizontal axis we are measuring the level of the activity (L) involved: How long the factory runs, how big the garden is, how loud the music is, how many cigarettes are smoked.

A private autonomous actor ignores any external effects and chooses the optimal level of activity by comparing her private costs and her private benefits at the margin. We learned before that marginal costs increase and marginal benefits decrease with the level of activity. We will label these as marginal private cost (MPC) and marginal private benefit (MPB) to emphasize that these are the costs and benefits felt directly by the private actor.

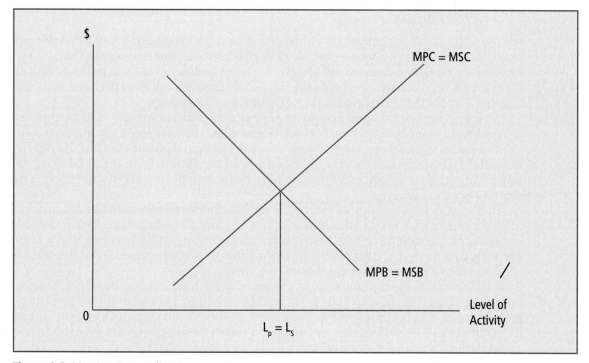

Figure 9.3.1A No Externality Case

As you can see in Figure 9.3.1A, so long as at the margin the benefit is greater than the cost, then that is a level of activity worth doing. But as one does more and more of the activity, marginal benefits fall and marginal costs rise. Thus, the net benefit at the margin shrinks until, at the point where the marginal benefit equals the marginal cost, there is no net benefit at the margin. To go further would mean doing the activity when marginal cost is higher than the marginal benefit—which makes no sense. So the optimal level of private activity (L_p) is where marginal private cost equals the marginal private benefit.

Now let's distinguish some terms. Social costs and social benefits are the full costs and benefits created by an activity. Social costs include both the private costs to the individual undertaking the activity *and* any external costs to others. Social benefits include both the private benefits to the individual undertaking the activity *and* any external benefits to others. If there are no external costs or benefits, then the only costs and benefits are the private ones. In that case the full social costs and benefits are equal to the private costs and benefits. In terms of our margins, in the absence of any externality we can write

(in the case of no negative externality)
marginal social costs = marginal private costs
MSC = MPC

and

(in the case of no positive externality)
marginal social benefits = marginal private benefits
MSB = MPB

The optimal social level of activity (L_S) is where marginal social costs equal marginal social benefits. In this case of no externality the marginal social and marginal private cost lines are the same, and the marginal social and marginal private benefit lines are the same, so the optimal social level of activity (L_S) is the same as the optimal private level of activity (L_p). Not surprising, since if a private activity does not affect anyone else then what is best for the individual is also best for society.

9.3.9 Representing Externalities Graphically—A Negative Externality

For the purposes of our analysis, we have defined a negative externality as an additional, external cost (EC) and a positive externality as an additional, external benefit (EB). On our externality graph therefore, we will identify any such additional costs or benefits with an EC or an EB respectively. For simplicity we will assume that all external costs (EC) and external benefits (EB) are constant no matter the level of activity.

Now let's suppose that an activity generates a negative externality and no positive externality. In that case EC > 0 and EB = 0. Graphically, this case looks like Figure 9.3.1B.

The marginal social cost (MSC) line is above the marginal private cost (MPC) line. The vertical distance between them is the exact size of the external cost, EC. The marginal social benefit line is the same as the marginal private benefit line (MPB) since there is no external benefit, EB = 0.

In this case, what is the optimal level of activity for the private individual (L_p)? Since a private actor only considers her private costs and private benefits, the optimal level of her activity is just as it was when there was no externality. It is still where the MPC = MPB. The EC is called external costs precisely because the private actor does not take them into account when choosing the optimal level of activity.

OK, that is still the optimal level of private activity, but now that there is a negative externality what level of activity is socially optimal? From a social point of view things have changed. Benefits are the same because there is no EB, but costs are higher by EC and the optimal social level of activity has changed to reflect these higher costs. What is the new optimal social level of activity (L_S)? Since from the social perspective all costs and benefits count, the optimal social level of activity is where the MSC = MSB.

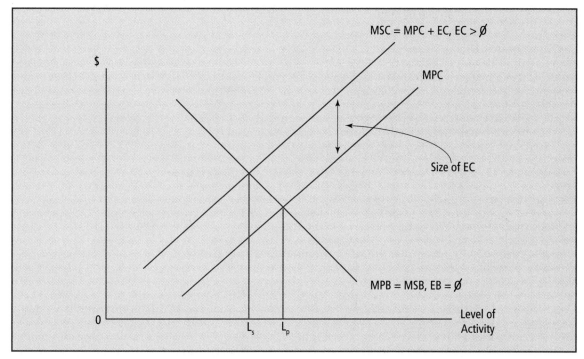

Figure 9.3.1B Negative Externality Case

9.3.10 Negative Externality, Efficiency, and Equity

Our analysis demonstrates that when there is a negative externality, the level of activity that a private actor undertakes is greater than the level of the activity that is socially optimal (Lp > Ls). This is so because the private actor does not take the external costs into account.

For each unit of activity from L_S to L_P, while the private individual is doing better with each unit because the MPB is greater than the MPC, society as a whole is doing worse because the MSB is less than the MSC. Thus from a social point of view this private level of activity is inefficient.

A negative externality is a market failure that creates inefficiency because the private actor is not taking all the costs into account.

9.3.11 Positive Externality, Efficiency, and Equity

A positive externality also causes inefficiency and equity effects. Figure 9.3.2 shows a positive externality case.

In this case the marginal social benefit (MSB) line is above the marginal private benefit (MPB) line. The vertical distance between them is the exact size of the external benefit, EB. The marginal social cost line (MSC) is the same as the marginal private cost line (MPC) since in this case there is no external cost, EC = 0.

What is the optimal level of activity for the private individual (L$_p$) now? As always it is where the MPC = MPB. As with external costs, the private actor does not take external benefits into account when choosing the optimal level of activity.

In this positive externality case what is the optimal social level of activity (L$_S$)? The optimal social level of activity is where the MSC = MSB.

In this case the level of activity that a private actor undertakes is less than the socially optimal level of that activity. This is so because the private actor does not take the external benefits into account. As in the negative externality case, this difference between what is socially optimal and what the private actor will actually do causes an inefficiency in the market.

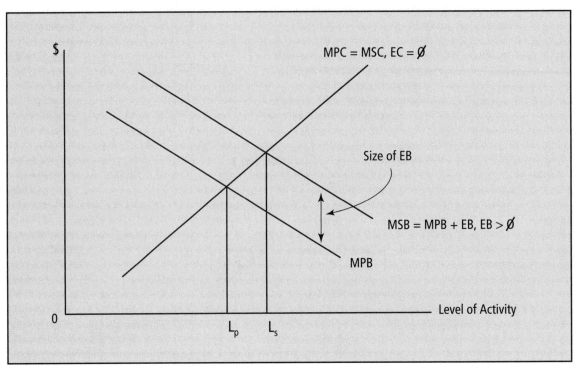

Figure 9.3.2 Positive Externality Case

9.3.12 Risk Externalities

Some cases of negative externalities are pretty obvious because we can perceive them directly, for example some kinds of air pollution, or water pollution, or noise pollution. In other cases they are not so obvious. One kind that is not so obvious is a risk externality—that is creating a risk for bystanders.

Picture this: You are at a party consuming alcohol. This may not be a good thing for your body, but it is your body and your body is ultimately your private business. Is your alcohol consumption any of my business?

It could be: When the party breaks up it is time to go home. How are going get home? You drove to the party, your car is right outside, you live a few miles away, it is a nasty night for a walk . . .

You calculate your EPV of driving rather than walking. Keep in mind that your choices are based on perceptions. At this point, since your mind is affected by the alcohol, your calculations are based on a distorted perception of reality. You think, "Hey, I've driven this route a million times, I can do it in my sleep, there's no one out at this hour, it's not that far . . . it's not a problem . . . I'll drive." So off you go, ever so carefully aiming your car between the white lines.

Just about that time, at the house across from my house, the parents come home, pay my kid for babysitting, thank her, and off she heads for home. As she crosses the street you come around the corner—just a little too fast. Before you realize there is someone there, you have run down my kid.

This is just a story, but for many kids it is a reality. Lots of kids are killed by drunk drivers. All the folks who drove the cars that killed those kids got behind the wheel of a car in an impaired state. They really thought it would be OK. It was certainly not their intention to kill a kid. They almost certainly did not know the kid they killed. But they will never forget that face. Their choice to drive drunk created a risk for every bystander along their way—this was a risk externality . . . and in their case the risk became a reality.

9.3.13 Risk Externalities and Technology

Or how about this one: One day—now I think the gist of this is true but lord knows I have no memory so we will just consider it a plausible story—anyway, one day I am watching TV and on comes a story about an genetically altered bacterium that when sprayed on plants it multiplies, coats the plants, and reduces the temperature at which they are harmed by frost. This is a big deal with huge commercial applications. If such an organism can protect fruit crops in California and Florida from just a few more degrees of cold, it could save growers a lot of money. During the report there was a video clip showing fruit being sprayed as part of a test of the organism's performance. The reporter solemnly noted that the scientists had taken precautions to ensure that the experiment was controlled so the organism would not escape into the general environment.

I wondered, as I watched, how extensive those precautions were. I mean, after all, precautions cost money and the experimenters have limited resources. Obviously, they would limit their expenditures on precautions based on their sense of the probabilities of the risks. The probabilities of a release into the general environment might have been very low and the organism they were testing might have a very short life, so the probability of risk may have seemed small. But organisms mutate. Suppose that in this batch there was a variant that lived much longer and somehow that variant, carried by a breeze, got out of the test area. If such an organism actually established itself outside the test area and started to multiply . . . well, in the extreme, a spread of such an organism globally would change the ecology of the earth and the earth's environment much faster than any estimates on global warming caused by burning fossil fuels.

Scientific experimentation causing unintended consequences for innocent bystanders is not a new concept. Mary Shelley's *Frankenstein* was published in 1818. What is new or what at least seems to be growing exponentially with the advent of biotechnology is our ability to create new technology that can have significant unintended consequences. This makes externalities—in particular risk externalities—a particularly interesting concept in this day and age.

Again, the model raises interesting questions by systematizing our thinking. It does not answer these questions, but it alerts us to ask them and it provides us with a systematic way of analyzing the possible answers.

9.3.14 Market Failure—Conclusion

When individuals or firms act in a way that optimizes their own private well-being, they may generate effects that unintentionally benefit or cost bystanders. If property rights are not defined or are not enforceable, no market will form. Without a market there is no signal, no price to make each actor feel the full effect of the costs and/or benefits of her activity. In the absence of a market price the actor can ignore her external effects. This is a market failure. As a consequence of market failure, while private activity is privately optimal, it is not socially optimal. Activities with negative external effects are overdone and activities with positive external effects are underdone.

This externality issue brings us back yet again to the theme of sustainability. If there is a problem with global environmental sustainability much of that problem is a consequence of negative externalities, and under the current model of production these externalities inevitably increase with economic growth. Since global economic growth is accelerating as aspirations for material well-being from citizens in China and Russia and India and other emerging economies compete with to those continuing aspirations in traditional global economic giants like the U.S., Japan, Germany, England, so too negative externalities are expanding at an accelerating rate on a global scale.

If the current model of growth generates increasing externalities is that model sustainable, or is it self-limiting? Will our pursuit of material consumption generate a level of negative externalities that will ultimately consume us? Or is this concern just much ado about nothing because the problem is not so big as the purveyors of sustainability panic would have us believe and the markets are much more responsive than the market naysayers given them credit for?

These questions about market failure bring us to the role of government. If markets can fail, does that mean government should step in to solve the problem? Now we turn to the role of government in the micro workings of a liberal, market economy. Is there a role, and if "yes," what is it?

We will focus on policy at a national level. We will see how complicated national policy can be and we will examine the debate about whether government intervention is a wise idea. As we explore this debate at the national level, imagine how much more complicated such policy debate is at a global level.

10.0 THE MICROECONOMY AND THE GOVERNMENT

10.1 INTRODUCTION

10.1.1 Potential Roles for Government

In his 1962 book titled *Capitalism and Freedom*, Milton Friedman—winner of the 1976 Nobel Prize in Economics—writes that

> the organization of economic activity through voluntary exchange presumes that we have provided, through government, for the maintenance of law and order to prevent coercion of one individual by another, the enforcement of contracts voluntarily entered into, the definition of the meaning of property rights, the interpretation and enforcement of such rights, and the provision of a monetary framework. . . . We may also want to do through government some things that might conceivably be done through the market but that technical or similar conditions render it difficult to do in that way. These all reduce to cases in which strictly voluntary exchange is either exceedingly costly or practically impossible. There are two general classes of such cases: monopoly and similar market imperfections, and neighborhood effects.

In the first part of this statement Friedman is reasserting what Adam Smith said almost 200 years ago. As Smith put it: Commutative "[j]ustice . . . is the main pillar that upholds the whole edifice [of society] . . . [S]ociety cannot subsist unless the laws of justice are tolerably observed." (*TMS*, 86) Ensuring commutative justice is an essential role for government in a liberal, market-based society. But is there more to government's role? In the second part of the quotation Friedman cites two other things "[w]e may also want to do through government": Dealing with "monopoly and similar market imperfections" or, in other words, dealing with market power, and also addressing "neighborhood effects," that is, addressing market failures. Should government intervene to solve these market problems?

And what about equity? Is the government's only job to ensure an efficient system, or should the government ensure some degree of equity at either the starting line or the finish line in the race for wealth?

10.1.2 Preview to Policy Debate

There are two principles that underlie the debate about the role of government in the economy. First there is the question as to whether the economy needs any help from the government. Secondly there is the question as to whether, assuming the markets do not work perfectly, government intervention is a potential solution or is just an invitation to a bigger problem.

In order to set the scene for the debate, let's review a few cases of market problems and the difficulty of doing policy to constructively address these problems. Then, having reflected on how challenging role of good government intervention can be, we will turn to the philosophical debate between those who think it is worth the challenge because government can contribute to solutions and those who think policy intervention is a pointless effort and that more often than not government is itself a large part of the problem.

10.2 GOVERNMENT INTERVENTION IN THE MICROECONOMY—CASES AND ISSUES

10.2.1 Government Solutions for Externalities Issues

At a theoretical level, solving an externality issue is a trivial problem. All you have to do is correctly measure the external effect. For example, Figure 10.2.1 shows a negative externality. The size of the externality is EC. If you can measure EC accurately and then impose that cost on the private actor, what happens to the MPC line?

In effect imposing the EC on the private actor means adding the EC to the private costs. Having done that, all costs including those that were formerly external are now internal costs. This is called *internalizing the externality*. Picture it: Once the externality is internalized, the private actor's MPC line rises to the level of the MSC line, and the optimal level of private activity (L_P) moves to the socially optimal level (L_S).

Alternatively, if the government can determine the size of the externality then it can determine how far the private level of activity is from the socially optimal level. With this information it can regulate the activity to a socially optimal level.

Either way it's a piece of cake, *IF* the size of the externality can be measured. But it cannot. The signal that would measure it, the price, is precisely the missing signal that causes the externality problem in the first place. So absent a direct measure, any solution requires a *proxy* or substitute measure. But substitute measures are problematic at best.

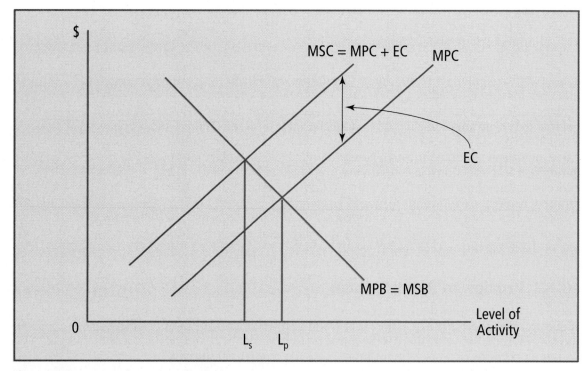

Figure 10.2.1   Negative Externality Case

10.2.2 Solving an Externality Problem—A Case

Suppose (this is not a true story) my family has a home in a beautiful, secluded, tree-filled area along a lovely little stream. Our house is well over 150 years old. It has been in my family since my great-great-great grandmother and grandfather built it shortly after they were married. Their blood, sweat, and tears are in the broad wooden planks of our floors and in the beautiful woodwork that surrounds our windows and doors.

This house has been our family's little piece of heaven for the last 150 years. For a 150 winters we've been sitting by the big fireplace watching the flames dance, listening to the sap pop, smelling the sweet scent of the cherry wood, and sharing the warmth of each other and the fire. For that many summers we've been enjoying quiet evenings on the big broad porch listening to the wind in the willows and watching the fireflies dance for mates. I watch my kids play in the pristine stream that runs in front of the house—just as so many generations of my family have done before me. I love this place so much. It is what the term "home" means to me.

Then one day Acme Better Chemical Company builds a big plant upstream. Not long after, our stream is not a pristine path through heaven, it is a sewage canal and the stench makes the area virtually uninhabitable. My few neighbors and I decide to sue the Acme Corporation to stop the pollution. Courts are one avenue we can use to try to solve private interest coordination problems when the market fails. An agreement is reached that there must be an abatement plan to reduce the pollution. The Environmental Protection Agency (EPA) will design the plan.

A government agent comes to my door. She says to me: "I took economics. I know the externality graphs, so I know exactly how to solve this problem. I just need to know how big the externality is. So, please tell me your estimate of the cost the plant is imposing on you?" I look her straight in the eye and say, "About $100,000,000,000." She stares at me in disbelief and says. "Excuse me?" I calmly explain, "My heart and soul are wrapped up in this home. Here I feel like the richest person in the world. So if that's how I feel then I estimate that the value of the loss of pleasure to my heart and soul caused by this foul stuff is about as much as the richest person has. I'm guessing Bill Gates has almost $100,000,000,000, so that is my honest best estimate of my cost."

She stares at me, shakes her head, and walks away. So much for the "It's a piece of cake." solution. Remember: Anybody who says it's simple is either simple minded or thinks you are. Sure, it may look easy on the graphs, but in real life it is hard, very hard. So what is the government to do? In most cases it tries to estimate the size of the effect using a proxy. In the case just described what would most likely be chosen as the best measurable proxy for the effect on me is what the pollution does to the market price of my house. But while it is a measurable proxy, it is not a very good proxy. Markets are premised on voluntary exchange and I do not want to sell my house precisely because the market does not value it as much as I do. Absent a good proxy, the government agent just has to make a fair guess. It is not the precision of rocket science, and it is not easy. . . . All the more so when the externality costs are imposed on the well-being of future generations whose voices are not heard.

10.2.3 Government Solutions for Market Power Issues—A Labor Market Case

Now consider this market power issue. In his discussion of the wages of labor Adam Smith wrote:

> What are the common wages of labour depends every where upon the contract usually made between those two parties [(masters and workers)], whose interests are by no means the same. The workmen desire to get as much, the masters to give as little as possible. The former are disposed to combine in order to raise, the latter in order to lower the wages of labour.

It is not, however, difficult to foresee which of the two parties must, upon all ordinary occasions, have the advantage in the dispute, and force the other into a compliance with their terms. The masters, being fewer in number, can combine much more easily [and . . . i]n all such disputes the masters can hold out much longer. A landlord, a farmer, a master manufacturer, or merchant, though they did not employ a single workman, could generally live a year or two upon the stocks which they have already acquired. Many workmen could not subsist a week, few could subsist a month, and scarce any a year without employment. In the long-run the workman may be as necessary to his master as his master is to him; but the necessity is not so immediate. (*WN*, 83-4)

So according to Smith, in labor negotiations employers often have an advantage.

In modern societies the response among workers to this market power of employers is to organize, to create unions as a countervailing force so that negotiations are power to power. But collusion in order to create power in the market, whether among firms or among workers, is a violation of our nice assumptions. Thus it reduces efficiency and causes changes in equity. So is there a role for government when such market power problems emerge? Some would argue that government should use its power to break down concentrations of private power wherever they emerge so that the market system can approximated the no power condition of the nice assumptions. Government should be the impartial referee or umpire that insures that the "race for wealth" is fair for all. Others argue that the very power the government exercises that would make this possible is never exercised impartially and that government is inevitably part of this power problem . . . not part of the solution.

10.3 GOVERNMENT INTERVENTION AND EFFICIENCY— THE PHILOSOPHICAL DEBATE

10.3.1 Introduction

Every government has an economic policy. If it taxes, or spends, or regulates at all, it is tweaking that web of connections that is the micro market system. In doing so it is influencing how that system will resolve itself into a general equilibrium. On the other hand, if it does not do anything that is a policy too. It is choosing to let the system work itself out on its own—with all the potential promise and all the possible problems of a market system.

But just because a government has a policy, that does not mean it has a thoughtful policy. Often a hands-off policy simply reflects a thoughtless neglect of the situation, and a hands-on policy is just a day-to-day *ad hoc* (case-by-case) reaction to unfolding events. Coherent policy, whether hands off or hands on, involves the careful application of systematic analysis based on a thoughtful model and a philosophical foundation.

We have developed a rich tool for systematic microeconomic analysis. But remember, the model is not a set of answers, nor does it generate answers. Its strength lies in systematizing your thinking so that you appreciate the web of connections, recognize the paths of possible connections, ask rich questions, and think systematically about alternative answers before you arrive at answers.

Let's assume you have defined your microeconomic policy objectives as Pareto optimality and equity. There are several philosophical questions you must answer for yourself before you decide what role, if any, you believe government should play in this complex web we call a microeconomy.

1. How well do I believe the market system really works? How closely do the conditions of the microeconomy actually approximate our nice assumptions?
   and
2. How much do I trust government to carry out thoughtful policy?

A second set of questions follows from this concern about government:

1. Do I trust government at all? If intervention is allowed, would government power simply become another tool used by interest groups (like Smith's Mercantile interests) to create or enhance market power? Is government a source of constructive solutions or is it a rent-seeking/rent-maintenance structure that must be constrained?

   and

2. Even if I assume that government's intent can be trusted, can government be wise enough to intervene efficiently and effectively? The web of economic connections is very complicated. Is it so complicated that it is unreasonable to think that wise policy is even possible?

Honorable, intelligent people who share a belief that our model is a reasonable representation of the way the economy works can nevertheless disagree on the role of government because they answer these questions differently. And to make matters more complicated, many people believe there is no absolute answer to these questions. They do not see markets as good and government bad, or vice versa. Rather their perspective on markets and government varies with the context.

In what follows we will use the polar cases—markets are good and government bad, or vice versa—to frame the debate. But remember, most economists' opinions are really complex combinations of these cases related to context.

10.3.2 Interventionist v. Non-Interventionist Policy

Our model tells us that if all of our assumptions including the nice assumptions actually hold, then the self-adjusting micro market system realizes a Pareto optimal General Competitive Equilibrium. If that is the case then the best policy to achieve efficiency is non-intervention. Non-interventionist policy is often called *laissez faire*. This term was coined by an eighteenth-century French economist, Vincent de Gournet, who was arguing for the dismantling of government obstacles to free trade. In effect, *laissez-faire*, means "leave the markets alone to work their magic." Combining a faith in markets with a belief that government is part of the problem not part of the solution is the philosophical position that underlies the *laissez faire* or *non-interventionist* approach to policy.

There are others, however, who believe that while markets may work well at some times and in some areas; due to market failure and/or market power there are inevitably times when and/or places where the system is distorted. As we have seen, these distortions lead to inefficiencies. A belief that these distortions and the accompanying inefficiencies are a significant problem, combined with a belief that government is capable of constructive policy, is the philosophical foundation of the *interventionist* position.

10.4 DISTRIBUTIVE JUSTICE AND THE ROLE OF GOVERNMENT

10.4.1 Problems of Definition

The debate about the role of government in the microeconomy is further complicated if we add to the efficiency objective an equity objective. Clearly the government can, by taxing and spending, redistribute well-being in society. It can do so by simply transferring wealth, taxing one group and giving the money to another, or it can do so by taxing one group and spending on programs that benefit another. Redistribution can also be accomplished by regulating the behavior of one group to the benefit of another. For instance, rent controls limit how much landlords can charge and, in effect, redistribute income from landlords to renters. There are, however, potential problems with government intervention in the name of equity.

The most fundamental problem is determining a definition of equity. Some folks who are doing well may say that this current state of affairs is just fine thank you, while those who are poor cry foul. If those who see inequity in the current distribution call for change, those who are doing well may believe their position is threatened. Obviously, in this case a social consensus on a definition of equity is very difficult, if not impossible.

These conflicts over equity challenge government in a liberal democratic society, because government becomes the contested space within which those who value or reject the status quo work to protect or to change it respectively. If government tries to satisfy the claims of all segments of the population, this may be possible for a short period but it is doomed to failure in the longer term. As we have learned, demands can be limitless but resources are finite. Government cannot legislate scarcity out of existence.

10.4.2 Problems of Implementation—The Rent Control Example

Let's assume for a moment that a generally acceptable definition of equity is agreed upon. The government still faces the challenge of implementing a policy that will realize that goal because many such policies can have perverse efficiency effects. Remember, anytime the government taxes, spends, or regulates, it is potentially affecting the market's efficiency.

Take for example the rent control case cited earlier. Figure 10.4.1 represents the market for apartments after rent controls that put a ceiling on rents at R_c are imposed. The effect is an excess demand for apartments.

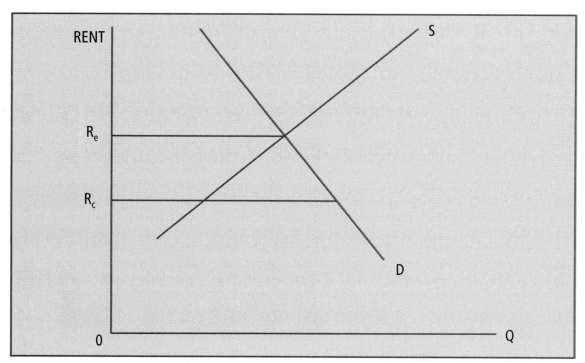

Figure 10.4.1 Rent Control Case

Since rent controls are the law the automatic market adjustment mechanism—price adjustments that bring the market back into balance—is not able to eliminate the shortage. The shortage becomes a long-term problem.

If controls were lifted, rents would rise to R_e. As rents rise the quantity supplied would rise (new apartments would be built) and the quantity demanded would fall (fewer people could afford the price of housing). Here we have an efficiency/equity trade-off. In order to get the efficiencies of the apartment market, some people would be priced out of the market for apartments.

If we can agree on some standard of equity, the question of government intervention becomes: How do we realize the equity standard at the lowest possible cost in terms of efficiency?

10.4.3 Are Equity and Efficiency Inevitably a Tradeoff?

In theoretical terms, the answer is straightforward. As we heard in a quotation from Kenneth Arrow cited earlier: "[T]heory teaches us that the final allocation will depend on the distribution of initial supplies and of the ownership of firms. If we want to rely on the virtues of the market but also to achieve a more just distribution, the theory suggests the strategy of changing the initial endowments rather than interfering with the allocation process at some later stage." So equity and efficiency are not an inevitable trade-off. Redistribution of endowments is possible.

But, this redistribution of endowments solution returns us to the problem of consensus. How can we get individuals to agree on redistribution of endowments if someone will lose based on any definition other than the status quo, and many reject the status quo? There has been no social consensus on what distributive justice is or how to approximate it. So in practice government intervention for equity purposes is often, when it is done at all, an *ad hoc* process with all the attendant efficiency problems that implies.

10.4.4 Conclusion on the Micro Policy Debate

Do all these problems of policy mean that *laissez-faire* is the clear winner in the debate over microeconomic government policy? No. It just means that coherent, constructive policy is a challenge.

The debate over whether government should intervene in the economy continues because there continues to be disagreement among economists and within the general public over how well the market economy works, how well the government works, and how fair the status quo is. This debate plays itself out in the form of social and political competition. Those who take varying positions in the debate compete for control of society's institutions so that they can shape the future to conform to their vision of an ideal society. This competition can be peaceful as it is in most American political campaigns; or it can be violent as it has been and remains in many parts of the world, or it can be played out in both ways simultaneously as it was in the old South Africa or in the U.S. civil rights movement during the 1950s and 1960s.

10.5 CONCLUSION ON MICROECONOMICS—A REVIEW

10.5.1 From Individual Choice to Complexity

We began the development of our microeconomic model by defining and arranging terms and specifying some assumptions. With that foundation we built a microeconomic model for a simple Robinson Crusoe society. We developed a decision rule that represented how a lone individual with limited resources would allocate those resources in order to maximize utility. Our rich version of this rule emerged as we successively relaxed assumptions in order to build the issues of production, time, and risk and uncertainty into the decision rule.

Next we examined the forces that give rise to complexity. We found that the benefit of the division of labor - increased social product - makes everyone better off as long as there is a mechanism for coordinating the exchange of the surpluses produced by all the participants. The market system, adjusting on price signals, provides such a mechanism. If it works perfectly, it ensures that all individual decisions to produce and consume and to save and invest are efficiently coordinated.

10.5.2 Coordination Under Our Nice Assumptions

In order to understand how markets work their magic, we analyzed the concepts of supply and demand, the role of price as the signal on which coordination is based, and the concept of market equilibrium. We found that under our nice assumptions the market system outcome in a complex society is analogous to that in a Robinson Crusoe society: The coordination of decisions to supply and demand and to save and invest is perfect; all productive resources offered for use are put to use in the most efficient technique of production available; for every good or service, the quantity supplied will be equal to the quantity demanded; and all individuals will derive the maximum utility from their share of society's initial endowment.

We identified the outcome of the general system under these nice assumptions as a Pareto optimal General Competitive Equilibrium.

10.5.3 From GCE to the Other Possible Outcomes—Market Power and Market Failure

Having examined this case, we began to relax our assumptions. First we analyzed the impact of a market power on the efficiency and equity of the system. We found that efficiency was diminished and that distribution, and therefore equity, is affected. We noted that market power is often generated by social and political institutions that skew the distribution of society's opportunities to the advantage of some members of society and the disadvantage of others. Thus market power is a concept that connects the study of economics to the study of other social sciences. This connection makes it clear that while the tools of the economist are indispensable for a complete analysis of social forces, only when those tools are used in conjunction with the tools of sister social sciences can an analysis of society be complete.

Another problem of the market system that we identified is the failure of markets to develop under some conditions. In cases such as externalities or public goods there is no mechanism for coordinating individual choices, so a socially suboptimal condition results.

10.5.4 The Microeconomy and the Role of Government

We have seen that the market system has one great virtue. When it is working well and is unencumbered, it is the most efficient system for allocating society's resources and thus for generating the greatest wealth for the nation. This is indeed a great virtue . . . so great that much of the world, having seen the material well-being that market systems can create, is moving to markets. As I write this, billions of people in China, in India, in Russia, and in other nations are leaving behind old systems of economic coordination—tradition or central planning—in the hopes of capturing the magic of markets.

But even under our ideal efficiency conditions, a market system lacks another great virtue that many people mistakenly ascribe to it—it is not inherently just. Markets are amoral choice coordinators. Under the best of market conditions, our nice assumptions, the coordination is perfectly efficient, but the fairness of the outcome depends entirely on the fairness of the distribution of society's initial endowment and opportunities among individuals. And as we have seen, the system can be distorted in ways that allow some individuals to exploit others.

So, as the world moves more and more to a global market system, is there a role for government in that process? We have identified two basic positions on this issue: non-interventionist and interventionist. Those who believe that the market system works well and that government will inevitably make matters worse if it intervenes advocate a non-interventionist, *laissez-faire* policy. Those who believe that the efficiency and/or equity and/or sustainability problems of the economy are significant and that government can be a constructive force advocate government intervention. In presenting this debate we noted that while many economists lean toward one view or the other, most are not absolutist about this. Rather, they treat each policy proposal as a separate case.

Now we have completed our model of the microeconomy. It is time to change perspectives and look at the economy as a single wholeness . . . from a macroeconomic perspective.

11.0 INTRODUCTION TO MACROECONOMICS

11.1 OVERVIEW

11.1.1 The Basic Distinction Between Micro and Macro

Up to this point we have been studying microeconomics, focusing as if through a microscope on individual people, individual enterprises, individual markets, and the web of connections that weaves them together.

In micro we constructed a complex model of a market economy that allowed us to understand that:

- Based on price signals a market can coordinate the autonomous choices of individuals in a complex world.
- The market system is like an econosystem. As an ecosystem is to living things, similarly a market system is a complex web of connections among markets within which activity in any one market affects events in all other markets.
- The market system can determine how the resources from our social endowment are used.
- The efficiency with which the market system allocates these resources depends on the degree to which there is market power or market failure in the system.
- The market system can determine what we pay for things—their values; and how much we make for our contributions to the market process—our share of the distribution.
- And finally that the equity of the market system's distribution depends on our definition of justice, the distribution of the social initial endowment among individuals, and the impact of power and failure in markets.

Now we shift our focus from this micro perspective to a macro perspective. In macroeconomics we will construct another model. Instead of a model representing a complex web of connections, this macro model will represent the entire market system, the entire econosystem, as a single entity. In macro we will explore a different set of questions. Instead of the micro issues of individual people, enterprises, and markets, in macro we are interested in aggregate questions about how the economy, the entire econosystem, is functioning as a whole.

- Is it producing up to its full capacity? And if not, why not?
- Is it providing employment for all who want to participate? And if not, why not?
- Is it possible for one to make a living without worrying about price rises or price falls making living complicated and/or hard? And if not, why not?
- Is perpetual growth of the production and consumption sustainable? And if not, why not?

11.1.2 Why Study the Economy at the Macro Level: Aggregating the Micro Reality to Get a Feel for the Wholeness of Society's Experience.

From this macro perspective all the people and markets lose their individual identity as we look at the whole web as a single unit. To appreciate the distinction between micro and macro perspectives, and to see how the macro perspective can help us to understand human events, consider some examples.

Figure 11.1.1 represents a macro perspective on war. There you see war in a whole sense—people, lots of people, die. In this picture the people are an abstraction reduced to numbers of gravestones. Those gravestones are markers for the men and women, the fathers and mothers, the sons and daughters, the blacks and whites, the Christians and Jews and Muslims, the generals and captains and sergeants and privates, all the individual people, each unique, who died for their country. But in this picture we don't see them as the unique individuals they are, they are simply represented as one among the many similar stones. What we see here is not the individuals, but the wholeness, the macro reality of war—lots of people die.

Courtesy of Corbis Images

Figure 11.1.1 A Macro Perspective on War

The micro reality of war looks like Figure 11.1.2. Individual human beings die. A person who was someone's daughter or son, someone's husband or wife, someone's mom or dad, someone's dear friend—a person is lost forever. The reality of war is a micro reality—the real fighting and suffering and dying takes place person by person. So, too, the joys of life: the loving, the growing, the becoming . . . Living is done at the micro level.

Figure 11.1.2 A Micro Perspective on War

But it is impossible to represent the wholeness of a social experience, like a war or an economic depression, person by person. These experiences are too big for that. So we represent the wholeness of such events by adding up the elements, by "aggregating" the individual realities into a form we can digest—like a number of people who died in World War II (by one estimate it was over 52,000,000), or a number of Americans who were unemployed at the depth of the Great Depression (by one estimate it was over 12,830,000 people).

Obviously macro representations can never do justice to the fullness of the micro realities. But it is often valuable to step into the macro perspective and study a subject at that level if only to get a sense of the wholeness of the subject. As we do so, however, we must keep clearly in our mind that behind the macro concepts and numbers we talk about there are many, many real people, and that ultimately the measure of any human event, whether it be war or peace, or, as, we will study here, depression or full employment, lies not in macro numbers but in the individual lives of the thousands or millions of people that those numbers are supposed to represent.

11.1.3 Why Study the Economy at the Macro Level: The Macroeconomic Perspective—The Whole as Greater than the Sum of Its Parts

Macroeconomics is a valuable tool for aggregating the micro reality to get a feel for the wholeness of society's experience. But there is more to the value of the macro perspective. It is not only a whole perspective, it is a distinct perspective that is valuable for its difference.

Macroeconomics is to microeconomics as the study of a forest is to the study of its trees. A forest is made up of trees, but it is more than the sum of its trees. There are characteristics of a forest, such as size, maturity, and growth rate that transcend any particular tree. Yet because these characteristics have implications for the strength and stability of the forest as a whole in the face of environmental disturbances, they have a bearing on the well-being of every tree in the forest.

The same can be said about the relationship between the micro and the macroeconomy. There are characteristics of any whole economy, such as size, maturity, and growth rate that transcend any individual. Yet because these characteristics have real implications for the strength and stability of the economy in the face of disturbances, they have a bearing on the well-being of every individual in that economy. We study micro and macroeconomics separately because the nature of the issues at each level is different. We do not study them separately because they are independent of one another. To consider them so would be as absurd as considering the forest independent of its trees.

11.1.4 Why Study the Economy at the Macro Level: Micro v. Macro—Summary

While the whole is in some sense greater than the sum its parts, the microeconomic system is the foundation of aggregate, macroeconomic events. We will see, for example, that if the micro system moves toward a Pareto optimal General Competitive Equilibrium, this will be reflected at the macro level as an economy moving toward producing the greatest feasible wealth for the nation and full employment. We will also find that if we relax our nice assumptions, the resulting inefficiency we found in the microeconomy will be reflected in the form of less-than-full-capacity production and the presence of unemployed resources in the macroeconomy.

11.1.5 Macro Analysis—The Basic Questions

Our macroeconomic model is designed to explore four basic aggregate questions:

1. Why doesn't the economy always produce up to its full capacity? For example, the U.S. had huge unrealized capacity during the Great Depression of the 1930s. What caused the problem? Why did it end? Can it happen again?
2. Why are some of society's resources (like people) sometimes unemployed? What causes unemployment to persist? During the Depression unemployment was very high for many years. What caused the problem? Why did it end? Can it happen again?
3. What causes the cost of living to go up, making living hard? For example, in the U.S. during the 1970s inflation made it difficult for many people to make ends meet. What caused the problem? Why did it end? Can it happen again?

4. Is it possible to live in an economy that is always at or moving toward full capacity and full employment with a nice, steady cost of living? And if so, how do we achieve that?
5. Is perpetual growth of the global economy sustainable? If not, is the human prospect a dismal one?

11.1.6 On Policy

These questions inevitably bring us to the issue of government policy. Some economists believe that each of the problems cited is caused by flaws in the market system and that government can play a constructive role in fixing each problem and thus in achieving the full capacity, steady price level economy envisioned in the fourth question. There are other economists who believe that in each of these cases the problem is essentially the product of foolish government policy, and all would be well if the government would simply keep its hands off the economy. As we did in micro, we will refer to these respective positions as *interventionist* and *non-interventionist*. Obviously these are polar cases. In fact, most economists take a position somewhere along a continuum between these two poles. While each economist probably has a bias toward one pole or the other, opinions about the role of government in specific cases are generally based on the specific issues of the case.

The goal here is not to convince you that either pole or any particular position along the continuum between the poles is right or wrong. The goal is to equip you to use the macro model to analyze your world and to see how thoughtful people can arrive at different views on the policy implications of the macro model. You will see that the basis for these differences lies in different assumptions. It is up to you to decide on your own assumptions and therefore your own views about policy.

11.1.7 Preview of What is to Come

In studying macroeconomics we will follow the same approach we used in studying microeconomics. We will begin by defining the terms necessary to build a model. We will then proceed to assemble the model. Once our macroeconomic model is constructed, we will practice with it by applying it to cases—in particular we will apply it to historical cases like the period that encompasses the Great Depression, World War II, and the immediate post-War period. The more you practice with the application of the model, the more adept you will become at applying it to today's news and today's commentaries about tomorrow's possibilities.

The goal here is to make you proficient with this economic model, this tool kit. If you can use it to analyze events of the past, then you will be in a position to understand its strengths and limitations and thus to put it to good use as you "look out the window" at events of today and the possibilities of tomorrow.

As I have told you before, these economic tools are like a hammer in a carpenter's tool kit. A carpenter cannot build much of value without a good hammer, but there is not much she can build with only a hammer either. Similarly, these economic tools alone are not sufficient to build a thoughtful analysis of the world around you, but they are essential to such work.

The educated carpenter works with a full tool kit. The value of the hammer is realized in skilled hands by combining it with a saw and a level and other key tools. With a full tool kit the carpenter builds things of lasting value. Similarly, if you combine the economic tools we will develop here with a rich appreciation of social and political theory and hone your skill with them by applying them in the context of history and anthropology, the tools you will develop here can become a part of a valuable tool kit for understanding your world as it has been, as it is, and as it might become in the years ahead.

11.2 Defining Terms

11.2.1 Introduction to Defining Terms

In order for you to understand the macroeconomic analysis that follows we have to be sure we are speaking the same language—in other words, you need to be clear about what I mean by the words I use. So as with micro, we start our exploration of macroeconomics by defining some terms. The first term we need to define relates to national production.

11.2.2 National Production—The Concept

The broadest measure of a nation's production and the term we will use to represent that production is *Gross Domestic Product* (hereafter *GDP*). The GDP is defined as the value of all the new production in the nation during a given year. We will distinguish between two measures of GDP: *Full, sustainable capacity GDP* and *Actual GDP*

Full, sustainable capacity GDP is the greatest level of production that the whole economy can maintain given the current endowment. If we imagine the size of a pie as representative of how much the nation can produce with its total initial endowment (all of its labor, natural resources, and capital), then full, sustainable capacity GDP is the biggest pie the nation can consistently produce.

Consider a non-economic example of this "full, sustainable" concept: The best pace you can sustain for many miles of traveling by foot is your full, sustainable pace. You can go slower, but then you would not be performing up to your capacity. You can sprint much faster, but you cannot sustain that level for the long haul. Full sustainable capacity is the best pace you can maintain. Full, sustainable capacity GDP is the best pace of production that an economy can sustain given the current endowment. Since this implies that resources are being used most efficiently, full sustainable capacity GDP is the level of production the macro economy achieves when the micro economy is functioning at Pareto optimality. One of the macroeconomic questions we will explore is: What determines a nation's full, sustainable capacity GDP?

This "full, sustainable capacity" term is pretty cumbersome. So to make our story easier to tell and easier to follow, from here on we will use the shorthand *full GDP* to represent full, sustainable capacity GDP.

In contrast to full GDP, the actual GDP is how much the nation is currently producing. Comparing the actual GDP to the full GDP is a gauge we use to measure the productive health of the economy. If the actual GDP is close to or at full GDP, then the macroeconomy is considered productively healthy. If, on the other hand, actual GDP is well below the full GDP, then productive resources must either be lying idle or they are being used inefficiently, or both—a very unhealthy condition.

Economists refer to an economy as productively healthy when the actual GDP is at or is approaching full GDP. But, if the actual GDP has been falling for over six months (two consecutive quarters of a year as economists say) that is called a *recession*, and if there is a prolonged, deep decline in the level of GDP that is called a *depression*.

11.2.3 National Production and National Well-being, a Caveat

While it is used as a gauge of national economic health, we need to be careful when we think of GDP as an indicator of the well-being of individuals in a society or as an indicator of general social welfare. Does more GDP necessarily mean that the people in that society are better off? We need to examine this proposition before we go on so we that we can keep the relationship between macro events (changes in GDP) and micro realities (individual human well-being) clear.

A growing GDP does mean more production, but more for whom? If as GDP expands a few rich people get richer while many more of the citizens get poorer, then that may not be a "better" society. Remember, aggregate measures obscure the underlying micro reality. In this case, the level of GDP is not a direct measure of the general standard of living in a country because this macro measure obscures the microeconomic distribution of wealth.

Another problem with GDP as a measure of social well-being is that this implies that increased human production invariably improves our world. This is, however, open to question. If we "harvested" all the trees in the world, GDP would reflect this "productive" activity. But this increase in productivity would come with dramatic, negative ecological consequences. If we then proceeded to burn all those harvested trees to produce energy, we might benefit from the energy. But we might also need to produce air filters to protect our lungs from the soot produced, and also dikes to keep back the rising sea levels caused by the global warming.

In this "tree" case, GDP would be expanded by the harvesting and burning as well as by the production of the filters and dikes to protect us from the externalities of our own production. But does this increase in GDP that reflects expenditures to protect ourselves from the negative externalities of our production and that comes at the expense of the viability of the planet for future generations represent a social welfare gain? This raises a question about the sustainability of continuous growth in the GDP, a question we will return to shortly.

GDP is a useful tool for keeping track of a nation's economic condition. But with GDP and with all the other macro concepts to come, we need to use them with a thoughtful appreciation for their strengths and their weaknesses. As with any aggregate variable, we must be careful to look behind this aggregate number if we want to understand the underlying micro reality: How are individuals in a society doing?

Now let's turn our attention to some labor-related terms

11.2.4 Labor-Related Terms—Labor Force

A nation's most precious resource is its people. Why is this resource sometimes less than fully utilized? Why are there times when people who want a job cannot find one, and what causes those times when this situation of unemployment becomes desperate—like during the Great Depression? What do we need to do as a nation to provide people the opportunity to make a livable, honest living from their labor?

In order to discuss labor and these labor-related questions we need to define some more terms. But first a note: Our definitions here are theoretical, and we will treat them as if they are easy to measure. Later, when we get to the technical definitions that the government actually uses to measure these concepts, we will see that measuring is at best problematic. But for now, as we develop our model, we will use the following theoretical definitions:

Labor force is the term we will use for all those persons who are participating in or who are looking for an opportunity to participate in the nation's productive activity. Clearly, people who do not want a job should not be counted in the labor force. We refer to this group as *voluntarily unemployed*. For example: If you had a job, worked and saved for many years so that you could retire, and then you do retire, you become voluntarily unemployed. Or if one day you win the lottery and decide to quit your job and live off your winnings, you become voluntarily unemployed.

Those people who want to participate in the nation's productive activity and are therefore in the labor force fall into two categories: *employed* and *unemployed*. The employed are those folks who have jobs, and the unemployed are those who do not have a job but want one. From here on when we use the term "unemployed" we are referring to these folks who want a job but do not have one—not to the voluntarily unemployed.

We represent the unemployment situation in an economy by a statistic called the *unemployment rate*. It measures the percentage of the labor force that is unemployed. The unemployment rate in the United States has ranged from highs during the Great Depression of as much as 25% to lows during World War II of as little as 1%. In order to understand what numbers like this mean for the economy we need to examine the concept of unemployment further. Combined within the unemployment rate number you hear in the news there are, in fact, three different kinds of unemployment, each distinguished by its cause.

11.2.5 Labor-Related Terms—Frictional Unemployment

Frictional unemployment is the case in which people are looking for jobs and there are appropriate jobs out there for them—they just have not found the jobs yet. Frictional unemployment exists because the *job search* process takes time.

Consider yourself for example: I assume you are working toward a degree, and you are hoping that your degree will help you get a good job. If, as you leave your graduation ceremony still decked out in cap and gown, you see a sign in the window of the local fast food restaurant that says: "Help wanted, apply within. " . . . Do you rush in and grab the job? It is a job. It is honest and respectable work. But it is not the job that you had in mind when you spent those long nights studying for an economics final exam. This job is not why you invested all that time and money in your human capital, in your education. You pass it up. You search for a better job.

Let's assume there is a good job out there for someone with your skills. Unless you're incredibly lucky, it is going to take you some time (and sweat) to find it. In our language, while you are searching you are frictionally unemployed.

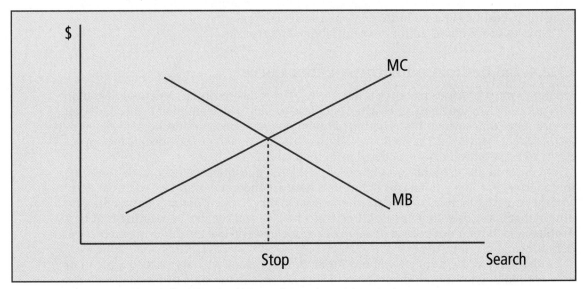

Figure 11.2.1   Marginal Benefits/Marginal Costs of Search and Stop Point

As you search you collect information, you adjust your expectations. ("OK, so I can't get a job in San Francisco.") In our economic terms, as shown in Figure 11.2.1, you keep searching until the rising marginal costs of further search (résumés, gasoline, stamps, ulcers, wages lost, risk of losing an available offer, and so on . . .) finally equal the falling marginal expected benefit of further search (the chance of getting a better offer).

In the aggregate, that is as a macroeconomic phenomenon, the quicker the search process can be completed the smaller the number of people who will be searching and thus the lower the frictional unemployment will be. But in healthy, growing economy the frictional unemployment will never be zero because job search does take time. Indeed, it is good for the economy when people take the time, as described in Figure 11.2.1, to find the optimal job because that insures that our labor and human capital resources will be allocated most efficiently.

The frictionally unemployed are those folks for whom there is a job that matches their skills, they just have not searched long enough to fine it yet . . . but they will.

11.2.6 Labor-Related Terms—Structural Unemployment

Another kind of unemployment is *structural unemployment*. As with frictional unemployment, the problem of structural unemployment is not a lack of jobs. With frictional unemployment the issue is search time; in the case of structural unemployment the problem is a mismatch between people's and jobs' requirements. Structural unemployment occurs because any healthy, growing economy is constantly going through technological transformations. For instance, when the economy went from carriages to cars, there were plenty of buggy whip makers who lost their jobs, and without some retraining they could not take the new mechanics jobs that became available. More recently, structural unemployment resulted when industrial jobs in some areas were disappearing even as high-tech jobs in other areas were expanding.

The only way to avoid structural unemployment is to keep the economy static. There was very little if any structural unemployment in feudal society. But a static society is clearly not desirable. Since structural unemployment is inherent in a changing economy, we can expect to find some structural unemployment in any dynamic, growing economy. It can be reduced by more speedily adjusting the skills of workers, but it cannot be eliminated.

11.2.7 Labor-Related Terms—The Natural Rate

Because economists expect to find both frictional and structural unemployment in a dynamic, healthy, growing economy they refer to the sum of these as the *natural rate of unemployment*. These forms of unemployment are a *natural* part of a dynamic, healthy, growing economy. Since even in the best of times economists expect that there will be some frictional and some structural unemployment, economists equate *full employment* with the natural rate of unemployment—NOT with zero unemployment.

If you see or hear or read an economist's assertion that, "Things are good. The unemployment rate is only 4.5%, so the economy is at full employment," that may not sound sensible. You might say to yourself: How can she say the economy is at full employment when there's 4.5% unemployment? Now you can understand. This economist believes that 4.5% is the natural rate. In the language of economists full employment does not mean the economy is at zero unemployment. It means the economy is at the natural rate of unemployment.

11.2.8 Labor-Related Terms—Demand-Deficient Unemployment

There is one more kind of unemployment, and this kind is one of the villains in our macro story. It is called *demand-deficient unemployment*. Recall that in the case of both frictional and structural unemployment there are enough jobs for everyone who wants one; the problem is one of searching or matching. Demand-deficient unemployment occurs when there are just not enough jobs for everyone who wants one. A central goal of macroeconomic policy is to avoid or eliminate demand-deficient unemployment, because its cost to society is high.

If the natural rate is 4% and the actual unemployment rate is 5%, that difference represents the demand deficient unemployment. It sounds like a very small number—1%. But that number represents the productive potential of literally millions of workers going to waste as they search or train in vain for a job. And the cost is really much greater than the lost production of this untapped human potential. Unemployment undermines self-esteem, it breeds dependence and depression, and, in the extreme, desperation. If a parent cannot find a job, her children will not have access to proper nutrition or health care. If a partner or parent who cannot find a job loses self-esteem, the other partner and/or the children suffer with that loss. For all in the family, unemployment makes life difficult at best and tragic at worst. The full costs of unemployment are both the social production lost and the individual suffering incurred when people who desire work cannot find a job.

The classic American case of soaring demand deficient unemployment is the period from 1929 to 1933 when the unemployment rate soared from 3.2 to 25 percent. Think about that. That transformation of the economy from one with lots of jobs to one of desperation took only four years. That is the time it takes to go through college. Imagine entering as a freshman in a world going wonderfully well and leaving college (if you could afford to stay) into a disaster. That is indicative of how quickly the macroeconomic conditions can change.

This dramatic rise in unemployment was the most tragic manifestation of that period called the Great Depression. Clearly, this rise in the unemployment rate was not due to frictional or structural problems as we have defined them. There were simply not enough jobs for millions of people who were ready, willing, and able to work—people who were desperately searching for work.

The Great Depression set the agenda for post-World War II economic thought. The primary policy objective of the generation of economists who came of age during the Depression was to avoid its repetition. That generation has largely passed from the scene and new issues dominate the current agenda, but any economic theory must still be judged by the standard: What does it tell us about the Depression experience? As you will see, each of the competing versions of "mainstream" macroeconomic theory—the interventionist and the non-interventionist—has an explanation for the Depression, and the debate over what really happened during the 1930s still goes on. Our purpose here is to understand the model and the sides in the debate, not to resolve the issue.

11.2.9 Price Level: Inflation and Deflation

Demand-deficient unemployment is not the only serious problem a macroeconomy can face. Another is *inflation* or *deflation*. Inflation is a rise in the overall level of prices in the economy and therefore a fall in the purchasing power of money. Deflation is a fall in the overall level of prices and therefore a rise in the purchasing power of money.

Let's be sure to distinguish a macroeconomic change in the price level from a microeconomic relative price adjustment. At the micro level, individual prices are constantly rising and falling—and this is good because each price must constantly adjust to signal changing supply and demand conditions and thus the changing value of a product or factor in the market. Under our nice assumptions such relative price changes provide signals that make it possible for individuals to allocate their resources and make purchases efficiently. These microeconomic relative price adjustments do not necessarily imply any change in the overall level of prices. Some rising prices may be offset by other falling prices.

Conversely, a rise in the price level need not imply any change in microeconomic relative prices. The price level, as the name implies, is the general position of prices in the economy at any point in time. If all prices doubled then the price level doubles, but relative prices remain the same. In fact if all prices rose by the same proportion the only thing that loses value in the economy is money. If prices doubled, that inflation reduces money's purchasing power by half.

11.2.10 Price Level: The Cost of Inflation/Deflation

Inflation or deflation imposes two kinds of costs on an economy—an efficiency cost and an equity cost. We will focus on inflation in our examples of these costs.

Undermining the usefulness of money constitutes the major efficiency cost of inflation. As explained earlier, money emerges in a market economy because it allows for more efficient exchange than a barter system. Money takes on three roles: a medium of exchange, a store of value, and a unit of account. When inflation is high money loses value quickly, so people are less willing to hold money or accept money or to use it as a measure of value. Thus inflation undermines money's role as a store of value, a medium of exchange, and a unit of account.

When inflation is plaguing an economy unpredictably it undermines lending and thus investing. Lenders have to wait to get their money back, and while they wait inflation eats away at the value of the money they will be paid back. If they are confident that they know what inflation to expect, they can build a charge into their loan rate to cover the expected inflation. If, however, inflation is unpredictable and they are not sure, then they have to charge a lot to cover the worst possible case, or they can avoid the risk by not lending at all. Since most investors in new equipment or education or the like need to borrow, such high charges or constrained lending means less investment. As we will see, less investment undermines the macroeconomy.

And finally, in the worst case when sustained inflation gets very *very* high people abandon the use of money altogether. In such an environment holding money for even a short period can mean a loss of almost all value. In this kind of inflation, called a *hyperinflation*, money is useless as a store of value, a medium of exchange, or a unit of account because its value is falling so quickly. By one account, during the early 1920s in Germany there was a period when the price level was doubling every two days.

These are examples of the efficiency costs of inflation. In each case the efficiency benefits money brings to an exchange economy are eroded by inflation.

There are also equity costs to inflation, because inflation can redistribute wealth. Anyone who is being paid a constant amount of money—a fixed wage for a job or fixed interest on a loan or a fixed retirement benefit—will lose in the face of inflation because the value of the money she receives is less and less as time goes on. For example, I started teaching junior high school in 1973 at a salary of $7,300/year. During that period inflation was high, but for three straight years I got a zero raise. On the face of it I made the same amount the second year as I did the first, but did I really? Suppose inflation was 10%. How much was that second year's salary really worth compared to my first year's salary? My checks still added up to $7,300, but the 10% inflation cost me $730 in buying power. The real value of my salary went down.

As noted above lenders worry about inflation too. If you are lending money, you lose with inflation because the money you get back is worth less than the money you lent. Lenders can try to protect themselves from this by charging more interest if they expect inflation, but this in turn creates efficiency costs since it makes loans more expensive and therefore investment less likely.

While lenders have to worry about inflation, if you are a borrower you have to worry about deflation. In a deflation, the money you are paying back is worth *more* than the money you borrowed so in effect it costs more and more to pay back the loan.

11.2.11 Indexing

One way people who are receiving payments like wages or interest try to protect themselves from loss in the face of inflation is by *indexing* the payments. An indexed payment is one that is automatically adjusted with changes in the price level. It is called indexing because indexes are a common measure of the price level changes. We will see how indexes are constructed shortly.

So, for example, if my wage is indexed and in a given year inflation goes up by 10%, my salary goes up 10% automatically to keep up with inflation. The index keeps the buying power of my wage constant. I could of course also try to negotiate a wage increase on top of the index adjustment so that my buying power goes up.

Loans can also be indexed. If, for example, I am paying a mortgage and my loan is indexed, my payments go up with inflation.

In effect indexing adjusts the nominal or face value of the payment in order to keep the real value of the payment constant.

11.2.12 Real versus Nominal Values

These terms *real* and *nominal* are new terms for our vocabulary. The distinction between them is important, so let's examine it carefully. A nominal value is the face value of anything. It is the value in name only, ergo "nominal". A real value is the underlying true value.

For example, suppose you are in a romantic relationship with someone who says she or he loves you and only you. Ah, the joy. . . . Then two nights later as you walk along basking in that joy, you hear from a bench in the shadows that same loving voice sharing those same melodious words. "Geeze," you think to yourself "that certainly sounds familiar." Sneaking a peek you discover that you are not the one and only, but alas you are one among the many. Nominally, you have been told you are loved. Really, don't count on it. In love as in all things, face values (nominal values) can be deceiving.

This distinction between nominal and real values is emphasized for two reasons. It is important during the development of our macro model. In addition, it is very important that you understand this distinction if you are to be an informed reader of current or historical macroeconomic data and/or an informed observer of debates over macroeconomic policy. As with love, so too with money: The face value of something measured in money may not clearly reflect its real value. Any macroeconomic variable that is measured in dollars or in dollars per something else (like per year) has a nominal and a real value. When you read or hear such variables used, to have any real idea of what they represent you need know if the values being cited are in nominal or in real terms. If you don't know that, you don't really know much of anything about what the data mean.

Consider GDP.

11.2.13 Real versus Nominal GDP

Look at this data on GDP in Table 11.2.1.

TABLE 11.2.1 GDP AND PRICE LEVEL DATA 1981–1982
(Source: Standard & Poors/DRI Basic Economics Tape)

YEAR (By Quarters)	GDP	PRICE LEVEL (GDP Deflator, 1992 = 100)
1981 - 3rd Quarter	3183.5	62.95
1981 - 4th Quarter	3203.1	64.10
1982 - 1st Quarter	3193.8	64.99
1982 - 2nd Quarter	3248.9	65.83
1982 - 3rd Quarter	3278.6	66.75
1982 - 4th Quarter	3315.6	67.45

How does it look like the economy is doing? Given these data it looks pretty good . . . wouldn't you say so? After all, there is only one small dip in GDP from the fourth quarter of 1981 to the first quarter of 1982, otherwise it's all about growth . . . or is it?

During this whole period the price level was rising. So what do you really know about the state of the economy during this period? Nothing until I tell you whether the GDP data you are looking at is real or nominal. If it is real, then this is indeed a pretty good growth period with only one dip. If it is nominal, you cannot tell much of anything. The GDP in Table 11.2.1 is nominal.

OK, now look at this data in Table 11.2.2—it shows the unemployment rate and the real GDP during this period.

**TABLE 11.2.2 NOMINAL GDP, PRICE LEVEL, REAL GDP, AND UNEMPLOYMENT RATE DATA
1981–1982**
(Source: Standard & Poors/DRI Basic Economics Tape)

YEAR (By Quarters)	NOMINAL GDP	PRICE LEVEL (1992 = 100)	REAL GDP (1992 Dollars)	UNEMPLOYMENT RATE (%)
1981—3rd Quarter	3183.5	62.95	5056.80	7.4
1981—4th Quarter	3203.1	64.10	4997.10	8.2
1982—1st Quarter	3193.8	64.99	4914.30	8.8
1982—2nd Quarter	3248.9	65.83	4935.50	9.4
1982—3rd Quarter	3278.6	66.75	4912.10	9.9
1982—4th Quarter	3315.6	67.45	4915.60	10.7

Pretty dramatic stuff, huh? These data reflect the fact that the 1981–82 period saw the U.S. suffer the worst economic downturn since the Great Depression—the first time unemployment went above double digits since the Depression. So you see, those original GDP numbers were nominal and they masked the underlying real downturn.

Nominal values of economic statistics are measured in current dollars—that is, in the face values when the measurements are taken. On the face of it a dollar in 1981 looks the same as a dollar in 1982. But in fact there was inflation during that period, so the real buying power of a dollar changed. During that period the real amount of GDP also changed. The combined effect of real and price changes is wrapped up in one number—the nominal value.

In this case, in all quarters except the end of 1981, the price level is rising faster than the real GDP is falling. Given this dominant price level effect, even as the real GDP is falling the face value of GDP, the nominal GDP, is rising. Now look at the real GDP—you can see it falls significantly. During this period the country was in a severe recession, but you would never know that from looking at the changing value of nominal GDP.

Nominal GDP is not a good measure when comparing the value of GDP across time. Changes from year to year in nominal GDP may reflect changes in real production (the actual physical output), changes in the price level, or changes in both. An increase in real production increases nominal GDP. An increase in the price level increases nominal GDP. The problem with comparing nominal GDP from year to year is that if the nominal value changes, we cannot know whether the change represents a real change in society's production, a change in the price level, or both.

11.2.14 The Real versus Nominal Distinction—Its General Importance

As with GDP, so too with all variables measured in money. Real values are the only values useful for comparisons over time and space. Nominal values are not useful for such comparisons unless they are accompanied by information about changes in price level that allows you to convert them into real terms. So be a wise consumer of economic statistics. Whenever someone cites such data, ask yourself: Is this real or nominal? If it is nominal, do I have the price level information necessary to factor the price effects out of the nominal to make it real?

Now let's look at the kind of price level information you need and how you can use it to adjust nominal values.

11.2.15 Price Index as a Measure of the Price Level

The government uses several methods to measure the price level, these include a *price index* and a *price deflator*. Here we will focus on how a price index is constructed because the price level measure that most people read or hear about in the news is the *consumer price index* or the *CPI*.

The CPI is supposed to measure the level of prices for the products consumers buy, so it includes milk but not missiles. You can envision the construction of the CPI as follows:

The government begins by identifying the items it expects to find in the "*market basket*" of a "normal" household. Obviously in the technical process of creating this index, issues like what is a normal household and what goes in the basket are problematic at best. We will address this issue in Chapter 19.

The concept of a market basket is broadly defined to include all the things a family consumes, not just those things one can buy at a supermarket. So in addition to food it includes units of clothes, housing, transportation, entertainment, and other consumer items.

For our purposes, in order to give a simple example of how the index is constructed, we will assume that a normal household lives like a grad student . . . on 10 jars of peanut butter, 10 jars of jelly, 100 loaves of bread, 10 dozen doughnuts, 100 gallons of milk, four sets of clothes, a bike, a cheap apartment, and a black-and-white TV.

Now imagine that the index developer has two price-scanning machines: One machine has prices from a *base year* built into it. The base year is whatever year the developer decides she is going to choose as the orientation point—price level changes will all be measured relative to the price level in the base year. The other scanner has prices from the *target year* built into it. The object is to see how the price level changed from the base year to the target year.

The index developer begins by pushing the market basket up to the scanner with the base year prices and determining the aggregate or total price of the market basket in the base year. See Table 11.2.3.

TABLE 11.2.3 CALCULATING THE COST OF THE MARKET BASKET IN THE BASE YEAR

BASKET ITEM	UNIT PRICE ON SCANNER IN THE BASE YEAR IN DOLLARS	COST IN BASE YEAR IN DOLLARS
50 jars of peanut butter	2.50	125.00
50 jars of jelly	1.50	75.00
100 loaves of bread	2.00	200.00
10 dozen doughnuts	5.00	50.00
100 gallons of milk	1.50	150.00
4 sets of clothes	40.00	160.00
a bike	50.00	50.00
a cheap apartment	3,600.00	3,600.00
a black-and-white TV	40.00	40.00
BASE YEAR TOTAL COST OF THE MARKET BASKET = $4,450		

Next she pushes the basket up to the scanner with the target year prices and determines the aggregate or total price of the market basket in the target year. See Table 11.2.4.

TABLE 11.2.4 CALCULATING THE COST OF THE MARKET BASKET IN THE TARGET YEAR

BASKET ITEM	UNIT PRICE ON SCANNER IN THE TARGET YEAR IN DOLLARS	COST IN TARGET YEAR IN DOLLARS
50 jars of peanut butter	3.00	150.00
50 jars of jelly	2.50	125.00
100 loaves of bread	2.50	250.00
10 dozen doughnuts	6.00	60.00
100 gallons of milk	2.00	200.00
4 sets of clothes	50.00	200.00
a bike	60.00	60.00
a cheap apartment	4,000.00	4,000.00
a black-and-white TV	50.00	50.00
TARGET YEAR TOTAL COST OF THE MARKET BASKET = $5,095		

She then divides the target year total by the base year total and multiplies by 100 (the multiplication transforms the decimal into a number scaled on 100). In our case the number (rounded) is:

$$5095/4450 \times 100 = 114$$

Thus in our sophisticated analysis 114 is the price index for the target year. Notice, if we target the base year itself the index is going to be 100.

$$4450/4450 \times 100 = 100$$

In effect, we can think of that price index of 100 in the base year as representing 100 cents, or a dollar. The index for any target year tells us how much money it takes in that target year to buy what a dollar buys in the base year. In our example it takes 114 cents in the target year to buy what 100 cents buys in the base year.

A price index, or alternatively a price deflator, is a number that represents the level of prices for a group of items in any year relative to the level of prices for those items in the base year. The "group of items" may be as large as all items in the economy or as small as only the items related to medical care. We have already learned about the CPI. In what follows we will refer on occasion to the *GDP Deflator*. The CPI is a measure of the price level for consumer items. The GDP deflator is a measure of the price level for all items included in the GDP.

With these indexes or deflators we can measure inflation from one point in time to another by simply calculating the percentage change in a particular price index or deflator over that period. For example, in our example above the inflation from the base year to the target year was:

$$(114–100)/100 = .14 \text{ or } 14\%$$

These price indexes or deflators are also the tools we need to transform nominal economic values into real values.

11.2.16 Adjusting a Nominal Value to Make It Real

To see how to take price level effects out of nominal values, we begin with the fact that nominal values combine two effects: real and price. Mathematically, we can represent the combined effects embodied in nominal values as follows:

Nominal value = (Real value) × (Price level)

Clearly, for a constant real value, as the price level changes the nominal value will too. In order to factor out this price effect, we can divide both sides of our equation by the price level. Doing so we end up with:

(Nominal value)/(Price level) = Real value

So in order to get real values, we need only divide the nominal value by an appropriate measure of the price level. As noted above, if we are measuring real consumer spending over time we can use the CPI. If we are measuring real GDP over time we can use the GDP deflator. The real data from the recession of the early 1980s in Table 11.2.2 are based on nominal measures of GDP adjusted with the GDP deflator. You can see by comparing the nominal and real values for GDP that adjusting for the price level is important—VERY important!

Now that we have our terms in place, let's use them to build our macro model. We begin by developing our Macro Picture—the representation of the macroeconomy that will be the central framework for our analysis.

12.0 The Basic Macro Model

12.1 Introducing Our Macro Picture

12.1.1 The Micro Graph versus the Macro Picture

> "Analytic effort starts when we have conceived our vision of the set of phenomena that caught our interest . . . The first task is to verbalize the vision or to conceptualize it in such a way that the elements take their places with names attached to them that facilitate recognition and manipulation, in a more or less orderly schema or picture."
> Joseph Schumpeter, *History of Economic Analysis*, 1954

When we studied the microeconomy we used a supply and demand graph to represent each individual market, and to analyze the activity in and among those markets. In our micro graphs the axes were price and quantity and the graph represented two relationships between these two variables—one based on the demanders' attitudes and one based on the suppliers' attitudes.

Now we want to analyze the economy from a different perspective—a macro-economic (aggregate) point of view. We need a picture that captures the macro-economic perspective as clearly and effectively as our simple supply and demand graph did the microeconomic perspective. But how do we sum up so much in a single picture? It is not as difficult as it might seem. A little picture can capture the essence of a complex scene if the details can be summed up and conveyed in efficient terms. That is in effect what we have done by defining real GDP and the price level. Real GDP aggregates the quantities of final products exchanged in the millions of micro markets. The price level represents the overall level of the prices determined in these millions of micro markets.

Since the questions we explore in macro . . .

- Is the economy producing at full capacity, at full GDP? And if not, why not?
- Is the economy providing employment for all who want to participate? Is it at full employment? And if not, why not?
- Is it possible for one to make a living without worrying about price rises making living hard? Is it possible to keep the price level pretty steady so people don't have to worry about the value of the money they'll be getting in the future? And if not, why not?

. . . all relate to real GDP and the price level, so a graph with real GDP and price level as the axes can capture the essential macro questions we want to explore.

Our Macro Picture, therefore, looks as shown in Figure 12.1.1, with price level (P) on the vertical axis and real GDP (Y) on the horizontal axis, with Y_F standing for the point along the Y-axis at which the economy is at full employment or full GDP.

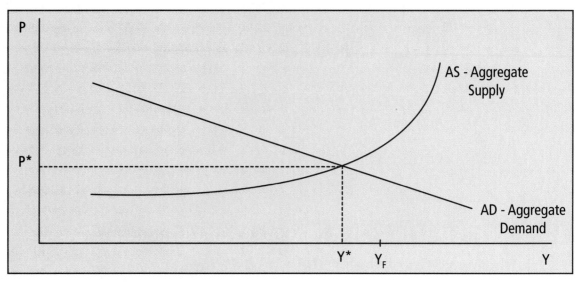

Figure 12.1.1 Our Macro Picture

12.1.2 Examining the Macro Picture

As shown in Figure 12.1.1, we will represent two macroeconomic relationships: *aggregate demand* (AD) and *aggregate supply* (AS). The intersection of these lines locates the point that represents the current condition in the macro economy. Given the AD and AS drawn in Figure 12.1.1, the current price level is P* and the current real GDP is Y*.

The aggregate demand line (AD) traces the relationship between the price level (P) and the real GDP (Y) demanded. The aggregate supply line (AS) traces the relationship between the price level (P) and the real GDP (Y) supplied. By examining the AD and AS relationships in detail, we will be able to understand why each line is shaped as it is and what conditions shift each line. Once we have mastered this we will be in a position to analyze how the forces that shift each line affect the macroeconomic conditions. This in turn will allow us to address the basic macroeconomic questions and analyze the debate over macroeconomic policy.

To get a feeling for the value of this graph as an analytical tool, let's preview how the Macro Picture can help us. In particular let's see how the Macro Picture represents that classic historical period we will use often as a case study: the time from the beginning of the Great Depression to the middle of World War II.

12.1.3 Look What We Can Do With the Macro Picture

For reasons we will explore in detail shortly, the Depression was caused by a dramatic decline in AD as represented in Figure 12.1.2. You can see there that as AD falls real GDP falls. This, in turn, means unemployment rises because we use less of our capacity (lower Y). That means more unemployed factors, including people. In Figure 12.1.2 the shift in AD also causes deflation, a falling price level. Falling AD, falling real GDP (Y), rising unemployment, and a falling price level—this is just what unfolded in the U.S. economy as the Great Depression seized hold of the nation. Our Macro picture represents this very effectively.

Then in the late 1930s World War II began. At first it raged in Europe and Asia with the U.S. as an observer. After the attack at Pearl Harbor on December 7, 1941, the U.S. became fully engaged.

War generates a lot of demand in the economy as the nation produces the material for battle. The war expanded AD immensely, increasing real GDP and bringing unemployment

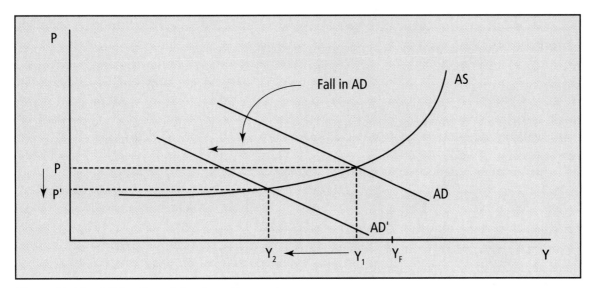

Figure 12.1.2 Fall in AD and the Great Depression

down to an amazingly low level. Figure 12.1.3 shows this expanding of AD, the growing real GDP, and the falling unemployment just as it occurred in the U.S. as World War II engulfed the nation.

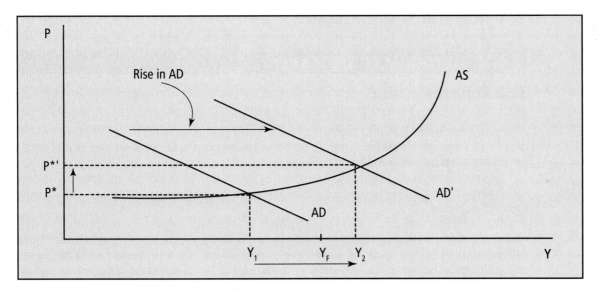

Figure 12.1.3 World War II and Expanding AD

Again, our Macro Picture represents the aggregate effects of these events very nicely. However, we need to understand the underlying forces that move AD to appreciate the economic impact of the events of this period more fully. Once we understand the forces that move AD, we will understand why the Macro Picture works so well.

Now let's look at a classic aggregate supply shock to the economy. For reasons we will explore in detail later, aggregate supply is moved by economy-wide changes in the cost of inputs into production. A broad rise in input costs shifts AS up. In Figure 12.1.4 we see what happens when AS shifts up: The economy experiences inflation, falling real GDP, and more unemployment. A classic case of such an event was the oil price shocks that hit the U.S. economy in the 1970s. Those shocks did indeed bring inflation, falling real GDP, and more unemployment. So the Macro Picture represents this case very effectively too.

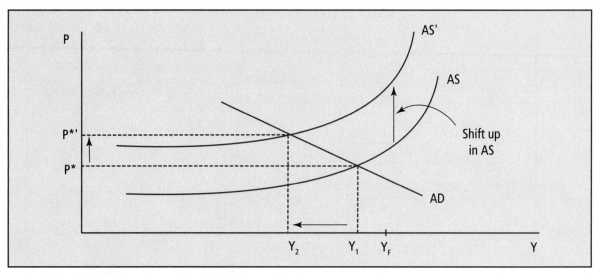

Figure 12.1.4 Oil Price Shocks and AS Shifting Up

The point here is that our Macro Picture is a very valuable tool for representing macroeconomic events. But to understand what it is representing we have to understand why the aggregate demand and aggregate supply are drawn as shown, and what forces move aggregate demand and aggregate supply. That brings us to the next step in our study: An examination of the AD and AS relationships.

We begin with the AD relationship.

12.2 AGGREGATE DEMAND

12.2.1 Introduction

Aggregate demand (AD) is the sum of all the *new* cars and books and haircuts and CDs and concerts and computers and factories and schools and roads and fighter planes and so on . . . all these goods and services that individuals and private enterprises and governments are prepared to purchase in a given year.

The real level of aggregate demand in the economy (Y) depends, therefore, on how much these individuals, enterprises, and governments are prepared to spend and on how much things cost.

The total nominal amount that individuals and enterprises and governments plan to spend is called the *aggregate expenditure* in the economy. Since aggregate expenditure (AE) is a nominal value—it is measured in current dollars—for any given level of aggregate expenditure the higher the price level (P) the less real GDP that amount of aggregate expenditure will buy.

The AD line represents the relationship between real GDP demanded (Y) and the price level (P) for a given level of aggregate expenditure (AE). In functional form we can write the AD relationship as

$$Y = AD (P \mid AE)$$

which means: the real GDP demanded (Y) is a function (AD) of the price level (P), given the level of aggregate expenditures (AE). The AD line that represents this relationship slopes down to the right because for a given level of aggregate expenditure (AE), as the price level (P) falls that amount spent (AE) buys more and more real GDP (Y).

In this AD relationship, aggregate expenditure is the shift variable. If aggregate expenditure rises then at any given price level (P) there is more spending taking place and so more real GDP can be purchased.

As shown in Figure 12.2.1, more AE will buy more at P_1, at P_2, and at P_3. Generalizing this idea, an increase in aggregate expenditure shifts the AD line to the right. If the aggre-

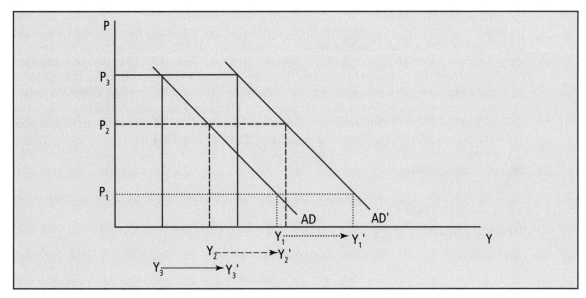

Figure 12.2.1 Increase in AE Shifting AD to the Right

gate expenditure falls, then at any given price level (P) there is less spending taking place and so less real GDP can be purchased. Generalizing, this change is represented by a shift of AD to the left. Since aggregate expenditure is the key to shifting aggregate demand, in order to understand the underlying forces that move aggregate demand we need to examine the components of aggregate expenditure.

12.2.2 Components of Aggregate Expenditure

There are six components of aggregate expenditure. Each is measured in nominal terms.

$$AE = C + I + G - T + X - M$$

"C" represents *consumption*: C stands for the total expenditures individuals make as consumers, purchasing things like clothes, food, concert tickets, new cars, and haircuts.

"I" represents *investment*: I stands for the total expenditures private enterprises make for items such as new plants, equipment, and inventories.

"G" represents the *government spending*: G stands for the total amount the government spends on roads, schools, the military, etc.

"T" represents net *government taxation*: T stands for the total funds the government takes out of the hands of individuals and enterprises in the form of taxes. We call it "net" because we need to exclude government taxation that merely passes resources from one person through the government to another person. Such transfer payments do not reduce the amount of funds in the hands of private citizens, they just change the hands that hold the funds—Social Security is the largest example of such a transfer program.

Notice that while we put a plus sign in front of G, we put a minus sign in front of T. Government spending (G) adds to aggregate expenditure, because every dollar the government spends is one more dollar of aggregate demand for our nation's production. In contrast, except for those dollars that are merely transferred, every dollar the government collects in taxes (T) reduces aggregate expenditure because it reduces the amount that individuals and enterprises have to spend on our nation's production. We call the combined effect of G and T the *net government budget position* (G–T). If (G>T), then the net government effect is to add to aggregate expenditures; if (G=T), then the net government effect on aggregate expenditures is neutral; and if (G<T), then the net government effect is to reduce aggregate expenditure.

"X" represents *exports*: X stands for the total amount of expenditures foreign buyers make for a nation's products.

"M" represents *imports*: M stands for the total amount of expenditures that domestic residents, enterprises, and government make for the products of other nations. Here again we see a plus, then a minus sign. Exports (X) are an addition to aggregate expenditures in an economy because they are additional expenditures on that nation's production—coming from outside that nation. Imports (M) are a subtraction from the nation's aggregate expenditure because they are expenditures that are leaving the domestic economy and being spent on the production of another nation. The combined effect of exports and imports (X-M) is the referred to as the *trade balance*. If (X>M), then the net trade balance effect is to add to aggregate expenditures; if (X=M), then the net trade balance effect on aggregate expenditures is neutral; and if (X<M), then the net trade balance effect is to reduce aggregate expenditure.

12.2.3 Summary

To summarize:

$$Y = AD (P \mid AE)$$

while

$$AE = C + I + (G - T) + (X - M)$$

Replacing AE with its actual components, we can rewrite the functional form of the AD relationship as:

$$Y = AD (P \mid C, I, G, T, X, M)$$

where the "given" variables to the right of the vertical line (C, I, G, T, X, and M) are the shift variables with respect to the AD relationship. A change in any one of these variables shifts the AD line.

Those that are additions to aggregate expenditure (C, I, G, and X) shift AD to the right when they increase. An increase in any one of these means there is more aggregate expenditure at any given price level and thus more real GDP demanded as shown in Figure 12.2.1. The increase in government spending (G) that came with World War II is an example of this.

A decrease in any of these variables (C, I, G, and X) shifts the AD to the left as shown in Figure 12.2.2.

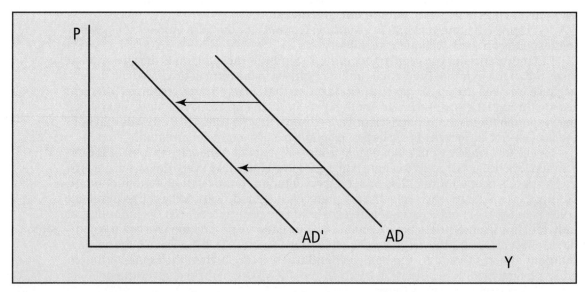

Figure 12.2.2 *Ceteris Paribus*, Falling Consumption (C), Investment (I), Government Spending (G), or Exports (X); or Rising Taxes (T) or Imports (M) Shifts AD Left

Also reflected in Figure 12.2.2 is the fact that those variables that are subtractions from aggregate expenditure (T and M) shift AD to the left when they *increase*. This is so because an increase in either of these means there is less aggregate expenditure on domestic production at any given price level and thus less real GDP is being demanded. A decrease in one of these variables (T or M) shifts the AD to the right. For example, *ceteris paribus*, a reduction in taxes means more funds in private pockets to spend, so AD shifts out.

To see the power of a shift in action let's return to our classic case, the Great Depression, and look at the impact of falling investment (I) on AD and the macroeconomy.

TABLE 12.2.1 THE GREAT DEPRESSION
From Economic Report of the President, 1954, Tables G-2, G-16
(Billions of dollars, 1953 prices)

YEAR	INVESTMENT (I)	REAL GDP (Y)	UNEMPLOYMENT RATE
1929	34.2	175.9	3.2
1930	23.3	159.2	8.7
1931	14.7	147.7	15.9
1932	3.3	125.3	23.6
1933	3.7	123.4	24.9

Table 12.2.1 reflects the fact that the Depression took hold in the United States from 1929–1933 as the level of investment plummeted to almost nothing. As investment contracted dramatically GDP followed. In turn, with falling production there were fewer and fewer jobs so unemployment soared.

As shown in Figure 12.2.3—in terms of our Macro Picture, *ceteris paribus*, the dramatic fall in I caused AD to move left. With this the real GDP fell. Hand in hand with such a fall, unemployment rises. Later we will study the sources of the forces that caused Investment to fall. For now we can see that if we understand the forces that move AD around in our Macro Picture, we can represent real events like the Great Depression very powerfully.

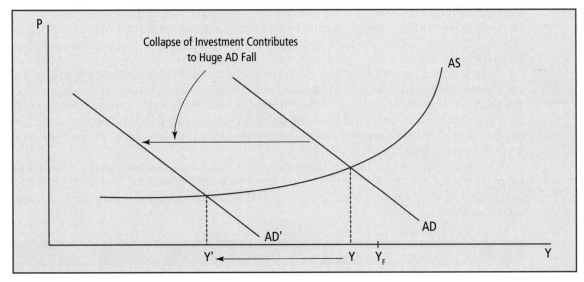

Figure 12.2.3 The Great Depression

12.2.4 Now You Try It

Now you try it: On December 7th 1941, the Japanese military attacked Pearl Harbor. This thrust the United States into World War II. As the United States mobilized for the war government spending increased dramatically. Soldiers were outfitted and trained, guns, tanks, ships, and planes were manufactured, and people previously excluded from factory jobs (women and minorities) were recruited and trained. Take out a scratch piece of paper, draw a Macro Picture with an initial condition that represents the high unemployment of the Depression, then draw a new AD line that reflects how this sudden and dramatic increase in G, *ceteris paribus*, caused by the war moved the macroeconomy. . . . OK, now let's see if you are getting this:

The effect of the military spending associated with the United States' entry into World War II was a government-stimulated expansion of AD. As a result of this dramatic increase in G, the U.S. went from the Great Depression to one of the lowest levels of unemployment in its history. Figure 12.2.4 represents this as a shift in AD to the right, increasing real GDP and decreasing unemployment.

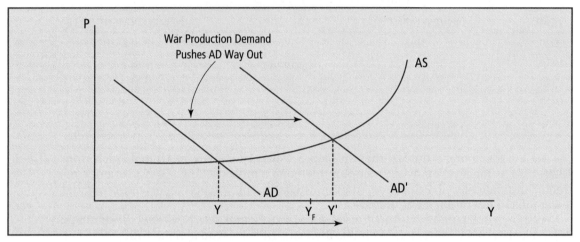

Figure 12.2.4   From the Great Depression to World War II

The wartime expansion was in fact so dramatic that, as shown in Figure 12.2.4, it pushed the economy to produce beyond its full sustainable capacity. Wartime is a classic example of this case of production beyond full sustainable capacity. Such production is not sustainable for the long run because people and factories are being worked long hours, "for the duration" as the wartime language called it. This pace of production could not be sustained indefinitely.

Also notice in Figure 12.2.4 that given the shape of the AS line, a shape we will examine shortly, we would expect this high level of AD to stimulate inflation. In fact, however, the price level did not continue to rise during the war. It didn't, because knowing such inflation could be expected and knowing inflation would undermine national morale, for the duration of the war the government imposed price controls and rationing on the home front in order to keep inflation in check.

Two things should be clear at this point: First, AD is an essential piece of our macro story. And second, since telling the macro story depends on AD *and* AS—if we are going to tell the full story we also need to understand aggregate supply. So now let's turn our attention there.

12.3 AGGREGATE SUPPLY

12.3.1 Intro to LAS

The *aggregate supply* line represents the relationship between the price level and the real GDP produced in the economy. There are actually two different aggregate supply lines.

One represents the *long run aggregate supply* conditions. The term "*long run*" as we define it here is not a certain amount of time. It is the macro condition that is reached when given the current social endowment all microeconomic adjustments have been completed under our nice assumptions. Thus *it is the macroeconoimic condition when the microeconomy has reached a Pareto optimal, general competitive equilibrium.*

If the microeconomy is at this most efficient condition, then the macroeconomy is producing as much as it can—the biggest possible pie, to use that image. Thus, as we define it here, the long run is the macroeconomic condition when the economy has reached full GDP or full employment.

How much actual time this could take depends on the underlying micro conditions. If market power and market failure are not problems, micro adjustments can be pretty rapid, and the macro long run can be achieved that rapidly. If power and/or failure are big problems, the micro system might never reach Pareto optimality, and thus the macroeconomy would never reach the long run condition. So, getting to the long run condition might be a month or a year or a lifetime, or it may never happen at all. But whatever you may think about the micro adjustment process and the possibility of reaching the macro long run condition, for our purposes when we refer to the long run we mean an economy that has reached Pareto optimality at a micro level and full GDP or full employment at the macro level.

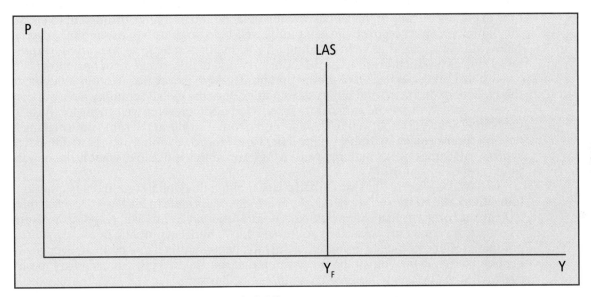

Figure 12.3.1   Long Run Aggregate Supply (LAS)

We represent the long run aggregate supply line (LAS) graphically as shown in Figure 12.3.1—a vertical line at full employment, Y_F, in our Macro Picture. It is vertical because the full, sustainable capacity is determined by the society's current endowment: the quantity and quality of available natural resources, labor, and capital. Since in the long run as we have defined it here we always reach the full-employment real GDP (Y_F), the LAS is a vertical line at Y_F. It is independent of the price level.

12.3.2 LAS Shift Variables—The Very Long Run

Since society's endowment (natural resources, labor, and capital) and technology determine the level of Y_F (and thus its relative position on our Macro picture x-axis), clearly any change in this available endowment and/or technology will change the level of Y_F and in turn shift the LAS line. We define the *very long run* as the period in which the endowment and/or technology change thus shifting the LAS.

When the LAS shifts to the right this is referred to as *economic growth* because it represents a growth in the economy's full sustainable capacity. In a growing economy the LAS is steadily shifting to the right because over time the social endowment is growing as population grows, capital "deepens" with successive periods of investment, the pool of available natural resources expands with exploration and discovery, and improving technology increases the productivity of this growing endowment.

It is possible for Y_F to shift rapidly in either direction. A contraction of Y_F can occur with tragic speed as the result of natural disasters like an earthquake or a hurricane, or due to human disasters like war. Extraordinarily rapid growth in Y_F can occur during periods of accelerated investment, dramatic innovation, or immigration. But the current standard model suggests that the desirable case is steady growth of GDP at a rate that makes possible a growing standard of living for our growing population.

Is that goal for the human prospect sustainable?

In 1798 in his *Essay on Population*, Thomas Robert Malthus imagined that the human prospect is a world of misery because, by his calculations, population growth would inevitably outstrip production growth (i.e., population would grow faster than Y_F). Mainstream economists have long dismissed this "Malthusian" logic arguing that Malthus overestimated the growth rate in population and underestimated the capacity of economies to grow. The ensuing 200+ years seem to vindicate this optimistic response to Malthus. Population has grown but, globally, production has outstripped it. So while too many people still live in poverty many more live in varying degrees of material well-being. As I write, vast populations of India and China and Russia and other growing economies are beginning to enjoy the fruits of the global division of labor and exchange through markets, so the human prospect seems to be expanding well-being rather than expanding poverty. The key to this success has been avoiding what economists refer to as *the stationary state*, for as long as production grows the Malthusian world of misery need not be a threat.

But this brings us back to a theme that has weaved its way through our analysis: Is this global expansion of production sustainable? Does the global economy have the sustainable capacity to expand sufficiently so as to provide increasing well-being for those in the United States, Europe, Japan, Canada, and so on . . . while at the same time making it possible for the citizens of India, China, Russia and other developing nations to ultimately achieve this same level of material well-being? And, if this is feasible, what is the opportunity cost of this growth?

In 1848, long before there was broad concern about this global sustainability question, John Stuart Mill addressed concerns about the stationary state in his book *The Principles of Political Economy*. In a chapter titled "Of the Stationary State" Mill responds to those who argue that that humankind has addressed the Malthusian problem because material production can continue to grow sufficiently to adequately feed and cloth an ever growing population. Reflecting on the proposition that the material growth necessary to satisfy a growing population is indeed sustainable, Mill writes:

> There is room in the world, no doubt, and even in old countries, for a great increase of population, supposing the arts of life to go on improving, and capital to increase. But even if innocuous, I confess I see very little reason for desiring it. The density of population necessary to enable mankind to obtain, in the greatest degree, all the advantages both of co-operation and of social intercourse, has, in all the most populous countries, been attained. A population may be too crowded, though all be amply supplied with food and raiment. It is not good for man to be kept perforce at all times in the presence of his species. A world from which solitude is extirpated, is a very poor ideal. Solitude, in the sense of being often alone, is essential to any depth of meditation or of character; and solitude in the presence of natural beauty and grandeur, is the cradle of thoughts and aspirations which are not only good for the individual, but which society could ill do without. Nor is there much satisfaction in contemplating the world with nothing left to the spontaneous activity of nature; with every rood of land brought into cultivation, which is capable of growing food for human beings; every flowery waste of natural pasture ploughed up, all quadrupeds or birds which are not domesticated for man's use exterminated as his rivals for food, every hedgerow or superfluous tree rooted out, and scarcely a place left where a wild shrub or flower could grow without being eradicated as a weed in the name of improved agriculture. If the earth must lose that great portion of its pleasantness which it owes to

things that the unlimited increase of wealth and population would extirpate from it, for the mere purpose of enabling it to support a larger, but not a better or a happier population, I sincerely hope, for the sake of posterity, that they will be content to be stationary, long before necessity compels them to it.

It is scarcely necessary to remark that a stationary condition of capital and population implies no stationary state of human improvement. There would be as much scope as ever for all kinds of mental culture, and moral and social progress; as much room for improving the Art of Living, and much more likelihood of its being improved, when minds ceased to be engrossed by the art of getting on.

Mill raises an important issue. Assuming that we can expand global economic production to accommodate a growing population, do we want to? Is growth the only or the desirable solution to the Malthusian prospect of an overpopulated world in misery; or is growth, ironically, a path to just such a world? All choices have opportunity costs and the cost of such an expansion to a larger global productive capacity might be the very nature of the earth that we hold dear. And in this day and age the question of opportunity cost is even more complex. Not only do we face the prospect Mill envisions, that growth for the purposes of material expansion might result in an earth that is not so sweet a place to live. Today we face the prospect that such growth is not in fact sustainable because it will make the earth unlivable.

These issues of growth and sustainability are incredibly complex. We all want to live better, and those across the globe who see how well we live have a legitimate right to aspire to our standard of living. So how do we constructively address these aspirations in a sustainable way? Is it possible given the current model of production and consumption? Is there an alternative model that would make it possible? Is it impossible? When we consider the very long run, these questions and the issues they raise must be addressed.

Our objective in this introduction to economic ideas and issues is to master the current mainstream model so that you can thoughtfully and systematically inform yourself about and add your voice to the conversations/debates on current events and policies. In the analysis that follows we will assume the LAS is stationary and focus on "long run" questions: Given the resource base of the economy (i.e., given the social endowment), what forces move the macroeconomy toward or away from full employment? What forces cause inflation or deflation? Since the LAS serves as our orientation line with respect to full employment and inflation in our Macro Picture, it is a key reference line in our analysis.

But, as we consider the policy debates regarding long run economic challenges, keep in mind that these policies must be informed by the very long run consequences that follow from them. Long run policies are a long run to a dead end if they do not address the very long run issue of sustainability.

12.3.3 Short Run Aggregate Supply (AS)

Another key macroeconomic question we will address is: What forces cause the price level to rise or fall? What causes inflation or deflation? The line that will be crucial in our analysis of inflation or deflation is the *short run aggregate supply* line, which we will label AS and which we will often refer to simply as the aggregate supply line.

We have defined the long run as the condition in which all the micro adjustments are completed under our nice assumptions. In contrast, the *short run* is the condition in which some of those microeconomic market adjustments have not been completed. Specifically, we will assume that in the short run the factor markets have not adjusted. Thus, along a given short run aggregate supply line, factor prices (for example, wages) are constant.

In our Macro Picture the short run aggregate supply line (AS) looks as shown in Figure 12.3.2. It represents the relationship between the amount of real GDP the economy is actually supplying, Y, and the level of output prices, P, when factor prices (in other words, input prices like wages) are constant. The shape of the AS line indicates that, for a given

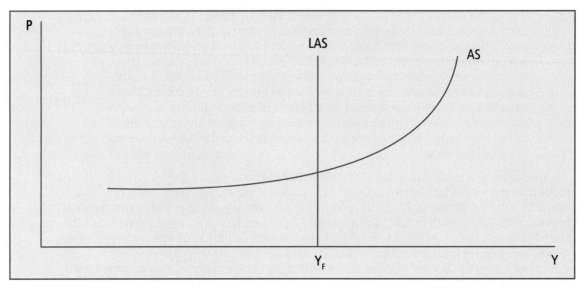

Figure 12.3.2   Short Run Aggregate Supply

level of factor prices, as the economy is pushed to produce more and more real GDP—it can do so at first without any effect on the output price level, P. But as AS approaches the LAS line it turns up, reflecting the fact that at some point producing more real GDP causes the output price level (P) to begin to rise. The sharp upturn in AS represents the fact that pushing production beyond full GDP (Y$_F$) causes significant inflation in the output price level. But if factor prices are constant, why does expanding production at some point stimulate inflation? To understand this let's analyze the AS line in three segments from left to right, examining what is going on along each segment.

12.3.4 Analysis of AS's Shape—Intro and the "k" segment

Figure 12.3.3 shows the AS line divided into segments labeled: *k, l*, and *m* respectively.

Anywhere along the *k* segment of the aggregate supply line the real GDP supplied is significantly below full-employment real GDP, Y$_F$. In this case there are large quantities of

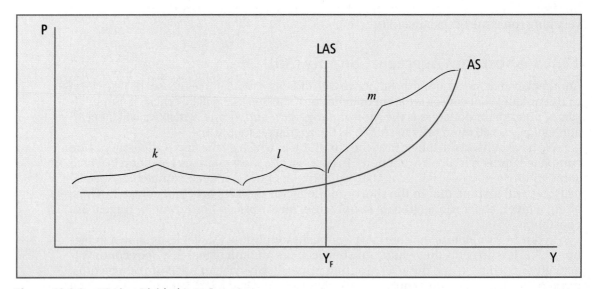

Figure 12.3.3   AS Line Divided Into Segments

idle factors—many closed factories and unemployed workers. Economists often refer to this as an economy with a lot of "slack" in it. In the Great Depression the economy was far to the left along the AS line—not producing much with lots of empty factories and unemployed workers.

To move along the AS line to the right represents expanding the real GDP produced. This can be accomplished by putting these idle factors, these people and factories, to work. All the factors necessary to produce are there. Drawing these factors—such as workers who are ready, willing, and anxious to work—into the production process is as simple as offering them an opportunity. Since, as we have assumed, factor prices are constant during this expansion along AS, there is nothing in this process of expansion along the *k* segment of the AS line that puts any pressure on the cost of producing. Therefore along this *k* segment, as real GDP supplied increases the prices of products, and thus the general output price level, P, remains constant. We can see an example of this in the case of the latter years of the Great Depression. As production expanded, the country pulled in lots of slack with no pressure on the price level.

12.3.5 Analysis of AS's Shape—the "l" segment

Along the *l* segment things begin to change. As the real GDP supplied approaches full GDP (full-employment), production bottlenecks *may* begin to occur because it is unlikely that all sectors of the economy will reach their capacity at precisely the same time. Bottlenecks put cost pressures on the production process as enterprises need to wait for intermediate goods to arrive. For example, bottlenecks in the steel industry would raise prices in the automobile industry. Cost pressures from such bottlenecks may show up in the economy as higher output prices. The *l* segment of AS represents this by the way it starts to turn up as the AS approaches the LAS—pushing the economy to produce more real GDP, Y, is causing higher price level, P.

The AS line will start to rise when production cost pressures begin, and these pressures *may* begin even before the macroeconomy has reached full, sustainable capacity (Y_F). Then again, they may not. As we will see when we get to policy, a debate about the shape and length of this *l* segment of the AS line *plays a central role* in the larger debate about when and if the government should intervene in the macroeconomy.

The shape of this segment determines how far the economy can be pushed without causing inflation and where the *l* segment ends determines when the economy has reached its full, sustainable capacity. Beyond that point the economy enters the *m* segment of the AS line.

12.3.6 Analysis of AS's Shape—the "m" segment

Along the *m* segment of the AS line the economy has passed the limits of its full, sustainable capacity (Y_F). The macroeconomy can do this for some period of time, but it cannot sustain this level of production given the current endowment because people and machines are being worked harder than they can sustain in the long run (just as you can sprint, but you cannot sustain that pace for long). Labor works overtime, factories are run on extra shifts, and inferior resources (like marginal land) are brought into use. All of these pressures drive up the short-run costs of production (for example with overtime pay) even as basic factor prices remain constant.

These cost pressures show up in the microeconomy as higher output prices and in the aggregate macroeconomy as a rising price level—inflation. The more we try to push the economy beyond its sustainable capacity the greater these pressures get. In the vernacular, economists say that these pressures are causing the economy to "heat up." The steep upturn in the AS represents the fact that at some point more pressure creates lots of heat (inflation), but very little light (production). For instance, people who are already working 60 hours a week (40 at regular pay and 20 at double pay) would have to be paid triple pay to get them to work 10 more hours a week. But those last 10 hours put in by exhausted workers would produce hardly anything. The rising **m** segment of the AS line shows that putting too much pressure on the economy produces little more than inflation.

TABLE 12.3.1 WORLD WAR II AND THE MACRO ECONOMY
From Economic Report of the President, 1954, Tables G-2, G-16, A-1
(Billions of dollars, 1953 prices)

YEAR	REAL GDP	UNEMPLOYMENT RATE (%)	INFLATION (%)
1939	187.9	17.2	-1.0
1940	205.7	14.6	2.0
1941	239.2	9.9	5.9
1942	271.7	4.7	6.5
1943	305.9	1.9	2.6

A classic example of this can be seen in the case of World War II. Table 12.3.1 reflects the fact that as the war began and heated up, so, too, did the economy as the home front strained to produce as fast as possible to supply the troops. The real GDP increased dramatically and unemployment fell to amazing lows. At the outset the heat, inflation, also began to show up. The only reason it stopped was because the government put rationing and price controls in place to stop what would have otherwise been an inevitable and disheartening inflation. But if the nation was going to run as market economy these government controls on prices were not sustainable. After all, price controls shut down the very mechanism that a market economy works on: price signals. Only the exigencies of war made these policies acceptable, as the term went, "for the duration."

12.3.7 Analysis of AS—Shape Review, and Shifts

To review: the three segments shown in Figure 12.3.3 make up the short-run aggregate supply line, AS. The AS line represents the positive relationship between the output price level (P) and real GDP supplied, when basic factor prices are constant. The relationship is positive because as output approaches and surpasses Y_F pressures on the cost of production grow. *The shape of the AS and the position of Y_F are central to our analysis.* At many steps along the way, as I describe shifts in AD that take us along the AS line I will often note: The inflationary consequence of the AD shift depends on the shape of the AS line. This is so because the AS represents how production cost pressures show up in output prices and more generally in a rising price level as more demand pressure is put on the economy.

In the case of the AS line factor prices have been assumed constant. In the case of the LAS line, all adjustments including factor prices have been completed under our nice assumptions. But what about the intermediate case: How do we represent changing factor prices in our Macro Picture?

While along a given AS line the factor prices are constant, changing factor prices are the shift variables of the AS line. Rapid changes in technology—by changing the basic structure of production costs—can also shift the AS line, but we will focus on factor prices because historically these have been the most volatile source of AS shifts. So, for example, if wages across the economy rise this general rise in a basic factor price will shift the AS line. How?

Widespread wage increases raise costs of production across the entire economy. To the degree they can, suppliers pass along these cost increases by charging higher output prices. Graphically a rise in factor prices shifts the AS line up, as shown in Figure 12.3.4. This is so because for any level or real GDP supplied the output price level would be higher. Conversely, a fall in factor prices shifts the AS line down, because for any level or real GDP supplied the output price level would be lower.

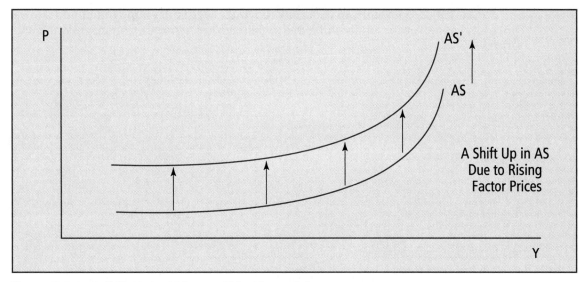

Figure 12.3.4   A Shift Up in AS Due to Rising Factor Prices

12.4 COMBINING AD, LAS, AND AS

12.4.1 Presenting Our Macro Picture and Reviewing Its Value

Now that we have developed our AD, AS, and LAS tools for macro analysis, let's put them together in our Macro Picture and use them as a tool kit to represent the macroeconomy. The value of our Macro Picture is that it can represent any particular macroeconomic condition, or changing macroeconomic conditions. Let's look at some cases:

Figure 12.4.1 represents an economy suffering increasing unemployment due to a falling aggregate demand.

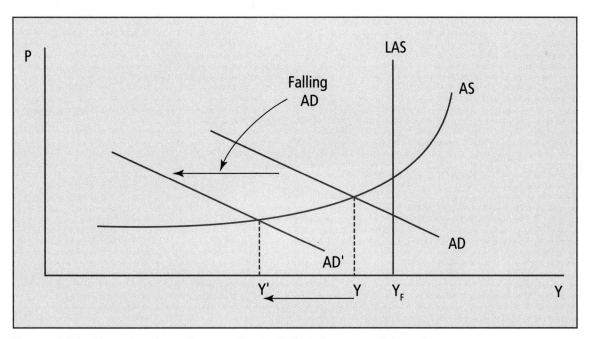

Figure 12.4.1   Increasing Unemployment Due to Falling Aggregate Demand

Figure 12.4.2 represents an economy moving toward full employment and a lower price level as aggregate supply shifts due to falling costs of production from lower factor prices.

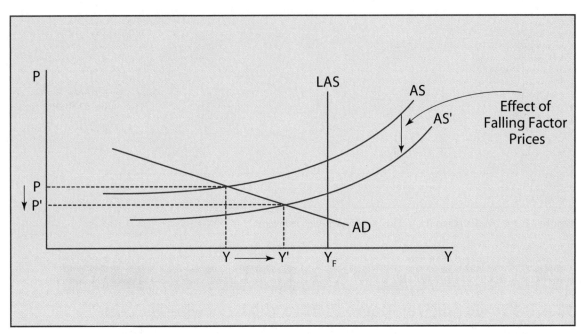

Figure 12.4.2   Falling Unemployment and Falling Price Level As AS Shifts Down Due to Falling Factor Prices

Figure 12.4.3 represents an economy experiencing inflation and increasing unemployment due to rising costs of production caused by a widespread rise in factor prices.

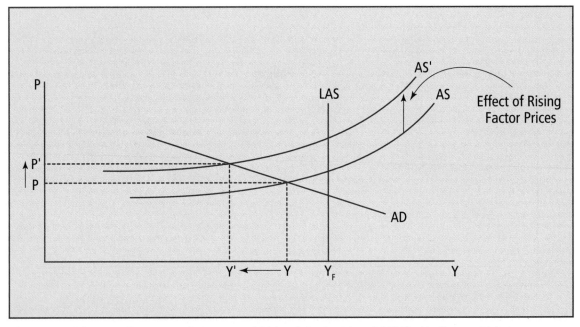

Figure 12.4.3   Increasing Unemployment and Rising Price Level as AS Shifts Up Due to Rising Factor Prices

Figure 12.4.4 represents an economy in which expanding aggregate demand is lowering unemployment to levels even below the natural rate. This pressure on the production system to keep up this unsustainable pace is causing inflation.

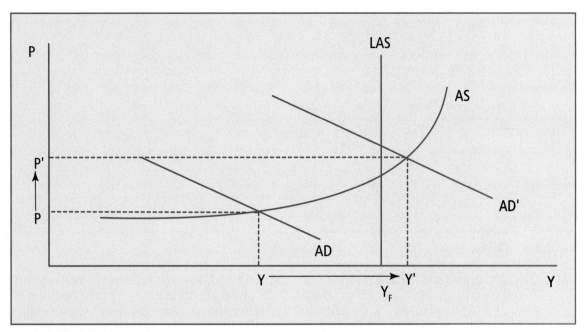

Figure 12.4.4 Falling Unemployment and Rising Price Level Due to Increasing Aggregate Demand

12.4.2 A More Complex Case—The Wage-Price Spiral

And finally consider this more complex, very interesting case that has actually occurred, that could happen again, and that our Macro Picture can represent very nicely.

Suppose you are working, making $55,000 a year, and that the current economic condition is the case shown in Figure 12.4.4: a *tightening labor market*—in other words there are plenty of jobs, but there is also inflation.

What is happening to the real value of your wages? If the nominal value of your wages is constant the real value, and therefore your standard of living, is going down. Is this a big deal?

Suppose inflation is 10% this year. How much buying power—in dollars—will you lose this year? If your nominal wage is $55,000, 10% of that is $5,500; so you are taking a real hit to your lifestyle as inflation eats up the buying power of your money. What do you do? You ask for a raise. After all, the labor market is tight, so there are plenty of other jobs. If your employer wants to keep you she has to in effect bid for you. To be attractive that bid, the wage offer you get, ought to at least keep you up with inflation, and probably more.

And you are not alone—all workers are in the same boat, so all workers have the same incentive as you do: To ask for a wage increase that at least protects them from inflation. And given the tight labor market, most workers (but not all—there are inevitably some sectors, especially low-skilled sectors of the labor market, that are left behind)—anyway, most workers are in the same good position you are to bargain for a higher wage.

Now if across the economy workers are bargaining for and getting a higher wage, *ceteris paribus* this dynamic shows up in our Macro Picture as represented in Figure 12.4.5. Widespread wage increases mean widespread factor price increases and therefore higher costs of production. This shows up in our Macro Picture as a shift up in AS.

With this wage story in mind, let's go back to the condition that set off this general wage rise—an increasing AD is lowering unemployment, and the pressure that it puts on the economy sets off inflation. Graphically the condition in the economy moves from condition #1 (Y_1, P_1) to condition #2 (Y_2, P_2).

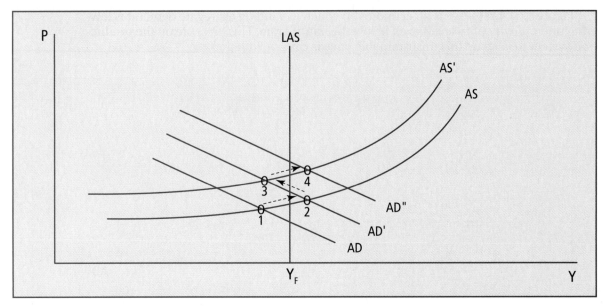

Figure 12.4.5 A Wage-Price Spiral

Now let's add the wage response we just described. As wage demands to keep up with inflation permeate the economy the AS shifts up taking the economy from condition #2 (Y_2, P_2) to condition #3 (Y_3, P_3) reflecting the higher output prices required to cover higher costs. But now the workers have higher incomes to cover the higher costs, so at least in nominal terms consumption (C) expands increasing AD—moving the economy from condition #3 (Y_3, P_3) to condition #4 (Y_4, P_4). And with this rising price level workers continue to ask for higher wages, raising AS, which is followed by expanding AD as workers use their higher wages to consume. Well, you can see where this is going: Around and around the spiral goes as wages chase prices and prices reflect higher wages. Indeed this economic dynamic is referred to as a *wage-price spiral*.

A wage-price spiral is a very perverse reality that takes on a life of its own and is hard to stop. Clearly and reasonably workers want to keep up with rising prices, and just as clearly and just as reasonably enterprises want to keep up with rising costs. Both are reasonable responses to the situation, but the combination of these motives feeds into the spiral. Neither the workers nor the enterprises want to be the first to say "enough" and stop asking for higher wages or prices respectively—each wants to at least catch up with the very last move on the other side of the process. And so it goes.

This dynamic is all the more virulent when workers do the reasonable and rational thing: Ask that their wages be indexed. If they get an indexed wage then the feedback loop from prices to wages is automatic and quick, making the spiral all the more dynamic.

This is not a story of good versus evil: good workers versus evil capitalist pigs, or greedy unions versus noble entrepreneurs. This is a story of both workers and enterprises simply trying to keep up with inflation—a reasonable objective on both their parts. Having said that, it is a very difficult problem to eliminate, and like demand-deficient unemployment, one we want to avoid.

12.4.3 What Next?

As these cases demonstrate, we have constructed a model that allows us to richly represent many macroeconomic conditions. However, the model offers us no basis for analyzing these cases because while we have identified the forces that actually move AD and AS, we have not analyzed the sources of these forces. In order for the model to come alive as a powerful analytical tool, we must examine the sources of the forces that shift AD and AS, and that in turn move the macroeconomy. So now we turn to our attention there. We begin on the aggregate demand side. What are the sources of the forces that move AD?

13.0 AGGREGATE DEMAND

13.1.1 Sources of the Forces that Determine the Level of C

One of the forces that moves AD is a change in the level of consumption, C. So what are the sources of the forces that determine the level of consumption?

For the average individual we can represent a person's consumption as being based on the standard of living she thinks is consistent with her long term financial prospects. For example, if you have been making $50,000 a year and you can reasonably expect to be in that income bracket for the foreseeable future, you tend to consume based on that expectation.

If you are making that $50,000 and you get a windfall of $15,000 from your great uncle's will or if you have $15,000 in sudden, unexpected healthcare costs not covered by insurance—you may have a blip in your consumption up or down respectively. But, in general even as you have these ups and downs from year to year in your consumption, if you are like our assumed "average" consumer you will tend to "smooth out" your consumption to fit your expected long term income status. This is true whether you are making $50,000 or $20,000 or $150,000 or $7,000,000 a year. Indeed, the essence of *personal financial planning* is arranging consumption, saving, and financial investment patterns so that your long term ability to consume (your standard of living) will be at least constant and, hopefully, improving, given the prospect that sometime in the future you will retire and your wage income will go to zero.

So the first thing we can say about consumption, C, is that in the aggregate it is a function of long term expected income status or what economists refer to as people's perception of their *permanent income*. In order for people to achieve this smoothing, they spend out of their current income and, if necessary, they spend out of their accumulated wealth or they may borrow.

13.1.2 Sources of Consumption Spending

The amount of current aggregate income in the economy is determined by the amount of production in the economy, because the funds paid for that production are people's incomes. The current nominal income can, therefore, be represented by price level times the real GDP ($P*Y$). This measures how much was spent in the economy and therefore how much income was earned. If we let a lower case "b" stand for that share of current aggregate income that people use for consumption, then the level of consumption, C, is determined in part by

b (PY)—this is the share of current aggregate income that is spent on consumption

For most folks this spending out of current income is the whole story of their consumption, but in the aggregate we have to remember that there are some people who are smoothing out their consumption levels by spending out of their perceived wealth. I say "perceived" wealth because while some of it is "money in the bank", some of this wealth is based on the perceived value of assets like stock holdings or a house that do not have a determinate value until they are sold.

The most common form spending out of wealth is that done by those who do so as retirees. Laid off workers may also spend down their wealth. The rate of this spending will depend on whether they perceive it as covering the transition to an expected new good job or to easing the glide down to a lower paying job. Another source of spending out of "wealth" is that done by folks who see their stock or house assets grow significantly in value. They may expand consumption based on this perceived increased in wealth. This *wealth effect* can also be negative. It can cause contraction of consumption when the perceived value of assets fall.

We will call this consumption out of accumulated wealth *autonomous consumption* and identify it with an upper case "A." Adding this autonomous consumption, A, to the consumption based on current income, b(PY) we have an equation that represents the sources of consumption, a consumption function:

$$C = b(PY) + A$$

Now, with this consumption function, we are in a position to identify and explain one of the sources of the forces that moves the macroeconomy: *Consumer confidence.* If consumers see their prospects as brightening then their perceived permanent income goes up and with it their level of consumption goes up also. As C increases, *ceteris paribus*, this increases aggregate expenditures, shifting out AD—increasing real GDP. Since C is itself a function of real GDP (Y), these positive expectations become to some degree self-fulfilling. As people spend more they create more income, just as expected.

13.1.3 Post-War Example of the Power of A and a Transition to I

A classic example of the power of consumption and in particular of autonomous consumption, A, can be found in the immediate post-World War II period.

From the early 1930s until World War II the U.S. economy endured that disaster known as the Great Depression. After December 7, 1941, the huge increase in government spending as the nation mobilized for and fought the war created a huge increase in aggregate demand. Unemployment plummeted from Depression-level highs to levels that were certainly below the natural rate.

As the war drew to a close and victory was finally in sight, concerns turned from winning the war to the state of the world in the post-war period. Domestically, this concern was focused on the economy. Factories were beginning to demobilize since there was no longer a need for producing tanks and planes and guns and so on for the war. It seemed to many that without the war effort to create the aggregate demand and in turn the jobs, the economy would slip right back into the Depression that had preceded the war. Where would the demand come from to make it worthwhile for those factories to retool to make cars and can openers and civilian clothes, and so on? Where would the demand come from to keep the people in the factories working?

At least in part, it came from A—from autonomous consumption. During the war incomes were high but rationing made it difficult to consume, so there was an effective forced saving. At the end of the war with the hope of peace and high expectations for new lives ahead, the wealth accumulated during the war was used to start new lives and new families (these were the years of the baby boom). The unleashing of this pent-up demand from the war years, along with the good fortune that the infrastructure of production was untouched by the war, helped the economy move into a post-war period that was not a return to the Great Depression.

But while consumer confidence and autonomous consumption can move the economy, they cannot sustain growth by themselves. A major engine in the economy and a key determinant of its overall direction is investment, so next we turn our attention there: What are the sources of the forces that determine the level of investment, I, and in turn move the macroeconomy?

13.2 INVESTMENT

13.2.1 Introduction:

The level of investment—and here we mean the level of investment in real things like plants, equipment, education, inventories—the level of this investment is determined in what we will refer to as the country's *long term capital market*. It is in this capital market that individuals and enterprises get the funds they need to make investments.

Investments cost money. It is the rare individual or enterprise that has enough funds to cover the costs of an investment, so more often than not a loan is needed in order to make an envisioned investment a reality. (Maybe you are taking out a loan to pay for this investment in your education.) The capital market, if it is working well, coordinates the desires of those who need funds with the resources of those who have funds that they are willing to loan.

We will refer to the funds that pass through this capital market as *financial capital* or *liquidity*. Unlike real production capital (a produced means of production fixed in its form as a building or a machine or an education), financial capital can take any shape we pour it into—it is like a liquid. The funds exchanged in the capital market flow from lenders to borrowers, and the borrowers in turn pour those funds into thousands of different channels (paying for blueprints and backhoes, or books and CDs . . .) as the real investments they envision take shape.

Borrowing financial capital or liquidity is a key step in developing real investments. The capital market coordinates the exchange of this liquidity between lenders and borrowers. In doing so the capital market plays a central role in making investment possible. Financial institutions like banks or mutual funds play a very significant role in do the day-to-day job of making this coordination process work. They are the *financial intermediaries* of the financial system.

The kinds of real investments we are talking about (like building a factory) generally take a significant amount of time between the loan being made and the investment actually paying off, so borrowers need a lot of time to pay the loan back. In practice it is not uncommon for such loans to be for as long as 20 to 30 years. In our story we will use these 20 to 30 year loans as our standard for real investment loans, which is why we refer this as the *long term* capital market. Now let's represent this market graphically.

13.2.2 The Long Term Capital Market—The Basic Picture

The capital market graph looks as shown in Figure 13.2.1.

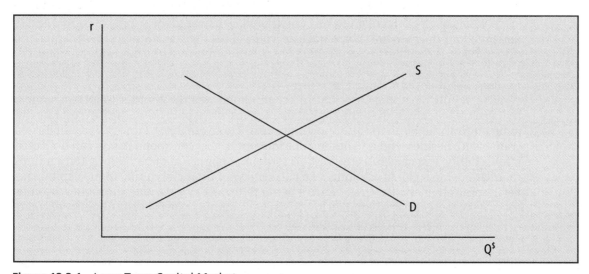

Figure 13.2.1 Long Term Capital Market

The horizontal axis represents quantity of financial capital (designated $Q^\$$). Moving to the right along the line represents increasing amounts of these funds. Keep in mind that since we are measuring in actual dollars, the horizontal axis is a nominal scale.

The vertical axis represents the nominal interest rate (r). This interest rate is the "price" of the financial capital or, if you will, the price of liquidity—moving up the vertical axis represents an increasing interest rate or a higher price of liquidity.

The supply and demand lines in this market, as in all markets, represent the attitudes of suppliers and demanders respectively. So, what determines the attitude of the suppliers and the demanders in this capital market and thus the shape and location of these lines? Let's look at each in turn.

13.2.3 Supply

The supply line (S) represents the attitude of people with funds to loan. Look at Figure 13.2.2.

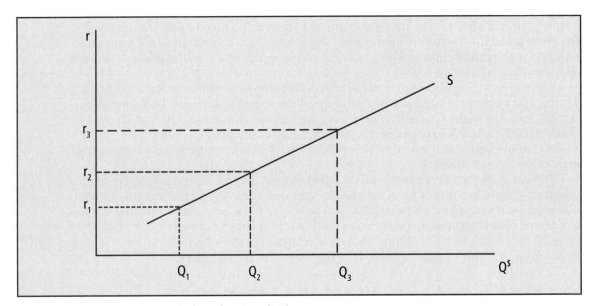

Figure 13.2.2 Long Term Capital Market Supply Line

If you take any particular interest rate (r), follow it over to the supply of capital line (S) and then look down to the horizontal axis, you will see the specific amount of capital that the suppliers are willing to loan at that particular interest rate (the quantity supplied, $Q^\$$). Look at several different interest rates. You can see that as the interest rate rises, *ceteris paribus*, the quantity supplied increases. Why?

The supply of capital comes from accumulated wealth. In order to attract some of that accumulated wealth to the capital market, the price paid for it, the interest rate, has to be more attractive than the opportunity cost. There are a lot of things you can do with your wealth besides lend it to others for a long term: You can spend it, you can hold on to it for security, you can lend it for a short term in anticipation of better long term interest rates later, or in a global economy you can send your financial capital to the capital market in some other country in search of a better return. *Ceteris paribus*, the higher the interest rate the better a capital market looks, so as the interest rate rises the quantity of capital supplied increases, just as our graph represents it.

13.2.4 Demand

The demand line (D_I) represents the attitude of those who want to borrow funds in order to make real investments. To understand their attitude we must keep in mind that these investments are all about the future. You invest in the production capital (physical capital—like a factory, or human capital—like an education) now, but the payoff only comes later. Entrepreneurs, people with vision, envision investments that they believe will pay off in the future. At any time there are many potential investments possible, each with a different expected rate of return. For example if in a year you expect to make $110 on a particular $100 investment made today, your expected rate of return on that investment is 10%. (Note that word "expect"; it is a big player in our story.) The expected monetary benefit of any investment is measured by its expected rate of return, and at any given time there are an array of potential investments available with a range of expected rates of return that prospective investors can rank from high to low.

While the attractiveness of an investment is its expected rate of return, its costs are right up front. And while entrepreneurs have vision they seldom have the liquidity to make that vision a reality, so they need to borrow financial capital—they need to borrow liquidity. The interest rate is the price they pay for the liquidity they borrow. Clearly borrowing for an investment only makes sense if the expected rate of return (the expected benefit) is higher than the interest rate one has to pay (the cost) to make the investment. The demand for capital line represents the fact that as the interest rate rises fewer and fewer investments have an expected return that beats the interest rate, so, *ceteris paribus*, as the interest rate rises the quantity of capital demanded for the purposes of investments falls.

Note: Here we use D_I because for now the only demand we are considering in the capital market is the demand for the purposes of private investments in production capital. There are other demanders in this market. In particular we will see that government borrowing can have a significant impact on the capital market, but we are not ready to deal with that yet. For now we are going to assume that all demand for capital is for the purposes of private investment in productive things like building a new shopping mall or a computer factory or an education.

13.2.5 Combining Supply and Demand

Combining the supply and the demand for capital, we see in Figure 13.2.3 that where the capital market reaches an equilibrium the long term nominal interest rate (r) and the nominal level of investment (I) are determined.

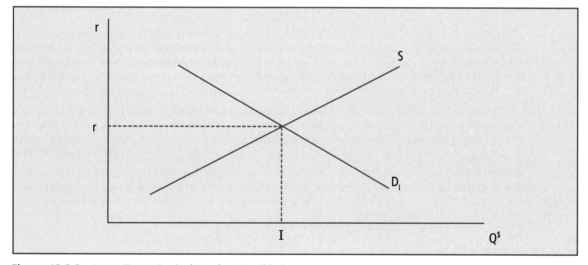

Figure 13.2.3 Long Term Capital Market Equilibrium

This level of nominal investment (I) is a part of the total expenditures in the economy that determine the level of aggregate demand and in turn affect the macro conditions in the economy.

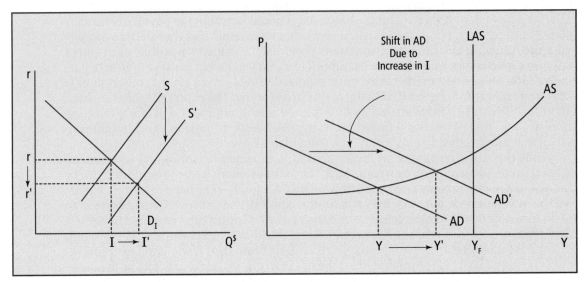

Figure 13.2.4 Capital Market Supply Shift Down, and Macro Consequences, *ceteris paribus*

Clearly changing attitudes in the capital market, represented graphically by shifts in supply or demand, result in changes in the level of investment and in turn affect macroeconomic conditions. This connection between the capital market and the macroeconomy is going to be central to our story so let's take a moment to explore this connection graphically.

Suppose for example that, *ceteris paribus*, suppliers in the capital market decide to charge less for their capital: financial capital will be cheaper. In Figure 13.2.4 we see that the supply in the capital market shifts down. In other words, for any given quantity of financial capital the lenders charge less. Given this shift in attitude, we see on the graph that the long term interest rate, r, falls and the level of investment, I, rises. This in turn expands the aggregate demand (AD): increasing real GDP (Y), expanding employment (reducing unemployment), and possibly causing inflation depending on the shape of the AS line.

Consider another case: If, *ceteris paribus*, the demanders in the capital market decide they want to borrow less capital, then at any given interest rate there is less quantity of financial capital demanded. In Figure 13.2.5 this is represented by a shift in the demand for capital line to the left: At any given interest rate the borrowers want to borrow less. Given this shift in attitude we see on our graph that the long term interest rate (r) falls and the level of investment (I) falls also. This in turn reduces the aggregate demand (AD): decreasing real GDP (Y), increasing unemployment, and possibly causing deflation depending on the shape of the AS line.

In these examples the process started with a shift in capital market supply or capital market demand. In order to understand the *sources* of the forces that change the level of investment (I) and affect the macroeconomy, we need to identify the variables that change the attitudes of suppliers or demanders and thus shift capital supply or capital demand.

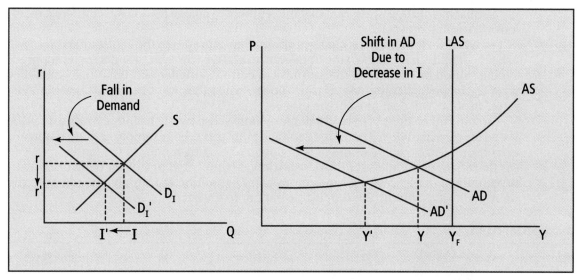

Figure 13.2.5 Fall in Capital Market Demand, and Macro Consequences, *ceteris paribus*

13.2.6 Shift Terms

But first let me clarify the terms I just used to describe shifts in supply and demand. In our first example I said supply shifted "down." In our second example I said demand shifted "left." Why "down"? Why "left"? Let's examine these shift terms so we will use the language the same way and thus speak the same language.

If we think of suppliers as concerned with the return they will get on their loan, a change in their attitude can best be represented by the following question they ask themselves: "Do I want to charge more or less for my capital?" If a change in attitude moves them to charge more, then at any given level of capital supplied the price of the funds—the interest rate—will be higher. As shown in Figure 13.2.6, at any given quantity level, Q, they will charge more. Since this is true at all quantities, graphically this shift in attitudes looks like a shift "up" in supply.

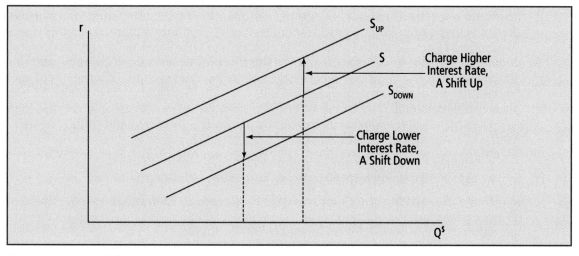

Figure 13.2.6 A Shift in Long Term Capital Market Supply

Similarly, a change in attitude that moves them to charge less—a lower interest rate—looks like a shift down.

So when we are analyzing changes of suppliers attitudes in the capital market we will use the quantity axis as our frame of reference, and we will refer to shifts in the supply of capital caused by changes in the attitudes of current suppliers as shifts "up" when they want to charge higher interest rates or "down" when they want to charge lower interest rates. Or so we will do it most of the time.

In some other kinds of cases it will make more sense to use the interest rate axis as the frame of reference when discussing capital supply shifts. For example, if there is entry or exit of suppliers of capital (more or fewer people bringing money to the market), we can say that at any given interest rate there is a larger (with entry) or smaller (with exit) quantity supplied. In this case we can refer to entry as shifting the supply line out or to the right, and exit as shifting the supply line back or to the left.

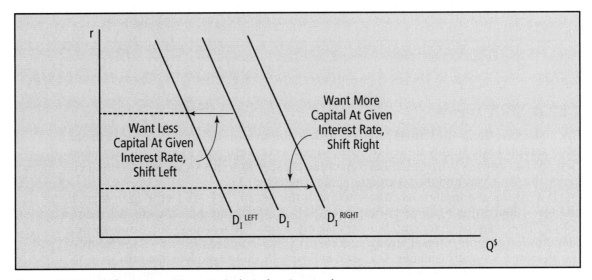

Figure 13.2.7   Shifts in Long Term Capital Market Demand

On the demand side the attitudes can generally represented by the question, "How much capital do I want to borrow at the going rate?" If a change in attitude moves them to borrow more, then at a given interest rate the quantity of capital demanded will increase. As shown in Figure 13.2.7, at any given interest rate they borrow more. Since this is true at all interest rates, graphically this shift in attitude looks like a shift to the right in demand. Similarly, a change in attitude that moves them to borrow less at any given interest rate looks like a shift left. So we will refer to shifts in the demand of capital caused by changes in the attitudes of current demanders as shifts "right" if they want more capital or "left" if they want less capital.

The crucial issue when discussing capital market supply or demand shifts is to orient yourself by one axis or the other so that you can interpret a shift as:

- larger or smaller quantity at any given interest rate—shifts right or left, or
- higher or lower interest rate at any given quantity—shifts up or down.

Now that we have our shift terms in place, what are the shift variables that move S or D in the capital market and in turn affect the entire macroeconomy? Let's begin on the supply side with some basic information about capital supply.

13.2.7 Capital Market Shift Variables—Supply

A fundamental determinant of the level of interest people charge for their long term capital is their perception of the risk that they won't get their funds back—the risk of default. For example, because the perception of risk of default is different with respect to you and me, to General Motors and to the U.S. government, we each pay a different interest rate for exactly the same long term loan. The U.S. government pays the least—a rate called the U.S. Treasury bond rate—because it has a great record for paying back when it borrows and it has been doing so for a very long time. You and I, while we are both fine upstanding citizens, do not have the record or the resources of the U.S. government. Since we look a lot riskier, we will pay more interest for the same loan. In this regard General Motors is more like the government than you and me, so it pays a rate above but closer to the government rate—a rate called the prime rate. Keep in mind: If any one of us—you, me, General Motors, or the government—defaulted on a loan, after that we would be known as very risky and we would have more trouble borrowing in the future—and if we could borrow, it would be at much higher interest rate than before.

As shown in Figure 13.2.8, there are in effect an array of long term capital supply lines—lines for folks like you and me, lines for big firms like GM, and lines for governments.

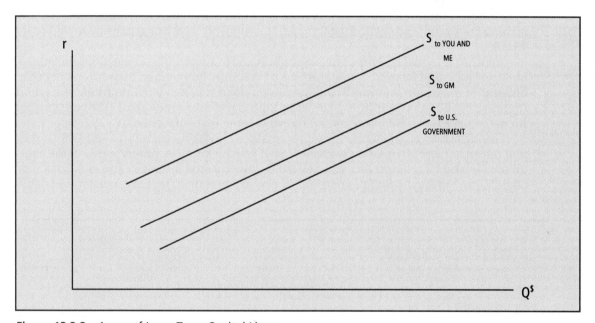

Figure 13.2.8 Array of Long Term Capital Lines

The differences among these rates do change as events affect people's perceptions about the relative security of individuals, private enterprises, or governments. And keep in mind that different governments have different risk factors associated with them—so for example because Russia is seen as more risky, it pays more than Germany for an identical loan. But we want one supply of capital line to represent this array, so we are going to use the U.S. Government Treasury Bond rate (the rate the U.S. Government pays for long term loans) as representative of the array.

Now with these terms in place let's examine the variables that determine the level of the long term capital supply and that cause it to shift as they change.

13.2.8 Long Term Supply Shift Variables—The Short Term Supply of Capital

Among the factors that determine the level of the long term capital supply is the *short term* level of supply. Why? Because when people lend they give up control over their funds. People prefer to get that control back sooner rather than later. For that reason people are generally more comfortable with making short term loans. Therefore, *ceteris paribus*, short term loans carry a lower interest rate than long term loans.

We will use a less than one year loan as our standard for short term. Since, *ceteris paribus*, these short term loans are supplied at lower rates than long funds are, the level of short term interest rate line establishes a base or floor for the long term supply line. Onto this base several "premiums" or extra costs are added to determine the level of long term supply line. Let's draw a short term capital supply line (lower case s) on our graph and then add on those premiums in order to see how the level of the long term capital supply line (S) is determined.

13.2.9 Long Term Supply Shift Variables—The Premiums

One essential difference we have already noted that makes the long rate line higher than the short rate line is that short term loans do not require nearly as much waiting until you get control of your loaned funds back. Long loans involve a long wait and they charge a premium for this waiting. Adding that *waiting premium* to the short term capital supply line is the first step in locating the long term capital supply line on our graph shown in Figure 13.2.9.

Another essential difference between short and long rate lines is the different vulnerability of short and long loans to the affects of inflation. Remember, inflation reduces the amount of real value that funds will buy. If you loan funds at a 5% nominal rate and if there is a 5% inflation before you get your funds back, how much *real* return did you get (in percentage terms)? Zero. All of the return is eaten up by inflation.

Clearly, what you care about when you make a loan is the real return—a 1,000% nominal return is a loser if inflation is 2,000%. So if you are going to supply funds in the capital market you want to protect yourself from any expected inflation. You can do this by charging an *expected inflation premium*. Suppose you wanted to make a real return of 3%

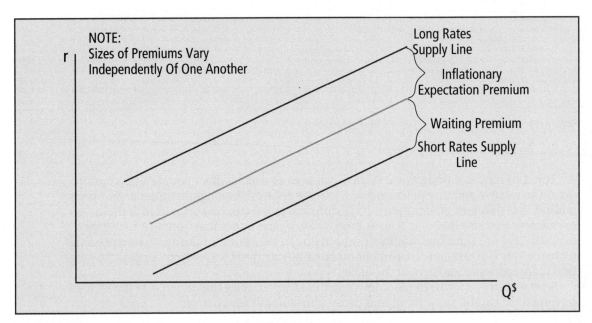

Figure 13.2.9   Short Rate Floor and Premiums That Make Long Rates

on your loan and you expected inflation to be 2%; what nominal interest rate would you have to charge in order to expect to meet your goal? 5%: 2% to cover the expected inflation and 3% more for the real return.

Now if inflation is not either currently high or expected to become high very soon, inflation is not a big threat to short term loans because there is very little time for moderate or low inflation to erode the value of the funds. It is a very different story with long term loans, however. In the span of several years the level of inflation in an economy can rise dramatically. On a long loan one has to consider that possibility and build in protection from that risk. With this in mind long term lenders add an *inflationary expectations premium* to the charge for supplying their funds in the long term market. Adding this additional premium to the short term capital supply line is another step in locating the long term capital supply line on our graph.

13.2.10 Long Term Supply Shift Variables—Cases

So now we have identified three factors that determine the level of long term capital supply line (S): The level of the short term supply line (lower case s), the waiting premium, and the inflationary expectations premium. Since a change in any one of these can change the level of the long term capital supply line, these are key shift variables with respect to long term supply line. In order to practice with this idea, consider the following examples:

1. Suppose the short rate supply line goes down (don't worry about exactly how much). *Ceteris paribus*, in which direction does this short rate change shift the long term supply of capital line?—Given the premiums, the falling short rate line pulls the long line down.

2. Now suppose that inflationary expectations shoot up for some reason. *Ceteris paribus*, in which direction does this change in inflationary expectations shift the long term supply of capital line?—Given the short rate supply line and the waiting premium, the increasing inflationary expectations shift the long rate supply line up.

3. Finally let's try a combo effect. Suppose the short rate supply line goes up and at the same time inflationary expectations go down. *Ceteris paribus*, in which direction does the combined effect of the raising short rate supply line and the falling inflationary expectations shift the long term supply of capital line?—It can go either way depending on which factor dominates. If the short rate supply line shift dominates inflationary expectations, the long rate supply line shifts up. If inflationary expectations dominate the short rate supply line shift, the long rate supply line shifts down. This combined movement, reflects a degree of complexity that we will see more and more as we get into macro: There are often forces at work in opposite directions and the net effect of these forces depends on their relative strength.

13.2.11 Long Term Shift Variables—Entry or Exit

Now we need to introduce one more shift variable with respect to the long term capital supply line: Entry into or exit out of a country's capital market.

As shown in Figure 13.2.10, entry of more funds into a nation's capital market adds to the quantity supplied at any given interest rate so it shifts S to the right. Exit subtracts from the quantity supplied at any given interest rate so it shifts S left.

One source of entry is an increase in accumulated wealth within the country. A growing economy creates more wealth and thus more potential funds for the capital market. Alternatively, funds exit a nation's capital market as accumulated wealth in the nation decreases. For example, a corrupt or incompetent banking system can through graft or lack of care destroy or waste on unproductive investments a significant amount of national wealth, thus diminishing the available financial capital.

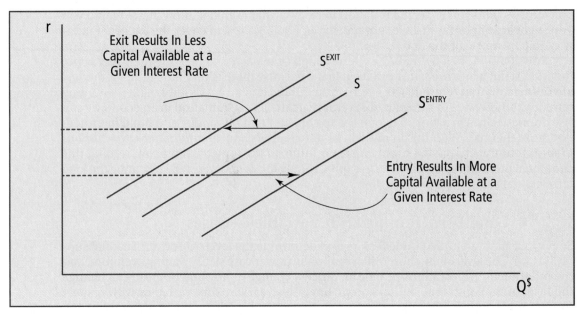

Figure 13.2.10   Capital Market Entry or Exit

Another source of entry or exit is movement of wealth among opportunities. If people get nervous about the stock market, they may move their assets toward the financial capital market (often referred to as the *bond market* since in this case people are buying the IOUs called bonds), expanding the supply there. Conversely, if people get excited about the stock market, they may move their assets out of the bond market and into stock market, contracting the capital market supply.

A significant source of entry or exit, and often the most volatile source (that is, the one which can cause changes most quickly) is flows of funds from one country's capital market to another country's capital market. These *international capital flows* as they are called are playing a bigger and bigger role in the economies of individual nations as national economies become more and more woven into a global system—something that is happening very rapidly with the amazing advances in global communications.

We often see flows into a country when conditions there seem to be improving so much that it seems full of opportunities and thus people see this as a great place to put funds. We also see flows *into* a country when political or economic instability in another country (maybe a dramatic, unwelcomed change in leadership or a surge in inflation there) makes folks with funds in that unstable place nervous and so they move their funds to a safe haven to escape the risk.

Now let's do an example graphically. Suppose a country has an international capital flow into its capital market. As shown in Figure 13.2.11, *ceteris paribus*, the expansion in the supply of liquidity from this capital flowing in shifts the supply of capital to the right, lowers interest rates, and makes more investment (I) possible in the country receiving the funds. If the holders of international capital send their funds and make the actual investment themselves, this is called *foreign direct investment*.

In the Macro Picture the increase in I resulting from the influx of capital adds to aggregate demand shifting AD out. This means more real GDP and less unemployment. The effect on the price level depends on the shape of the AS line. As it is drawn here, there is some inflation.

Obviously as the funds flow into one country they must be flowing out of another. We see flows *out* of a country when political or economic instability in that country makes folks with funds there nervous. In the face of such nervousness, funds are sent elsewhere to escape the perceived increasing risks. Funds also flow out of a nation's capital market when conditions in another country become, relatively speaking, more promising. In that

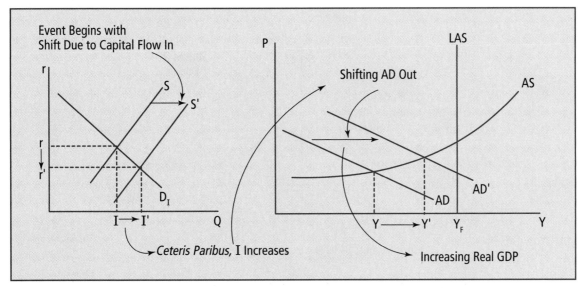

Figure 13.2.11 International Capital Flow In, and Macro Consequences, *ceteris paribus*

case the other country's capital market appears to be an advantageous place to move funds, so liquidity flows out to that other market.

Ceteris paribus, such a contraction in the supply of liquidity due to a capital flow out raises interest rates. This in turn reduces investments (I) since some are no longer worthwhile at these higher interest rates. The decrease in I reduces aggregate demand. This means real GDP falls and there's more unemployment. The effect on the price level depends on the shape of the AS line.

We have seen that changes in short term capital supply, changes in inflationary expectations, changes in domestic wealth, and/or international capital flows can each shift the supply of long term capital and in turn affect a nation's entire macroeconomy.

Now let's look at the demand side of the capital market.

13.2.12 Capital Market Shift Variables—Demand

One of the most significant forces that moves the demand for long term capital and in turn affects the level of investment and the overall macroeconomic conditions is expectations in the economy. Remember: The quantity of capital demanded at any given interest rate represents the number of investments that offer expected rates of return that can beat the price of liquidity—the interest rate. As investors' expectations become more and more positive, more and more investments look good at any given interest rate.

As shown in Figure 13.2.12, increasingly positive expectations shift the demand for capital (D_I) to the right.

Ceteris paribus, with expanded demand the interest rate (r) rises as borrowers bid for the funds; but this bidding is for funds to make new investments. This expanding investment (I) increases AD, increases real GDP (Y), and increases employment. Its effect on the price level depends on the shape of the AS line.

Conversely, a depression of expectations causes D_I to shift left. As a result, *ceteris paribus*, the interest rate falls as borrowers withdraw from bidding for the funds. This lack of bidding reflects a fall in investment (I) which reduces AD, and in turn decreases real GDP (Y) and increases unemployment. Again, the effect on the price level depends on the shape of the AS line.

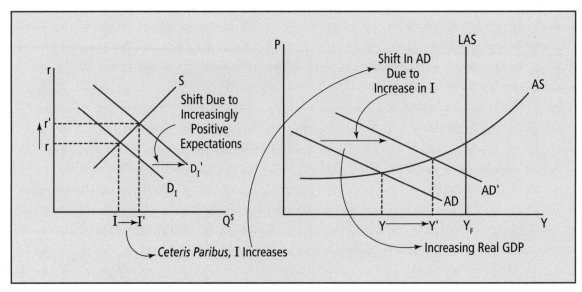

Figure 13.2.12 Shift in Capital Market Demand to the Right Given Increasingly Positive Expectations and, *ceteris paribus*, the Effect of This on the Macroeconomy

OK, it is time for some practice.

Suppose that a country has been suffering from a long and violent internal struggle, a struggle between the forces that control the government and army and other forces that want to change the character of the nation's governance or that simply want a share of the land on which to form an independent country with its own government. There are plenty of real cases of such a scenario around the globe, from the Middle East to Central America to Africa to Eastern Europe and so on. This kind of struggle keeps investment in the nation depressed because the risks of destruction of the investment and the difficulties of carrying on business discourage many investments.

Now suppose the two warring factions are able to achieve a mutually acceptable solution that brings peace to the nation—a peace that people truly believed will be real and enduring. *Ceteris paribus*, how does the prospect of peace affect the long term capital market and the aggregate economy? First let's focus on the capital market itself. Given the scenario just described, what will happen in the capital market?

The prospect of peace makes that nation a more stable place and makes the prospects for a productive future much greater, so expectations become much more positive—shifting the capital demand to the right. This new stability and the new opportunities may also attract more foreign capital shifting capital supply to the right. The net effect of these two shifts on the interest rate (r) are not clear, but what is clear is that under this scenario investment (I) expands.

How will this capital market activity affect the aggregate economy? *Ceteris paribus*, an increase in I will shift AD out, expanding real GDP and lowering unemployment. The effect of inflation depends on the shape of the AS line and where the activity is along that line.

Let's try another case . . . the Great Depression.

As the name implies, the Depression was a period of deeply depressed expectations. How does a depression of expectations affect the capital market?

Depressed expectations mean people see the future holding fewer and fewer good opportunities. With fewer good opportunities ahead, there is less and less reason to borrow money for investments. The demand in the capital market shifts to the left. Investment (I) falls and with less bidding for the available liquidity, the interest rate falls also.

What are the implications of this for the macroeconomy? Falling investment reduces aggregate demand, AD shifts left. As AD falls the real GDP falls and unemployment rises.

The effect on the price level depends on the shape of the AS line. There was deflation during the Great Depression.

Now let's look at some actual data. Table 13.2.1 shows changes in real investment, real GDP, and the unemployment rate as the Depression took hold in the United States from 1929–1933.

TABLE 13.2.1 THE GREAT DEPRESSION
From Economic Report of the President, 1954, Tables G-2, G-16
(Billions of dollars, 1953 prices)

YEAR	INVESTMENT (I)	REAL GDP (Y)	UNEMPLOYMENT RATE
1929	34.2	175.9	3.2
1930	23.3	159.2	8.7
1931	14.7	147.7	15.9
1932	3.3	125.3	23.6
1933	3.7	123.4	24.9

As people began to reassess their expectations about the future in 1929, the optimism of the 1920s was replaced with pessimism. Pessimism is only a perception, but *perceptions can have real effects*. Feeding on itself the pessimism transformed into depression—there is a reason economists call the economic catastrophe of this period the Great "Depression."

Table 13.2.1 shows that as the Depression took hold of the national psyche the level of investment plummeted to almost nothing. As investment contracted dramatically GDP followed, and in turn with falling production there were fewer and fewer jobs so unemployment soared.

People with no hope don't invest, and with the absence of investment there is little reason to hope—it's a real dilemma driven by perceptions and expectations that create real effects that in turn feed the perceptions and expectations. While there was clearly a lot more going on (we'll return to this Great Depression example later), this depression of expectations at the outset of the Great Depression contributed to the depth of the downturn. At this point you have the tools to understand this process—we have covered a lot of ground in our analysis of economic ideas and issues.

13.3 THE TRADE BALANCE

13.3.1 Introduction

We have just seen how investment can be a major mover of aggregate demand. Now let's look at another significant determinant of AD—the trade balance (X-M).

International trade exists for the very same reason that domestic trade exists. There are, as we have seen, *gains from trade* when individual people or nations specialize and then exchange surpluses. So long as channels of exchange are open, markets form in order to coordinate the exchange of these surpluses. In international trade, as in domestic trade, the most basic determinant of the amount of trade that goes on is the underlying conditions in the markets for the items traded.

To see this, let's look at one international trade market—trade in French wine between France and Germany, and examine how the trade in that market works.

We will assume that there are only two countries involved in this market: France and Germany. The market is represented in Figure 13.3.1.

The determinants of trade in French wine between these two countries include:

1. The attitude of French wine producers. This attitude is represented graphically in Figure 13.3.1 by the French wine supply line,

2. The attitude of domestic demanders, that is, the French demanders of French wine. This attitude is represented graphically in Figure 13.3.1 by the domestic demand line, and

3. The attitude of German demanders of French wine. This attitude is represented graphically in Figure 13.3.1 by the German demand line. There is no German supply line because the product is from France.

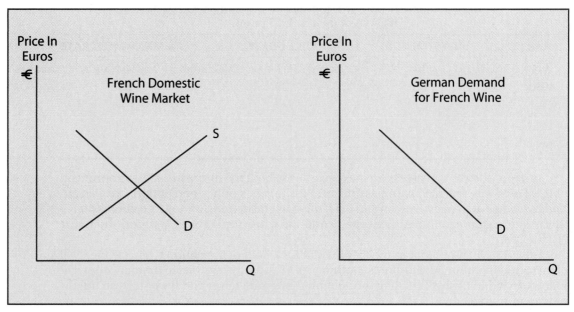

Figure 13.3.1 French Wine Market—In France and in Germany

Adding the German demand to the domestic demand, as shown in Figure 13.3.2, gives us the full demand conditions. This, in the context of domestic supply conditions, determines the market price and the total quantity exchanged.

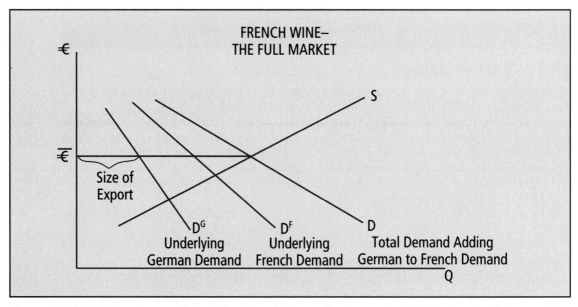

Figure 13.3.2 Adding German Demand to French Demand to Represent Full Market Conditions, and Identifying the Amount That Goes from France to Germany

Then to determine the share of this total that that goes into international trade, we take the price over to the German demand line to identify the German share of the quantity demanded. This is the size of the French export and German import of French wine.

13.3.2 Introduction to Foreign Exchange Markets

But this case of international trade is uniquely easy because these two nations use the same currency, the Euro. In principle the process of determining the level of trade in any item between any two nations is the same. In reality it is significantly complicated by the fact that in all international trade except among the euro countries, different countries use different currencies.

Take for example the trade in French wines between France and the United States.

In the case of trade with Germany, adding the German demand to the French demand (as we did in Figure 13.3.2) to determine the total market demand was simple. It was simple because the vertical axes that measure price in Figure 13.3.2 matched—both are measured in euros. But in the case of French/U.S. trade the price is measured in different currencies. The U.S. uses dollars, not euros like France or Germany. In order to "add" U.S. demand to the market for French wine, we first need to transform the U.S. dollars into the euros of France. To put it more simply, before you can buy a bottle of French wine your dollars have to be exchanged for euros.

"But wait," you say, "I can purchase French wines, South African diamonds, Sudanese sandals, Indian cottons, Italian shoes, Chinese paintings, Japanese cars, Mexican art, and lots of other international items right here in town—with U.S. dollars." That may be so, but somewhere up the line of trades that led to your final purchase, dollars had to be exchanged for euros, or South African rand, and so forth. The people in those other countries who produce the imports you buy do not live in a dollar-denominated market. They need their domestic currency to shop in their world, and so they need to be paid in their domestic currency.

How about if you travel internationally and visit these other countries? Somewhere along your journey you will have to exchange your currency so that you can pay for things with a currency acceptable in the country you are visiting. This exchange of currencies, be it for tourism or for importation of goods or services or for any other purpose, takes place in the *foreign exchange market*.

Currency exchange is central to the process of international trade, so in order to understand international trade we need to analyze how a foreign exchange market works. For simplicity, we will assume a two-currency world in which the only foreign exchange market is between the U.S. dollar and the European euros.

13.3.3 Analyzing the Foreign Exchange Market

There are two perspectives from which we can represent the foreign exchange market between dollars and euros. One, shown in Figure 13.3.3, is with a picture in which euros are the commodity to be bought and sold with the price of euros measured in dollars.

The supply line in this picture represents people holding euros and their attitude toward exchanging them for dollars. The more dollars they are paid for a euro (in other words, the higher the dollar price of euros), the greater the quantity of euros they will supply.

The demand line in this picture represents the attitude of those who want to buy euros. The cheaper the euros (in other words, the lower the dollar price of euros), the greater the quantity of euros they demand.

The price in this market specifies how many dollars one has to offer in exchange for one euro. It is the *exchange rate* for euros priced in dollars: dollars/euro. At any given exchange rate (in this case dollars per euro), there will be a quantity of euros supplied and a quantity of euros demanded. If the exchange rate is a price that is allowed to adjust freely, then the foreign exchange market will reach an equilibrium at which the quantity of euros supplied equals the quantity of euros demanded.

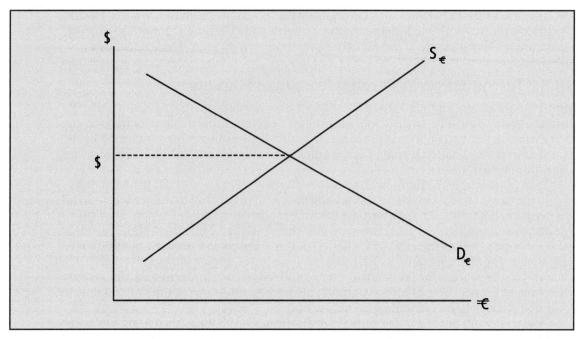

Figure 13.3.3 Foreign Exchange Market: the Euro-Dollar Market with Euro as the Commodity Priced in Dollars

13.3.4 An Alternative Perspective on the Foreign Exchange Market

An alternative perspective on this same market for exchanging euros and dollars can be represented by a picture in which dollars are the commodity to be bought and sold with the price of dollars measured in euros. Figure 13.3.4 shows both perspectives.

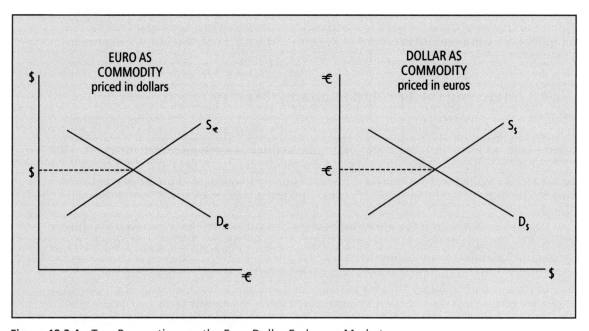

Figure 13.3.4 Two Perspectives on the Euro-Dollar Exchange Market

The right graph in Figure 13.3.4 represents the euro-dollar exchange market when we think of the dollar as the commodity. In this case the supply line represents people holding dollars and their attitude toward exchanging them for, being paid in, euros. The more euros they are paid for each dollar (in other words, the higher the euro price of dollars), the more dollars they will supply.

The demand line in this picture represents the attitude of those who want to buy dollars with euros. The cheaper the dollar (in other words, the lower the euro price of dollars), the greater the quantity of dollars they demand.

Again, the price is the *exchange rate*. But now it is the exchange rate for dollars priced in euros: euros/dollar. And again, if the exchange rate is allowed to *float*, which means "to adjust freely," the foreign exchange market will reach an equilibrium at which the quantity supplied equals quantity demanded.

13.3.5 The Relationship Between These Two Perspectives

Now let's examine the relationship between these two perspectives on the foreign exchange market between dollars and euros.

To give this a real context, imagine you are leaving tomorrow to spend a semester at a European campus of SU Abroad (Syracuse University's International Programs Abroad). It's a great experience. Have a wonderful time!

Anyway, wanting to be prepared, you stop at a bank to buy some euros. . . . In doing so you are supplying dollars to the foreign exchange market in order to demand euros. As shown in Figure 13.3.5, your action is represented in our two foreign exchange graphs as a move to the right of the demand for euros line and a move to the right of the supply of dollars line. Your action is reflected in both graphs because in fact these graphs are two perspectives on the same action—supplying dollars in order to demand euros.

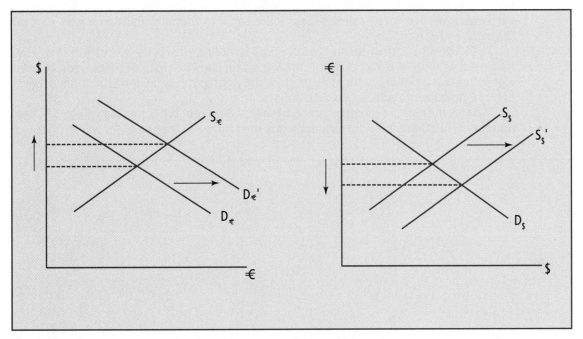

Figure 13.3.5 Expanding the Supply of Dollars and the Demand for Euros

When you come home, you will sell the euros you have left for dollars. As represented in Figure 13.3.6, when you do so you are at one and the same time supplying euros and demanding dollars. Graphically the supply of euros line shifts right and the demand for dollars line shifts right.

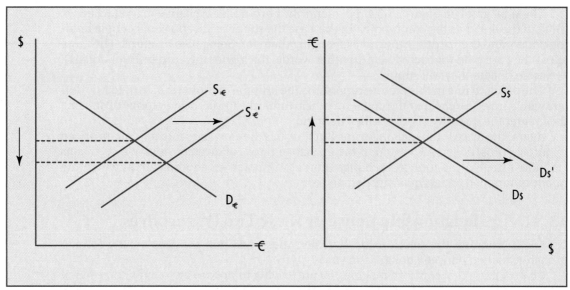

Figure 13.3.6 Expanding the Demand for Dollars and the Supply of Euros

Falls in demand and supply work the same way. A fall in the demand for euros implies a fall in the supply of dollars. A fall in the demand for dollars implies a fall in the supply of euros.

The point to keep in mind is that while we can represent the exchange of dollars and euros from two perspectives, these are two views of exactly the same market. And notice something else about these two perspectives on the euro-dollar foreign exchange market. Since they are just two different perspectives on exactly the same market, the two exchange rates they give—one in euros/dollar and the other in dollars/euro have to mean the same thing. And they do.

In Figure 13.3.7, the rate on the left graph in dollar/euro is the reciprocal of the rate in the right graph in euros/dollar. If the left graph shows a price of $2/euro or, in other words, it takes 2 dollars to buy 1 euro, then the right graph will show that it takes 1 euro to buy 2 dollars, or a price of ½ euro/dollar.

What is the actual exchange rate as of today? Find out. What was it a year ago? Check that out. More than likely the exchange rate has changed.

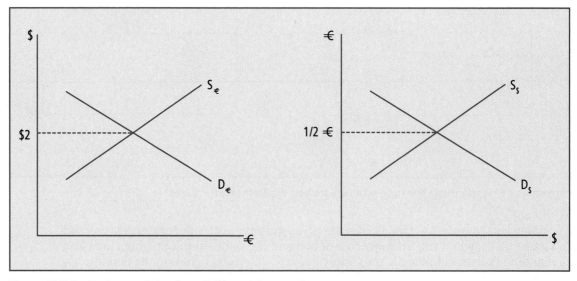

Figure 13.3.7 Exchange Rates from Different Perspectives

Why do exchange rates change? How do changing rates affect trade and the trade balance? These are the questions we need to address next.

13.3.6 Representing and Understanding Changing Exchange Rates

An exchange rate is simply the price between two currencies in the foreign exchange markets, and as with any market it is shifts in supply and demand that change the price. If the demand for euros increases (and so too, by definition, the supply of dollars) there will be a new exchange rate. Consider this case:

Suppose for some reason the demand for euros does increase as shown in Figure 13.3.8. What happens to the dollar price of the euro? As the demand for euros expands, *ceteris paribus*, the dollar price of euros goes up. It costs more dollars to buy a euro. Given this, what must be happening in the picture representing the other perspective? As people with dollars demand more euros, the supply of dollars expands. What happens to the euro price of dollars? It goes down.

Now suppose this market did adjust as shown in Figure 13.3.8 and the new dollar price of the euro is $4. What is the new euro price of the dollar? It is ¼ euro/dollar, because if 4 dollars buys 1 euro then ¼ euro buys 1 dollar. When, as in this case, the dollar price of the euro goes up and the euro price of the dollar goes down, economists refer to this as the euro getting *stronger* and the dollar getting *weaker*.

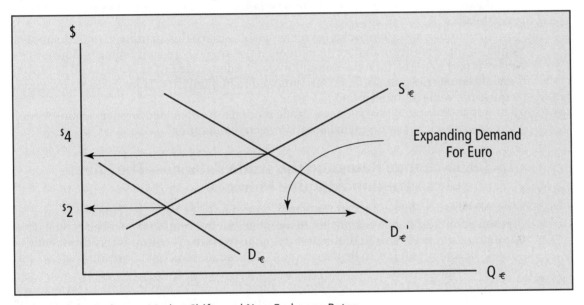

Figure 13.3.8 Exchange Market Shifts and New Exchange Rates

13.3.7 Stronger versus Weaker Currency—The Micro Issue

The euro is called "stronger" because a euro will now buy more dollar value. A $400 piece of Native American art sitting on a shelf in New York City costs a European tourist 200euro at the original exchange rate of 0.5euro/$. Now with the change in the exchange rate to 0.25euro/$, even though it still has the same price tag, $400, the art costs the tourist 100euro. A stronger currency is like putting all the other country's items on sale. In this case it is a 50% off sale—a very nice deal.

And as the euro is getting stronger, the dollar is by definition getting weaker. Even as that European tourist is enjoying the strength of her currency as she shops in New York, if you are at SU Abroad in Europe you are hurting. Suppose the place you rented in September is 400euro a month. When you arrived the exchange rate was $2/euro so your flat cost you $800 a month. But now that the exchange rate has gone to $4/euro, the same 400euro a month flat now costs you $1,600 a month. And food is more too. You can see why we call this a weaker currency.

So strong currencies are good and weak currencies are bad—right?

Right! If you are a purchaser of items from another nation, a buyer of imports from that place or a tourist there—you are personally better off if your currency gets stronger with respect to that nation's currency. For you, everything they sell is on sale.

So strong currencies are good and weak currencies are bad—right?

Wrong! If you are a seller to people in another nation, a seller of exports to that place or catering to tourists from there, you are personally worse off if your currency gets stronger with respect to that other nation's currency. Everything you sell goes up in price to your customers even though you get paid the same amount in terms of your own currency. So you sell less and make less.

The point here is that from a micro perspective the effect on you of a stronger or weaker currency depends on how you make your living and what you buy. But what are the implications of strong and weak exchange rates for that macroeconomic, aggregate variable we are investigating—the trade balance?

13.3.8 Exchange Rates and the Trade Balance—The Simple Case

If the only reason people ever bought currencies in the foreign exchange market was for exports and imports and if exchange rates were allowed to float, then the trade condition would always be moving toward exports equaling imports, and therefore a trade balance of X-M=0.

Remember, a flexible exchange rate adjusts to make the quantity of dollars supplied equal to the quantity of dollars demanded. If the only buying and selling of dollars is for exports and imports, then the amount of dollars demanded in order to buy U.S. exports exactly equals the amount of dollars supplied to buy imports. Thus the value of exports equals the value of imports and X-M=0.

But we know that the balance of trade is often out of balance for many countries and in some cases it is way out of balance. How can that happen?

13.3.9 Exchange Rates and the Trade Balance—The Effect of International Capital Flows

It is possible for the balance of trade to be out of balance because trade is not the only reason people exchange currencies. Remember that international financial capital flows around the world in search of the best risk adjusted rate of return. As this capital moves across boundaries it has to be transformed. This financial capital flows through the foreign exchange market.

For example suppose, *ceteris paribus*, there is an expansion in demand for financial capital in the U.S. This shift in demand, shown in Figure 13.3.9, increases the interest rate and the rising interest rate attracts a greater quantity supplied. Now suppose some of this new quantity supplied comes from Europe. As financial capital moves from Europe to the U.S., euros have to be exchanged for dollars because U.S. financial assets like bonds are denominated in dollars. This is represented in the foreign exchange market graph, see Figure 13.3.9, as an expanding supply of euros and an expanding demand for dollars. How does this shift in the foreign exchange market affect the dollar? It makes it stronger. *Ceteris paribus*, what does this stronger dollar do to U.S. imports? They would go up because the dollar buys more. How about to U.S. exports? They would go down because U.S. items are more expensive for foreigners.

So if an expansion of demand for financial capital in the U.S. raises relative interest rates in the U.S., how, *ceteris paribus*, does that affect the trade balance? *Ceteris paribus*, the rate rise attracts international financial capital. The flow of capital into the U.S. strengthens the dollar. The stronger dollar increases imports and decreases exports. The trade balance (X-M) becomes less positive or more negative.

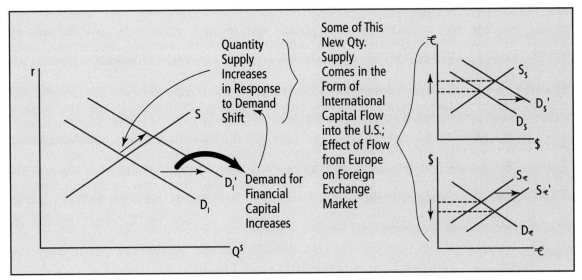

Figure 13.3.9 Expanding Demand in the Capital Market, Capital Flow in to Meet that Demand, Effect of that Capital Flow on the Exchange Rate

This same effect would occur if international financial capital flowed into a country in order to take advantage of very attractive opportunities in a surging stock market.

13.3.10 Exchange Rates and the Trade Balance —The Effect of International Capital Flows II

Now you try it.

Suppose that while the rest of the world remains steady, confidence in the U.S. economy declines significantly. How does this change in attitude affect the U.S. capital market? On a scratch piece of paper represent this case graphically in the capital and foreign exchange markets and predict how it will affect the trade balance.

As we saw when we examined the capital market, a decline in confidence reduces the demand for financial capital. Those who imagined attractive opportunities to make good returns on real investments in things like new factories or new equipment see fewer of those opportunities ahead. So they demand less financial capital.

With this fall in demand in the U.S. capital market, what happens to the interest rate? It falls. As it falls what happens to the quantity of financial capital supplied? It goes down because the price, the interest rate, is no longer high enough to keep all that capital in the market. So where does the capital that leaves the U.S. financial market go? Some of it goes to capital markets in other countries where the risk-adjusted return now looks better.

Let's assume that some of it goes to Europe. How does this affect the dollar/euro foreign exchange market? The capital moving out of the U.S. financial market in search of a better deal expands the demand for euros, increasing the dollar price of euros. So in this case is the dollar stronger or weaker? Weaker; it buys fewer euros. As a result, *ceteris paribus*, what effect can we expect this capital flow out of the U.S. to have on the U.S. trade balance? It will make the trade balance less negative or more positive as we buy fewer imports and sell more exports.

13.3.11 Exchange Rates and the Trade Balance—The Effect of International Capital Flows—Countervailing Forces

Now think about this one: Once this outward flow of financial capital begins are there any market forces that, under normal circumstances, could slow down the flow and ultimately stop it before it became a hemorrhage?

The answer is: "Yes, there are". Let's see what they are and how they work.

The story we have been telling began with falling confidence in the U.S. economy. This caused an outflow of financial capital from the U.S. in search of a better risk adjusted rate of return. As this capital flows out it weakens the dollar. This means the euro gets more expensive.

A progressively more expensive euro makes it more and more expensive for capital to leave the U.S. because dollars have to be exchanged for ever more expensive euros in order to leave. Furthermore, this capital flow out of the U.S. is a capital flow into Europe. As capital flows into Europe that expands the supply of financial capital there. *Ceteris paribus*, this lowers the interest rate there. Thus as financial capital flows from the U.S. to Europe, the cost of going (the exchange rate) goes up and the advantage of going (the European interest rate) goes down. At some point this rising cost and falling benefit of capital movement will eliminate the advantage of leaving. At that point the flow will stop. The international capital market will have reached a new equilibrium that reflects the revised level of confidence in the U.S. economy.

13.3.12 Global Financial Panic and Trade

But this self-adjusting mechanism has its limits. The adjustment process just described assumes that there is time for information to flow and to be thoughtfully processed. However, in our age of global communications and instantaneous transactions, there is sometimes not enough time for thoughtful processing of information.

Suppose you work in the international capital markets. You sit at a computer monitor all day making money by making electronic transactions that move financial capital around the globe. Suppose also that there is a nation called Zapland that has attracted significant international financial capital, including some of yours. Suddenly a newswire report like "Unrest in the streets in Zapland; Prime Minister resigns!" or "Largest Zapland Banks Reveal Insolvency!" flashes up on your screen. The credibility of the Zaplandese government and/or of its financial system is in a nose dive. This news makes markets *very* nervous. The market *will* respond to this new information. If you are behind the rest of the market in responding you can lose a lot of money very quickly.

You hear a voice in your head saying: "Get the hell out of there NOW! Sell out!" So you pull the trigger. You move everything you can out of there and into a safe haven—like the U.S. or Europe. You are not alone. Everyone else sitting at a similar screen wants to be the first one out—not "the last one out is a rotten egg" fool. You and they have independently acted rationally, given that the speed of the competition gives you virtually no time to process information. But the aggregate effect of your actions is a global financial panic.

Just such a panic occurred in the late 1990s. It began in mid-1997 with news of financial instability in Thailand. Since financial institutions from other nations in East Asia had interests in the Thai banks, that raised questions about the stability of banks in other East Asian countries. Questions quickly became concern, concern quickly became cautionary withdrawal of financial capital. Withdrawal of capital reduced the liquidity to the very banks that were in a shaky condition to begin with, so some of those faced collapse. News of possible banking collapses transformed cautionary withdrawal into a full-scale panic. Capital fled to safe havens like the U.S. or Europe. In the context of a panic mentality, every possible problem in any nation suddenly looms large and capital flees. Fear becomes a self-fulfilling expectation as possible problems become very real.

In 1998 this global financial panic sent huge amounts of financial capital racing to leave any country that seemed risky. Since the speed of transactions was so fast, there was little time to assess country-specific risk. In some cases the risks were significant, and in some cases they were probably not so significant. But in the panic, financial capital fled virtually all the economies that got associated with what was called "the Asian contagion." The name reflected the fact that the panic originated in East Asia, but by the end of the year the impact of the panic that started in Asia had spread as far as Brazil.

As capital fled these countries there was a rapid fall in the value of their currencies relative to the dollar. Furthermore with collapse of confidence and the outflow capital there was a dramatic contraction in those economies as investment vanished. Since these countries fell into recession or depression and their currencies were terribly weakened they were in no position to buy U.S. exports. Indeed, given the strong dollar the U.S. imported a great deal from them, contributing to a U.S. trade deficit that by the end of 1998 was at its highest level in history to that date. But this increase in exports to the U.S. was not enough to jump start these struggling economies. Exports can help an economy, but exports alone are not a sufficient foundation for a healthy economy. With little financial capital available and few plans to invest in new productive resources, for these struggling economies this increase in exports to the U.S. was too little, too late. This was a very painful time for those nations.

13.3.13 Summary of the Trade Balance (X-M)

Now let's review what we've learned about the determinants of the trade balance.

Absent any government intrusions, trade in any particular item is determined by the underlying market conditions in the producing country, the exchange rate that determines the currency-adjusted price for the consumers in other countries, and the demand conditions in those other countries. The aggregate effect of all this trade is the trade balance. If exchange rates are allowed to float and if the only action in the foreign exchange market is for the purposes of trade, then the value of exports will equal the value of imports, so trade will be balanced at X-M=0.

However, international capital flows change this. For example, suppose a country initially has a trade balance at X-M=0, but then for some reason its risk-adjusted interest rates rise relative to the rest of the world. The higher risk-adjusted interest rates attract financial capital. This inflow of capital strengthens the currency. The stronger currency makes imports rise and exports fall. The trade balance becomes negative: X-M<0.

The point to keep in mind is that the trade balance of any nation can be significantly affected by international flows of financial capital. So the determinants of a nation's trade balance and the direction of trade's affect on the nation's Aggregate Demand and the macroeconomy include both the underlying market conditions for items of trade and the global financial capital conditions.

We have examined how investment and trade move AD and the macroeconomy. Now let's explore the last major mover of AD—the government budget position.

13.4 THE GOVERNMENT'S BUDGET POSITION

13.4.1 How the Government's Budget Position Is Determined— General Principles

A government's budget position is the net aggregate effect of how much it spends and how much it taxes: G-T. The process by which a government goes about determining its budget position (G-T) depends on the nature of the government: A congressional/presidential system as in the U.S., a parliamentary system as in many other democracies, a dictatorship, or some other form.

In the U.S. the government's budget position is determined by the Congress and the President through a budget process that begins with a Presidential proposal, weaves its way through both Houses of Congress in parallel processes, converges though a joint committee of both Houses into a single budget bill, and then goes to the President for her signature. If she signs it, there is a budget. If not, negotiations ensue until she agrees with the Congress on a budget, or until Congress can pass a budget over a Presidential veto. While some players are obviously more powerful in this process than others (the President, the Speaker of the House, the Majority Leader in the Senate, certain chairs of crucial committees in each House), ultimately there are 536 people (the President, 100 Senators, and 435 House Members) who have a hand in determining the shape of the U.S. budget.

13.4.2 How the Government's Budget Position Is Determined—Specific Realities

In every government there are specific individuals who have the responsibility and the power to determine the government's budget. But the deliberations and decisions of these people do not take place in a vacuum. Powerful outside forces surround and sometimes engulf the process. In the U.S., interest groups with the financial means can leverage access to the decision-making process through political action committee (PAC) contributions to political campaigns, by media campaigns, and/or by stationing their lobbyists among the standing army of lobbyists that line the halls of Congress.

On rare occasions, dramatic international events can impose themselves on and define the direction of the budget decision-making process as when the Japan attacked Pearl Harbor on December 7, 1941. Japan's attack was an unparalleled shock to the United States security. It set off an unprecedented expansion in government spending as the United States geared up for war very quickly. The government budget position went from a slight deficit in 1940 to a huge deficit in 1944. This is represented in our Macro Picture as the dramatic shift in AD as shown in Figure 13.4.1.

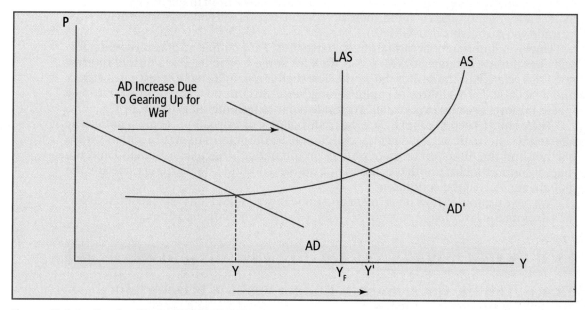

Figure 13.4.1 Gearing Up for World War II

We would expect this shift in AD to be accompanied, as Figure 13.4.1 suggests, by a dramatic fall in the level of unemployment and a rise in prices. In fact, during this period the unemployment rate did fall dramatically to a level below what can reasonably be considered the natural rate. At the outset prices rose just as dramatically. But then the government stepped in with a program of price controls and rationing to put a lid on that momentum.

A government's budget position is a political decision made in the context of both domestic needs and interests, and international realities. Once the budget position is determined its net effect contributes to the level of AD and in turn to the nation's macroeconomic conditions.

14.0 AGGREGATE SUPPLY AND THE TRANSITION TO POLICY

14.1 SOURCES OF AGGREGATE SUPPLY SHIFTS

Now that we have explored the sources of the forces that determine the level of aggregate demand, let's do the same for aggregate supply.

Recall that along a given short-run aggregate supply curve (AS) factor prices are constant. It is changes in these factor prices that shift AS. Such changes may be gradual as when wages are slowly rising. Or, they may be sudden and dramatic as when the Organization of Petroleum Exporting Countries (OPEC) shut off United States access to imported oil during the 1970s. At the time OPEC controlled much of the global oil production and was functioning as a very effective cartel working to determine how much oil was sold and to whom.

The response to the OPEC action in the U.S. was a quick, dramatic reduction in the supply of oil. With the sudden contraction of supply, oil prices shot up. Very few factors of production other than labor are as fundamental and widely important to our economy as the oil we use in fuels, plastics, pharmaceuticals, and many other products. When the price of such an essential and broadly used factor rises the impact may be felt economy wide. Graphically, this broad impact is represented by a rise in the AS line as shown in Figure 14.1.1.

In the OPEC case the sudden, dramatic oil price increase caused the AS line to shift up and as a consequence the country experienced inflation and a fall in the level of

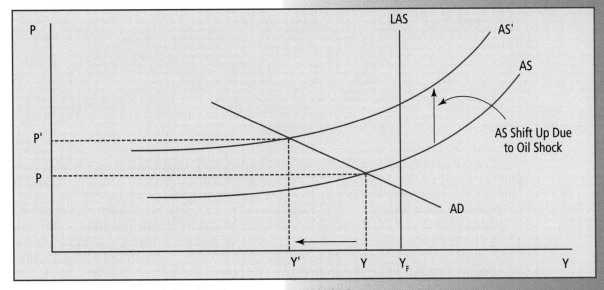

Figure 14.1.1   The OPEC Oil Shock and Aggregate Supply (AS)

real GDP with the associated rise in the level of unemployment. There were in fact, two separate OPEC-induced aggregate supply shocks during the 1970s, in 1973 and in 1979. The OPEC supply shocks were not the only shocks to the aggregate economy during these periods, but it seems clear that they were the most significant and contributed to the unemployment and inflation the U.S. economy suffered during this period.

International events are not the only source of supply shocks. Terrible weather might increase the cost of producing agricultural goods. A broad and dramatic failure of national computing networks due to a virulent virus could significantly drive up costs of production across the economy. Whatever the source, anything that broadly and dramatically affects the prices of factors of production and thus the general cost of production causes an aggregate supply shock to the economy.

14.2 TRANSITION TO POLICY

Now we have developed a mature model for representing the macro economy: our Macro Picture. We have examined the shapes of the AD, LAS, and AS lines. We have identified the sources of the forces that move these lines and in turn shape conditions in the macroeconomy. With this solid analytical framework in hand we can now answer one of our basic macroeconomic questions: Why are society's available resources sometimes less than fully utilized? Or in more common terms: Why is there unemployment?

Our model makes the answer to that question straightforward. As shown in Figure 14.2.1, if the economy is initially at full employment, any supply shock that shifts AS up (such as the OPEC oil price rise) or any demand shock that shifts AD down (such as a fall in investment as shown in Figure 14.2.2) will cause the actual GDP to fall below full GDP (Y_F). If this happens, the unemployment rate will be above the natural rate and there will be demand-deficient unemployment.

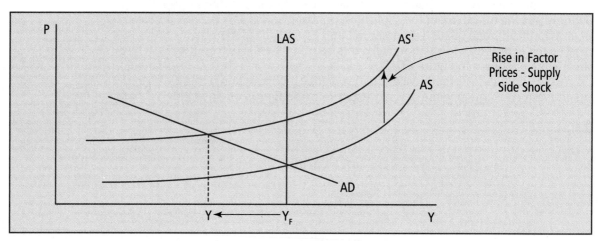

Figure 14.2.1 Macro AS Shock that Gives Rise to Unemployment

This answers the question as to why unemployment might occur, but there is then another question that follows: Why would unemployment persist? The answer to this question lies in the microeconomic foundation of the macroeconomy.

In what follows we will see that if our nice microeconomic assumptions hold, unemployment will not persist. The smoothly and quickly adjusting micro markets that those assumptions ensure eliminate unemployment in all factor markets and therefore in the whole macroeconomy. We will find, however, that if the nice assumptions do not represent reality, then in a world of significant market power and/or market failure the slow or incomplete or nonexistent adjustment of micro markets can lead to persistent macro unemployment.

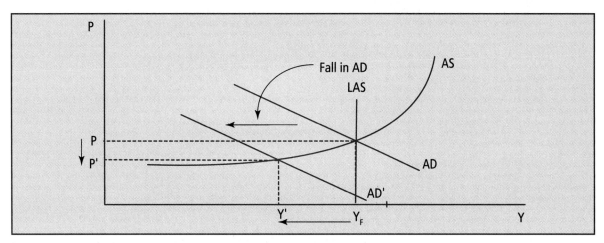

Figure 14.2.2 Macro AD Shock that Gives Rise to Unemployment

Recognizing and understanding this connection between the micro foundations and the macro implications for an economy is crucial. It is central to the analysis of how a macroeconomy can be expected to function, and thus it lies at the heart of the debate in modern mainstream economics over macroeconomic policy.

Let's examine this micro/macro connection by contrasting the working of the macroeconomy with and without the nice microeconomic assumptions.

15.0 POLICY: THE PROMISE AND THE PROBLEMS

15.1 BACKGROUND TO POLICY DEBATE, THE MICRO/MACRO CONNECTION

15.1.1 Introduction

The "nice assumptions" that gave us the Pareto optimal General Competitive Equilibrium at the micro level were:

1. No market failure—markets exist where needed and they adjust smoothly and quickly when needed.
2. No market power—a fair race with equal access to information and markets

As we saw when we developed the LAS line in our Macro Picture, when these nice assumptions hold the smoothly and quickly adjusting microeconomic processes they imply brings the macroeconomy smoothly and quickly to full employment. Now that we have our full tool kit in place we can demonstrate this micro/macro connection graphically.

15.1.2 Macroeconomic Response to Unemployment Given the Nice Microeconomic Assumptions

In Figure 15.1.1 the graph on the left represents a less than full employment condition in the macroeconomy. Here the actual GDP, Y^*, is at less than full GDP, Y_F, so we know that there is demand deficient unemployment in the economy. We also know by definition that along the AS line shown the factor prices are constant (e.g., the wage is constant). So the circumstance shown here represents conditions prior to adjustments in the factor markets.

What has this Macro Picture got to do with microeconomic realities? As we learned at the beginning of our study of macro, any macroeconomic condition is just an aggregation of the conditions in millions of individual microeconomic markets. Thus if as we show it here the macroeconomy is experiencing demand-deficient unemployment, there must be conditions in micro markets—specifically, the thousands of individual labor markets—that add up to macro demand-deficient unemployment. What must those conditions be?

The graph on the right in Figure 15.1.1 represents a generic micro labor market. The typical micro labor market looks as shown in Figure 15.1.1 when the macroeconomy is at less than full employment. The individual labor markets (e.g., the market for bricklayers, or nurses, or MBAs) must be experiencing an excess supply of workers, or, in other words, a quantity demanded that is not sufficient to absorb the quantity supplied—all the workers who are looking for a job at the going wage.

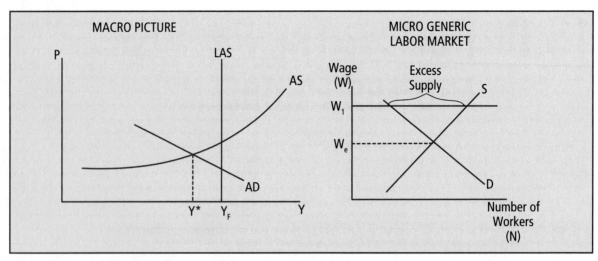

Figure 15.1.1 Macro Demand-Deficient Unemployment and Its Underlying Micro Conditions

The excess supply in each micro market exists because the wage, W_1, is above the equilibrium wage, W_e. As long as the wage remains at W_1 there will be an excess supply of, or a deficiency of demand for, this kind of labor. If this is the condition in individual labor markets throughout the economy, in the aggregate it adds up to a macro condition of demand-deficient unemployment. In effect, macroeconomic demand-deficient unemployment is the aggregate evidence of excess supplies of workers in thousands of individual labor markets. Now consider the adjustments that occur at the microeconomic level if our nice assumptions are weak assumptions. We will focus on our generic micro labor market as representative of the general case.

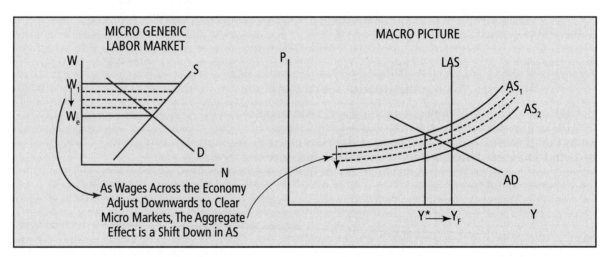

Figure 15.1.2 Macro Demand-Deficient Unemployment, Underlying Micro Conditions and Adjustments Under Our Nice Micro Assumptions

As shown in Figure 15.1.2, there is initially an excess supply of labor in the micro markets. As we learned in micro, given our nice assumptions markets respond to such a disequilibrium by adjusting. How is that going to happen in this case? The unemployed workers begin bidding for employment. How do they do that? They offer to work for a wage that is lower than the going wage. What does this process look like in our micro labor market picture?

As we learned in micro, markets adjust on a price signal. In this case, the price involved is the price of labor, the wage. We learned that the signal will adjust to clear the market.

In this case, the bidding for jobs by unemployed workers will lower the wage and in the process eliminate the excess supply of labor in this market.

How does this microeconomic adjustment process show up on the graph representing the macroeconomic model? Recall that the wage is a factor price and as factor prices change the AS line shifts. A fall in factor prices, such as a broad-based fall in wages, shifts the AS line downward.

In the case before us the unemployment present at Y* represents thousands of micro labor markets in disequilibrium, an excess supply condition. Under our nice assumptions this disequilibrium sets off microeconomic adjustments: A fall in the price of labor, the wages. These broad-based falling factor prices are represented at the macro level as shown in Figure 15.1.2 by a shifting down of the AS line. The microeconomic adjustments continue until the individual labor markets are cleared: Each market in equilibrium and all the excess supplies eliminated. While our example is in terms of labor, this process holds for all unemployed factors: labor, capital, or natural resources.

When all the micro factor markets are cleared the macroeconomy is at full employment. This is represented in the Macro Picture by the fact that when the micro adjustments are complete the AS has shifted from AS₁ to AS₂. At AS₂ the macroeconomy is at full employment.

In this process the microeconomic adjustments necessary to eliminate the excess supplies of unemployed factors lower the costs of factors and this lowers the costs of production. This, in turn, lowers product prices because, in the perfectly competitive markets we are assuming here, as production costs go down competition forces product prices down. Therefore as the Macro Picture demonstrates the price level falls.

Does this process leave workers better off or worse off? In the aggregate we can say that everyone who now wants a job can now find one, and that even as wages fell, prices did also, so real wages may be the same. But some people who were in the labor market left as wages fell. And, while real wages may be the same on average, there are almost certainly winners and losers because wage adjustments in different markets may be smaller or larger depending on market elasticities. Here, as in all macro analysis, we cannot know the micro consequences without looking through a microscope. What we can say is that there is a very important connection between microeconomic markets and macroeconomic conditions, and that under our nice assumptions micro adjustments bring the macroeconomy to full employment.

15.1.3 Macroeconomic Response to Inflationary Pressure Given the Nice Microeconomic Assumptions

Now let's examine an adjustment process from the opposite direction.

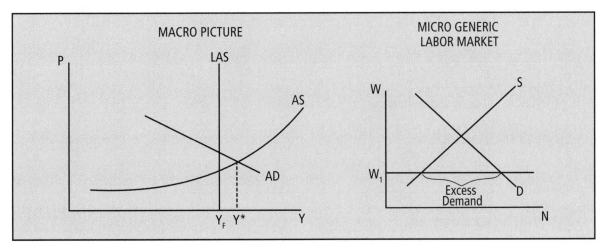

Figure 15.1.3 Macro Inflationary Pressure and Its Underlying Micro Conditions

Suppose, as is shown in Figure 15.1.3, AD is very high, causing inflationary pressures. In this short-run circumstance the resources of society are being used to a degree that is not sustainable in the long run. This pressure on the productive capacity of the economy is reflected at the microeconomic level as excess demands for the available factors of production. In analyzing the adjustment process we will focus, as before, on a generic labor market.

An excess demand is represented graphically as shown in Figure 15.1.3. Given our nice assumptions, markets respond to such a disequilibrium by adjusting. How is that going to happen in this case? In this tight labor market the enterprises begin bidding for workers. How do they do that? As reflected in Figure 15.1.4, they offer higher wages. What does this process look like in our micro labor market picture?

As we saw in our study of microeconomic markets, when there is an excess demand the price signal will adjust upward to clear the market. In this case the wage level in millions of microeconomic labor markets (e.g., bricklayers, teachers, mechanics) rises until quantity supplied and quantity demanded in every individual market are equalized. W_1 is the wage prior to adjustment. At that wage excess demand exists. W_e is the wage after adjustment. The adjustment eliminates the excess demand.

How does this microeconomic adjustment process show up in our Macro Picture? Recall that the wage is a factor price and as factor prices change the AS line shifts. A rise in factor prices, such as a broad-based rise in wages, shifts the AS line upward. As shown in Figure 15.1.4, the microeconomic adjustments will continue until the micro factor markets are cleared. At the macroeconomic level this is reflected in a shift from AS_1 to AS_2, at which point the economy is in a long run, full-employment condition.

In this process the microeconomic adjustments necessary to eliminate the excess demands for factors raised the costs of factors and, in turn, the costs of production and the product prices—as represented in the higher price level in the Macro Picture. So does this process leave workers better off or worse off? In the aggregate we can say that everyone who now wants a job can find one, and that even as wages rose prices did also so real wages may be the same. But again there are almost certainly winners and losers because wage adjustments in different markets may be smaller or larger depending on market elasticities. Here as before we cannot know the micro consequences without looking through a microscope. But what we can say yet again is that there is a very important connection between microeconomic market processes and macroeconomic conditions, and that under our nice assumptions micro adjustments bring the macroeconomy to full employment.

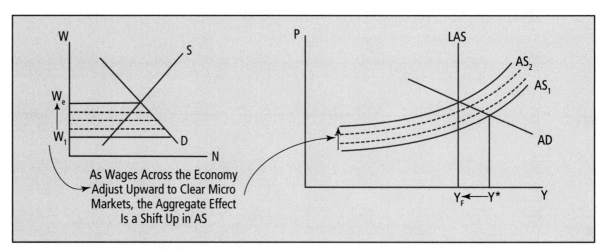

Figure 15.1.4 Macro Inflationary Pressure, Underlying Micro Conditions, and Adjustments Under Our Nice Micro Assumptions

15.1.4 Macroeconomics and the Invisible Hand

What we have just demonstrated is the amazing self-adjusting potential of a market system to bring the entire economy to a full employment position. This is precisely the story that Adam Smith first told so powerfully in his *Inquiry into the Nature and Causes of the Wealth of Nations* in 1776. Notice the title tells you that his story is about *The Wealth of Nations.* What we have just seen is something Smith understood very well. The aggregate material well-being of a nation, the wealth of a nation, depends on the micro foundations on which that aggregate reality is built. If the "invisible hand," as Smith referred to it, is guiding the micro process without any impediment then it follows that the macro result will be excellent: Full employment. Ultimately, the level of efficiency in the microeconomic adjustment system determines how quickly the macroeconomy will eliminate demand-deficient unemployment or too much pressure. This should not be surprising. As has been emphasized all along, micro and macro analysis are different perspectives on the same economy. If the economy is working efficiently at the micro level, this will be reflected at the macro level.

In the terms of our analysis, the power of the invisible hand is determined by how realistic our nice assumptions are. If our nice assumptions are realistic the micro system is as efficient as possible. In that case macroeconomic problems are quickly and automatically eliminated by microeconomic adjustments. On the other hand, to the degree that market power and/or market failure are a problem the micro system will not work efficiently, and in turn the macroeconomy will not automatically move toward full employment at a stable price level. Indeed, if the micro system is not working properly it is possible for the macro economy to become stuck in a perverse condition such as high unemployment.

So what is the role of government in this economic system?

15.1.5 The Role of Government

The Preamble to the United States Constitution reads:

> We the People of the United States, in Order to form a more perfect Union, establish Justice, insure domestic Tranquility, provide for the common defence, promote the general Welfare, and secure the Blessings of Liberty to ourselves and our Posterity, do ordain and establish this Constitution for the United States of America.

This Preamble defines the purpose of the government as envisioned by those who wrote that United States Constitution. That Constitution lays out the structure of the government, including the responsibilities of each branch within that structure and the boundaries of federal government power. Since 1787 amendments have changed and Supreme Court decisions have interpreted the words of the Constitution. Since 1787, however, the Preamble has remained the same—always defining the common purpose. All this raises a practical question: Given the structure of government, what should the role of government be in order to fulfill its purpose? Next we examine the government structures that control United States macroeconomic policy, and we examine the debate about how macroeconomic policy should be managed in order to realize the purposes of government as laid out in the Preamble.

There is indeed a sharp debate between the non-interventionists and interventionists as to whether the government has any role to play in the economy. The non-interventionists believe that the micro system works pretty well, thank you, and that government just screws up the processes, so *laissez faire* (from the French for "to let to do"—in other words, let it work itself out on its own) is the way to go. The interventionists believe that we cannot depend on the system to work in all cases so there are times when thoughtful government policy is the wise course.

The non-interventionist response to the interventionist is that "thoughtful policy" is an oxymoron—that the arrogance of a government that claims to know the answers to every problem is part of the problem, not part of the solution. The best guidance for the course of economic events comes from the informed decisions of autonomous individuals pursuing their own interest. Government intrusion is a threat to liberty.

The interventionist response to the non-interventionist is that a faith in the invisible hand is a naïve faith with dreadful consequences if followed. In response to the suggestion that if we just wait for the long run adjustments to fix things, John Maynard Keynes reportedly replied, "In the long run we are all dead," as in: Waiting for the long run is like waiting for a ship to come in that isn't coming. And while you wait people suffer and lose faith, thus undermining the fabric of liberal society.

As our analysis of policy unfolds keep in mind that while our case is the United States economy, our model is applicable to any economy. You should read the news of the day and look at how the ideas we are examining here inform your understanding of the issues that are unfolding in the United States, in South Africa, in Lebanon, in Mexico, in Iran, in India, in Russia, in China, in every corner of the globe. Later we will expand our story to a global perspective, so your immersion in current international events will pay off when we get to what is called "open economy macro."

Now let's examine macroeconomic policy: The tools and the debate. We begin with a brief review of the promise of the macroeconomy—the ideal for which a nation strives, and the kinds of macroeconomic problems that can and actually do occur.

15.2 THE PROMISE AND THE PROBLEMS

15.2.1 The Promise

Most economists agree that the long run ideal for a macro economy is to have full employment (the natural rate of unemployment) and a stable price level. So, as we examine macroeconomic policy this will be the goal we ascribe to policy makers. But keep in mind that while achieving this goal ensures the greatest wealth for the nation, it does not ensure a just distribution of that wealth among individuals. And even if this long run ideal is achieved, as population grows and as many nations strive to enjoy the level of material well-being we enjoy, the prospect of very long run growth in production (Y_F moving to the right) raises important questions of sustainability. For now we will set this issue aside and focus on the long run policy objectives: Full employment and stable price level.

Historically, these objectives are rarely achieved. Aggregate demand and/or aggregate supply shocks can lead to macroeconomic problems that range from mild to catastrophic. In order to understand the nature of these potential problems, we begin by reviewing some of the most difficult macroeconomic problems the United States has faced in recent years.

With those challenges in mind we will then turn to the central questions of long run macro policy: What macroeconomic tools does the government have at its disposal? Should the government use these tools to intervene and fix problems, or is government intervention itself a source of the problems?

15.2.2 The Problems—Aggregate Demand Shocks and the Phillips Curve

Until the 1970s most economists believed that all shocks to the macro system were caused by shifts in aggregate demand. This was based on the assumption that the aggregate supply line is fixed. Given this perspective all possible macro problems can be represented by shifts of the AD line along the given AS line. This means that the macroeconomy can experience either unemployment without inflation if AD is falling, or full employment with inflation if AD is rising.

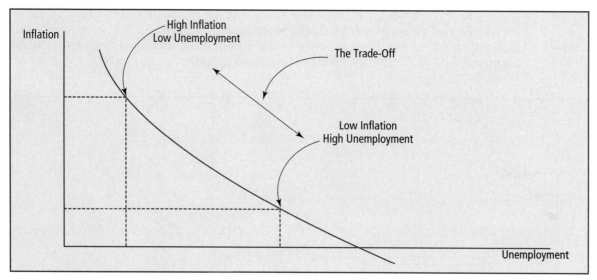

Figure 15.2.1 The Phillips Curve

This either/or proposition with respect to inflation and unemployment was presented in a 1958 paper by an economist named A. W. Phillips. He presented it not as a theoretical relationship but as an empirical one based on analysis of historical data. Nevertheless, it became the foundation of a theoretical trade-off that came to be known as the *Phillips curve*.

The Phillips curve shown in Figure 15.2.1 reinforced the view of most mainstream economists that government faced a policy trade-off: The price of lower unemployment was inflation, and the price of lower inflation was unemployment. The Phillips curve represents this trade-off very simply.

This trade-off view of the economic problems of inflation and unemployment was held so long because it seemed to be consistent with actual experience. Recall that the Great Depression can be represented as a point to the far right of the Phillips curve with very high unemployment and no inflation, while the expanding AD of World War II took the economy up the Phillips curve to very low unemployment and an initial surge of inflation until the government put the lid on it with rationing and price controls.

The experience of the 1960s seemed to reinforce this Phillips curve perspective. Government spending on domestic programs such as Medicare and Medicaid expanded in an effort to realize President Lyndon Johnson's Great Society. Spending on the Vietnam War also increased dramatically in 1965. This spending surge was not offset by major tax increases. Thus we find that during this period AD shifted out, and as a result unemployment fell from 6.7 percent in 1961 to 3.5 percent in 1969, while the inflation rate rose from 1.0 percent in 1961 to 5.4 percent in 1969.

This condition of rising prices at full employment set off that especially perverse phenomenon we learned about earlier: a wage-price spiral. Recall that as the price level rises, the value of anything measured in nominal terms falls. Wages are always measured in nominal terms because today's wages are paid with today's money. Thus, with inflation the real value of a wage falls. Workers feel this effect and respond by demanding higher wages—a demand that employers have to take seriously when full employment makes labor markets tight.

At first these demands are made contract by contract: Each new contract negotiated includes a wage catch-up. However, as inflation continues, it becomes built into the expectations of the wage earners. When you expect inflation, you seek to avert its effects by building automatic inflation adjustments directly into your wage contract, so you negotiate an indexed wage.

All these increases in nominal wage levels shift the aggregate supply curve up. As we learned earlier, the wage-price spiral looks as shown in Figure 15.2.2. At each new condition the price level has increased—the inflation continues, which reaffirms the expectations and the wage demands, which in turn feeds the inflation, and so on.

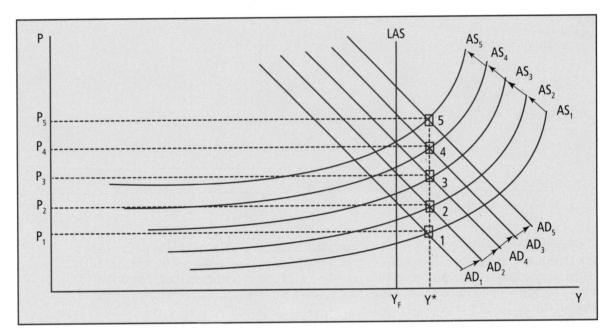

Figure 15.2.2 Wage-Price Spiral

15.2.3 The Problems—Dislodging the Phillips Curve: Aggregate Supply Shocks

These inflationary expectations are what underlie our last case, unemployment with inflation, a condition referred to as *stagflation*. It is possible to have a situation in which there is demand-deficient unemployment and yet those who remain employed are still fighting to maintain real value of their wages. This case can be represented in our Macro Picture as shown in Figure 15.2.3.

As in the full employment case, the track of the economy is straight up so actual GDP, Y^*, is constant and all that is changing is the price level, P. In this case, however, $Y^* < Y_F$, so it is inflation with demand-deficient unemployment, or stagflation.

When Jimmy Carter ran for president against Gerald Ford in 1976, he cited the 1975 statistics that reflected economic stagflation: the unemployment rate was over 8 percent and the inflation rate was over 9 percent. Mr. Carter added these two values together and called it a "misery index." The misery index was over 17 percent that year, and Carter won the election.

This concept came back to haunt Mr. Carter, however. When he ran for reelection in 1980 against Ronald Reagan, Reagan pointed to 1979 figures showing the unemployment rate close to 6 percent and an inflation rate over 11 percent, for a misery index that was still over 17 percent. Mr. Reagan won that election.

Clearly, in the opinion of American voters neither Mr. Ford nor Mr. Carter solved the country's macroeconomic problems. Unfortunately for their political careers, they both faced a macroeconomic problem that took them and their advisors into uncharted territory. Conventional, Phillips curve-based logic held that unemployment and inflation were an either/or proposition. Mr. Ford and Mr. Carter faced the worst of both worlds, stagflation. An expectationally fueled inflation seemed to survive even in the face of increased unemployment. To make matters worse for both men, each saw their efforts to reduce

16.0 MONETARY POLICY

16.1 THE INSTITUTIONAL CONTEXT

16.1.1 Introduction—The Fed

One of the primary macroeconomic policy tools a government has at its disposal is monetary policy. *Monetary policy* is based on government's ability to manipulate of the supply of financial capital or liquidity.

In most countries a central bank manages monetary policy. In Europe a *European Central Bank* manages the monetary policy for all the countries that use the euro. Some central banks are fairly independent agencies and some are less so.

The example we will explore in order to understand the workings of a central bank and monetary policy is the monetary authority of the United States, the *Federal Reserve*. The *Fed* as it is commonly called was established by Congress and can be abolished by Congress. It is not a constitutional institution. Nevertheless it has enjoyed significant independence from direct political control. One reason for this is its structure.

The Fed is led by a Chair who is appointed by the President and must be approved by the Senate. The Chair serves a 4-year renewable term, so the President who appointed her may be gone by the time the question as to whether she will be reappointed comes up. Under the leadership of the Chair, the Federal Reserve Board runs the Federal Reserve System. This Board has seven members including the Chair. As with the Chair, the members of the Board are appointed by the President and must be approved by the Senate. They serve a 14-year nonrenewable term, so they enjoy great independence from the shifting winds of political interests.

The Federal Reserve System was established in 1913 in order to bring coherence to the nation's banking system after a series of crises. It is divided into 12 districts, each served by a Federal Reserve Bank. While private banks nominally own the Fed, the actual decision-making power rests with the Fed's *Board of Governors* and with a larger body called the *Federal Open Market Committee* or *FOMC*. The FOMC is composed of the seven Board members plus the presidents of five of the district Federal Reserve Banks. The FOMC, under direction of the Fed Chair, determines the nation's monetary policy.

16.1.2 Distinguishing the Fed from the Treasury Department

It is important to keep in mind that the Fed and the United States Treasury Department are entirely separate government agencies. The Fed is an independent agency. The Treasury is a Department of the Executive Branch under the President. It is the Treasury Department that collects the federal taxes and pays the federal government's bills. If the government's tax revenues are not sufficient to pay those bills the government budget position (G-T) is in deficit. In that case the Treasury borrows money to cover that deficit by selling Treasury bonds or bills. These are in effect IOUs that promise a payback on specific terms. They are sold in the open market to any individual or institution that is willing to hold the government's debt paper and in effect loan the government money.

The open market in which bonds are bought and sold is the financial capital market that we learned about earlier. Governments and businesses sell new bonds to borrow financial capital. These bond sellers are demanders of capital, offering a bond as an IOU in exchange for the financial capital. Individuals or institutions buy bonds in order to make an interest return on their financial capital. These bond buyers are suppliers of financial capital, taking a bond as an IOU in return.

To understand how the *bond market* works, consider a very simple, hypothetical example: Suppose the Treasury offers a bond for sale that costs $10,000, that pays $1,000 interest/year for 20 years, and that returns the $10,000 principle at the end of the 20-year life of the loan. A person who buys that $10,000 20-year bond is looking at earning 10% interest every year because the $1,000 interest each year is 10% of the $10,000 loaned.

If during the life of that 20-year bond the person holding it decides she needs the money or that she can do better in another investment, she can sell that bond on the open market to someone else. Since the amount the bond pays each year is a constant $1,000/year, the less the buyer pays for the bond the more interest the buyer will be earning, or alternatively the more the buyer pays for the bond the less interest the buyer will be earning. So in terms of our example, as the 20-year bond price rises the interest rate yield on that 20-year bond falls, and vice versa. As a general principle, bond prices and interest rates move in opposite directions.

So what does all this information about Treasury bonds and the open market for bonds have to do with the Fed? A lot! But to understand why, we still need to develop some more institutional information. We need to look at how a financial system works.

16.1.3 How the Financial System Works

A *financial system* is the arrangement of institutions that coordinate the intentions of suppliers and demanders of financial capital. Remember, in any market the attitudes and intentions of suppliers and demanders are determined independently, and the price adjusts to bring these intentions into balance. The financial markets work just this way and work efficiently to the degree that market power and market failure do not distort the process. But in the financial capital market suppliers and demanders rarely interact directly. Maybe you have borrowed money from your parents, but more likely if you needed a very large loan, like a college loan, you went to a financial institution like a bank.

Banks are one of the intermediaries that carry out the transactions of the financial system. In most cases it would be very costly in time and legal fees for an individual with money to lend to find others who want to borrow and then to negotiate terms of the loan. Banks and other *financial intermediaries* make it their business to attract financial capital and then to lend it to those who need financial capital. Banks attract the capital by paying interest for it. They make a return by lending that capital to someone else at a higher rate of interest. If the financial system is perfectly competitive, then as in any other market all participants will make only a normal return on their investment.

The web of financial institutions that make up the financial system coordinate the exchange of capital in the financial capital market. We will focus on how a bank functions.

16.1.4 Banks and Reserves

Banks hold *assets* and have *liabilities*. An asset is anything you have that has value in the market. If you have a car, or a marketable painting, or cash, you have an asset. A liability is a claim by others on your assets. If you have a loan, you have a liability. Your *portfolio* is all the assets and liabilities you have. A portfolio can be represented by a *t-account*. Figure 16.1.1 shows a very simple representation of a new bank's portfolio.

Suppose you deposit $200 cash in this new bank. Now the bank's t-account looks like the t-account shown in Figure 16.1.1. On the left in that t-account we see the bank has

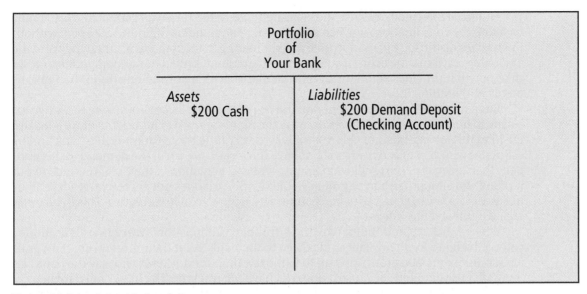

Figure 16.1.1 A Bank's Portfolio

assets of $200, the $200 cash you deposited. On the right we see the bank has a $200 liability because you can come in and withdraw your $200 if you choose to. If the bank just puts this money in its vault and sits on it, you and the bank can both feel absolutely secure knowing that it has all the money it is liable for right in the vault.

This is called a *full reserve system*. *Reserves* are the *liquid assets* of a bank. Liquid assets are those that can change form quickly without losing value. Financial capital is a very liquid asset. You can immediately get a dollar's worth of value for every dollar of financial capital you exchange for something else in the market. That is why we refer to it as liquidity. In contrast, a house is a very illiquid asset. If you own a house that is assessed at $100,000 you can presumably get that much for it on the open market, but not quickly. It takes time to find a full-price buyer. If you need to sell your house in a hurry, you will not get $100,000 for your house. You'll get a lot less.

Financial institutions need to hold some of their assets as reserves, that is in a liquid form, in order to cover the normal day to day withdrawals that occur. If they only have illiquid assets they would lose money every time they had to sell such an asset to cover a withdrawal.

If your bank has liabilities of $200 and reserves of $200, then it has reserves to cover all the claims on its assets. In that case the bank is holding full reserves. But as we just saw, a bank makes it return by taking your deposit and loaning that liquidity out at interest. Banks do not want to hold full reserves, and they don't. What a prudent bank tries to do is keep a portion of its assets in liquid form . . . as reserves to cover anticipated day to day transactions, and loan out the rest. The portion a bank holds as reserves depends on the flow of withdrawals it can reasonably expect. On a normal day relatively few people withdraw money, so the portion of assets held as reserves does not normally have to be very large. When banks function this way, holding a portion of assets as reserves and loaning out the rest to make a return, this is called a *fractional reserve system*.

16.1.5 Fractional Reserve Systems

A *fractional reserve system* is very good for an economy because it allows financial capital to be constantly active. It provides a mechanism for getting the financial capital from someone who does not want to use it right now (the depositor) to someone who wants to put it to work (the borrower). When you put your money in a bank someone else can put it to good use to start a business or develop a new product or get an education. Thus, by keeping financial capital constructively engaged this system serves society.

Financial intermediaries are the clearinghouse of the financial capital market. If they facilitate the coordination between suppliers and demanders of financial capital without themselves distorting the market (like discriminating in making loans), then they provide a valuable service to the economy. So long as the system is ruled by fair competition rather than power it provides all financial intermediaries with a normal return on their investments and nothing more.

But a fractional reserve system does have a down side. There is a strong incentive for a bank to hold inadequate reserves because the more capital it loans out the more it makes. Pushing this is risky business because it leaves very little room for error. If a bank underestimates withdrawal activity it will not have the reserves to meet the demand. If this happens the bank has to start selling off illiquid assets at a fraction of their market value to put its hands on enough cash to pay off its liabilities. Since it does not get full value for its illiquid assets, its books go out of balance. Its assets are less than its liabilities. This in turn can create a snowballing effect.

When word gets out that a bank is in trouble its depositors worry that their money will not be there for them. They quickly go to the bank to get their money out. If a significant number of depositors show up to withdraw their funds there is no way the bank can meet all these demands because it does not have full reserves. The bank "fails" to meet its obligations. If one bank fails, that makes depositors at other banks nervous. They fear that their life savings for college, a home, or retirement will vanish. These nervous depositors go to their banks to withdraw funds. Others see them doing so and join in out of fear that all the funds will be gone if they do not get there soon enough. They run to withdraw. This *run on the banks* can cause even prudent, responsible banks that are holding normally adequate reserves to have liquidity problems and fail. As more banks look shaky or fail, people get more and more nervous. Concern turns into *panic*. Under a fractional system, even the most responsible banks are doomed when confronted with a run on their resources. Because all banks hold only fractional reserves, a collapse of confidence and expectations of further bank failures is self-fulfilling.

16.1.6 Fractional Reserve Systems and the Fed

The Fed was established in 1913 to regulate major United States banks so that they function responsibly. Today all banks are required by Fed regulations to keep a certain percentage of their assets in the form of reserves. This *reserve requirement*, along with Fed regulation of bank practices, ensures that banks do not take on irresponsible levels of risk. These policies are designed to ensure that the U.S. banking system is run prudently. Nevertheless, at the beginning of the Great Depression panic overwhelmed this regulatory system. Even prudent banks cannot survive a panic. That traumatic national experience gave rise to the Federal Deposit Insurance Corporation (FDIC), which insures individuals' deposits up to a certain amount. The logic of this program should be clear. The FDIC is intended to allay the fears of depositors and thereby reduce the likelihood of a run on the financial institutions.

But the regulations of the Fed and the insurance of the FDIC may not always be sufficient to stop a panic. The best insurance against panic is maintaining confidence that banks are not at risk of collapse. The Fed can use its Open Market Operations to do this. It can also use Open Market Operations to influence the course of the macroeconomy. Now, with the institutional context in place, let's look at the hows and whys of Fed policy and the debate as to whether it should ever intervene.

16.2 THE IMPLEMENTATION OF MONETARY POLICY

16.2.1 The Fed and Open Market Operations

The primary policy tool the Fed has at its disposal is called *Open Market Operations*. This policy gets its name from the fact that its implementation is accomplished by the Fed buying or selling U.S. Government Treasury bonds in the open market. The Fed carries out

Open Market Operations by buying Treasury bonds from or selling Treasury bonds to banks.

When it buys, the Fed replaces a less than fully liquid asset in the banks' portfolios, Treasury bonds, with a fully liquid asset, financial capital. As a result these banks have more assets in the form of reserves. If they are already holding reserves adequate to cover their reserve requirement these new reserves are *excess reserves*.

These banks do not want to hold excess reserves because excess reserves are assets that could be put to work earning a return. The quickest outlet for excess reserves are overnight loans to other banks that need more reserves to bring their daily accounts up to the reserve requirement. The market among banks for this overnight borrowing of reserves is called the *Federal Funds Market*. The interest rate paid for these overnight loans of reserves is called the *Federal Funds Rate*. When the Fed buys in the open market the immediate effect of this expansion in the supply of available reserves in the banks is a fall in the Federal Funds Rate.

If the Fed sells Treasury bonds to banks, it replaces a fully liquid asset in the banks' portfolios—reserves, with a less liquid asset—the bonds. As a result there are fewer reserves in the banking system. As the supply of reserves in the banks contracts, the Federal Funds Rate rises.

Since the Fed is not concerned about profits or losses, it can always sell low enough to find a buyer and always buy high enough to find a seller. It puts more reserves into the system (by buying bonds from banks) to lower the Fed Funds Rate; it takes reserves out (by selling bonds to banks) to raise the rate. The Fed uses Open Market Operations to set the Fed Funds Rate at a level it deems helpful to the economy.

The Fed Funds Rate is the key tool the Fed uses to implement its policies. There is, however, another tool it can and occasionally does use to put more emphasis on a policy move. That is the Discount Rate.

16.2.2 The Fed and the Discount Rate

Any bank can go directly to the Fed to borrow reserves. The interest rate the Fed charges banks for reserves is called the *Discount Rate*. (This is a proper name for this loan; it is not the same thing as our micro concept of the discount rate.) In theory the Fed can influence the amount of reserves in the banks by raising or lowering the Discount Rate. A lower Discount Rate makes borrowing cheaper so more reserves flow into the financial system. A higher Discount Rate makes borrowing more expensive so less reserves flow into the financial system. In practice, however, banks do not borrow very often or very much directly from the Fed, so the Discount Rate is not a significant policy tool of the Fed. Changes in the Discount Rate are usually done to keep it from getting too far out of line with the Federal Funds Rate, since both are sources for bank borrowing.

But why use these tools at all? Let's look at some cases in which interventionists might urge the Fed to intervene and the non-interventionist argument against such intervention.

16.3 POLICY ISSUES—FINANCIAL CRISES

16.3.1 A Financial Crisis

Suppose an economy gets caught up in a *speculative bubble*. This is period of dynamic economic activity when the perception of many is that there is a lot of money to be made.

As we learned in micro, choices are driven by perceptions, and perceptions may or may not reflect underlying reality. In a boom mentality, people begin to believe that asset prices, prices on things like stocks or real estate, will go up and up. That mentality leads to speculation. People buy stocks and real estate on the assumption that they will be able to sell it at a higher price later. Such speculation leads to higher and higher prices, which reinforces the perceptions that the boom is continuing—and to the perception that you would be a fool to miss this opportunity to make some easy money. Such speculation can run asset prices up very high very quickly.

It is normally impossible for underlying economic activity to expand real production nearly so quickly, so the real value underlying the speculative boom lags behind the paper value of assets. The expansion of paper values is like a bubble that can burst at any time. The pin that bursts the bubble is generally some event that brings more sober assessments of the relationship between real economic activity and asset prices.

For example, a financial institution might fail because in the flush of success and optimism its leaders begin to think they are "oh so smart." Seduced by their own conceit, they make some very risky decisions. They get burned. This news hits the wires. Reporters smell blood and begin to shed light on other such financial institutions that have similar risky portfolios. Suddenly people are wary. They want to get out while their assets are at a high value. As people begin to sell to get out of the market, asset values fall. It becomes a "last one out is a rotten egg" market, because the last one out will have a portfolio that stinks. People try to sell quickly before it is too late. Once this panicky selling sets in, it is too late. The bubble has burst.

Once the bubble bursts the economy can implode. Other irresponsible banks fail. As banks fail they call in loans to liquidate their assets. Individuals with loans from these banks may not have the funds to pay off the loan, especially if the borrowed money is tied up in speculation. Individuals declare bankruptcy. Even responsible banks can get caught up in the crisis as their assets lose value. As the financial system implodes the supply of financial capital for the purposes of real investment dries up, sending long term interest rates higher and choking off investment. As Investment (I) contracts, Aggregate Demand contracts sending the real economy into recession or even depression.

16.3.2 A Financial Crisis and the Fed

So what can the Fed do to avoid this disaster? If banks or other financial institutions look like they are at risk the Fed can step in to provide them with the reserves they need to stay afloat. If the Fed can keep the panic from starting it may be able to spare the economy the disaster of the financial collapse and the subsequent real collapse when the bubble bursts.

In the fall of 1998 there were financial crises around the globe—in the Far East, in South America, in Russia. The global financial panic, the "Asian contagion" as it was called since it started in Asia, seemed to be spreading. It had not spread to the U.S. financial market, but many feared it would. The Fed's response is reflected in this press release from the Fed dated September 29, 1998:

> The Federal Open Market Committee decided today to ease the stance of monetary policy slightly, expecting the federal funds rate to decline ¼ percentage point to around 5-1/4 percent.
>
> The action was taken to cushion the effects on prospective economic growth in the United States of increasing weakness in foreign economies and of less accommodative financial conditions domestically. . . .

This "less accommodative financial conditions domestically" reflects the Fed's concern that the international financial crisis could tighten up access to capital in the U.S. In order to allay domestic concerns the Fed used its Open Market tool to pump more liquidity into the capital market. On November 17th of that year the Fed lowered the Fed Funds Rate another ¼ percentage point, noting in the press release that day that "[a]lthough conditions in financial markets have settled down materially since mid-October, unusual strains remain." So we see that the Fed can use its Open Market Operations tool to offset sudden, destabilizing contractions of liquidity in the financial system. In this 1998 case it intervened to simply allay fears of such a contraction.

16.3.3 The Debate Over Fed Intervention in a Financial Panic

In the face of an emerging financial crisis the Fed can step in to try to stop the problem before it becomes a panic that brings down the financial system and, in turn, the economy. It can do so by providing liquidity to the financial system so that institutions that might otherwise fail have the resources necessary to stay afloat. And as importantly if not more so, by making a public show of support for the financial system the Fed may be able to allay fears that might grow into panic and in turn bring down an otherwise solid financial system.

It can do this, but should the Fed do this? The interventionists say, "Yes, of course. To allow the economy to collapse is absurd. There is more than paper involved here; the livelihoods of millions of families rest on the foundation of a solid financial system. That foundation must be maintained."

The non-interventionists disagree. They say, "No way. If the Fed saves the fools who have been engaged in speculation from their own stupidity this time, it just encourages them to act foolish next time because they'll assume the Fed will bail them out again. Doing this creates what economists refer to as a *moral hazard* problem: If you don't feel the consequences of your irresponsible action, you're not likely to change your behavior. Let the market pick the winners and punish the losers, not some government central bank bureaucrats."

I hope you can see in this case as we have seen in others before: Both sides in this debate have a compelling logic. Policy choices are usually not so simple or clear as some suggest. When it comes to policy in our complex world: Anyone who says it's simple is either simple minded, or thinks you are.

With that in mind we turn to another dimension of Fed policy: Aggregate demand management. With its policy tools the Fed can exert significant power over aggregate demand and in turn over the macroeconomy. We want to see how. Then we want to explore the inevitable debate: Should it?

16.4 POLICY ISSUES—AGGREGATE DEMAND MANAGEMENT

16.4.1 Aggregate Demand and the Fed

We have seen that the Fed can use Open Market Operations to expand or contract the amount of reserves available to the banks and thereby control the Federal Funds Rate. Now let's see how this power translates into significant potential influence over aggregate demand and in turn macroeconomic conditions.

In order to tell this story we need to return to our long term capital market picture shown here as Figure 16.4.1.

Remember, the floor on which the long term capital supply line is built is the short term supply line. The differential between the short rate and the long rate lines is determined by the waiting premium and the inflationary expectations premium. If these premiums remain constant then a change in the short rate supply line shifts the long rate supply line in a similar fashion.

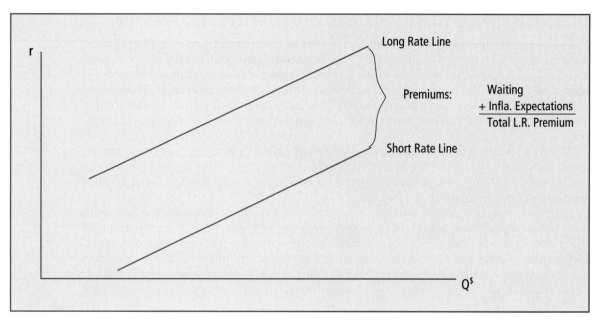

Figure 16.4.1   Long Term Capital Market

Ceteris paribus, a rise in the short rate line shifts the long rate line up while a fall in the short rate line shifts the long rate line down as shown in Figure 16.4.2.

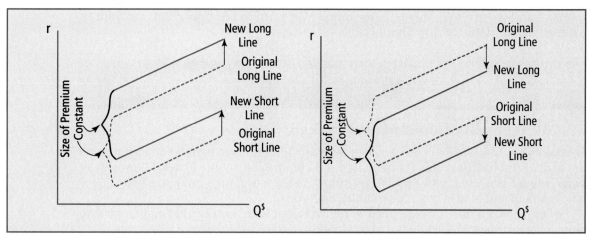

Figure 16.4.2   Long Rate Line Shifts as Short Rate Line Changes, *Ceteris Paribus*

The Fed Funds Rate is in fact the short rate floor—it is the shortest of short rates—and it is a floor the Fed can manage. When the premiums remain constant, Fed manipulation of the Fed Funds Rate translates into Fed manipulation of the long term capital supply line. And to the degree the Fed can manipulate the long term capital supply line it can often significantly influence the equilibrium interest rate in the long term capital market, the level of investment, the level of aggregate demand, and the state of the macroeconomy.

16.4.2 Unemployment—the Interventionist Policy

Suppose for example the macroeconomy is in the less than full employment condition shown in Figure 16.4.3. On the left in Figure 16.4.3 are the underlying capital market conditions.

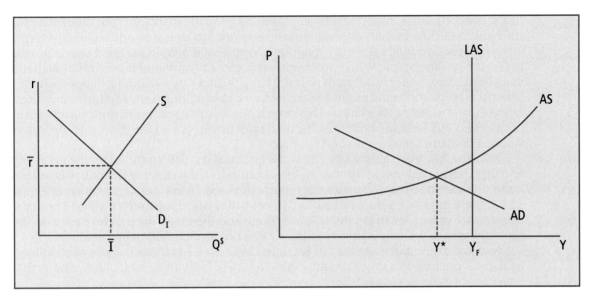

Figure 16.4.3 Macro Conditions and the Long Term Capital Market

Now suppose the Fed uses Open Market Operations to lower the Fed Funds Rate. (Figure 16.4.4 shows the story unfolding graphically.) *Ceteris paribus*, what happens in the capital market? If the Fed uses Open Market Operations to lower the Fed Funds Rate, the short rate line goes down. *Ceteris paribus*, this brings the long term supply line down.

What happens to investment (I)? *Ceteris paribus*, it goes up. As Fed policy shifts the long term supply line down, *ceteris paribus*, the long term equilibrium shifts to a lower long term interest rate and a higher level of investment (I). How does this increase in investment (I) show up on our Macro Picture? The increase in investment adds to aggregate demand, shifting it to the right. As aggregate demand expands the level of real GDP increases and unemployment decreases. (Figure 16.4.4)

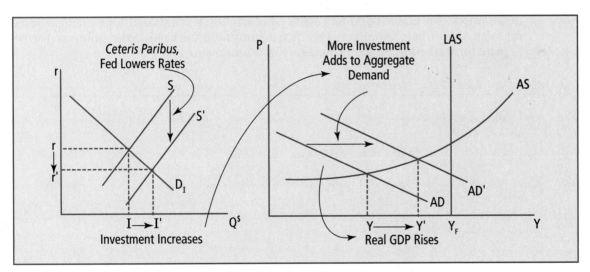

Figure 16.4.4 Fed Intervention in the Capital Market and Macro Reponse, *Ceteris Paribus*

This is, at least, how it is suppose to work *ceteris paribus*, but *ceteris* is rarely *paribus*. For example, a Fed policy to lower the long rate supply line will not increase investment if, as the long term supply line is shifted down by the Fed, the long term demand line is moving to the left due to declining expectations and/or due to capital flight from the market.

In a very depressed economy when people see no good prospects, it is possible for a central bank make moves that take equilibrium long rates to near zero and still not generate any stimulus. Low long rates only generate investment if people see good opportunities to use the cheap capital. When prospects seem gloomy and long term capital demand vanishes and no matter how low the central bank pushes rates—nothing happens. In this situation it is possible one might see the peculiar case of long term equilibrium interest rates being at or below short rates. This occurs because movements of the long term supply and demand lines are both pushing long rates down, but on the short side there may still be a demand keeping the short rates up.

For now, however, let's assume that the Fed uses its tools to stimulate the economy and that there is a demand for that financial capital, so the effect of the policy is indeed increased investment and expanded aggregate demand. In that case, as it shows in Figure 16.4.4, there might be a shot of inflation. Interventionists argue that *if* the Fed's policy is targeted accurately it can get the stimulus done and then take the pressure away as the economy gets to full employment, so there need not be an inflation problem.

Non-interventionists see the "if" just cited in "if the Fed targets its policy accurately" as akin to "once upon a time" in a fairy tale—a leap of faith into a land of naïve hope that never has been and never will be.

16.4.3 Unemployment—the Non-Interventionist Says Intervention Is Not Necessary and the Interventionist Reply

The non-interventionist looks at the same initial condition and says "Hey, this kind of thing is inevitable. It's unfortunate, but the best medicine is no medicine. Just give it some air and it'll heal itself." Because the non-interventionist has faith in the market system she believes that the underlying micro adjustments are going to kick in and fix things. We have seen the logic already. (Figure 16.4.5 shows the story unfolding graphically.)

The micro reality underlying a demand-deficient macro condition is thousands of micro labor markets with the excess supplies of labor. If our nice assumptions hold, then these micro labor markets will adjust toward equilibrium and as they do wages across the economy go down. In our Macro Picture these micro adjustments are reflected by a shift down in aggregate supply. When all the micro adjustments are complete under our nice assumptions, the macro condition is full employment. It is a straightforward logic based on a rich philosophical tradition: Our nice assumptions are weak assumptions so we can depend on markets to be good coordination mechanisms.

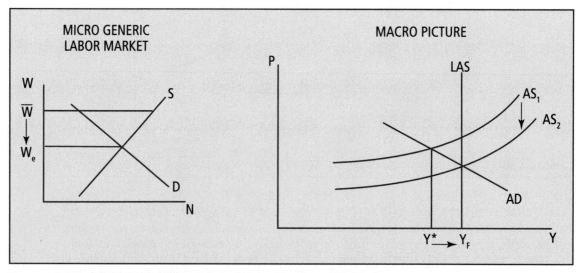

Figure 16.4.5   Non-Interventionist Story of Unemployment Elimination

But it is a position that is not shared by all.

The interventionist looks at the same reality and says, "Wait! Wait for what? For all these unemployed folks to suffer enough to start losing faith in the liberal free-market system that promised them opportunities and a better life? The markets are not always there when we need them, and they're obviously not doing the job now. We can fix this problem. The Fed should intervene with Open Market Operations: Buy in the open market, lower the Fed Funds Rate, lower long rates, increase investment, expand AD, and put people to work. The solution is in our hands and we have an obligation to act."

To which the non-interventionist replies. "Sure, and 'if' the Fed's policy is targeted accurately we'll have full employment with a stable price level. That's a wonderful story. It ranks right up there with another of my favorites that begins: 'Once upon a time there was a brilliant bureaucrat. . . .' Get real; the likelihood that the Fed is going to target this just right is near zero, and the potential problems of getting it wrong are very significant."

16.4.4 Unemployment—the Non-Interventionist Cites Problems Intervention Can Cause and the Interventionist Reply

Picking just the right level of stimulus is very tricky. First of all, the Fed cannot even be sure where the target is. The target is full employment. Graphically that is right at the LAS line. But in fact the natural rate is not a number we know, it is a number that we estimate or, more accurately, that we guesstimate. Honest folks have honest differences of opinion about what that number is. It is not odd for two economists to look at the same reported unemployment rate and argue respectively that the economy needs more stimulus and that the economy is already over stimulated. Suppose the reported unemployment rate (in itself a problematic number, but more on this later) is 5%. An economist who believes the natural rate is 4.5% would call for more stimulus. An economist who believes the natural rate is 5.5% would call for less stimulus.

Then there is the problem of the shape of the AS line. Even if the target is known, if the AS line begins to slope up prior to reaching the LAS—that is, if inflation kicks in before full employment—a Fed stimulus meant to lower unemployment might set off inflation even before the target is reached. Since we cannot really know the shape of the AS line, we cannot be sure about how real this threat is.

The debate over intervention is driven in part by different assumptions about the structure of the economy. These different assumptions lead to different answers to the questions: What is the natural rate? What is the shape of the AS line?

It is virtually impossible to resolve these differences empirically, that is, based on past data, because the past is not necessarily a good guide for understanding current conditions. Since the economy is a dynamic system its structure (and thus the natural rate and the shape of the AS) is constantly changing. The best we can do is make intelligent assumptions, but such assumptions can and do vary. Not surprisingly the interventionists tend to assume a low natural rate and a flat AS line thereby seeing the need for intervention more often. And not surprisingly the non-interventionists tend to assume a natural rate close to current conditions and an AS line that reflects early inflation, thereby seeing no need for intervention and significant inflationary danger in doing so.

But policy is trickier yet. Even if the Fed knew exactly what the actual natural rate target is and what the AS line really looks like, it is difficult for the Fed to be sure about how much to lower the Fed Funds rate to get the desired investment (I) stimulus. This is tricky because the response of the long term capital market to changes in the Fed Funds Rate depends on the capital market elasticities, on what else may be affecting the long term supply line (capital flows in or out), and on what is happening on the long term demand side. The Fed cannot know the answers to these questions when it implements policy, it can only make thoughtful assumptions.

The non-interventionists argue that the economy is simply too complex to be managed thoughtfully. An economy is a complex web of connections so intervening anywhere has ripple effects in many directions. Intervention can cause perverse unintended consequences. Some of these cannot be foreseen, and some can be foreseen but not measured. For example, a Fed policy aimed at stimulating investment can also affect the nation's trade balance.

16.4.5 Unintended Consequences

If the Fed lowers interest rates to stimulate investment that can affect international capital flows. *Ceteris paribus*, falling interest rates in the U.S. will cause capital to flow out of the country, because relative risk adjusted interest rates elsewhere begin to look better. This flight of capital contracts the domestic supply of capital, so if the Fed is going to actually add to the liquidity in the domestic capital market it has to add enough to offset any potential flight and then some. With capital flight and capital demand elasticities to guesstimate, deciding how much liquidity to inject into the financial markets is tricky. If the Fed overdoes it and puts too much stimulus in, that makes for a serious problem. And this international capital flow issue gets even more complicated.

As capital flows out of the country the dollar gets weaker. A weaker currency makes exports rise and imports fall. This change in the trade balance (X-M) adds to Aggregate Demand.

Let's review what is happening: As the Fed lowers interest rates to encourage more investment (I) and thereby stimulate the economy, it may set off capital flows out of the country that also make the trade balance (X-M) more stimulative. This double stimulus may lead to an over stimulus.

If for whatever reason the Fed over stimulates the economy, we have a new problem. Too much stimulus can overheat the economy and set off an inflationary spiral. You know the story: Expanding Aggregate Demand pushes the economy toward full employment. The price level begins to rise. As the economy nears full employment workers are in a position to demand higher wages. They do so in order to keep up with rising prices. Higher wages mean higher factor prices, so AS shifts up. The stimulus continues to keep the economy at full employment so AD shifts out. And so it goes, around and around in a spiral with all the perverse consequences that inflation brings to those on fixed incomes, to those trying to borrow for long term investments, and to those with financial capital who want to protect its real value. The United States suffered from such a wage-price spiral in the late 1970s. Let's look at the background to this spiral and how events played out to end it.

16.4.6 Background to the 1970s Wage-Price Spiral

As the United States entered the 1970s, inflation was creeping up due to the Aggregate Demand pressures of expanded government spending that came with the 1960s combination of the Great Society programs and the Vietnam War. In August 1971, anticipating the coming elections and appreciating the public frustration with the corrosive effect of inflation on standards of living, President Nixon surprised the nation by announcing a national product and factor *price freeze*. The freeze did stop most of the inflation while it was in force, but most economists agree it provided a short term solution at a significant long term cost.

In order to work the freeze had to be a surprise. If people had expected it, there would have been a frenzy of wage and price increases as folks tried to get wage and price increases in before the freeze was imposed. Since it was a surprise some folks were caught in a position they considered "behind"; maybe they were about to get a wage or price hike and now they were trapped behind those who got theirs just before the freeze. All those folks who got caught behind were of course anxious to catch up. The longer they waited the more catching up they felt they needed to do. So the freeze was like a locked lid on a pot of boiling water with no pressure release valve. A lot of explosive price pressure built up under it.

Furthermore, the freeze was by definition not a long term solution. Think about it. What is the basic signal on which the coordination mechanism of the whole market system works? Prices. Freezing product and factor prices turns off the signals that run the system, so in effect it shuts down the entire market system. The longer the system is shut off, the more distortions occur due to lack of signals. If ours is going to be a market economy, freezing the price signals is not a long term solution to inflation. In 1973 the freeze was lifted and not surprisingly inflation jumped up. Then came the oil price shocks from an OPEC embargo on oil sales to the U.S. The oil shocks shifted AS up increasing inflation and adding unemployment to the mix. By 1975 the economy was suffering a severe stagflation. Inflation was over 10% and unemployment was as high as 9%.

Happily, by the middle of 1979 the unemployment rate had come down below 6%. However, the improving employment conditions made it possible for wages to chase prices. So even as the unemployment rate was down, inflation was up to over 11%. The U.S. economy was in a classic wage-price spiral. Under the leadership of Chairman Paul Volcker, the Fed used its policy tools to squeeze this inflation out of the U.S. economy. Let's see how this was accomplished.

16.4.7 Squeezing Inflation Out of the Economy—Mr. Volcker's Recession

In May of 1978 the Discount Rate was at 7% and the Fed Funds Rate was just over 7%. By March 1980 the Discount Rate was 13% and the Fed Funds Rate was over 17%. This dramatic rise represents a concerted effort on the part of Volcker and the Fed to significantly cut back access to liquidity. It worked. By 1980 Investment (I) had fallen significantly. With this contraction in aggregate demand, inflation began to fall and unemployment began to rise. Inflation went from over 14% in early 1980 to below 4% by the end of 1982. Unemployment went from around 6% in mid 1980 to over 10% by the end of 1982. Mr. Volcker's Fed policy took time to bite, there was a lag between implementation and impact, but it worked. It eliminated the inflation. The price was very high, however. The low inflation was achieved by creating the worst unemployment since the Great Depression. Figure 16.4.6 represents these unfolding events.

The wage-price spiral is shown in Figure 16.4.6 as the economy tracks from condition 1 to 2 to 3 to 4 to 5. Then, as the Fed raised the Fed Funds Rate and the Discount Rate this raised long term interest rates, reducing investment (I). This fall in I took the steam out of aggregate demand at AD_5.

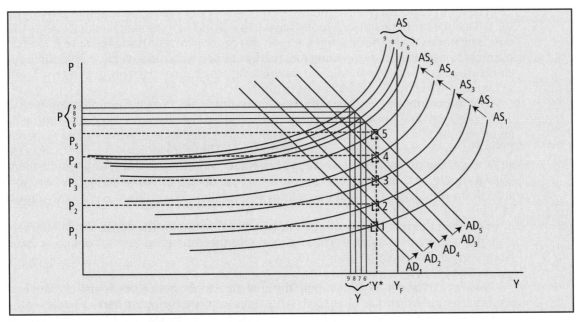

Figure 16.4.6 Volcker's Squeezing Out Inflation

Initially, even as AD stops AS continues to rise because workers look at the prices that have been rising and the higher wages they have been getting to keep up with the price rises, and they continue to demand these wage increases. This stage is represented by the movement of AS from condition 5 to 6 to 7 to 8 in Figure 16.4.6.

Notice that when AD stops moving up, the tracking of the conditions in the macro-economy is no longer vertical—pure inflation. As AS goes up the current condition begins to track along the now-fixed AD line (5 to 6 to 7 to 8). Along this path, inflation slows down and unemployment begins to rise. These consequences take time to unfold. They lag behind the policy implementation, but they happen.

As AS continues to track along the now-fixed AD, unemployment rises further. At some point unemployment reaches a level at which workers are much more worried about keeping jobs than they are about keeping up with inflation. At that point AS stops rising. In terms of our graph we have reached condition 9, the condition that the actual economy reached in mid 1982: very low inflation, very high unemployment.

Mr. Volcker understood that the consequence of squeezing the capital market would be a recession and high unemployment. Nevertheless, he saw it as the only way to squeeze the juice out of the wage-price spiral. Given that the target was inflation, it worked. Was it wise? That depends on whether you believe there was an alternative policy path out of the wage-price spiral that would have caused less pain.

16.4.8 Conclusion on Monetary Policy

The non-interventionist points to this pain and says the best policy is to avoid the problem in the first place, and the best way to do this is to get the government out of the economy. These problems began with interventionist government policies and they ended with interventionist government policies. If the government had not been involved, the path of the economy would not have taken this horrible turn. The non-interventionist says: "I'll put my faith in the invisible hand of the market rather than the visible hand of some government bureaucrat who can really screw things up."

Following this non-interventionist logic, the best monetary policy is to fix the amount of liquidity in the system and then just let it run. To achieve this, some non-interventionists advocate that the nation go to a *gold standard.* A gold standard fixes the amount of available liquidity by tying it to the amount of gold the government holds. Since gold holdings are fairly constant, this keeps the amount of liquidity in the system fairly constant.

The interventionist believes that tying monetary policy to a gold standard is like tying the wheel of a car in position: A foolish move in a world of natural and global events that create obstacles and pitfalls along the road the economy must navigate. Sure it is tricky business to steer the economy along that road, but responsible intervention is possible and sometimes necessary. We should not leave our fate to chance based on an ill-advised faith in markets. We should be the masters of our fate.

The interventionist asserts to the non-interventionist: "Yes, government can be part of the problem, but it can also be part of the solution. Waiting is no solution. Waiting for an unseen hand to solve our problems while millions suffer is to abrogate the responsibility of a government to the citizens it represents. There are tools we can use to allay the suffering. Certainly these tools are only as effective as the craft of those who handle them, but we should not shun the tools because we have seen them used badly. We have also seen them used well. They can be helpful and we should learn how to use them more carefully and constructively."

To which the non-interventionist responds, "Praying for the constructive intervention of government is as mythical as praying for the constructive intervention of Zeus: Great story of hope, but no basis in reality."

And so the debate goes.

Notice that the debate is not about the analytical tools. Both sides in mainstream economics use the same tools of analysis—the ones we are developing here. The difference is ultimately philosophical. Non-interventionists put a great deal of faith in the market, in the invisible hand, and have little faith in government. Interventionists believe that we should not leave our fate to the sometimes undependable markets, and that when they fail us government can be constructive.

These are not simple issues. There are no simple answers. Anyone who says it's simple is either simple minded, or thinks you are.

These issues are, however, of the utmost importance. The philosophy of those who hold the power of government determines how the government will respond to any perverse macroeconomic condition. The well-being of millions, even billions, of people, including you and me, depends on getting it right.

But enough for now about monetary policy; let's turn to fiscal policy. As you will see, and it should be no surprise, while the tools are different, the essence of the debate over policy remains the same.

17.0 FISCAL POLICY

17.1.1 Introduction—Fiscal Policy and The Budget Process

As we saw at the beginning of our macro study, the government's budget position (G-T) can have a major impact on the aggregate economy. *Fiscal policy* is the government's policy with respect to its budget position.

If the government runs a big budget deficit, *ceteris paribus*, this adds a lot of demand to the aggregate economy and is very stimulative. If the government runs a big budget surplus, *ceteris paribus*, this takes a lot of demand out of the aggregate economy and is very contractionary. So as the government determines its budget, it not only determines the micro issues of who will benefit from its programs and who will pay for them. It also determines its aggregate budget position, and thus its fiscal policy and the impact of its actions on the macroeconomy.

The process that determines the United States government budget position begins with the President. She submits a proposed budget to Congress. Each House of Congress then determines through a committee process, floor debate, and a vote what it actually wants to do in terms of spending and taxing. The work of the Senate and the House of Representatives then goes to a joint Congressional committee that irons out any differences between the two plans. When a single plan finally receives a majority vote in both the Senate and the House, it is sent to the President for her signature. If she signs it, the federal budget is determined. If she vetoes it, Congress can override her veto if both the Senate and the House can muster a two-thirds vote to do so. Failing that, the process goes on until a budget agreement can be reached among the Senate, the House, and the President.

Budgets cover one year. Budgets include all the taxes on individuals and corporations and so on and all the spending on education and the military and agriculture and space programs and so on. In addition, as long as there is a national debt part of the spending in each new budget is dedicated to paying the interest on that debt. A national debt is a cumulative effect of the years in which a government's budget was in deficit—it spent more than it has taxed (G>T). Even if in a given year the budget position is a surplus (T>G), as long as there is a debt the government is borrowing and it pays interest on the borrowed financial capital. Recall the Treasury bonds we talked about in monetary policy. Treasury bond sales are the government's way of borrowing money.

As a given year's spending and taxing authority ends, a new budget is required in order for the government to have the authority to continue to tax and spend. If there were no new budget the government would have to shut down. If the government failed to pass a budget the Treasury Department would not be able to pay that interest, and the government would go into default on its debt obligations. A default undermines the confidence of people with financial capital to lend. As a consequence capital becomes either harder to borrow (the interest rate is higher) or possibly even impossible to get. The U.S. government has never defaulted, so it has excellent access and terms for borrowing financial capital. Smaller and/or less economically and/or politically developed nations have a much more serious problem in this regard. Their access to and terms for financial capital are often very difficult. The smaller and less established a nation's political and economic institutions, the more tenuous its relationship with the international financial capital market. I note this here to anticipate an issue that we will take up when we get to the international dimensions of macro: The vulnerability of nations, especially those with less-developed political and economic structures, to flows of international financial capital. For now, however, our focus is on the U.S. case as representative of how a government budget position affects a macroeconomy, *ceteris paribus*.

17.2 THE IMPLEMENTATION OF FISCAL POLICY

17.2.1 Fiscal Policy Intervention—How it Works

Suppose the economy is in recession as represented in initial macro condition in Figure 17.2.1. Millions of people are out of work, families suffer, and there is much unutilized capacity in the economy. If the President and Congress agree to, they can use fiscal policy to address the problem. The implementation process is very straightforward.

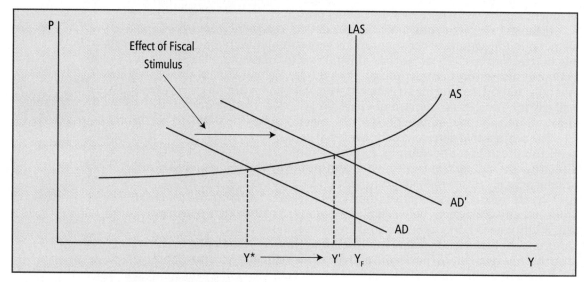

Figure 17.2.1   Recession and Fiscal Stimulus

The government can stimulate the macroeconomy by changing its budget position: moving to a lower surplus, moving from surplus to balance, moving from surplus to deficit, moving from balance to deficit, or moving to a bigger deficit. In all cases it means increasing (G-T). This can be accomplished by increasing spending (G), lowering taxes (T), or any combination of changes in G and T that increases the budget position (G-T) and adds aggregate demand stimulus to the macroeconomy.

On our Macro Picture in Figure 17.2.1, this move to a more stimulative government budget position shows up as a shift to the right in aggregate demand. As you can see, such a shift increases real GDP (Y) and reduces unemployment.

A carefully planned intervention can move the economy to full employment. However, with the potential benefit come potential problems. One is immediately obvious from our picture. The intervention may cause a shot of inflation depending on the shape of the AS line. There are other potential problems as well—problems that relate to the financial capital market.

17.2.2 Fiscal Policy Intervention to Stimulate the Macro Economy—A Potential Problem

Whenever the government runs a deficit in order to stimulate the macroeconomy, it has to make up the difference between G and T (G>T) by borrowing. As we have seen, the source for the money the government needs to borrow is the capital market. The government must enter the capital market and compete with private borrowers for the available capital. In doing so the government adds to the demand for financial capital.

In our capital market picture we have been using D_I for the demand line. This represents the private demand for financial capital. Now we add the government's demand which we will designate D_G. So the total demand in the market is now D_I plus D_G. In our capital market graph the government entry into the market shifts demand line to the right as shown in Figure 17.2.2.

Given the current supply condition (S), this increasing demand causes the price (the interest rate) to rise (r_0 to r_1) as demanders bid for the available capital. The quantity supplied increases in response to the higher price, and the total amount of financial capital exchanged increases (TQ_0 to TQ_1).

Since the government's credit rating is better than anyone else's, it can bid up the price as high as is necessary to get the capital it needs. In the process of this bidding, however, some private bidders are priced out of the market. The investments they had in mind do not offer a rate of return that can cover such high interest rates. In the vernacular of economists it is said that the government bidding "crowds out" these private bidders who are trying to get capital for private real investments.

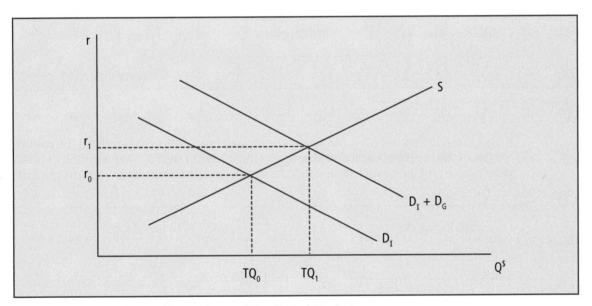

Figure 17.2.2 Government Borrowing and the Capital Market

17.2.3 The Crowding-Out Effect—The Basics

We can see this *crowding-out effect* in our capital market picture shown in Figure 17.2.3. Prior to the government's entry into the capital market, the interest rate is r_0 and the total capital exchanged is TQ_0. Since all of this capital is going to private investment, the initial level of investment, I_0, is equal to TQ_0.

After the government enters the market in search of funds, private investors' demand for capital (D_I) is augmented by the government's demand (D_G). At this new level of total demand the interest rate rises to r_1 and the total amount of capital exchanged increases to TQ_1. Notice, however, that at the new higher interest rate r_1 private investors now only want funds for investment equivalent to I_1. This is because nothing has changed about their attitude, their demand for capital—it is still D_I, and at this higher interest rate fewer investments have a rate of return that beats the interest rate so fewer investments are worthwhile.

We see then that when the government enters the capital market to borrow, while the total amount of capital exchanged increases, the share going to private investment decreases. This decline in the amount of investment (I) caused by the entry (or increase) of government demand for available capital is the crowding-out effect.

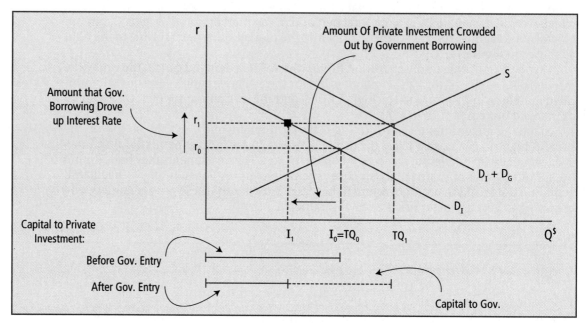

Figure 17.2.3 Crowding-Out Effect

As shown in Figure 17.2.4, the size of the crowding-out effect depends on the responsiveness of the supply of capital to changes in the interest rate. In other words, it depends on the elasticity of the supply of capital. If the supply of capital is inelastic, the government's

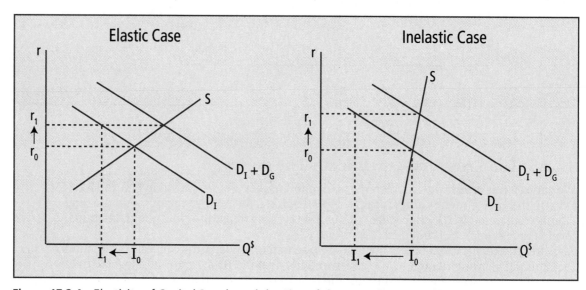

Figure 17.2.4 Elasticity of Capital Supply and the Size of the Crowding-Out Effect—Cases

entry will increase interest rates significantly but the total quantity of capital supplied will not go up very much. In this case the government gets most of the capital it needs by crowding out private investment.

If, on the other hand, the supply of capital is elastic, the government's entry will be met by a rapid expansion of the quantity of capital supplied. The effect on interest rates will be small, and the crowding-out effect will also be small.

17.2.4 Government Borrowing and Capital Market Supply-Side Responses

When a government expands the demand for capital the response on the supply side of the capital market may go beyond changes in quantity supplied. A government's activity in the capital market and/or the political and economic circumstances surrounding that activity can change the underlying attitude of suppliers to that nation's capital market. If suppliers believe the government is pursuing wise policy and general conditions will improve, this confidence may lead them increase the amount of financial capital they supply to the nation's capital market. In this case the effect of increasing demand from the government will be offset in part by the increasing supply, and to the degree this occurs crowding-out is diminished. If on the other hand the government's borrowing is seen as irresponsible and it makes suppliers less confident, the suppliers may withdraw their capital from the market making it necessary for the government to bid up interest rates to very high levels to attract the funds it needs. In this case the crowding-out effect, the decline in private investment (I), can be dramatic.

17.2.5 Government Capital Market Activity, International Capital Flows, and Trade

Whether the supply-side response to government activity in a nation's capital market is a change in quantity supplied and/or a change in supply, some of this supply-side flow of financial capital is inevitably an international flow. And as we learned earlier, international flows of capital have an effect on exchange rates and, in turn, on trade.

Suppose, *ceteris paribus*, the United States runs a big budget deficit. As shown in Figure 17.2.5, domestic interest rates rise as the government bids for financial capital. Some of the supply necessary to meet that demand flows in from other countries. As that liquidity flows in to benefit from the attractive interest rates, it has to go through the foreign exchange market. As international suppliers of financial capital buy dollars in order to get

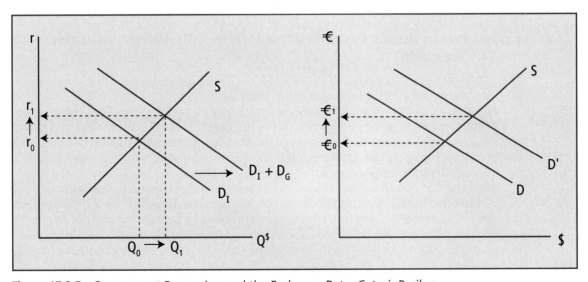

Figure 17.2.5 Government Borrowing and the Exchange Rate, *Ceteris Paribus*

in on the good interest rates in the U.S. capital market, the price of the dollar goes up. This flow of international capital will continue until the attractiveness of the high U.S. interest rates is ultimately offset by the increased price of the U.S. dollar.

To the degree this flow supplies the U.S. government's needs it reduces the crowding-out effect, but at the same time this flow makes the dollar stronger so it affects the nation's trade position. A stronger dollar makes it easier to import and harder to export. As exports (X) fall and imports (M) rise, the U.S. trade position (X-M) worsens taking aggregate demand out of the economy. Some argue that the huge trade deficits of the 1980s were directly related to the huge government budget deficits of that period.

17.2.6 Government Capital Market Activity and the Fed

All the potential problems of government borrowing (crowding-out, higher interest rates, international capital flows, higher exchange rates, perverse trade effects) can be avoided if the Fed "monetizes" the deficit. In effect, this means the Fed expands the supply of liquidity in the capital market to meet the demand generated by a deficit. In that case, the supply shifts out with demand, the interest rate remains the same, and private investment remains the same.

The problem with monetization of the deficit is that it is in effect an expansionary monetary policy, and it could set off the inflation demonstrated earlier. This is especially so if the Fed allows the money supply to expand in an unrestrained fashion.

17.3 THE FISCAL POLICY DEBATE

17.3.1 Fiscal Policy Intervention— The Non-Interventionist Response: "It's not necessary"

The non-interventionists look at all these potential problems and the possible role of the Fed and say: "No! Stop! There's great danger in this interventionist course, and besides intervention isn't necessary."

Those who argue for *laissez-faire* believe that the mirco market adjustment system will work as needed to solve the problems that we see in the aggregate as less than full employment. Macro unemployment implies excess supplies of workers in individual micro labor markets. The prices in these markets, the wages, fall to clear these markets. As the micro markets clear with falling factor prices, in our Macro Picture AS starts shifting down. When the micro adjustments are complete the macroeconomy is back to full employment. (See 15.1.2-15.1.4 to review this analysis.)

17.3.2 Fiscal Policy Intervention — The Non-Interventionist Scenario

The non-interventionist points to all the potential problems and argues that intervention is not only not necessary, it is fruitless and distorting.

Running a deficit to stimulate the economy causes crowding-out. Thus the stimulative effect of increasing the government's budget position (G-T) will be offset at least to some degree by the contractionary effect of reduced investment (I). And furthermore, this represents replacing private choices about where to spend with public choices, always a bad idea to the non-interventionist.

Of course it is possible that international capital will flow in and provide some of the liquidity needed by the government, thus reducing the crowding-out effect. This does not save the policy, however, because it reduces one problem by generating another. While the capital flow reduces crowding out, it also in strengthens the dollar reducing the nation's international competitiveness and hurting the trade balance (X-M)—another contractionary effect.

So, says the non-interventionist, pick your poison: crowding-out or trade deficits or worst of all both. Whatever the scenario, the effort of the government to stimulate the economy with fiscal policy is not necessary and is difficult to implement because the stimulus sets into motion forces that create contractions elsewhere. And if the stimulus is indeed strong enough to overwhelm the contractionary side effects, it might lead to inflation: An inflation that could turn into a wage-price spiral if the central bank is foolish enough to try to protect the capital market from crowding-out by monetizing the deficit.

The non-interventionist believes an interventionist fiscal policy is a disaster waiting to happen.

17.3.3 The Interventionist Response

The interventionist responds: As the Preamble to the United States Constitution asserts, the government has been established to "promote the general welfare." Waiting for the economy to fix itself while millions of our fellow citizens suffer the material and mental pains of unemployment is an irresponsible abrogation of our national responsibility. Markets are often good coordinators of individual choices, and in most cases the government should let the markets work their magic. But there comes a time when it is obvious that the market system is not going to solve our problems. When that time comes, we have tools that can be helpful.

Can they be used wisely? Yes? Have they always been used wisely? No. Have they ever been used wisely? Yes. If a good tool has been used badly does that mean it should be thrown away? No. It should be put into thoughtful hands so that it can serve us. If you don't like the government we have, vote it out of office and pick wiser leaders. But don't tie the hands of those leaders. Let them use the tools to do the job when there is a job to be done. Thoughtful policy is a good way to solve bad problems. It is our collective responsibility to those of our fellow citizens who have no job to act. It is easy to say "wait for the markets to adjust" when you are an economist with a job. For the laid-off parent with no paycheck "wait for the markets to adjust" has a very hollow sound.

17.3.4 The Non-Interventionist on "Thoughtful Fiscal Policy"

The non-interventionist responds: Ultimately every family will be better off if we put our faith in the markets rather than government because thoughtful fiscal policy is an oxymoron. The whole mechanism for implementing fiscal policy makes it so.

Recall, the budget determination process in the United States is a political dynamic with the President, the Senate, and the House of Representatives as the players. Since each of these players may have different micro and macro agendas for the federal budget, the budget process is an institutional tug of war among them. This contest is further complicated by the fact that there are two parties in each House of Congress with factions within each party, and there are factions within the White House staff. On top of all this the individual members of the Senate (100) and the House (435) are tugged in 535 different directions. They must respond to the interests of their general constituency and also to the special interests of those with the power (e.g., the money) to influence the course of their next election.

At all levels and at all stages, there is a potential tension between the macroeconomic (aggregate) policy with respect to the government budget position and microeconomic (disaggregate) policy with respect to who is to benefit from the government's expenditures, who is to receive preferred tax treatment (an implicit expenditure), and who is to pay taxes and how much? For example, a Senator or House member may want to cut taxes on products from her state or district while at the same time she wants to expand an Air Force base there to create more jobs. Less taxes and more spending is a very popular political position, but the sum of these micro motives can lead to a macro result that no one intends or likes. Budget deficits may be driven not by a thoughtful macro policy objective, but by an aggregation of micro incentives that dominate macro considerations in the political process.

In the United States, the only player in the budget process who has a truly national constituency is the President. If she does not hold the other 535 players accountable for the macro consequences of their micro decisions, then the macro result is simply the unintended aggregate consequence of these micro decisions. In that case there is a macro policy . . . after all, any budget embodies a macro policy. It is not, however, a policy based on thoughtful consideration of its consequences. Rather it is a macro policy based on micro motives.

If such a dynamic leads to a large budget deficit, there may be a consensus among the players that it would be wise macroeconomic policy for the government to reduce its deficit. Yet micro realities make achieving that very difficult. It is hard to cut spending, because to do so means that someone loses benefits. Each Senator or House members says. "OK, let's cut an Air Force base, but let's cut the one in YOUR area." It is also hard to eliminate tax breaks, because to do so means that someone loses benefits. It is hard to raise taxes, because to do so means that someone must pay more. Again the individual Senators or House members say "Fine, let's eliminate some tax breaks or raise some taxes, just don't do it to my constituents or my donors." Yet, if the government satisfies everyone: Spending rises, taxes fall, the deficit grows . . . and as we have seen this can create undesirable macroeconomic consequences that eventually affect everyone.

The non-interventionist believes that the only way to protect the nation from the dominance of micro motives over rational macro policy is to ensure that the government cannot abuse its power to tax and spend. Some non-interventionists argue that the way to do this is to pass a constitutional amendment that requires the federal government to have a balanced budget. As a gold standard is to monetary policy, so the constitutional requirement of a balanced budget is to fiscal policy. Together these are the Holy Grail of some non-interventionists' policy pursuits.

17.3.5 The Interventionist on "Thoughtful Fiscal Policy"

The interventionist believes that locking fiscal policy into a balanced budget by constitutional amendment is as foolish as tying monetary policy to a gold standard. Allowing no discretion in policy is like not allowing the captain and crew of a ship to adjust the rudder and the sails. Natural and global events shift the winds, stir up the waters, and often present the ship of state with challenges from other states. Sure, history and the sea floor are strewn with records of captains and crews who could not handle their ships. It does not follow, however, that a ship is better off when the hands of the captain and crew are tied. A wise captain and crew have saved many a ship from disaster.

The non-interventionist responds that the analogy to a ship is cute but irrelevant. Ships do not self-adjust to the conditions, markets do. A fair criticism says the interventionist, if markets always worked as smoothly and as quickly as conditions require, but they do not. And when they don't, to pretend they do is an invitation to disaster. The interventionist believes that government policy can be constructive and can ameliorate the aggregate, macro effects of problems caused by natural or national or global dislocations—dislocations that will not be solved smoothly and/or quickly by markets due to distortions in micro markets—market power and market failure.

17.3.6 The Philosophical Foundations of the Policy Debate Revisited

At this point you should note two things about this debate over government economic policy. Both are very are important to keep in mind: First of all, the positions I am describing are the poles, the two extreme positions in the debate. In fact, very few economists are at either pole. Most lean one way or the other, but the positions they take in real cases depend on the circumstances.

Secondly, there is a symmetry to this debate.

Both the interventionists' and the non-interventionists' positions ultimately rest on a lack of faith. The interventionists lack faith in the invisible hand's ability to solve all the problems that emerge in the economy. The non-interventionists lack faith in the government's ability to solve the any problems that emerge in the economy.

And both the interventionists' and the non-interventionists' positions ultimately rest on a leap of faith. The interventionists have faith that the government can be constructive, that it can solve problems in the economy. The non-interventionists have faith that the invisible hand is constructive, that it solves problems in the economy.

Both sides in the debate use the same tools of analysis—the tools you have learned about in these pages—to make their case. It is their assumptions that differ. Both sides in the debate can point to historical cases/data that they feel support their position and disprove the other, but neither can point to any absolute evidence that resolves the debate once and for all.

We will return to this issue of resolving the debate at the end of our study, but now we turn to the last dimension of policy and in some ways the most complicated: International Trade.

18.0 Trade Policy

18.1 Trade Policy Tools

18.1.1 Introduction

As we expand our analysis to the global perspective, we open up the analysis to the pull and tug of global events . . . in which case we are doing what is called "open economy macro." Global economic analysis is fundamentally different from national economic analysis because we live in a world of sovereign nation states.

In any given nation, individuals interact within the policy environment determined by the government of that nation. In the global economy there are still many individuals, but there are also many sovereign governments, and the policies of any one government cannot be directly imposed beyond its boundaries. This makes trade policy more complicated than monetary or fiscal policy, because in the global economy, as nations determine their trade policies other nations have the power to respond. As a result, global economic relations are a strategic game among nation states.

It is a game in which global rules can and have been negotiated. However, the rules are at best incomplete, the meaning of the rules is often debated, and sometimes the rules are violated. In all cases, national sovereignty makes interpretations of the rules and/or the rules themselves hard to enforce. So as it is true for monetary policy and fiscal policy, it is all the more so for trade policy: Anyone who says it's simple is either simple minded, or thinks you are. Yet in this domain of policy, as in the others, the issues are of the utmost importance. In the past, conflicts over trade have led to wars.

In this global strategic game, nations have several tools they can use to try to affect their global trade position. Let's examine the tools and the problems involved in using them.

18.1.2 Trade Policy Tools—Competitive Edge on Costs and Indirect Government Intervention

A nation can try to out-compete its rivals for markets.

As with any private enterprise, *ceteris paribus*, a nation can change its competitive position in the global economy by lowering its cost of production (its cost structure) and in turn offering a better price. As we saw in our micro analysis of markets, this can be accomplished by increasing efficiency and/or by lowering factor costs. As we also saw in that micro analysis, however, in a perfectly competitive environment (that is, under our nice assumptions) no such advantage can be sustained. Competitors, in this case other nations, will respond in kind eventually, eliminating any profits that being ahead of the market may have temporarily created.

But in the global economy, as in the domestic economy, advantages can be sustained if competitors play by different sets of rules. Nations can create market power for themselves by shaping domestic policies to create international advantages. For example, adopting different domestic policies regarding acceptable production conditions is one way to do this: Nations that have no child labor restrictions, no limits on hours of work, no worker safety rules, and/or no environmental protection standards are at a real advantage over nations that impose any of those conditions on themselves, because those with no rules on acceptable production conditions enjoy a much lower cost structure. Absent any global agreement on acceptable production conditions, advantage always goes to the lowest cost producer and this encourages a "race to the bottom" in terms of standards.

18.1.3 Trade Policy Tools—Competitive Edge on Consumer Satisfaction

Ceteris paribus, a nation can also change its competitive position in the global economy by making its products more suitable to the consumer tastes of the times. For example, building cars that are very simple and inexpensive was the key to the Volkswagon Beetle's success in the U.S. in the 1960s and 70s. Developing a reputation for quality and dependability was a key to Honda's and Toyota's success in the 1970s and 80s. But as we learned when trade was introduced into Aggregate Demand, an imbalance in trade cannot be sustained unless there is an offsetting capital flow.

Honda's and Toyota's success in the 1980s was facilitated and sustained in part by the huge U.S. government budget deficits of those years. Government capital market borrowing to cover those deficits sent U.S. interest rates up, attracting foreign capital, and strengthening the dollar. So not only did the Japanese have products U.S. buyers liked, during those years those products were in effect "on sale." Since the Japanese were happy to sell cars in the U.S. and then lend the dollars they made back to the U.S. government, the U.S. trade deficit with Japan began to grow dramatically.

18.1.4 Trade Policy Tools—Red Tape and Regulations: Direct, Very Subtle Government Intervention

That deficit was made worse by another tool of trade policy: Nations can make it more difficult to sell in their market by creating much red tape and many regulations as obstacles to foreign products. Such policies raise the *transaction costs* of doing business with that country. As the U.S. trade deficit with Japan ballooned in the 1980s, the U.S. complained that the Japanese government was a master at creating such obstacles, and the U.S. government demanded more access to Japanese markets.

Governments can complain all they want about such obstacles, but given national sovereignty only the nation that creates them can remove them, and such obstacles are often hard to remove for domestic reasons.

In some cases the obstacles have been created by political leaders in order to protect the interest of a powerful domestic group. Thus they are the product of domestic rent-seeking behavior. So long as that interest group remains politically powerful, it is difficult for the government to remove the obstacle. In other cases the trade regulations may reflect a domestic belief that there is a good reason to regulate a certain kind of trade, such as protecting consumers from products that might be harmful. Whether a rule represents rent-seeking red tape or a reasoned concern is in the eye of the beholder. What the outsider calls an obstacle, the insider might claim to be a reasoned and reasonable regulation. If Europe says it will not accept food from the U.S. produced using certain biologically engineered processes, the U.S. may respond that this is unreasonable. But then what?

As occurred in the U.S. trade relationship with Japan during the 1980s and 90s, success on one side set off reactions on the other. As the United States imported more and more Japanese cars, U.S. auto makers lost market share and U.S. auto workers lost jobs to foreign imports. Lost jobs made people angry.

Widespread public anger over foreign imports is an energy that feeds political activity. Candidates begin to call for a strong, effective response. Such a response can take either subtle or more "in your face" forms.

18.1.5 Trade Policy Tools—Exchange Rate Manipulation: Direct, Subtle Government Intervention

One direct but somewhat subtle action a nation can implement to improve its trade position is to manipulate its own currency to make it weaker. A weaker currency improves the nation's competitive price position in the global market. There are two ways a nation can accomplish this: By direct intervention in the foreign exchange market or by changing domestic interest rates.

Every government has access to its own currency. Most also have a store of financial reserves held in the form of currencies from other countries (for example the U.S. has a stock of euros and yen and so forth), and/or a stock of gold which can be exchanged for any currency. Governments can use the resources of this portfolio to participate in the foreign exchange market. If, for example, the U.S. wants to weaken the dollar with respect to the yen, it can sell dollars for yen in the foreign exchange market. By expanding the supply of dollars to the foreign exchange market, it shifts out supply and drives down the yen price of dollars.

Monetary policy can also weaken a currency. A lower domestic interest rate that causes a capital flow out can accomplish this.

However, both of these tools for manipulating the foreign exchange rate carry risks of undesirable domestic side effects and international responses. For example, if domestic interest rates are lowered to weaken the currency, the lower interest rates may also create an investment stimulus to the economy. If the policy works and the trade balance does improve this also stimulates the economy. As the currency weakens this makes imports more expensive, reducing foreign competition and making it easier for domestic producers to raise prices. The effect of the stimuli combined with the protection from foreign price competition can set off inflation.

18.1.6 Trade Policy Tools—Quotas: Direct, Not So Subtle Government Intervention

A more direct response to a trade problem is quotas. A nation can simply decree that it will not allow more than a certain number of units of a foreign commodity (like cars) to be imported.

While this does limit imports, it also invites the possibility of retaliation. The other nation replies: "If you restrict our access to your market, then we are going to do the same to you." The U.S. did impose quotas on Japanese cars in the 1980s, but only with Japanese acquiescence. That acquiescence reflected a real fear in both governments that if Japan did not agree to quotas, the political fury in the U.S. over imports and lost jobs would drive U.S. politicians to adopt the most dramatic "in your face" kind of retaliation: Tariffs.

18.1.7 Trade Policy Tools—Tariffs: Direct, "In Your Face" Government Intervention

Tariffs are, in effect, taxes on imports. The higher the tariff the higher the price of the import, and, *ceteris paribus*, the less will be bought. Demand for imports can be brought to a screeching halt with a high enough tariff. So, *ceteris paribus*, a tariff will solve a trade imbalance. But in global economic relations, *ceteris* is never *paribus*. The imposition of a tariff almost invariably invites retaliation. This in turn encourages a response. This process can quickly degenerate into a *tariff war*. In a tariff war, as in most wars, there are not so much winners as survivors—and even the survivors suffer dearly in the process.

Some economists argue that the economic slide that became the Great Depression would have turned around before disaster set in if the nations of the world had not become engaged in a tariff war as each tried to save jobs in its own market by restricting access to its market with tariffs. The United States' action in that war took the form of the Smoot-Hawley tariff.

So what is a reasonable international economic policy for a nation?

18.2 TRADE POLICY ISSUES

18.2.1 Global Economic Relations and Policy—Historical Background

As a truly global economy began to emerge with the age of nation states and exploration in the 15th and 16th centuries, trade became the focal point of European writing on economics and economic policy. During that period the Dutch were doing gloriously well with virtually no hinterland to develop. Their growing wealth was based on success at trade. Thus it appeared to many who wrote about economics and economic policy during that period that the wealth of a nation was determined by its success in trade.

The dominant view of trade during that period was that trade was a *zero sum game:* As in splitting up a pie, a bigger piece for you means a smaller piece for me and vice versa. It follows from this zero sum logic that in trade as in war there are winners and losers. Thus the key objective of policy in these early days of global trade was to figure out how to be a winner. This general position has since been called Mercantilism and the policy program that flows from this perspective is referred to as Mercantilist policy. The Mercantilist policies of the 17th and 18th centuries included keeping domestic wages low to help keep production costs low, restricting imports, developing strong navies to control trade routes, and establishing colonies to provide cheap raw materials. These kinds of policies were designed to create and sustain advantages, and sovereign nations with power were in a position to do just that.

In 1776 Adam Smith published his classic work titled *An Inquiry into the Nature and Causes of the Wealth of Nations.* This work is part of a larger moral philosophy in which Smith imagines and represents the constructive possibilities of liberal society. Liberal society is for Smith a world in which opportunities are not skewed by power, advantages are always vulnerable to competition, and when justice prevails the market system both domestically and globally is a *positive sum game*—one in which, if everyone plays by the rules, the pie gets bigger so all can benefit from the "game". In the *Wealth of Nations* he tries to demonstrate that constructive competition, that is competition under our nice assumptions, is good for all individuals and all nations. In the course of his presentation he dedicates a great deal of ink to debunking Mercantilist views.

18.2.2 The Promise of a Liberal System

Since Smith most mainstream economists have adopted his vision of a liberal order in which free, fair, and open trade is good for all. The promise of a free, fair, and open global economy is essentially a generalization of the desirable efficiency outcome that we learned in micro is possible for any economic system that functions under our nice assumptions: Pareto optimality. As we also learned in micro, and it still holds true at the global level, the distributive justice of such a system depends on the distribution of the initial endowments.

As the promise is the same, so too are the issues facing a global economy: Potential distortions of market power and market failure, and the justice of the endowment distribution. And was true in micro and other dimensions of macro policy, with respect to trade there are philosophical differences between interventionists and non-interventionists on the role of government in addressing these global trade issues. But while there is much similarity between domestic and global market analysis, one major distinction sets domestic policy apart from global policy. In the former case there is one ultimate center of power—

one government that makes the laws and that controls the police and the military. In the global economy, there are many such governments each implementing its own global trade policy. As a result, at the scale of the global economy, the interventionist hope for good government policy and the non-interventionist hope for no government intrusion are equally remote.

18.2.3 The Problems of a Liberal System: Power and Response

A liberal global trading system in which free, fair, and open global trade allows all to enjoy a just share of the gains from trade is the ideal of most mainstream economists. But mercantilist thinking is still very much alive and well when it comes to policy decision making.

That should not be surprising. A government can serve the interests of its constituents (whether that is an elite or the general public) and thus itself by creating and maintaining global power positions. The problem with playing the global trade game this way is that it leads to inherently unstable and often degenerative global relations. The losers in this Mercantilist world are always looking for the opportunity to undermine the power of the winners.

It is very easy for political rhetoric to stir up public resentment against imports because often those imports represent jobs lost at home. Workers who feel they are losing their jobs to workers in other countries clamor for protection from the invasion of foreign products. *Protectionism* becomes a popular political platform, and a trade war looms. But as noted before, in a trade war as in many wars it is often the case that everyone loses, for as barriers are erected to protect domestic producers, other countries retaliate with similar barriers. International trade is stifled. With the decline of international trade all the global benefits that come with specialization and the exchange of surpluses are lost. The gains from trade that we learned about long ago when we introduced the advantages of a complex society are lost.

John Maynard Keynes brought this issue into sharp focus in the concluding chapter of his classic work, *The General Theory of Employment, Interest, and Money*. As you read a brief selection from that work keep in mind that he wrote this in 1935, in the wake of a trade war, in the midst of the Great Depression, and as the shadow of World War II was beginning to envelop Europe:

> War has several causes. Dictators and others such, to whom war offers, in expectation at least, a pleasurable excitement, find it easy to work on the natural bellicosity of their peoples. But, over and above this, facilitating their task of fanning the popular flame, are the economic causes of war, namely, the pressure of population and the competitive struggle for markets. It is the second factor, which probably played a predominant part in the nineteenth century, and might again, that is germane to this discussion. . . .
>
> [W]hilst economists were accustomed to applaud the prevailing international system as furnishing the fruits of the international division of labour and harmonizing at the same time the interests of different nations, there lay concealed a less benign influence; and those statesmen were moved by common sense and correct apprehension of the true course of events, who believed that if a rich, old country were to neglect the struggle for markets its prosperity would droop and fail. [i.e., If such a nation did not play to win at the Mercantilist game, it would decline.] But if nations can learn to provide themselves with full employment by their domestic policy (and, we must add, if they can also attain equilibrium in the trend of their population), there need be no important economic forces calculated to set the interest of one country against that of its neighbours.

While many disagree with Keynes' domestic interventionist policy prescriptions, most mainstream economists would agree with his advocacy for solving the economic problems of nations domestically when the international markets are free, fair, and open. As did

Keynes, most mainstream economists see Mercantilism as a destructive trade strategy. But still, many governments see it as the way to satisfy domestic constituencies.

18.2.4 The Problems of a Liberal System: Powerlessness and Response

Caught in the crossfire of powerful trade strategies played by powerful, developed nations are the largely powerless developing nations. How are such nations to compete in the global economy if their endowment, especially their endowment of financial capital, is very meager? Many of these countries compete with cheap labor costs, but often this cheapness is achieved by discounting issues that in more developed nations are considered human rights—like a living wage, safe working conditions, no child labor, not poisoning the environment, and so on. . . .

And this one cost advantage a developing nation might have, cheap labor costs, is not alone enough to make such a nation globally competitive. Financial capital is required to start and maintain operations. With very little domestic financial capital, developing nations must attract financial capital from the outside. But as we have seen, this capital is very mobile and can be very fickle. It can abandon an economy overnight in a panic. In such a global panic a nation that has been struggling but that has been making reasonable decisions can get caught up in the crisis and see its hopeful prospects destroyed in the blink of an eye.

The international lender of last resort for countries in dire conditions is the International Monetary Fund (*IMF*). The IMF describes itself as follows (quotations that follow are from the IMF homepage (http://www.imf.org) as of this writing):

> The IMF is the world's central organization for international monetary cooperation. . . .
> The IMF's primary purpose is to ensure the stability of the international monetary system—the system of exchange rates and international payments that enables countries (and their citizens) to buy goods and services from each other. This is essential for sustainable economic growth and rising living standards.
> To maintain stability and prevent crises in the international monetary system, the IMF reviews national, regional, and global economic and financial developments. It provides advice to its 184 member countries, encouraging them to adopt policies that foster economic stability, reduce their vulnerability to economic and financial crises, and raise living standards, and serves as a forum where they can discuss the national, regional, and global consequences of their policies.
> The IMF also makes financing temporarily available to member countries to help them address balance of payments problems—that is, when they find themselves short of foreign exchange because their payments to other countries exceed their foreign exchange earnings.

Countries in desperate need of assistance do not always see the "advice" of the IMF as reasonable and the assistance generally involves a quid pro quo: "To get our financial capital you have to make the following policy changes . . ." So some countries feel like they are at the mercy of the IMF and its economic philosophy. The IMF's role in the global economy is powerful and controversial.

18.2.5 Conclusion on International Economic Policy

At a global level it is no longer possible to simply talk about interventionists and non-interventionists debating *the* government's policy. There is no single global government that is making policy. Many governments make policies, and the policy environment is a fluid space of constant action and reaction among these governments.

In an effort to bring some coherence to the global economic policy environment, institutions have been established to set global rules. An early effort the *General Agreements on Tariffs and Trade, GATT* as it was called, was established to encourage free and open global markets. GATT has since been replaced by the *World Trade Organization (WTO)*. The WTO describes itself as follows (quotations that follow are from the WTO's homepage (http://www.wto.org) as of this writing):

> The World Trade Organization (WTO) is the only international organization dealing with the global rules of trade between nations. Its main function is to ensure that trade flows as smoothly, predictably and freely as possible.
>
> The result is assurance. Consumers and producers know that they can enjoy secure supplies and greater choice of the finished products, components, raw materials and services that they use. Producers and exporters know that foreign markets will remain open to them.
>
> The result is also a more prosperous, peaceful and accountable economic world. Virtually all decisions in the WTO are taken by consensus among all member countries and they are ratified by members' parliaments. Trade friction is channeled into the WTO's dispute settlement process where the focus is on interpreting agreements and commitments, and how to ensure that countries' trade policies conform with them. That way, the risk of disputes spilling over into political or military conflict is reduced.
>
> By lowering trade barriers, the WTO's system also breaks down other barriers between peoples and nations.
>
> At the heart of the system — known as the multilateral trading system — are the WTO's agreements, negotiated and signed by a large majority of the world's trading nations, and ratified in their parliaments. These agreements are the legal ground-rules for international commerce. Essentially, they are contracts, guaranteeing member countries important trade rights. They also bind governments to keep their trade policies within agreed limits to everybody's benefit.
>
> The agreements were negotiated and signed by governments. But their purpose is to help producers of goods and services, exporters, and importers conduct their business.
>
> The goal is to improve the welfare of the peoples of the member countries.

Some regional arrangements have also been established. The *North American Free Trade Agreement (NAFTA)* is designed to create a fluid trading environment among the U.S., Canada, and Mexico.

But both the WTO and NAFTA suffer from the fact that ultimately the participants are sovereign nations that can interpret and even ignore provisions, and both are negotiated treaties that leave some key issues such as workers' rights and environmental protection standards in dispute.

The most dramatic transnational agreement on trading relations is the European Union's adoption of the euro. A single currency eliminates all the issues of foreign exchange, and combined with the elimination of other trade barriers it creates a truly seamless market. Trading between Paris and Berlin is now just like trading between New York and Los Angeles. This seamlessness comes at a dramatic price, however. Having a *common currency* means that the monetary policy of each participating nation is determined not that nation's central bank, but by the European Central Bank.

As we have seen, monetary policy is a *very* powerful macroeconomic tool. In effect, each of the participating nations has traded a significant part of its national sovereignty for the right to be inside the euro system. They have eliminated many of the issues of international trade by in effect creating, for monetary policy purposes, a federal European state. Power over fiscal and many other policy dimensions still lies in the hands of the national governments, but the power of monetary policy lies in the hands of a European government.

When Keynes wrote his *General Theory* these now-unified euro nations had recently suffered one horrific war, and Keynes correctly predicted that there "might again" be another war. A significant motive for the integration of these nations into a common market was to eliminate the very "competitive struggle for markets" cited by Keynes as the "economic causes of war." The price, national sovereignty, is, however, a very dear one.

As you can see, expanding our study to the global economy adds a new and significant dimension of complexity to all the intricacies we already encountered in the economic analysis of an individual nation's economy. Thus we can say of global economic policy as we have said before about national economic policy, but now with ever more emphasis: Anyone who says it is simple is either simple minded, or thinks you are.

18.2.6 Globalization and Sustainability

There is currently a sharp debate about the desirability of globalization: The progressive integration of national economies into an unfettered global market system with no governmental intrusion or impediments to trade.

The logic underlying advocacy for the globalization of the free market system is the same logic that explained why we do not live as many Robinson Crusoes—each providing all for ourselves . . . why, instead, we choose to live in a complex society: By dividing up the labor of society and exchanging our surpluses through a market coordination system we can, under our nice assumptions, all benefit from the gains from trade. The productivity of this scheme is desirable whether the system encompasses a village or a nation or the entire world.

Advocates of globalization believe that sustaining and expanding the reach of humankind's material progress depends on expanding the global nexus of markets. They make the case that just as the material well-being of the average citizen in the U.S. or Japan or Germany has improved dramatically based on this model—the latter two having progressed very rapidly from the ashes of World War II, so too this model is the best hope for material progress in places still mired in squalor: Give these nations access to the global economy and development will follow as access to global markets expands. The advocates for globalization point to dramatic expansion of China and India as examples of this promise.

This is the case for globalization, but as we have seen in the course of developing our model—an analysis is only as strong as its assumptions are weak. So to assess the case for globalization, it is important to assess the assumptions that underlie that policy position.

What follows are three of the assumptions that warrant particular attention and an analysis of the debate regarding these assumptions:

1. Free markets reward lower cost structures and this is not only good for developing nations and their people, it is good for all humankind.
2. The distribution of the global endowment including global capital holdings is taken as a given.
3. Market responsiveness and agility insures sustainability as global production expands.

Consider the first of these assumptions: "Free markets reward lower cost structures and this is not only good for developing nations and their people, it is good for all humankind." As we learned when we covered the magic of markets, under our nice assumptions the keenness of the competition rewards those with a lower cost structure. Globalization extends this competition by eliminating barriers among nations so that nations with generally lower cost structures are rewarded and those with higher cost structures must adjust or lose in the competition.

Advocates for globalization argue that this is precisely the incentive that free and open markets can and should encourage. It offers developing nations with cheap labor an opportunity to compete based on their low cost structure while encouraging developed nations to be creative with new capital intensive techniques that allow them to compete with the low wage producers. By forcing high and low wage nations to focus on their comparative advantages, this dynamic creates opportunities for developing nations while encouraging innovation in developed nations, thus spurring the positive sum competitive game that Adam Smith envisioned in his *Inquiry into the Nature and Causes of the Wealth of Nations.*

Skeptics of globalization see this dynamic very differently. They make the case that cost structure differentials among nations are not simply due to different pay scales. The cost structure differences all too often reflect differences in working conditions (e.g., worker safety) and environmental protection. In an unfettered competition, nations with high standards for worker safety and environmental protection would be at a significant competitive disadvantage compared to those nations in which there is little or no protection for workers and/or the environment. The skeptics argue that globalization is bad for workers and the environment because it rewards and thus encourages neglect of these protections. They argue that globalization is a short to mid-term strategy for wealth accumulation, but is not sustainable in the long run because it would lead to working class and environmental degradation.

Here again we hear the voices of polar cases: Globalization is absolutely good versus globalization is absolutely bad. And again I would remind you that most economists are not at either of these poles. Most economists take a position along the continuum between these two poles.

Many economists subscribe to the argument that the division of labor, exchange of surpluses through markets, and gains from trade makes as much sense between Calcutta and St. Louis as it does between New Orleans and New York, so it is good to have free trade . . . but they would add the caveat that trade is only constructive if it is free and fair. "Free" implies competition with unfettered access to one another's markets. "Fair" implies playing by the same set of rules, including the same standards for conditions like worker safety and environmental protection.

But while this position of the "middle ground" economist is easy to conceptualize, it is very hard to operationalize for several reasons. First of all, the concept of "fair" is itself very complicated. As noted above, one nation's conception of legitimate standards may be seen by another nation as a protectionist strategy in disguise. Second, some nations just do not want to play fair because they want to win at the mercantilist game of beggar thy neighbor by holding down domestic wages, ignoring unsafe working conditions, and trashing the environment. This leaves the competitors the choice of playing the game by these lowest standards of "rules", losing in the competition, or trying to create multilateral agreements to isolate the mercantilist players . . . all of which are problematic solutions.

Clearly, the division of labor, coordination of exchange through markets, and gains from trade, as first laid out in a systematic fashion by Adam Smith has produced those gains for a great deal of humankind. But capturing those benefits on a global scale in a world of sovereign nations with different strategies (e.g., mercantilism) and values (e.g., environmental protection) is a complex, daunting challenge. This challenge brings us back to the observation that, in the global economy as in the domestic economy, with regard to policy: Anyone who says it is simple is either simple minded or thinks you are.

The second assumption underlying the globalization case is the very same assumption that underlies the analysis of markets in the national case: "Given the distribution of the initial endowment." In this case, however, this distribution is with respect to nations rather than individuals.

A market system is premised on private property rights—for you must own what you are offering to exchange—so the resources must be owned and the shares of ownership are certainly not equal either among individuals or among nations. Given that an agreement to redistribute the shares of the global endowment is highly unlikely, the analysis must begin from the assumption that extant distribution of that endowment among nations (shares of labor, natural resources, production capital, and financial capital) is taken as given.

As we learned in micro, so too in this case, even under the best case for globalization . . . the global economy under out nice assumptions realizing a Pareto optimum . . . those nations that enjoy a larger share of the endowment will enjoy a larger share of the global production. This in turn raises issues of global distributive justice. Some developing nations argue that current distribution of global endowment is the product of hundreds of years of rent-generating exploitation through colonial control and/or hegemonic military domination and/or control over access to financial capital . . . and so the global "playing field" is not level but rather is tilted by history to the advantage of the more mature economies. Many of those who make such a case see globalization as a fancy new term for maintaining this exploitive relationship justified by mathematically impressive models and elegant images like the invisible hand.

The pro-globalization voices reply: Yes, these injustices of history are very real . . . BUT, rather than being the next stage of exploitation, globalization offers a path to escape from this historically oppressive relationship. Markets are, they repeatedly point out, dynamic systems. Within such a system it is very hard to maintain an advantage because agility and creativity offer constant opportunities for eroding the advantages embodied in the current arrangement of production and consumption. To use a term from Joseph Schumpeter, free markets are constantly buffeted by gales of "creative destruction". This dynamic of constructive change is the fruit of competition when it is free. It is the best hope for all in humankind who are willing to work hard to improve their condition because it rewards energy and creativity while destroying the long powerful but old and inert structures that lie in the way of change.

The anti-globalization voices dismiss this logic as a self-serving rhetoric from those who actually hold power, for it deflects the conversation away from the real problem of globalization which is the golden rule: "Them that's got the gold rule." According to the anti-globalization argument, those who control the vast majority of the global financial capital have the power to play a very successful rent-maintenance game while those in developing nations who are waiting for the gales of creative destruction are waiting for a perfect storm in an imperfect world. To which the globalization advocates respond: Global capital is a citizen of no nation. It is not pursuing any agenda other than its best risk adjusted rate of return. If creative energy emerges from new entrants into the global economic nexus, that capital will flow into those places that display that energy and creativity . . . thus nurturing the very dynamic that holds out the best hope for growth in these emerging markets and the best chance for improving the material well-being of those who were previously left out of the global market opportunities. To which the anti-globalization respond: Lovely, romantic story . . . but utilizing energy and creativity requires capital. In return for blessing an emerging nation with a bit of their capital the global capital holders take most of the benefits of the production out of the developing country. Globalization holds no promise that these countries can ever accumulate the means for independent sustained domestic development.

The last assumption underlying the pro-globalization case is that market responsiveness and agility insures sustainability as global production expands. This brings us back to the debate we developed in section 12.3.2 on the Very Long Run: Does the global economy have the sustainable capacity to expand sufficiently so as to provide increasing well-being for those in the United States, Europe, Japan, Canada, and so on . . . while at the same time making it possible for the citizens of India, China, Russia and other developing nations to ultimately achieve this same level of material well-being? And, if this is feasible, what is the opportunity cost of this growth?

Advocates of globalization argue that the market system will respond constructively to the incentives created by any perverse effects of global development for material production. For example, as fresh water dwindles relative to a growing population, its price will rise. This will spur research into more efficient ways to accomplish desalination. So the solution to water shortages will be provided by the very creativity that free market competition encourages. And in the process more jobs will be created by this new dimension of market activity. This is a classic example of the faith of those who believe in markets, a faith that underlies laissez-faire and the advocacy of rapid globalization: In the context of a free market system with all the energy and creativity that system unleashes, the "problems" we create for ourselves in one time frame become the opportunities we create for ourselves in a larger time frame. If one believes in that faith, sustainability is not a problem, it is a given because the agility of markets will sustain the progress of humankind.

Anti-globalization advocates do not share this faith in markets. They believe that markets are driving a deadly dynamic. Markets not only deliver for consumers, they encourage greater consumption in order to justify their existence. The 20th century saw the emergence of marketing driven consumer societies with seemingly insatiable appetites for more material goods. Globalization is the extension of this culture into the rest of the world. Anti-globalization voices believe that under the current models of production and consumption, the growth in global production that would be necessary to satisfy humankind's voracious appetite for consumption is not only not sustainable, it threatens the very existence of humankind because the environment that sustains human life is being destroyed.

To which the advocates of globalization respond: Most of humanity simply wants to enjoy the well-being that those of you who hug trees in your designer clothes enjoy. It is hypocritical at best to say they should not have that opportunity. . . . The anti-globalization voices respond: There will be no designer clothes for anyone to wear nor any trees for anyone to hug if we do not change the way we as humankind feed, cloth, and shelter ourselves.

To say this debate is about your future prospects is an understatement. As my dad would say: "It matters!"

The tools of our analysis do not resolve this debate. As always the value of the tools that we have developed here is that they give us a systematic way of thinking critically about these big ideas and issues so that we can individually add our voices to the conversation in an informed and thoughtful way.

19.0 CONCLUSION ON POLICY

19.1 SOME HISTORICAL BACKGROUND ON THE INTERVENTIONIST VERSUS NON-INTERVENTIONIST DEBATE

19.1.1 The Ricardo-Malthus Debate

The interventionist versus non-interventionist debate is an old one.

The patron saint of modern non-interventionism is Jean-Baptiste Say. Writing in 1803, Say popularized the idea that a market system can and does effectively coordinate all decisions, and thus it always assures that the economy will work efficiently. This belief, commonly expressed as "supply creates its own demand" (i.e., prices will adjust to efficiently clear markets), became known as *Say's law*.

Say's law implies that the market system outcomes in a complex society are analogous to those in a simple Robinson Crusoe society. Recall that in a Robinson Crusoe society the decisions of supplier and demander are perfectly coordinated because the supplier and demander are one and the same person. According to Say's law, a complex society exhibits the same nice coordination despite the dispersion of supply and demand decisions among many people, because the markets coordinate very effectively.

Two famous contemporaries of Say, David Ricardo and Robert Malthus, were among the first of the modern economists to engage in an interventionist versus non-interventionist debate. In an exchange of letters (quotations that follow from and on this exchange are from John Maynard Keynes' essay "Robert Malthus" in *Essays and Sketches in Biography*. New York: Meridian Books, 1956; pages 32–33) Ricardo wrote on January 24, 1817, that

> It appears to me that one great cause of our difference in opinion on the subjects which we have so often discussed is that you have always in your mind the immediate and temporary effects of particular changes, whereas I put these immediate and temporary effects quite aside, and fix my whole attention on the permanent state of things which will result from them.

In effect Ricardo is arguing that while there are periods of adjustment, as Say's Law suggests, the economy will ultimately move to a general competitive equilibrium and thus full employment. Malthus responds in a letter of January 26, 1817, that:

> I agree with you that one cause of our difference in opinion is that which you mention. I certainly am disposed to refer frequently to things as they are, as the only way of making one's writings practically useful to society, and I think also the only way of being secure from falling into the errors of the taylors of Laputa, and by a slight mistake at the outset arrive at

conclusions the most distant from the truth. Besides I really think that the progress of society consists of irregular movements, and that to omit the consideration of causes which for eight or ten years will give great stimulus to production and population, or a great check to them, is to omit the causes of the wealth and poverty of nations—the grand object of all enquiries in Political Economy. A writer may, to be sure, make any hypothesis he pleases; but if he supposes what is not at all true practically, he precludes himself from drawing any practical inferences from his hypothesis.

Malthus's critique of Ricardo's logic is that it is based on strong assumptions, assumptions that are not realistic. Since assumptions set the trajectory of one's subsequent logic, Malthus argued that this error in the beginning of Ricardo's analysis of markets leads to him to fall "into the errors of the taylors of Laputa and by a slight mistake at the outset arrive at conclusions the most distant from the truth." Malthus is referring to the tailors of Laputa in the story of *Gulliver's Travels* by Jonathan Swift who by working from some assumed ideal proportions of a human ended up making an outfit for the very real Gulliver that was not at all properly proportioned to his actual body.

Ricardo's error, according to Malthus, lay in assuming Say's Law. Given this assumption it inevitably follows that the market system moves toward a general competitive equilibrium and full employment. This logic inevitably leads in turn to a *laissez faire* policy. But that policy is, according to Malthus, misguided because it is based on a false foundation—the assumption of Say's law.

Ricardo never convinced Malthus, but he did convince the emerging community of economists. In 1817 Ricardo published his *Principles of Political Economy and Taxation*. Ricardo's *Principles* established Say's Law as a fundamental principle of economic thought for over a century. During that time mainstream economic analysis focused primarily on the microeconomic system. Given Say's Law it seemed that the real mysteries of analysis lay in mechanics of the micro world. All this changed with John Maynard Keynes' *The General Theory of Employment, Interest and Money* published in 1936.

19.1.2 John Maynard Keynes' The General Theory of Employment, Interest, and Money

In his 1933 essay on Malthus, Keynes wrote of the exchange of letters between Malthus and Ricardo (p. 33):

> One cannot rise from a perusal of this correspondence without feeling that the almost total obliteration of Malthus's line of approach and the complete domination of Ricardo's for a period of a hundred years has been a disaster to the progress of economics. Time after time in these letters Malthus is talking plain sense, the force of which Ricardo with his head in the clouds wholly fails to comprehend. Time after time a crushing refutation by Malthus is met by a mind so completely closed that Ricardo does not even see what Malthus is saying.

Keynes' *General Theory* (New York: Harcourt Brace Jovanovich, 1964; pp. v, viii, 18–20) opens with the following statement in the "Preface":

> This book is chiefly addressed to my fellow economists. I hope that it will be intelligible to others. But its main purpose is to deal with difficult questions of theory, and only in the second place with the applications of theory to practice. For if orthodox economics is at fault, the error is to be found not in the superstructure, which has been erected with great care for logical consistency, but in a lack of clearness and generality in the premises. Thus I cannot achieve my object of persuading economists to reexamine critically certain of

their basic assumptions except by a highly abstract argument and also by much controversy.

Keynes concludes the Preface by saying:

> The composition of this book has been for the author a long struggle of escape, and so must the reading of it be for most readers if the author's assault upon them is to be successful, --a struggle of escape from habitual modes of thought and expression. The ideas which are here expressed so laboriously are extremely simple and should be obvious. The difficulty lies, not in the new ideas, but in escaping from the old ones, which ramify, for those brought up as most of us have been, into every corner of our minds.

Keynes identifies the "habitual modes of thought and expression" from which he must escape as follows:

> From the time of Say and [David] Ricardo the classical economists have taught [Say's Law] that the supply creates its own demand. . . .

He cites some passages from the economic writings of John Stuart Mill (1806–1873) and Alfred Marshall (1842–1924) that support this proposition, and then continues:

> The doctrine is never stated to-day in this crude form. Nevertheless it still underlies the whole classical theory, which would collapse without it. . . . Post-war [World War I] economists seldom, indeed, succeed in maintaining this standpoint consistently; for their thought to-day is too much permeated with the contrary tendency and with facts of experience too obviously inconsistent with their former view. But they have not drawn sufficiently far-reaching consequences; and have not revised their fundamental theory.

What were the "facts of experience too obviously inconsistent with their former view" that suggested to Keynes that Say's law is not valid? They were the realities of the Great Depression. Keynes looked out the window in the 1930s and asked: How can a theory that is based on the belief that the market system works nicely be relevant to our present Great Depression experience?

His point was that while such a theory may be internally consistent given our nice assumptions, in the real world those nice assumptions apparently do not hold. This is the point he is making when he writes in his preface to *The General Theory* that "if orthodox economics is at fault, the error is to be found not in the superstructure, which has been created with great care for logical consistency, but in a lack of clearness and of generality in the premises."

According to Keynes, the "classical" model is based on strong assumptions that make it a model of a special case that does not exist in reality. He emphasizes this point when he writes that "[T]hese conclusions [those that derive from Say's law] may have been applied to the kind of economy in which we actually live by false analogy from some kind of nonexchange Robinson Crusoe economy." Keynes argues that the analogy is false because, as we have seen, in a Robinson Crusoe society coordination of supply and demand intentions is perfect by definition, but in a complex society coordination is by definition a complex process vulnerable to power distortions and failure.

The essence of Keynes' argument is that intervention may be necessary in order to correct breakdowns in this complex system. His model established the framework for modern macroeconomic analysis and his interventionist views rekindled the macroeconomic interventionist versus non-interventionist debate in the mainstream economics profession. Today there are many thoughtful, powerful voices on each side in this debate.

So why can't economists resolve this debate among themselves?

19.2 Why Can't Economists Resolve This Debate Once and For All: The Problem of Testing

19.2.1 Overview

The extreme non-interventionist and interventionist positions in the policy debate are not actually occupied by many professional economists. As I've tried to point out along the way most economists hold views that would place them somewhere along a continuum between absolute *laissez-faire* and eager interventionism. What is more, for any particular economist the position she takes along this continuum may vary as the specific policy issue under consideration varies.

It has been said that if you survey 30 economists on an issue you will get 60 opinions. Everyone will have a different view and the expression of each view will be couched in terms like: "On one hand . . . but then on the other hand . . . " President Harry Truman is said to have wished for a one-handed economist.

Why can't economists agree? Why doesn't someone prove once and for all that this view or that view, that any one view of the economy is the correct view? The lack of a definitive answer to the question "What is the Truth?" is due to the fact that testing a model is a challenge, and it is fair to say that in the social sciences there is no such thing as a perfect test.

This leads to two problems. First of all, since the testing methods are imperfect, error may escape even the eye of a perfectly unbiased observer. Second, since there are no perfectly unbiased observers, what is an error is determined in the biased eye of the beholder. As a result there can be competing tests and competing interpretations of test results. This in turn makes it possible for the competing interventionist and non-interventionist viewpoints, each with strong "evidence" supporting their respective positions, to coexist. This problem generally frustrates interested observers of the debate within economics. The student of economics and the consumer of economic advice want answers, not more debate. We cannot resolve this problem here. We can, however, examine the source of the problem so that we can understand it more clearly.

19.2.2 Operationalizing a Model

The economist who wants to test a model must first operationalize the model. This means that she must transform theoretical, abstract definitions of the variables she's using into technical definitions that can be measured. She must also specify the relationship between variables exactly. For example, if the number of hours people choose to work is predicted to depend on wage, education, experience, wealth, and so on, then a specification of the predicted relationship might look something like this:

$$\text{Hours} = 2.3 \ \text{Wage} + 1.5 \ \text{Education} + 1.5 \ \text{Experience} - .5 \ \text{Wealth} + \ldots$$

Such specifications are necessary because the predictions of a model can only be tested if the variables included can be measured and the model itself can be exactly specified. Unfortunately, this process of transforming a theoretical model into an operational model is imperfect at best and vulnerable to self-serving manipulation at worst.

19.2.3 Theoretical versus Technical Definitions

Consider the transformation of a theoretical definition into a technical definition. The former defines a concept that is used in the model. The latter defines a set of criteria we can use to measure the concept so that the explanation and prediction of the model can be tested. Ideally, the theoretical and the technical definitions are a perfect match. In reality, however, that is rarely, if ever, the case.

Those who collect the data (e.g., the government) must set the criteria for the technical definition with the practical problems (e.g., expense, availability, accessibility . . .) of data collection in mind. Because macro variables are aggregates (summations of lots of individual values) and because the microeconomy is so large and complex, technical definitions are generally only *proxies* (substitutes) for the theoretical definitions they represent.

Take for example the problems with operationalizing labor-related terms. One hears a great deal in the media about the unemployment rate. It is based on the government's measures of labor force and unemployment, and is calculated as follows:

$$\text{Unemployment Rate} = (\text{Number unemployed}/\text{Labor force}) \times 100\%$$

The labor force is technically defined as people from 16 to 65 years old who are not in an institution (e.g., in jail) and who are working, awaiting return to work (laid off), or actively looking for work. If you fit the first two criteria but not the third, you wouldn't be counted in the labor force. You'd be considered voluntarily unemployed. So even if you're doing very productive things outside the market process like housework or volunteer work, technically you're voluntarily unemployed. Clearly counting houseworkers or volunteers among the voluntarily unemployed is an artificial distinction in the technical definition of the labor force. To see how artificial it is, consider this case: If you are working for someone as a housekeeper you are an employed member of the labor force. But if you and your boss fall in love and get married, and you continue to do the same housework while she goes to work, you are now counted as voluntarily unemployed because your work is not part of a market exchange.

Another glitch in this measure relates to folks who in very bad times give up actively looking for work because of their despair at lack of success. These folks are referred to as *discouraged workers*. They want a job. They would take a job. But absent any apparent hope of finding a job they quit looking. In doing so, according to the statistics, they have left the realm of unemployed members of the labor force and joined the ranks of the voluntarily unemployed—along with the homemakers, volunteers, retirees and the independently wealthy.

And the problems of measurement of labor-related variables goes beyond the distinction of in or out of the labor force. Even if we can agree on who is working and in the labor force, there is a technical issue related to the distinction between employed and unemployed. An individual is technically considered unemployed if during the reference week (the week when the data are collected) she is either laid off, waiting to report to work, or is available for work and has actively looked for a job during the last four weeks. Technically, you are employed if you have worked at least 1 hour for pay or at least 15 hours at the family business or farm during the week the government does its labor survey. The problem with this measure is that it counts someone as fully employed if they are in some real sense underemployed. For example, you are counted as employed even if you would like to be working full-time but can only find part-time work.

These labor-related measurement problems matter a lot because one of the central questions in macro is: Will the economy automatically reach full employment—the natural rate of unemployment? Clearly, a test of that question depends not only on an agreement as to what is the natural rate—a debatable issue, because frictional and structural unemployment are hard to measure—but also on an accurate measurement of the overall unemployment rate. Unfortunately the measures we use are flawed.

Measurement problems also arise when the concept of gross domestic product is operationalized.

The technical definition of GDP has four criteria for inclusion. First, the production must be exchanged for money. This criterion is included because a common denominator is necessary if we are going to add up apples and oranges and other components of society's production. Since money is a unit of account and market price is a representation of value in money terms, it is easy to aggregate (sum up) the value of all products that are exchanged for money. Given this criterion exchanges not involving money, like housework for one's family or volunteer work, are not included in the measure of GDP. Following our earlier example, when you go from employed housekeeper to housekeeper-spouse, your production suddenly disappears from the GDP.

This criterion also excludes production exchanged through what is called the *underground economy*. The underground economy is primarily a barter system for service exchange: You fix my car and I fix your plumbing. Such exchanges are often used as a method of escaping income taxes because there is no paper transaction for Internal Revenue Service (IRS) agents to follow.

A second criterion for inclusion in technically defined GDP is that the transaction be legal. Payments for mafia hits or political bribes are not generally reported to the government. Because of the difficulty of collecting data on illegal transactions, they are excluded from GDP.

A third criterion is that the transaction be for current production. The logic here is that goods and services produced in previous years are not part of this year's product. Thus, a transaction for "old" products (e.g., a used car) is not included in GDP. It represents an exchange of preexisting product for money, not a payment for new production.

And lastly, only final goods are counted in GDP. This criterion avoids double counting. If the value of a loaf of bread was measured by adding up all the money transactions that occurred in its production and final sale—farmer to miller to baker to grocery to you—the sum would overstate the value because the price you pay at the last exchange includes all the other prices. Adding them in along with the final price would be double counting.

These, then, are the technical criteria the government uses for measuring the GDP. They leave out some important things. The government has recognized this and has made some exceptions in order to include things that are clearly too important to exclude. One example is the government's own production. Many of the services the government provides (e.g., schools and defense) are not sold to the consumer in a marketplace for money. Thus, according to the technical criteria, this production would be excluded from GDP. Since government production is so big an item in our economy, an exception is made and the value of government production is measured by and added into GDP at the cost of producing it. But while the exceptions capture some important things, many others such as the value of all the home production done by a member of a family for the family are still excluded. Thus the technical measure of GDP is only a proxy for the real GDP we talk about in theory.

Macro variables like the labor force variable and GDP suffer from such flaws, but at least we can be thankful that most key macroeconomic variables are actually measured. A common problem with microeconomic variables is that there are often no measures of the values of variables relevant to the model. This is so because there are so many things to measure in a microeconomic empirical test.

For example, if an economist wants to test her model's prediction that the number of hours an individual works per week depends on factors like wage, education, age, race, gender, health status, experience, and so on, she would need information from thousands of individuals on the number of hours they work each week, their wage, education, age, race, gender, health status, experience, and any other factors the model represents as relevant. That is a lot of numbers, and often the actual measures do not exist so proxies are used instead.

For instance, if there is no available measure of experience, some researchers use

$$\text{Age} - \text{Education} - 6$$

as a proxy. The logic here is that if one spends six preschool years and all school years outside the labor force, then the rest of life is spent in the labor force acquiring experience. The problems with this proxy should be obvious. It does not allow for the possibility of years outside the labor force after school, it does not account for variations in the quality and kinds of experience one can acquire, and so on.

Suppose a researcher has an actual measure of the number of years the individuals in her data set have been in school. At least she has an accurate measure of education, right? Wrong! Number of years in school is only a very rough proxy for education, because not all years are equal. A person who went to 12 years of quality schools and/or a person who spent 12 years working hard in school has a much better education than someone who spent those same12 years in schools that were lousy and/or if she was goofing off.

There are, in short, lots of problems with micro data, just as there are with macro data. These problems with technical definitions and data measurement contribute to the coexistence of competing theories. When definitions are not perfect, researchers with an agenda can choose proxies that help make the case they desire to prove. And even if the researcher is entirely impartial, the results are only as good as the data that go in. As the classic line goes: Garbage in, garbage out.

The problems with testing models do not end here. There are also testing flaws that arise in the process of specifying the relationships among variables once they are defined and in analyzing the data.

19.2.4 Multiple Variable (Multivariate) Regression Techniques

The technique most often used by economists to establish what is going on in the economy is called *multiple variable regression analysis*. To see how it works consider the following example.

For some vintages of wine, e.g., Bordeaux, the process of maturation is very slow. It is only many years after the harvest when the quality of the wine is finally established. Traditionally, the prediction of the quality of the wine that will come from a given year's harvest is based on tastes from the barrel as the wine is maturing. But this assessment of vintages is by no means an exact science.

Enter Orly Ashenfelter, a well-known labor economist and a wine enthusiast. Ashenfelter decided to apply the multivariate regression technique he uses to analyze economic data to the analysis of wine data. He had data on prices of mature Bordeaux wines for many years past. He also had data on the growing conditions for each of these past vintages: winter rain, harvest rain, and average temperature during the growing season. His theoretical model was, in fuctional form:

Quality (Q) = f(Winter Rain (WR), Average Growing Temperature (TMP), Harvest Rain (HR))

where Q is the dependent variable. Its value depends on the effects of the independent variables WR, TMP, and HR. Ashenfelter constructed a quality index based on his price data and operationalized his equation as follows:

$$Q = \text{ß}_0 + \text{ß}_1*WR + \text{ß}_2*TMP + \text{ß}_3*HR$$

where ß_1, ß_2, and ß_3 are parameters of WR, TMP, and HR respectively. Each parameter shows the sign and size of the effect of its respective variable on the dependent variable, Q. The parameter ß_0 captures the effect of all the variables that were not included but that do affect quality. If the equation is correctly specified and if we can determine the parameters, then multiplying WR, TMP, and HR by their respective parameters ß_1, ß_2, ß_3 and then adding ß_0 should give an accurate value for Q.

Computer programs that do multivariate regression analysis take this specification of the wine quality equation and test it with a data base of values for Q, WR, TMP, and HR. The result generated by the computer gives the sign of the parameter (is it positive or negative), size of the parameter (how big is the number), and the significance (does it really seem to matter in determining the dependent variable) for the parameters on each variable in the equation. Ashenfelter's results looked like this:

$$Q = -12.145 + 0.00117*WR + 0.6164*TMP - 0.00386*HR$$

The signs of the parameters (positive for WR and TMP, negative for HR) generated by this data analysis suggest that winter rain and higher growing temperatures improve quality while harvest rain lowers quality. If this analysis based on the data Ashenfelter had at his disposal is correct, then in any future year as soon as the grapes are harvested he should be able to plug in that year's numbers for WR, TMP, and HR and, given the parameters he's determined, predict the quality of the wine from those grapes once the wine is mature years later. It's this process of estimating parameters based on analysis of past data, which then in turn can be used to predict, that makes multivariate regression analysis such a popular tool for economic analysis.

Take the hours-worked issue cited earlier. Suppose a labor economist's theory suggests that in general, hours worked rise as a worker's wages rise and as her education and experience increase, but fall if her wealth increases. If the economist has a good database that includes hours, wage, education, experience, and wealth data for lots of individuals, she can run a regression on the specification:

$$\text{Hours} = \beta_0 + \beta_1 * \text{Wage} + \beta_2 * \text{Education} + \beta_3 * \text{Experience} + \beta_4 \text{ Wealth}$$

to see if the data support her theory.

Multivariate regression analysis is widely accepted and respected as a useful way to estimate the effect of independent variables on a dependent variable. If there is a problem with this technique, it lies not in the technique itself but in the way it is applied. The computer can only test on the basis of the data and the model specification it is given. As we have seen, because of the use of proxy variables, the data are often suspect. Another problem is that the specification of the model can be manipulated in order to achieve desired results.

Clearly, the economist testing the hours equation hopes that the regression results will be consistent with her model's predictions. Usually the economist is satisfied if the predicted sign is correct (e.g., for the example just cited, that the sign of the coefficient on wealth is indeed negative) and if all the variables that were predicted to be significant in determining the dependent variable, are, in fact, significant (the computer will report the level of significance for each independent variable).

Suppose the economist does the analysis described above and she gets the following results in which all the variables are found to be significant:

$$\text{Hours} = 3.3 - 1.3 * \text{Wage} + 1.5 * \text{Education} + 1.5 * \text{Experience} - .5 * \text{Wealth}$$

Education, experience, and wealth all behave as predicted, but not the wage. The wage has a negative sign rather than the positive one predicted.

She could accept this as a rejection of her theory, or she could adjust the specification a bit to see if that would change the outcome. For example, if she *re*specified the equation she puts into the computer as:

$$\text{Hours} = \beta_0 + \beta_1 * \text{Wage} + \beta_2 * \text{Education} + \beta_3 * \text{Experience} + \beta_4 \text{ Wealth}^2$$

The squared sign on the wealth variable would definitely change the results. If the new results are

$$\text{Hours} = 2.3 + 1.5 * \text{Wage} + 1.0 * \text{Education} + 1.3 * \text{Experience} - 1.2 * \text{Wealth}^2$$

the signs are now consistent with the theoretical prediction.

Is this legitimate? Has she just "cooked the data" or done "data mining" to get the result she wanted. Is the theory driving the data analysis, instead of the data testing the theory? It is a judgment call. There are plenty of times when an initial specification does not give a result consistent with theory. At that point it is up to the researcher to decide if there is a legitimate reason to change the specification. There can be legitimate reasons. It might well be that before the initial analysis the researcher did not consider effects that the unexpected result makes clear.

The key point here is that data analysis in the social sciences is not an exact science. It requires thoughtful judgment, and it benefits from flexibility in testing. But this flexibility also makes it possible for someone to manipulate the test until the results fit the predictions of her model. And it certainly makes it possible for honest differences to occur about how to test a model and what various test results imply. It is this lack of definitiveness in model testing that contributes to the endless debate in economics. No one can say with certainty that her model is Truth with a capital T, because no one has an absolutely faultless test to determine Truth.

19.3 CONCLUSION

Our analysis has demonstrated that under the ideal conditions (given our nice assumptions and a "just" distribution of the initial endowments), a market system will realize an efficient and just society. As Adam Smith put it: "Human society, when we contemplate it in a certain abstract and philosophical light, appears like a great, an immense machine, whose regular and harmonious movements produce a thousand agreeable effects" (*TMS*, 316).

The world Smith has in mind here is the world we refer to today as a General Competitive Equilibrium. In such a world the race is fair and the competition is constructive. All individuals strive for personal excellence, and in that pursuit we each serve ourselves and one another. If all hold a fair share of the initial endowment, the society will realize ethical and efficiency norms: Distributive justice and Pareto optimality.

Smith recognized, and we have demonstrated, that it is in fact very difficult to realize such a society because constructive competition is only possible if the competition is built on a more fundamental foundation of cooperation. For competition to be constructive, there must be universal cooperation in observing the basic standards of conduct that ensure a fair race. Smith wrote *The Theory of Moral Sentiments* to represent how these standards of conduct might be determined and established. He realized, however, that due to human frailty we never have, and possibly never will, realize them. He recognized, in short, that vice exists and undermines society's efforts to realize the ideal.

Continuing the quotation cited above, Smith writes that:

> As in any other beautiful and noble machine that was the production of human art, whatever tended to render its movements more smooth and easy, would derive beauty from this effect, and, on the contrary, whatever tended to obstruct them would displease upon that account: so virtue, which is, as it were, the fine polish to the wheels of society, necessarily pleases; while vice, like that vile rust, which makes them jar and grate upon one another, is as necessarily offensive. (*TMS*, 316)

Ironically, the rationality of individuals is the source of both virtue and vice in competition. It is the motive force for constructive competition and also for destructive competition.

We have seen that in a complex society the incentive to provide for the needs of others is based on self-interest: By specializing and generating a surplus, one can benefit by the gains from trade. As Smith states:

> It is not from the benevolence of the butcher, the brewer, or the baker that we expect our dinner, but from their regard to their own interest. We address ourselves, not to their humanity but to their self-love, and never talk to them of our own necessities but of their advantages. (*WN*, 26–7)

This is a virtue of rationality.

The flip side of rationality is that unbridled self-interest leads to rent-seeking. Individuals or coalitions of individuals often use their resources in pursuit of advantage rather than excellence. As Smith wrote:

> People of the same trade seldom meet together, even for merriment and diversion, but the conversation ends in a conspiracy against the public, or in some contrivance to raise prices. (*WN*, 145)

Either control of markets or control of the social and political institutions that distribute the opportunities that are paths to markets can be exploited in order to produce a rent. We have seen how such behavior distorts the distribution and undermines the efficiency of the microeconomy and results in macroeconomic problems.

It is precisely this two-sided nature of rationality that makes economics such an inexact science. Ironically, as the old comic strip character Pogo once put it: "We have met the enemy and they are us."

If the rationality of all individuals were constrained by an absolute commitment to a fair race, then in a sense both the interventionists and the *laissez-faire* advocates would be correct. The market system would work very nicely wherever markets existed, and the government of such a people would intervene wisely wherever markets failed. In the absence of such a perfect people, the *laissez-faire* advocates put faith in the market system, the interventionists put much less faith in the market system, and the vast majority of economists grope for answers in the face of the complex reality.

The analysis presented here does not give "answers" to basic economic questions like: What should the role of government be? The purpose of this text and the model we have developed is to empower you to be a more constructive critical thinker as you address these important questions—to think more systematically about the consequences of your own choices and the choices of your government.

The choices you make as an individual and as a citizen will to some degree shape the future for yourself and for your society. It should be clear that the choices that will shape your economic future are not simply those related to where to work and what to buy. While these are important, your choices as to what values to adopt and for whom to vote will be equally important.

Individuals do not always have the opportunity to make such choices. In a society with a totalitarian government and a command economy, there are no elections in which to choose leaders and no markets in which to choose exchanges. The dictator makes all choices. A benevolent dictator may choose justice but could never be so omniscient as to realize the efficiency of markets . . . and what assurance is there that the next dictator will be so benevolent? In a free society with a government of, by, and for the people, the people choose and there is the potential for justice and efficiency. However, it is only a potential. There are forces ("factions," Adam Smith called them) constantly seeking control in order to benefit from exploiting the advantages control bestows.

The fact that you are reading this text represents your connection to a complex society. The labor and capital of many individuals you will never meet are embodied in these pages. Complexity brings with it great benefits for those who enjoy the fruits of more productive human labor. But it does not come without costs. As Smith put it, in such a world "[a]ll the members of human society stand in need of each others assistance . . . [and] are likewise exposed to mutual injuries." The cost of complexity is vulnerability that comes with interdependence.

20.0 ON JUSTICE AND THE SUSTAINABILITY OF LIBERAL SOCIETY

20.1 INTRODUCTION

We have studied the market system. Humankind has been employing markets to coordinate exchange for a very long time, but societies that do most of the allocation of resources and the distribution of output based on market coordination are a very new phenomenon in humankind's long history.

A mature market coordination system is one dimension of a *liberal social order*, a social arrangement in which each individual is free to choose—no tradition binds her, no dictator controls her. In the ideal it is a system in which there is "liberty . . . for all".

But liberty is not a sufficient condition for a liberal society to sustain itself. A necessary condition for the sustainability of a liberal system is justice. It is for this reason that the preamble of the U.S. Constitution cites "establish Justice" as a first priority in order to "secure the Blessings of Liberty to ourselves and our Posterity".

In the thousands of years of humankind's history this new social/political/economic experiment called liberal society began to emerge in a recognizable form in the 17th and 18th centuries in northwestern Europe. Very early on as this new experiment unfolded people wondered: How do we build and sustain a constructive liberal society?

The early liberal philosophers understood very well that, for reasons you can understand in the terms of our model (strong incentives for rent-seeking and rent-maintenance), making this experiment work is a very tricky business. When individuals are free to choose and self-interest is the motive force, the incentive to seek rent-generating advantages is very powerful.

In the early years of this liberal experiment some of the great philosophers of the day believed that unconstrained individual freedom would unleash a war of all against all as free individuals participated in a no-holds-barred struggle with one another for personal gain—a rent-seeking war. This dire prospect for the liberal experiment became known as the Hobbesian abyss after Thomas Hobbes who most vividly imagined this unconstrained state.

A central question addressed by some of Hobbes' philosophical successors was: Can the benefits of liberal society—unfettered freedom and the energy, creativity, and productivity this freedom unleashes—be sustained? Can such a society avoid the Hobbesian abyss? This question is the focus of my research because it is a question that must still be addressed, especially so as much of humankind (including Russia and China) is unleashing the energy of a free market system.

The assumption that underlies my study of liberal society and shapes my perspective of how it might work more constructively is that human nature has not changed in the brief twinkle of an eye that the last few centuries represent in history of humankind's evolution. Certainly the context of human experience has changed dramatically in terms of technology, but human nature has not changed. So I look back at the work of some of my brilliant predecessors and I study how they imagined liberal society might be developed and sustained as a promising human prospect.

Given that human nature has not changed, those predecessors where struggling with the same fundamental questions of humankind's arrangements that we struggle with today. I study the history of economic thought and in particular the moral philosophy of Adam Smith because I think there is much we can learn from those who have addressed these questions before us.

20.2 ADAM SMITH AND COMMUTATIVE JUSTICE

Adam Smith believed that liberal society is sustainable if and only if at its foundation there is a system of commutative justice that defines and enforces fairness in our interactions with one another. Smith understood well that in a free society there are many opportunities and a huge incentive for individuals to exploit others, to take advantage of others and to come out materially ahead for having done so. Given this incentive, he believed that absent enforced rules of commutative justice liberal society would dissolve just as Hobbes predicted into chaos. In his first book, *The Theory of Moral Sentiments* published in 1759, Smith wrote as follows about the centrality of justice in a liberal society:

> Society . . . cannot subsist among those who are at all times ready to hurt and injure one another. The moment that injury begins, the moment that mutual resentment and animosity take place, all the bands of it [(society)] are broke asunder, and the different members of which it consisted are, as it were, dissipated and scattered abroad by the violence and opposition of their discordant affections. (*TMS*, 86)

This is the Hobbesian abyss. If you give people total freedom and there are no rules to constrain them from cheating, hurting, or injuring one another, people will all too often cheat, hurt and injure one another in pursuit of advantages. Freedom liberates both the most noble and the basest instincts in each of us. Those base instincts can easily dominate our interactions when self-interest is the only motive that drives us. There must be limits or there will be the abyss. In this spirit Smith continues:

> If there is any society among robbers and murders, they must at least, according to the trite observation, abstain from robbing and murdering one another. . . . Society may subsist, though not in the most comfortable state, without beneficence [by which he means human kindness towards one another]; but the prevalence of injustice must utterly destroy it. Justice . . . is the main pillar that upholds the whole edifice. . . . [S]ociety cannot subsist unless the laws of justice are tolerably observed. . . . (*TMS*, 86)

In his *Inquiry into the Nature and Causes of the Wealth of Nation*, Smith laid out the basic analysis of market efficiency and general competitive equilibrium that has been presented in the preceding pages. He understood very well the material benefits of a constructive, sustainable liberal system. But he also understood very clearly that markets do not function in a social/political vacuum. The central question Smith was trying to think through at this very early stage of the liberal experiment (the 1760–70s) was: How do we make a society of free individuals work constructively so that we can actually enjoy the benefits such a society has to offer? He believed that for the blessing of liberty to be sustained there must be liberty *and* justice for all, because liberty without justice leads to unbridled competition: A rent-seeking society and the abyss, the war of all against all.

Among Smith's contemporaries a group of French philosophers, the Physiocrats, were struggling with this same question Smith was examining: How can society give freedom and constrain greed? The Physiocrats' solution envisioned a "despotime legal" (an enlightened dictator) who would enforce standards of justice and thus maintain the structure of order within which liberty could flourish.

Smith rejected this solution. He understood that you cannot impose order from above and still enjoy the freedom that makes a society a liberal society. He appreciated that external control of the destructive forces of self-interest would require a web of control over everyday life that would destroy the very liberty that the enlightened despot was supposed to protect. If all individuals' ethics had to be policed, this would lead to a police state.

In Smith's vision of an ideal liberal society justice is not imposed upon us from above by a dictator. Rather it is imposed upon us from within by an internal "police"—a shared commitment to a common set of civic values. In Smith's vision the progress of liberal society, and thus its sustainability, depends on each generation building—through shared discourse and struggle—an ever more mature system of shared civic values, and then passing that more mature system of values on to the next generation for its subsequent contribution to this social maturation process.

Smith believed that while understanding history and applying reason can contribute to the discourse on ideal civic values, these ideal values are not directly knowable by reason. He believed that it is through thoughtful civic discourse and by trial and error that societal values mature, and that those societies which develop more constructive values are, *ceteris paribus*, more free, more productive, more able to sustain and protect themselves. Thus for Smith the key to societal maturation is an open, respectful discourse in which demagoguery is rejected.

20.3 JOHN STUART MILL AND DISTRIBUTIVE JUSTICE

Smith wrote in the last half of the 18th century, very early on in the liberal experiment. In his day the technological transformation often referred to as the industrial revolution was only just beginning. As that technological transformation grew, so too did the misery of the working class. During the first half of the 19th century many philosophers pointed to that misery as evidence that the liberal experiment of individual freedom and private property associated with this industrial revolution was a failure. They advocated, as an alternative, social structure schemes of communal living and ownership, communist systems that they believed would improve the condition of the working class. By 1848, when the industrial revolution was in full force, the misery it had created inspired revolutions across Europe. In 1848 Karl Marx and Fredric Engles published the *Communist Manifesto* calling for an end to the liberal experiment.

Also in 1848 John Stuart Mill published his *Principles of Political Economy*. Writing, as he put it, "[i]n an age . . . when a general reconsideration of all first principles is felt to be inevitable" (Vol. I, p. 261), Mill struggled with the same question Smith had: How do we develop and sustain a constructive liberal society? To set the scene for his response to this question Mill compares the potential of communism with "the [present] institution of private property." (Vol. I, p. 267) He begins by exploring "[t]he objection[s] ordinarily made to a system of community property and equal distribution of produce, [e.g.,] that each person would be incessantly occupied in evading his fair share of work." (Vol. I, p. 263) For each such objection to communism Mill offers an ameliorating consideration, and he concludes:

> But these difficulties, though real, are not necessarily insuperable. . . . If therefore, the choice were to be made between Communism with all its chances, and the present state of society with all its sufferings and injustices; if the institution of private property necessarily carried with it as a consequence, that the produce of labour should be apportioned as we now see it, almost in an inverse ratio to labour—the largest portions to those who have never worked at all, the next largest to those whose work is almost nominal, and so in a descending scale, the remuneration dwindles as the work grows harder and more disagreeable, until the most fatiguing and exhausting bodily labour cannot count with certainty on being able to earn even the necessaries of life; if this, or Communism, were the alternative, all the difficulties, great or small,

of Communism, would be but as dust in the balance. But to make the comparison applicable, we must compare Communism at its best, with the regime of individual property, not as it is, but as it might be made. The principle of private property has never yet had a fair trial in any country; and less so, perhaps, in this country than in some others. The arrangements of modern Europe commenced from a distribution of property which was the result, not of just partition, or acquisition by industry, but of conquest and violence: and notwithstanding what industry has been doing for many centuries to modify the work of force, the system still retains many and large traces of its origin. The laws of property . . . have not held the balance fairly between human beings, but have heaped impediments upon some, to give advantages to others; they have purposely fostered inequalities, and prevented all from starting the race fair. (Vol. I, pp. 267–8)

Mill's concern is with the distribution of the social endowment among individuals. In our analysis we have simply taken that distribution among individuals as given. With that given, we learned about Pareto optimality producing the greatest social product, noting that even in this most efficient case anyone who starts off with a small share of the social endowment ends up with a small slice of the social product. Our nice assumptions ensure efficiency, but nothing about them ensures distributive justice. The market system is amoral.

According to Marx the system of private property that goes hand-in-hand with a liberal order will inevitably lead to a progressively more unequal distribution of society's wealth: Even if the initial condition is consistent with our nice assumptions, those who enjoy a distributive advantage thanks to starting with a larger share of the social endowment will use their larger share of the distribution to generate market distorting rent-generating advantages. This growing power advantage will in turn lead to even larger distributive inequities and in turn more rent-seeking. According to Marx, this inevitable growing divide between the rich and poor will give rise to a working class revolt and the replacement of liberal society with a communistic regime.

Mill agreed with Marx that liberal society was generating an unjust outcome, but he did not believe that the failure of liberal society was inevitable. Mill argued that the source of the problem lay in the unfair distribution of the social endowment among individuals and that this is a problem that liberal society can solve. He wrote:

> That all should indeed start on perfectly equal terms, is inconsistent with any law of private property: but if as much pains as has been taken to aggravate the inequality of chances arising from the natural working of the principle, had been taken to temper that inequality by every means not subversive of the principle itself; if the tendency of legislation had been to favour the diffusion, instead of the concentration of wealth . . . the principle of individual property would have been found to have no necessary connection with the physical and social evils which almost all Socialist writers assume to be inseparable from it. (Vol. I, p. 268)

Then Mill imagines with the reader how it might be possible for the race for wealth to begin more fairly—not exactly equal, but much more roughly equal—so that it would truly be a race based on individual abilities and efforts, rather than a race the outcome of which is largely predetermined by advantages at the starting line. He continues:

> Private property, in every defence made of it, is supposed to mean, the guarantee to individuals of the fruits of their own labour and abstinence. The guarantee to them of the fruits of the labour and abstinence of others, transmitted to them without any merit or exertion of their own, is not of the essence of the institution, but a mere incidental consequence, which when it reaches a certain height, does not promote, but conflicts with the ends which render private property legitimate. (Vol. I, p. 269)

In other words, for someone to simply be given resources that put her ahead at the start of the competition is inconsistent with the whole philosophy of liberal society. The idea of a liberal order is that to succeed in the competition for wealth and to get ahead in life, you must work hard. Your personal rewards are supposed to derive from your own efforts. Mill sees inheritance as a classic example of an unearned advantage. As a liberal philosopher, he wonders: Why should anyone be allowed to inherit the accumulated wealth of previous generations if she had nothing to do with creating that wealth?

Not only is this unfair at an individual level, this unfairness has corrosive effect on liberal society: It empowers those with unearned advantages to exploit those advantages even further, while at the same time diminishing the incentive of those who suffer disadvantages to participate according to a set of shared civic values since the results seem to be so unfair. This perverse dynamic undermines the sustainability of liberal society. Mill suggests the following policy to address this corrosive process:

> Were I framing a code of laws according to what seems to me best in itself, without regard to existing opinions and sentiments, I should prefer to restrict, not what any one might bequeath, but what any one should be permitted to acquire, by bequest or inheritance. Each person should have power to dispose by will of his or her whole property; but not to lavish it in enriching some one individual beyond a certain maximum, which should be fixed sufficiently high to afford the means of comfortable independence. The inequalities of property which arise from unequal industry, frugality, perseverance, talents, and to a certain extent even opportunities, are inseparable from the principle of private property, and if we accept the principle, we must bear with these consequences of it: but I see nothing objectionable in fixing the limit to what any one may acquire by the mere favour of others, without exercise of his faculties, and in requiring that if he desires any further accession of fortune, he shall work for it. (Vol. I, p. 289)

20.4 COMMUTATIVE JUSTICE, DISTRIBUTIVE JUSTICE, AND SUSTAINABLE LIBERAL SOCIETY

So what are the necessary conditions for a sustainable liberal society? Combining the perspectives of two of the greatest philosophers of liberal society, Adam Smith and John Stuart Mill, suggests two necessary conditions: commutative justice and distributive justice.

Smith makes the case that a sustaining a constructive liberal society requires a citizenry that shares a commitment to common set of civic values; a system of commutative justice within which we all play by a shared set of mutually fair rules. Mill makes the case that distributive justice, not with respect to outcomes but with respect to distribution of the endowment, is essential. If the whole game is going to be played fairly, not only do people have to play by a common set of rules so the game itself is fair, the players have to begin from a roughly equal position if the outcome is to be fair.

These two dimensions of justice, commutative and distributive, are interdependent. If the race does not begin fair, if there is no distributive justice, it is highly unlikely that the people who suffer this injustice will feel any sense of commitment to society's rules of commutative justice—to the civic values. Similarly, if there is no system of commutative justice, a rent-seeking power struggle will unfold and distributive justice will never be achieved.

I would suggest that a policy for simultaneously building these commutative and distributive dimensions of justice in society might work as follows. After allowing individuals to inherit a "comfortable independence" from the passing generation, the bulk of that passing generation's wealth should be accumulated in a human capital account for use in nurturing the emerging generation with high quality health care and high quality public education. In doing so, society could diffuse wealth in a way that nurtures its citizenry.

I specify "public" education because, while parochial and private education is to be valued, as citizens we have a common interest in ensuring the access of all to a system of education that represents our *common civic* values. Religious, family, ethnic, or other group or personal values are a rich dimension of the diversity that invigorates liberal society, but as Smith (and his contemporaries, the founders of the United States who advocated a separation of church and state) understood very clearly: It is our *common civic* values that must form the foundation of the liberal order, for they are the glue that holds a liberal society of diverse individuals together.

20.5 Why Value This Liberal Experiment?

Adam Smith imagines humankind's ideal as "the liberal plan of equality, liberty and justice" (*WN*, 664). For Smith this ideal society is one in which the least of the working class are "tolerably well fed, clothed, and lodged":

> Servants, labourers, and workmen of different kinds, make up the far greater part of every great political society. But what improves the circumstances of the greater part can never be regarded as an inconveniency to the whole. No society can surely be flourishing and happy, of which the far greater part of the members are poor and miserable. It is but equity, besides, that they who feed, clothe, and lodge the whole body of the people, should have such a share of the produce of their own labour as to be themselves tolerably well fed, clothed, and lodged (*WN*, 96).

Smith believed that the liberal plan is the best social construct for the working class because when it is functioning constructively the freedom and security it affords each individual encourages the most productive use of resources. Furthermore, workers are most free and secure under this plan, and for Smith this secure independence is a key to human dignity and personal maturity.

Writing in the 18th century, Smith's ultimate concern is the well-being and dignity of the individual and he believes that a constructive liberal society is the best social construction for realizing the greatest well-being and dignity for each individual.

Writing in the 19th century, John Stuart Mill rejected communism not because he didn't think it could function, but rather because he believed that a world in which all activity was communal, a world in which each individual is always under the watchful eye of all others, would crush individualism. He values liberal society for

> those manifold unlikenesses, that diversity of tastes and talents, and variety of intellectual points of view, which not only form a great part of the interest in human life, but by bringing intellects into stimulating collision, and by presenting to each innumerable notions that he would not have conceived of himself, are the mainspring of mental and moral progression. (Vol. I, p. 271)

> No society in which eccentricity is a matter of reproach, can be in a wholesome state. (Vol. I, p. 271)

As did Smith in the 18th and Mill in the 19th, writing in the 20th century John Maynard Keynes valued the liberal experiment, and for very much the same reasons:

> [A]bove all, individualism, if it can be purged of its defects and its abuses, is the best safeguard of personal liberty in the sense that, compared with any other system, it greatly widens the field for the exercise of personal choice. It is also the best safeguard of the variety of life, which emerges precisely from this extended field of choice, and the loss of which is the greatest of all losses of the homogeneous or totalitarian state. For this variety preserves the traditions which embody the most secure and successful choices of former generations; it colours the present with the diversification of fancy; and, being

the handmaid of experiment as well as of tradition and of fancy, it is the most powerful instrument for human betterment (Keynes, 380).

As the 21st century unfolds before us, this relatively new social experiment, liberal society, is still very much an experiment. If it is to realize the potential for human dignity and creativity and betterment that these great minds of the 18th, 19th, and 20th century saw as its promise, it must be understood and nurtured by us, the citizens of today. Such nurturing begins with systematic understanding for critical thinking . . . that systematic understanding for critical thinking is the purpose of this text.

20.6 REFLECTIONS ON OUR MAINTAINED ASSUMPTIONS: ON COMMITMENT, DUTY, AND CITIZENSHIP

In the Preface to his *General Theory* (citations from the Harcourt Brace Jovanovich First Harbinger Edition, New York and London. 1964), John Maynard Keynes writes that "if orthodox economics is at fault, the error is to be found not in the superstructure, which has been erected with great care for logical consistency, but in a lack of clearness and of generality of the premises." He believed that to enrich the theory he had to "persuad[e] economists to re-examine critically certain of their basic assumptions. . . ." (Keynes, p. v)

At the very beginning of the course as I was setting forth our assumptions I wrote: "We're going to assume that the goal of everyone in life is to maximize utility." The term in economics for that character, that nature of being, is *homo economicus* or economic man. I said then that this will be a maintained assumption in our analysis.

Much of my research focuses on this assumption because I believe that such a human nature is not a stable foundation for a liberal order. If utility maximization was the only goal for all of us we would indeed live in the Hobbesian war of all against all, a very degenerative rent-seeking society. As described above, I have learned from Adam Smith that the force that holds the abyss at bay and that holds a liberal order of free individuals together is commitment—a commitment to civic values that transcends ourselves. Smith writes:

> The administration of the great system of the universe . . . the care of the universal happiness of all rational and sensible beings, is the business of God not of man. To man is allotted a much humbler department, but one much more suitable to the weakness of his powers, and to the narrowness of his comprehension; the care of his own happiness, of that is his family, his friends, his country: that he is occupied in contemplating the more sublime, can never be an excuse for his neglecting the more humble department. . . . The most sublime speculation of the contemplative philosopher can scarce compensate the neglect of the smallest active duty. (*TMS*, p. 237)

That last word, "duty," is central to Adam Smith's analysis of a sustainable liberal society. Our duty as an individual in a liberal society is to be a good citizen, to function constructively in our society so that society can function constructively for the rest of its citizens. This ultimately redounds to our own benefit. If everyone plays by the same constructive rules, we can all pursue our dreams confident that the only unwarranted constraints we face will be those nature imposes on us or that we impose on ourselves.

Smith did not believe, however, that the mature commitment to duty on which a liberal order depends can be based on self interest. He believed that we are more than *homo economicus*, that we are capable of commitments that transcend ourselves, and that while we are initially inculcated with a sense of duty based on self-interest of social acceptance we are capable as mature individuals of making commitments that transcend ourselves—the kinds of commitments that are the glue that hold a liberal order together. I think that there is evidence to suggest that we are indeed capable of such commitment behavior.

Consider this example from the news of March 27, 1998. "Just back from lunch in the cafeteria in the Westside Middle School in Jonesboro, Arkansas, Shannon Wright was calling her sixth-grade English class to order when the fire alarm sounded early Tuesday afternoon. The best bet was that it was another drill . . . so Mrs. Wright calmly but firmly ushered her children outside . . . Then the shooting started." Two boys were ambushing the students of Westside Middle School. "Spotting one of the shooters drawing a bead on 12-year-old Emma Pittman, Mrs. Wright jumped into the line of fire." Emma lived. Mrs. Wright died. "I think Mrs. Wright saw that bullet coming," Emma said, "She grabbed me by the shoulders and pushed me out of the way. I feel sorry for her." Mrs. Wright didn't think of herself. She acted instinctively, without calculation. She thought of her students. Mr. Wright said of his wife, "She never came home and talked bad about any of her kids. She just always enjoyed working with kids and helping kids." Jumping in front of a bullet to save a kid does not seem like calculated rational utility maximizing behavior. I believe it reflects commitment—the kind of commitment that Smith believed is the glue that holds liberal society together.

99.999% of the choices we make in life are like ice cream shop choices: Do I want chocolate or vanilla? They are not significant beyond the market interaction they represent. But every so often we are called upon to live up to our commitments. Those moments are extremely rare, but if we do not come through then the glue of society is less firm.

Consider another example. This is a Congressional Medal of Honor citation. The Congressional Medal of Honor is the highest recognition the United States gives for bravery in combat.

> Burr, Elmer J.
> > *Rank and organization:* First Sergeant, U. S. Army, Company I, 127th Infantry, 32nd Infantry Division.
> > *Place and date:* Buna, New Guinea, 24 December 1942.
> > *Entered service at:* Menasha, Wisconsin *Birth:* Neenah, Wisconsin
>
> > [First Sergeant Burr is half a world away from home spending Christmas Eve on the front line of World War II in Buna, New Guinea. Back home there's probably a family gathered around a Christmas tree thinking of him, praying for him, wishing he were warm and safe with them at home with those who love him. In any spare moment he had, he was doubtless thinking of them, thinking . . . praying . . . wishing . . .]
>
> General Order Number i66, 11 Oct. 1943
> > *Citation:* For conspicuous gallantry and intrepidity in action above and beyond the call of duty. During an attack near Buna, New Guinea, on 24 December 1942, 1st Sgt. Burr saw an enemy grenade strike near his company commander. Instantly and with heroic self-sacrifice he threw himself upon it, smothering the explosion with his body. 1st Sgt. Burr thus gave his life saving that of his commander. (Sharp and Dunnigan Pub., p. 273)

So while the rest of the family was sitting around sharing the joy of the season and wondering if he was ok, he was living up to his commitments.

And finally, consider these words from February 4th, 1968:

> Every now and then I think about my own death, and I think about my own funeral . . . I don't want a long funeral. And if you get somebody to deliver the eulogy, tell them not to talk too long . . . tell them not to mention that I have a Nobel Peace Prize . . . tell them not to mention that I have three or four hundred other awards. . . . I'd like somebody to mention that day, that Martin Luther King, Jr., tried to give his life for others. I'd like somebody to say that day that Martin Luther King, Jr. tried to love somebody . . .
>
> Say that I was a drum major for justice. Say that I was a drum major for peace. That I was a drum major for righteousness. And all the other shallow

things will not matter. I won't have any money to leave behind. I won't have the fine and luxurious things of life to leave behind. But I just want to leave a committed life behind.

Two months later Martin Luther King, Jr. was assassinated in Memphis.

Shannon Wright, Elmer Burr, Martin Luther King, Jr.—people who made heroic sacrifices . . . Herbert Behrend, Margaret Grout, Jesse Burkhead—some of my former teachers who spent their days making the lives of so many students richer . . . all those who do the good work of society "leave a committed life behind" and form the glue that makes this world of free people—our liberal experiment—sustainable.

That line at the end of the pledge of allegiance that many Americans memorize by rote:

". . . with liberty and justice for all."

That is the essence of sustainable success: Liberty only works where there is justice, and justice in a liberal society is only as strong as the commitment of the citizens to it.

The lesson that I take from Adam Smith's moral philosophy is that the markets we have analyzed in these pages can serve us well, but we cannot depend on markets alone to make liberal society sustainable.

What we have done here is develop a tool that can help us understand a very complex social system: Liberal society. But remember, economics is like a hammer in a carpenter's tool kit. It is an invaluable tool if you want to build a rich understanding of the human condition, of how societies work and how they evolve. But it is just one tool, and alone it is not very productive. If you want to get the most out of the economic analysis we have developed here, you will need to use it in concert with political and social theory, you will need to practice using these tools together by applying them to history and/or anthropology and/or current events. If you develop a full social science tool kit and hone your ability to use those tools together to study the human condition past, present, and future; you will have a tool kit that will enrich the rest of your life.

GLOSSARY

Absolute advantage—the ability to produce more of a good than the person or country one trades with using the same amount of resources.

Aggregate demand—AD—the sum of all the new items (cars, pencils, computers, food, roads, etc.) that individuals, private enterprises, and governments are prepared to purchase in a given year. The aggregate demand line shows the relationship between the price level and the real GDP demanded for a given level of aggregate expenditure. The six components of aggregate expenditure (consumption (C), investment (I), government spending (G), net government taxation (T), exports (X) and imports (M)) are the shift variables of aggregate demand.

Aggregate expenditure—AE—the total amount that individuals, private enterprises and governments plan to spend. Since it is measured in current dollars, aggregate expenditure is a nominal value. This in turn means the higher the price level, the less real GDP a given amount of aggregate expenditure will buy. Aggregate expenditure has six components: consumption (C), investment (I), government spending (G), net government taxation (T), exports (X) and imports (M). These components are the shift variables of aggregate demand.

Aggregate supply—AS—The aggregate supply line shows the relationship between the price level and the real GDP supplied. This line is also referred to as the short-run aggregate supply line. We assume that in the short-run the factor markets have not adjusted so that along a given short-run aggregate supply line factor prices (such as wages) are constant. Changing factor prices are, therefore, the shift variables of the aggregate supply line.

Allocate—to decide how you will use a resource.

Asset—anything you own that has exchange value in the market such as cash or a car. Liquid assets can be exchanged for another form of asset quickly without losing value, so for, example, money is a very liquid asset. Illiquid assets cannot be exchanged quickly without loosing value, so for example a house is generally an illiquid asset.

Assumptions—systematic abstractions from reality that allow one to reduce the complexity of the system being studied by taking some conditions as fixed and given. A strong assumption abstracts significantly from "reality" (e.g., assume you have at least $1,000,000,000), while a weak assumption is considered more realistic (e.g., assume you have at least $100). When we relax assumptions we move from a stronger to a weaker assumption.

Autonomous consumption—consumption out of accumulated wealth (either by spending one's savings or borrowing); spending funds that are not from one's current income.

Average cost—AC—the total cost of production divided by the total number of units produced. It is the generic measure of how much it costs to produce an item.

Barriers to entry—constraints in a market (such as economies of scale), which put potential new entrants to an industry at a disadvantage compared to existing firms. When barriers to entry exist, firms in the industry gain some market power.

Barter—the exchange of equivalents (commodities of similar value)—the exchange of goods and services for other goods and services of similar value. Barter requires matching, so that if you have surplus cloth and desire corn you need to find someone with surplus corn who needs cloth or you will need to arrange multiple trades (cloth for wheat then wheat for corn, etc.). Barter becomes increasingly difficult as trade becomes more complex.

Capital (production capital)—a produced means of production. Physical capital is embodied in a tool that makes us more productive such as a hammer or a computer. Human capital is embodied in ourselves and makes us more productive, such as obtaining an education or taking care of one's health. Production capital is different from *financial capital* (liquidity or money), which finances the exchanges that make production possible (buying and selling factors) and purposeful (buying and selling products), but is not used in the process of production itself.

Capital demand (financial)—the relationship between the long-term nominal interest rate and the quantity of financial capital demanded. It represents the attitude of people who want to borrow funds in order to make real investments (which are all about the future). A change in expectations about the future can shift the capital demand line.

Capital intensive techniques (production)—use relatively more capital than labor.

Capital market (financial)—coordinates the exchange of liquidity (financial capital or money) between lenders and borrowers; that is, the desires of those who need funds with the resources of those who have funds that they are willing to loan. This coordination is generally performed by financial institutions such as banks or mutual funds that are called *financial intermediaries*. In our story this term refers to the long-term capital market because the type of investment we are referring to (such as building a factory) generally takes a significant amount of time between the loan being made and the investment paying off—in fact, we assume 20 years in our story. The financial capital market is also sometimes referred to as the *bond market* because bonds are sold to acquire financial capital, and to buy a bond is to supply financial capital.

Capital supply (financial)—the relationship between the long-term nominal interest rate and the quantity of financial capital supplied. It represents the attitude of people with funds to loan. Three things determine the level of the long term capital supply: the level of the short term supply, the waiting premium, and the inflationary expectations premium. Entry or exit into or out of a country's capital market can also shift the supply line. Short-term capital supply is the relationship between short-term interest rates (such as for a 3-month loan) and the quantity of financial capital supplied—it establishes a floor on the cost of borrowing.

Ceteris paribus—other things being equal. This assumption allows a model builder to assume away any complicating conditions not specified by the model. But, the more important the conditions assumed away by *ceteris paribus* the less rich the model.

Circular flow diagram—a way to represent the general economic system. It shows the players in the system (individuals and firms), the markets in which the players interact (factor markets and product markets), and the flows that move through the system (factors, goods, services and money).

Command economy—a coordination system (mechanism for exchanging surpluses) in which a central authority determines what is produced as well as what is invested. Since decisions are made by a single person (or a small group of people), they are well coordinated, but since one person (or a small group) cannot know the desires of all others, the decisions are not efficient (they don't enable the attainment of the most utility from the available endowment).

Commodity money—items that function as money but also have value in and of themselves, such as gold.

Commutative justice—the fairness of the rules by which the "market game" is played.

Comparative advantage—the ability to produce a good at a lower opportunity cost than the person or country one trades with. As long as comparative advantages exist, trade is beneficial.

Complements—goods and/or services that are consumed together such as burgers and fries or peanut butter and jelly. Goods and services that are complements have a negative cross price elasticity of demand because as the price of one goes up (e.g., on burgers), you consume fewer of that item (smaller quantity of burgers) and in turn you have a smaller quantity demanded of the other item (smaller quantity demanded of fries, which you usually eat with your burgers). Keep in mind that the relationship between any two commodities is a personal perception, so the market responds to the weight of opinion. You might be the odd duck who likes to consume burgers only if you can't get fries, so for you they'd be substitutes.

Consumption—the act of deriving utility. Consumption does not only apply to things we use up, e.g., drinking a milkshake. We can also consume things that remain when we are done, e.g., viewing a work of art.

Coordination mechanism—a system for organizing the exchange of surpluses among individuals when the labor of society is divided up.

Cross price elasticity of demand—a measure of the responsiveness of the quantity demanded of a good to a change in the price of a related good, *ceteris paribus*. Cross price elasticity is calculated as the percentage change in quantity demanded divided by the percentage change in the price of the related good. A negative cross price elasticity of demand indicates the two goods are complements while a positive cross price elasticity of demand indicates the two goods are substitutes. While the sign determines whether the two goods are substitutes or complements, the magnitude determines the degree to which the change in the price of one good affects the quantity demanded of the other.

Consumer Price Index—CPI—a method used to measure the level of prices for the products consumers typically buy. To calculate the CPI, all the items a normal household typically consumes are identified. This is referred to as their *market basket*. It includes such things as food, clothing, housing, transportation and entertainment. The total value of the items in the "market basket" is then calculated in both base year dollars (a base year is a year chosen as a reference point for price level comparisons) and target year dollars (the year being examined). The CPI is the target year total cost of the market basket divided by the base year total cost of the market basket all multiplied by 100. The resulting number (CPI) essentially tells us how much money it takes in the target year to buy what a dollar bought in the base year.

Consumption—C—the total expenditure individuals make as consumers purchasing things like clothes, food, new cars, haircuts, etc. It is based on their perceived permanent income—the level of income they expect to enjoy for the foreseeable future. Since actual current income may vary from permanent income (perhaps due to large medical bills one year, or an unexpected inheritance another year), people tend to smooth their consumption by borrowing or spending out of accumulated wealth.

Crowding-out effect—a situation that occurs when the interest rate is driven up as a consequence of added demand for capital from the government due to a budget deficit. This higher interest rate makes it more expensive for private investors to borrow, thus reducing investment. The size of the crowding out effect depends on the elasticity of supply of capital.

Decision rule—a mathematical representation based on economic theory of how we make choices.

Deflation—a fall in the overall level of prices and therefore a rise in the purchasing power of money.

Demand—D—the current attitude of demanders (those who come to market to buy). It represents, *ceteris paribus*, the quantity demanded at various prices and can be represented in a demand schedule (table listing various price-quantity combinations) or a demand line (a graphical representation of the price-quantity relationship). A change in price will move one along the demand line, but will not affect the line itself (that is, a change in price does not affect the demanders' basic attitude toward the good or service). Shift variables such as—in the product market—income, tastes, and the price of related goods, change underlying attitudes and thus shift the entire product demand line.

Demand-deficient unemployment—a situation where there are not enough jobs for everyone who wants one. The classic American case of demand-deficient unemployment is the Great Depression when unemployment soared from 3.2 percent to 25 percent from 1929 to 1933. One goal of macroeconomic policy is to minimize demand-deficient unemployment because its cost to society is high.

Depression—a period during which there has been a prolonged, deep decline in the level of actual GDP.

Derived demand—factor demand is referred to as derived demand because of the fact that the demand for factors of production depends on the demand for the good or service that those factors are used to produce.

Diminishing marginal productivity—the assumption that, holding all other inputs constant, as one input increases the initial successive units of that input may add successively more to output, but eventually and inevitably each successive unit of that input adds less to output.

Diminishing marginal utility—the assumption that the utility we derive from the consumption of each successive unit of a good or service diminishes with each successive unit consumed.

Discount—to diminish value. This concept helps us understand how people assess the future in order to make choices now between alternative paths into the future. We assume that people discount the future.

Discount rate—a measure of the rate at which you discount the future—a waiting premium. For example, if *ceteris paribus* you would be willing to forgo $100 now for $125 a year from now, but not less, the 25% increase in return ($25) you require to get you to wait reflects your discount rate. *Ceteris paribus*, people with a high discount rate diminish the value of utility to be realized in the future more than do people with a low discount rate. There is no "right" discount rate. Every individual has her own discount rate depending on how she perceives the future.

Discount Rate (Fed)—the interest rate the Fed charges banks to borrow *reserves*. A lower (higher) discount rate makes borrowing cheaper (more expensive) so more (less) liquidity flows into the financial system.

Discouraged workers—those who are not currently working and would like a job, but who are not considered officially unemployed because they have given up looking for work believing it highly unlikely after unsuccessfully finding work. These people do not meet the technical definition of unemployed.

Disequilibrium—a situation where the market is out of balance—there is an excess supply or an excess demand. In a perfectly competitive market this is not a stable condition and prices will adjust to clear the market—rise if there is an excess demand, fall if there is an excess supply.

Distributive justice—the fairness of outcomes in the market process.

Division of Labor—when individuals take on particular activities in the process of production rather than try to do everything for themselves. The division of labor increases productivity for three reasons: by focusing on one task you get better at doing it; by staying at the task, time is not wasted moving from one activity to another; and by knowing your job well you can be inventive about doing it better.

Dynamic feedback system—an interdependent general system within which action in one part of the system generates quick, continuous information on how that action is unfolding so that the general system can respond quickly and continuously.

Economics—the study of how individuals make choices when faced with scarce resources, how individuals' choices are coordinated in an interdependent world, and under what conditions the coordination system is most efficient and most just. Economics is a necessary but not sufficient tool for systematic thinking about the world we live in.

Economies of scale—an increase in productivity (and therefore a shift down in the average cost curve) that occurs when all factor inputs are increased together—scale of production gets bigger. Economies of scale can lead to barriers to entry—smaller firms with higher average cost curves can't enter the market in order to compete for profits, so economies of scale can create market power.

Efficiency—the condition in which production provides each individual with the greatest utility from her share of the initial endowment of resources.

Elasticity—responsiveness. In the product market there is own price elasticity—the response of quantity demanded of a good or service to a change in its own price, cross price elasticity—the responsiveness of the quantity demanded of one good or service to a change in the price of another good or service, and income elasticity—the responsiveness of quantity demanded of a good or service to a change in income. In the factor market there is elasticity of input substitution—the responsiveness of the quantity demanded of one factor to a change in the price of another factor.

Elasticity of input substitution—the responsiveness of the quantity demanded of one factor to a change in the price of another factor. For example the responsiveness of the quantity of labor demanded to a change in the relative price of capital. The more easily and therefore the more quickly the substitution of one factor for another can be made as relative factor prices change—i.e., the more techniques there are in the available technology—the higher the elasticity of input substitution.

Employed—those people who have jobs (full or part-time).

Endowment—A society's endowment is the natural and human resources from which all goods and services for that society must be produced. A society's endowment is finite, but it is not fixed. It can expand with resource discoveries or contract as resources are used up or destroyed. Because a society's endowment is finite, there is scarcity.

Equilibrium—balance. In a market it occurs when, at the market price, the quantity supplied equals the quantity demanded so there is no excess supply and no excess demand. Equilibrium will be maintained as long as the conditions surrounding the market don't change; that is, as long as the supply and demand shift variables don't change. General equilibrium is the condition when all markets have achieved equilibrium simultaneously.

Equilibrium price—p_e—the price at which the intentions of suppliers and demanders are in balance and the market is in equilibrium.

Excess demand—a situation where at the market price the quantity demanded is greater than the quantity supplied. Often excess demand is revealed with long lines for an item and a willingness by some to pay more than the current market price for the item. Bidding can lead to a price rise that reduces and eventually eliminates the excess demand.

Excess reserves—any *reserves* (a bank's *liquid assets*) a bank has above and beyond the reserves required by government regulators. Banks don't want to hold excess reserves because that's money that can be working for them by being loaned out at interest.

Excess supply—a situation where at the market price the quantity supplied is greater than the quantity demanded. Often excess supply manifests itself as inventory buildups. This can lead to price reductions to move inventories which in turn reduces and can eventually eliminate the excess supply.

Exchange rate—the price of one nation's money in terms of another nation's money. For example the price of euros in terms of dollars represents an exchange rate between euros and dollars. If a currency is expensive in terms of another, it is said to be *strong* with respect to that other currency. On the other hand, if a currency is cheap in terms of another, it is said to be *weak* with respect to that other currency.

Expected present value—the present value of an option adjusted for one's perception of the risk associated with that choice.

Expected rate of return—the expected monetary benefit of any investment expressed as a percentage return per year. For example, if in a year you expect to make $110 on a $100 investment, your expected rate of return is 10%. *Ceteris paribus*, the higher the expected rate of return the more attractive the investment.

Exports—X—the total amount of *nominal* expenditures foreign buyers make for a nation's products. Exports are an addition to aggregate expenditure because they are additional expenditures on that nation's production—coming from outside that nation.

Externality—the unintended effect one actor's activity has on another. The situation occurs when property rights to resources are either not assigned or are not enforceable. For example, since air rights are often not assigned or are not enforceable polluters can use the air to dispose of waste, even as others desire clean air. If property rights were assigned and enforceable then an air market would form and a price would be paid to the owner for pollution access or fresh air access (depending on who owned it). But without assignment and enforcement of property rights a market won't form and therefore there is no price signal to balance the intentions of polluters and fresh air seekers. Externalities can be *negative* (such as air or noise pollution) because the activity imposes a negative effect—an unintended external cost on innocent bystanders that polluters don't have to take into account when determining the level of their activity. Externalities can also be *positive* (such as a private garden along a road) because the activity generates an positive effect—an unintended external benefit on bystanders that gardeners don't take into account when determining the level of their activity. When negative (positive) externalities exist, private actors undertake more (less) of the activity than is socially optimal because they don't take into account the external costs (benefits) and as a result the social outcome is inefficient. It also has equity implications.

Factors of production—the basic inputs we use to produce. They include natural resources, labor and capital.

Factor market—the context within which demanders of factors of production (labor, capital, natural resources) and suppliers of factors of production come together to exchange factors. The individual holding the shares of the social endowment are the suppliers and the firms are the demanders. The forces of supply and demand establish the prices for and quantities exchanged of the factors of production.

Federal funds market—the market among banks for overnight lending and borrowing of *reserves* to maintain their reserve requirements. The *Federal Funds Rate* is the interest rate paid on these loans.

Federal Reserve (Fed)—the monetary authority of the United States established by Congress in 1913 to regulate major United States banks so that they can function responsibly. Through *open market operations* the Fed establishes the monetary policy of the federal government. The decision making power rests with the Fed's *Board of Governors* and with the *Federal Open Market Committee* (FOMC).

Fiat money—things having no inherent commodity value (such as dollar bills) that function as money because the government says that by law they must be taken for all debts. The usefulness of fiat money depends on the willingness of people to accept it as money.

Financial capital—liquid assets that finance the exchanges that make production possible (buying and selling factors) and purposeful (buying and selling products). This is to be distinguished from physical capital—a produced means of production used in the process of production itself.

Financial system—the arrangement of institutions that coordinates the intentions of suppliers and demanders of financial capital.

Fiscal policy—the government's effect on the macro economy through its budget position—that is, by setting the level of taxes and government spending. Fiscal policy that increases aggregate demand is said to be *stimulative* while fiscal policy that decreases aggregate demand is said to be *contractionary.*

Foreign exchange market—the market in which demanders of a currency (the people who want to buy it) and suppliers of a currency (the people who want to sell it) come together to do business with each other. The price in this market, the *exchange rate* (e.g., foreign currency per dollar), determines the quantity supplied, quantity demanded and, if allowed to adjust freely, the equilibrium quantity of currency exchanged.

Fractional reserve system—a system in which banks hold a portion of *assets* as *reserves* and loan out the rest to make a return, thereby allowing capital to be constantly active.

Free rider—one who enjoys the benefit of a good or service without paying for it. It occurs with public goods since once someone pays and the good is provided everyone else can enjoy the full benefit without paying.

Frictional unemployment—the case in which people are looking for jobs and there are appropriate jobs available, they just haven't found the jobs yet. Frictional unemployment occurs because the *job search* process takes time. Because this is so there will always be frictional unemployment, even in the best of economic times.

Full employment—the situation when the *unemployment rate* equals the *natural rate* of unemployment, not when the unemployment rate is zero. With full employment there is *frictional* and *structural* unemployment, but there is no *demand-deficient* unemployment. When an economy is at full employment, the level of production is called *full GDP.*

Full reserve system—a system in which banks hold all deposits they take in as *liquid assets* in their vaults available for withdrawal by depositors. Banks don't want to hold full *reserves* because they make a return by taking in deposits and loaning that *liquidity* for interest.

Functional form—a way of describing a causal relationship between two variables. For example the demand relationship can be written: $Q^D = D(p)$ which states that the quantity demanded, Q^D, is a function D of the price, p.

Gains from trade—the increased utility made possible by specialization (through the *division of labor*) and trade (exchange of *surpluses*).

General Agreement on Tariffs and Trade—GATT—an early effort to establish and encourage free and open global markets. GATT has been replaced by the *World Trade Organization.*

General competitive equilibrium—the condition that the general market system (the complex web of connections of the whole market system) tends toward under ideal conditions—the perfect competition created by our nice assumptions. By general we mean including the whole market system, by equilibrium we mean that all the markets in the entire system are in balance, and by competitive we mean the balance has been achieved under perfectly competitive conditions and thus realizes Pareto optimality.

General equilibrium theory—the analysis of markets as a part of a web of connections, as part of a general system. In general equilibrium theory, all markets are part of a *simultaneous system*—a system in which all elements function as part of a larger whole. This scope of analysis was first formalized theoretically by Leon Walras in the latter part of the 19th century.

General equivalent—one commodity (historically gold is the classic example) that is generally accepted in barter for any other commodity.

Gold standard—setting a fixed ration between the quantity of money the government can issue and the government holdings in gold. Since gold holdings are fairly constant, a gold standard keeps the amount of *liquidity* in the system fairly constant.

Goods—things that provide utility when consumed, that are tangible, and that can be stored (such as food).

Government spending—G—the total *nominal* amount the government spends on roads, schools, the military, etc.

Gross Domestic Product—GDP—the value of all the new production in the nation during a given year. It is the broadest measure of a nation's production. *Full, sustainable capacity GDP* (full GDP) is the greatest level of production that the whole economy can maintain over the long haul (that is, the biggest pie the nation can consistently product) and implies the microeconomy is functioning at Pareto optimality; *actual GDP* is how much the nation is really producing. Economists compare actual GDP with full GDP to gauge the health of the macroeconomy.

Hyperinflation—a situation in which the price level rise is extraordinarily rapid. In such circumstances people will no longer want to use that nation's money because holding money for even a short period can mean a loss of almost all value. People switch instead to barter or the money of another more stable country.

Imports—M—the total amount of *nominal* expenditures that domestic residents, enterprises and governments make for the products of other nations. Imports represent a reduction to aggregate expenditures because they are expenditures that are leaving the domestic economy and being spent on the production of another nation.

Income elasticity of demand—a measure of the responsiveness of the quantity demanded of a good to a change in income, *ceteris paribus*. Income elasticity is calculated as the percentage change in quantity demanded divided by the percentage change in income. A positive income elasticity of demand indicates that the good is "normal," while a negative income elasticity of demand indicates that the good is "inferior." While the sign determines whether the good is normal or inferior, the magnitude determines the degree to which the change in income affects the quantity demanded.

Indexing—automatically adjusting wages, benefits or payments as the price level changes. These changes are often measured using indexes, ergo the term. *Ceteris paribus*, indexing adjusts the *nominal* or face value of a payment in order to keep the *real value* of the payment constant.

Inferior goods—goods for which, *ceteris paribus*, the quantity demanded decreases as income increases. Examples may include generic paper products or boxed macaroni and cheese. For an individual, whether a good is normal or inferior depends on personal preferences. The income elasticity of demand is negative for inferior goods because the quantity demanded falls as income rises.

Inflation—a rise in the overall level of prices in the economy and therefore a fall in the purchasing power of *money*. Inflation can be measured using price indexes (such as the CPI) or price deflators (such as the GDP deflator) by calculating the percentage change in the measure over a certain period of time. Inflation imposes *efficiency* costs—it undermines the usefulness of money as a medium of exchange, a store of value, and a unit of account, and if it is volatile it also reduces investment by creating uncertainty about the future. Inflation imposes *equity* costs—it redistributes wealth, for example, as it erodes the purchasing power for those with a fixed wage or fixed retirement benefit.

Inflationary expectations premium—an additional return required to cover the reduction in the *real value* of a *nominal* interest return due to expected inflation.

Interest rate (nominal)—r—the cost (in current dollars) of borrowing *liquidity*. It represents the *nominal* cost of borrowing *financial capital*. Also referred to as the long term nominal interest rate.

International capital flows—the flow of *financial capital* or *liquidity* from one country's *capital market* to another country's capital market. These flows are becoming more significant in their impact on individual nations as advances in global communications enable financial capital to flow across international boundaries much more quickly.

International Monetary Fund—IMF—the international lender of last resort for countries in a dire condition. The IMF lends money to members on the condition that they undertake economic reforms. The IMF has no direct authority over the economic policies of its clients, but is very influential because the monetary assistance can be withheld if the advice is not taken.

International/Intranational trade—international trade is trade between or among nations. Intranational trade is trade within a nation.

Intertemporal choices—choices made now that have consequences across time such as "Do I want to go to college?" Intertemporal choices require you to take a future flow of benefits and costs, and using your discount rate, telescope them back in to a single present value so that you can directly compare the benefits and the costs of alternative choices that have future consequences.

Interventionist—a belief that due to market failure and market power there are significant problems in markets, and that government is capable of constructive policy to address these problems.

Invest—to use saved resources in order to increase future productivity in the hopes of increasing future utility. The lower one's discount rate the more present value one sees in future utilities, the more willing one is to wait, and therefore the more likely one is to invest.

Investment—I—the total *nominal* expenditure private enterprises make for items such as new plants, equipment and inventories. Investment is determined in the country's long term *capital market* where individuals and enterprises get the funds they need to make investments. Also referred to as the nominal level of investment.

Invisible hand—the unseen process of the coordination that guides a market system to a coherent balance. The term was first introduced by Adam Smith in *The Wealth of Nations.*

Labor—the natural power humans have to exert themselves. It is a raw concept of human productive capacity.

Labor force—a term that refers to all people who are participating in or who are looking for an opportunity to participate in the nation's productive activity. It is the sum of the people who are *employed* and *unemployed.*

Labor intensive techniques—use relatively more labor than capital.

Laissez-faire—the idea that if left alone markets do a good job, and that government intervention hinders the workings of the markets. Also called a non-interventionist position.

Liability—a claim by others on your *assets*. If you have a loan, you have a liability.

Liberal system of free markets—a coordination system (a mechanism for exchanging surpluses) in which each individual gets a share of the social endowment as her private property with which she can do as she pleases, and in which she can freely exchange with whom she pleases when and where she pleases. When the system is functioning ideally (under our nice assumptions), participating in the market system allows her to get the most utility from her share of the endowment while at the same time it has the unintended consequence that she is forced to serve the preferences of others.

Liquid/Illiquid Assets—liquid assets can be exchanged for another form of asset quickly without losing value, so, for example, money is a very liquid asset. Illiquid assets cannot be exchanged quickly without losing value, so, for example, a house is generally an illiquid asset.

Liquidity—liquid assets (*financial capital)* that finance the exchanges that make production possible (buying and selling factors) and purposeful (buying and selling products).

Long-run—the macroeconomic condition that is reached when the microeconomy has reached a *Pareto optimal, general competitive equilibrium* (that is, when all the microeconomic adjustments have been completed under our nice assumptions). When this condition has been reached, the economy is at full GDP and full employment.

Long-run aggregate supply—LAS—a vertical line at full employment (Y_F). Since by definition the *long run* occurs when the economy has reached full employment and full GDP, the LAS is independent of the price level and therefore vertical. The level of GDP where LAS is vertical (full, sustainable capacity GDP) is determined by the society's initial endowment: the quantity and quality of available natural resources, labor, and capital.

Macroeconomics—the branch of economics that explores the economy as a whole and examines such topics as national production, unemployment, inflation and globalization.

Margin—in a succession of units, the marginal unit is the specific unit you're focusing on. According to economists, in all choices the process of choosing takes place at the margin as we ask ourselves: "Do I want this unit of a good or service?" or "Do I want to make one more of these?"

Marginal cost—MC—the additional increment of cost associated with producing one more unit of an output. It represents the actual cost of a specific additional unit. Because of our assumption of eventually diminishing marginal productivity, the marginal cost curve eventually increases (decreasing productivity at the margin increases cost at the margin). The upward sloping segment of the marginal cost curve is the individual firm's supply line.

Marginal product of an input—the change in output that occurs when one more unit of an input is used, holding all other inputs constant. For example, holding all other inputs constant, if auto workers are added to the line of an auto assembly plant, the additional output that comes from each successive worker put on the line is the marginal product of that worker.

Marginal utility—the additional increment of utility associated with consuming one more unit of a good or service.

Market demand—the horizontal sum of all individuals' demands. So, at any given price, the market quantity demanded is the sum of all the individual households' quantities demanded at that price. In addition to the shift variables that affect individual demand (changes in tastes, prices of related goods, income), changes in demographics (changes in the size and type of population) will also affect market demand.

Market failure—the condition that occurs when either markets don't form when needed to coordinate choices of interdependent actors or when a market exists but it does not function smoothly and quickly to do the coordination job. Market failure reduces the efficiency of the system, and it affects the equity.

Market power—the condition that occurs when an economic player (individual or firm) has some control in the market. Exercising market power is not a productive activity—rather it is a process of exploiting an advantage in order to gain a larger distributive share. Market power distorts the flow of market activity. It reduces efficiency because the actor with power is not as keenly sensitive to competition and need not be so efficient. It changes the equity because those with power get a larger share and those without the power end up with a smaller piece of the smaller pie. Market power can be either naturally occurring (perhaps as a result of natural gifts such as beauty or economies of scale in the production process) or artificially created (such as the system of advantage created by segregation).

Market supply—the horizontal sum of all individual firms' supplies. So, at any given price, the market quantity supplied is the sum of all the individual firms' quantities supplied at that price. In addition to the shift variables that affect individual supply (price of inputs, level of technology, and the environment of production), the entry and exit of firms into or out of the market will affect market supply.

Mercantilism—the position dating back to the 17th and 18th centuries that because trade is a *zero sum game* (a situation where the size of the pie is fixed and a larger slice for one means a smaller slice for another), there are winners and losers and the goal is to be a winner (through such things as restricting imports or controlling trade routes).

Microeconomics—the branch of economics that focuses on the behavior of individual decision-making units (individuals and firms) and how they interact through the market coordination system.

Model—a stylized representation of a complex system. According to Joseph Schumpeter, model building begins with a vision, which is formalized through analytic effort.

Monetary policy—a tool the government can use to affect the macroeconomy by manipulating the supply of financial capital or liquidity.

Monetization of the deficit—when the government central bank (e.g., the Fed) expands the supply of liquidity in the capital market to meet the demand generated by a government deficit so as to keep interest rates the same and therefore private investment the same. In other words, the Fed uses monetary policy to counteract the crowding-out effect of the government's use of fiscal policy.

Money—any item that serves as: a medium of exchange (accepted by others for any good or service), a unit of account (allows one to state the price of goods and services and to measure the value of one's holdings), and a store of value (allows one to hold value and exchange for goods and services in the future). Money is used to facilitate exchange in any complex market system.

Monopoly—a situation where there is only one seller in a market. A monopolist has market power because instead of facing the perfectly elastic demand line of perfect competition, she faces the downward sloping market demand. As a result she can choose the price/quantity combination that is most advantageous given her cost structure.

Monopsony—a situation where there is only one buyer in a market. A monopsonist has market power because instead of facing the perfectly elastic supply line of perfect competition, she faces the upward sloping market supply line. As a result she can choose the price/quantity combination that is most advantageous given product market demand conditions.

Moral hazard—a situation in which people choose more risky behavior because they believe that they are protected from the consequence of the additional risk. Examples include those who take on excessive risk in the financial markets believing that the Fed will bail them out, or those who take fewer precautions against auto theft because they're covered by insurance.

Multivariate regression analysis—a technique used to test a relationship between a dependent variable (the one being affected) and a series of independent variables (the ones affecting it) to see how significant, how big, and in what direction (positive or negative) the affects of the independent variables are on the dependent variables. It begins with the technical specification of the model so that relationships are explicit and variables can be measured. The specification of a model and of the proxies can be manipulated in various ways to make the results consistent with theoretical predictions. While there may be legitimate reasons to change the specification of the model or the proxies, doing so simply to obtain more anticipated results is considered "cooking the data" or "data mining."

Natural rate of unemployment—the sum of frictional and structural unemployment levels. It is the amount of unemployment one would expect to find in a dynamic, growing economy. The economy is considered to be at *full employment* when the unemployment rate is the natural rate of unemployment; that is, when the only unemployment is either frictional or structural.

Natural resources—all those things that come to us from, in, on, or around the earth such as water, oil, minerals, and trees.

Net government budget position—(G-T)—government spending minus net government taxation. A positive net government budget position adds to aggregate expenditure while a negative net government budget position reduces aggregate expenditure.

Nice assumptions—The assumptions of no market power and no market failure that ensure perfect competition and in turn a nice outcome with respect to efficiency: a Pareto optimal general competitive equilibrium.

Nominal GDP—the face value of production measured in current dollars and therefore reflecting both changes in real production (the actual physical output) and changes in the price level. Since changes in nominal GDP can reflect real effects or price effects or both, nominal GDP cannot be used for meaningful comparisons of the value of production over time.

Nominal value—the face value. Nominal values are measured in current dollars and are not immediately useful for comparisons over time because they have not been adjusted for changes in the price level. Since changes in nominal values can reflect real effects or price effects or both, nominal values cannot be used for meaningful comparisons of the values over time.

Non-interventionist—a policy position that the government should generally keep its hands off/out of the economy. This position is based on a faith in markets and a belief that more often than not government intervention causes more harm than good.

Normal goods—goods for which, *ceteris paribus*, the quantity demanded increases as your income increases. Examples may include good restaurants, nice clothes, quality cars, etc. For an individual, whether a good is normal or inferior depends on personal preferences. The income elasticity of demand is positive for normal goods because the quantity demanded rises as income rises.

Normal return—the amount of return in money (and also psychic satisfaction) required to just cover the opportunity cost (the best available option you forgo when you make a choice—perhaps working for someone else) of using resources (labor, human capital, financial capital, etc.) to run a business. It is the minimum that the business owner must "pay" herself to make staying in business worthwhile.

North American Free Trade Agreement—NAFTA—a regional arrangement designed to create a fluid trade environment among the U.S., Canada, and Mexico by eliminating barriers to trade like tariffs or quotas or administrative red tape.

Open economy macro—viewing macroeconomic issues from a global rather than a national perspective. It represents the global economy as a strategic game among nation states, since the policies of one government cannot be directly imposed beyond its boundaries.

Open market operations—the selling and buying of U.S. Treasury bonds by the Fed in the open market (that is, to or from banks). It is the primary monetary policy tool the Fed has at its disposal.

Operationalizing a Model—carefully specifying the actual relationship between variables in a model and transforming the theoretical, abstract definitions of those variables into technical definitions that can be measured so the model can be tested. This is by definition an imperfect process.

Opportunity cost—the best forgone opportunity you give up when you make any choice. It is the cost of choosing.

Optimize—to reach the best outcome. The optimal allocation is the one that maximizes utility. With constrained optimization, utility is maximized in the face of scarcity.

Own price elasticity of demand—a measure of the responsiveness of the quantity demanded of a good or service to a change in its own price, *ceteris paribus*. Own price elasticity is calculated as the absolute value of the percentage change in quantity demanded divided by the percentage change in the good's or service's own price. When the percentage change in quantity demanded exceeds the percentage change in price, the own price elasticity is greater than one and the demand for the good or service is said to be *elastic* (responsive). When the percentage change in quantity demanded is smaller than the percentage change in price, the own price elasticity is less than one and the demand for the good or service is said to be *inelastic* (not very responsive). The four things that together determine the own price elasticity of demand are: whether the good is a luxury or a necessity, the number and quality of available substitutes, the time frame, and the price of the good relative to one's wealth and income.

Pareto optimality—a situation in which there is no way to make one person better off without making someone else worse off. It implies that there is no slack in the production process, no way to squeeze more out of the resources to make someone better off without taking anything away from someone else. Pareto optimality is the standard of highest efficiency in a general market system that is achieved under our nice assumptions. The general competitive equilibrium represents the Pareto optimal case.

Partial equilibrium analysis—the examination of equilibrium conditions in and the dynamics of an individual market—as opposed, for example, to general equilibrium analysis that considers all markets simultaneously. Partial equilibrium analysis is an essential tool for policy analysis.

Permanent income—the average long-term income that people expect to receive over time.

Personal financial planning—The purposeful arranging of one's financial portfolio in order to achieve one's financial goals (e.g., buying a home, putting your kid though college, retirement, etc.) given one's discount rate and tolerance for risk.

Phillips curve—the graphical representation of the idea that government faces a policy tradeoff: the price of lower unemployment is inflation while the price of lower inflation is higher unemployment. It is based on the assumption that the aggregate supply line is fixed and that all macroeconomic problems can be represented by shifts of the aggregate demand line.

Portfolio—all the assets and liabilities you have, which can be represented by a *T-account*.

Preference ordering—a ranking of available choices in order of the utility they offer.

Present value—the value that any future flow of utilities has now. It can be calculated using the discount rate. Calculating the present value allows one to directly compare current choices that have intertemporal consequences.

Price deflator—a measure of price level. An example is the *GPD deflator*, which measures the price level for all items included in the GDP.

Price index—a number that represents the level of prices for a group of items in any year relative to the level of prices for those items in the base year.

Price level—P—the general position of prices in the economy at any point in time.

Price taker—the situation an individual or a firm faces under perfect competition. The market sets the price and, having no power, the individual or firm simply responds to it.

Process of production—the actual application of factors together to make a product. It is the period when factors are set in motion and production takes place.

Product market—the context within which demanders (individuals) and suppliers (firms) of goods and services come together to exchange. The forces of supply and demand establish the prices and quantities exchanged of all goods and services.

Profit—a return above a normal return. When total revenue exceeds total cost (recall costs include a normal return) a firm is making a profit. Profits signal that a market is a very nice place to be and in doing so it attracts competitors. Ironically, in a perfectly competitive market, as firms enter in pursuit of profits, the price in that market falls and slowly but surely the profits are eliminated.

Protectionism—the idea that domestic producers and workers need to be sheltered from the competition of foreign products through such things as imports and tariffs. Protectionist policies can invite retaliation thereby stifling international trade and losing the gains from trade that come with specialization and the exchange of surpluses.

Proxy—a substitute variable. A proxy is used when the true variable cannot be measured. For example, often in labor analyses there is not a good measure of a person's work experience, so a proxy is used: Age—education—6. This proxy represents the assumption that people work all years they are not in school after preschool begins at age six. Proxies are necessary because we often don't have a true measure of a variable, but they can be problematic. For example, the problem with using the proxy just cited for work experience is that it does not account for the types of work experience one has had (e.g., the quality of the experience), nor does it account for time spent out of the labor force or work experience accumulated while in school.

Public good—a good that is non-partitionable (it can't be broken into pieces like a candy bar) and non-excludable (once you provide it, you can't prevent anyone from using it). The classic case of a pure public good is national defense—it is non-excludable because if you live within the protected boundaries you are protected and non-partitionable because it would be virtually impossible to give some of parts of it to some families and other parts of it to other families.

Quantity demanded—Q^D—simply a number such as 5 or 25 that identifies the actual amount of a good or service a household would buy at a given market price.

Quota—a limit on the number of units of a foreign commodity (such as cars) to be imported.

Rational economic behavior—logical, internally consistent choices made to maximize a person's utility.

Real GDP—Y—the value of production measured in constant dollars (adjusted for changes in the price level) and therefore allowing for meaningful comparisons of the value of production over time.

Real value—the underlying true value. Real values are immediately useful for comparisons over time because they have been adjusted for changes in the price level and are measured in constant (comparable) dollars.

Recession—a fall in the real GDP for two consecutive quarters (six months).

Rent maintenance—the exploitation of institutional power in order to sustain a market advantage; that is, an effort to sustain a rent (a distributive return to power). Military and police enforcement of South African apartheid was a rent maintenance structure.

Rent seeking—an effort to artificially create an advantage in a market in order to obtain some market power and thus a rent. Artificial market power can be created by political institutions (e.g., lobbying for new laws that restrict competition) as well as by social institutions (e.g., gender stereotyping of career opportunities).

Reserves—a bank's *liquid assets* (those assets that can change form quickly such as financial capital). A prudent bank will keep a portion of its assets as reserves and loan out the rest to make a return.

Reserve requirement—the Fed regulation that stipulates the percentage of assets that banks must hold in the form of reserves. These levels are established so that banks do not take on irresponsible levels of risk by loaning out too large a portion of their liquid assets.

Returns to scale—the degree to which a change in the scale of production changes the level of output. Decreasing returns to scale occur when the scale of production is increased (say quadrupled) but output expands proportionally less (say only doubled). Increasing returns to scale occur when the scale of production is increased (say doubled) but output expands proportionally more (say quadrupled).

Risk—something that can affect the outcome of our choices that, based on our perceptions, we can associate with a specific choice and assign a probability to. For example, when I consider whether to cross the street I have some perception as to the probability that a car will hit me, or when I consider whether to parachute out of an airplane . . .

Save—to forgo using resources for immediate utility.

Say's law—the "Classical" idea put forth by Jean-Baptiste Say in the early 19th century that the market system coordinates very well and therefore no intervention is necessary. John Maynard Keynes argued in his *General Theory* published 1936 that as evidenced by the Great Depression, markets do not always coordinate so well and therefore interventions may be necessary to correct for any breakdowns in the complex system of markets.

Scale of production—the size of the process of production. Changing scale means increasing all the factor inputs in the same proportion to expand production.

Scarcity—the fact that available resources are limited and cannot satisfy all wants resulting in a situation where individuals are forced to make choices. While scarcity is often thought of in terms of limited funds to purchase desired goods and services, time is perhaps the most universally scarce resource.

Services—things that provide utility when consumed that are intangible and cannot be stored (like a haircut).

Shift variable—a variable that changes the whole character of a functional relationship when it changes.

Short run—the condition in which the microeconomic factor markets have not adjusted. Since in the short run the factor markets have not adjusted, along a given short-run aggregate supply line factor prices (such as wages) are constant.

Social benefits—the full benefits created by an activity, which include both the private benefits to the individual undertaking the activity and any external benefits to others.

Social costs—the full costs created by an activity, which include both the private costs to the individual undertaking the activity and any external costs to others.

Specialization—the division of labor across trades so as to increase productivity.

Speculative bubble—a period of dynamic economic activity when the perception of many is that there is a lot of money to be made. This leads to speculation—people purchase stocks and real estate on the assumption they'll be able to sell it at a higher price later. Since underlying economic activity cannot expand production as quickly as the rise in the paper value of assets due to the speculation, the expansion of paper values is like a bubble that can burst anytime. When people begin to sell to get out of the market, asset values begin to fall. A period of panic can set in when everyone wants to get out. Then the bubble bursts.

Stagflation—a situation where an economy is experiencing increases in both inflation and unemployment.

Structural unemployment—the case in which there are jobs but the skills and desires of job seekers don't match the available jobs. Structural unemployment occurs because as economies grow they constantly go through technological transformations and geographic relocations (for example the loss of industrial jobs in the Midwestern U.S. coupled with the expansion of high-tech jobs elsewhere). Structural unemployment is an inevitable part of a healthy economy, though it can be reduced by speedily adjusting the skills and location of workers.

Substitutes—goods that can be substituted for one another in consumption such as McDonalds hamburgers and Burger King hamburgers or Coke and Pepsi. Goods that are substitutes have a positive cross price elasticity of demand. As the price of one goes up—say for example Coke—you consume less Coke (quantity demanded falls) and in turn substitute more Pepsi (quantity demanded rises). So a rise in the price of one causes a fall in the quantity demanded of the other. Keep in mind that the relationship between any two commodities is a personal perception, so the market responds to the weight of opinion. You might be the odd duck who likes to consume Coke and Pepsi together, so for you they'd be complements.

Sunk costs—costs already paid for choices made—thus costs that cannot be recovered.

Supply—S—the current attitude of suppliers (those who come to market to sell). It represents, *ceteris paribus*, the quantity supplied at various prices and can be represented in a supply schedule (table listing various price-quantity combinations) or a supply line (a graphical representation of the price-quantity relationship). A change in price will move one along the supply line (change quantity supplied), but will not affect the line itself (won't change supply). Shift variables such as, in the product market, the price of inputs, technology, and the environment of production change underlying attitudes and thus shift the entire product supply line.

Surplus—more of a commodity than one desires. With the division of labor, an individual generates a surplus of that which she specializes in producing. Then by exchanging a portion of her surplus for portions of those surpluses of other items held by other producers, she can enjoy the full range of items she desires. Because of the increased productivity that comes with the division of labor, everyone benefits from this process—this is called the *gains from trade*.

T-account—a way to represent a portfolio by listing assets on one side and liabilities on the other.

Tariff—a tax on an imported good. A tariff can invite retaliation, potentially leading to a *tariff war*.

Tax burden/incidence—the identification of who really ends up paying a tax as opposed to who nominally pays the tax.

Taxation (Net Government Taxation)—T—the total funds the government takes out of the hands of individuals and enterprises in the form of taxes. This amount is net of any transfer payments such as Social Security that merely pass resources from one person through the government to another person.

Techniques—possible ways of producing an item by using different combinations of factors (labor, capital, and natural resources) in the production process. Labor-intensive techniques use relatively more labor than capital while capital-intensive techniques use relatively more capital than labor. When various techniques are available, input substitution means moving from a more capital-intensive to a more labor-intensive technique, or vice versa. Elasticity of input substitution measures the degree to which this substitution is possible.

Technical definition—a set of criteria that can be used to measure a theoretical concept so that the explanation and prediction of the model can be tested. Technical definitions are generally only proxies or substitutes for the theoretical definitions they represent.

Technology—a set of available techniques. Technology is like the book of blueprints for production processes, and techniques are the pages of that book.

Theoretical definition—a definition that is used in an abstract representation of a model. To test a model, a theoretical definition must be transformed into a technical definition.

Tight labor market—a situation where there are plenty of jobs, and workers are in great demand.

Total cost—TC—the amount of money the firm spends in the process of producing a given number of units. It is equal to average cost times quantity.

Total revenue—the amount of money a firm takes in from selling a given number of units of a good or service. It is equal to price times quantity. The own price elasticity of demand affects how total revenue changes as the price changes.

Total utility—the total satisfaction derived from consuming a specific quantity of a good or service. It can be obtained by summing the marginal utilities of all of the individual unit consumed.

Trade balance—(X-M)—the nominal value of exports minus imports. A positive trade balance adds to aggregate expenditure while a negative trade balance reduces aggregate expenditure. The trade balance is determined by the underlying market conditions in a given country, the exchange rate, and the demand conditions in the various countries. It can influenced by a change in any of these.

Traditional system—a coordination system (mechanism for exchanging surpluses) in which the patterns of the division of labor are based on social definition of place (e.g., gender) and these patterns are passed down from generation to generation. Traditional systems tend to be internally stable (patterns of behavior are very predictable), but externally unstable (tend to break down quickly when exposed to other systems).

Uncertainty—something that can affect the outcome of our choices but that does not affect our decision rule because we don't know how to factor it in. We can't factor it in because we have no idea what it might be or which choices it might affect, so unlike a risk we can't associate it with a specific choice and assign a probability to its occurrence.

Underemployed—a situation in which a person is working and so is technically considered employed, but is perhaps only working part-time but would like to be working full-time.

Underground economy—exchanges that take place without money changing hands; a barter system for exchanges sometimes used to avoid a paper trail and thus taxes. An example would be: you fix my car and I'll fix your plumbing.

Unemployed—those who don't have a job, but would like one and are actively seeking one.

Unemployment Rate—a measure of the percentage of the labor force that is unemployed. The unemployment rate in the U.S. has ranged from as little as 1% during World War II to as much as 25% during the Great Depression. The policy objective with respect to the unemployment rate is to reach the natural rate.

Utility—satisfaction. Economists assume the motive that drives individuals' choices is to maximize utility.

Value from the marginal product—V—the value (the amount of utility) derived from successive units of a factor input allocation, holding all other inputs constant. It is the sum of the marginal utilities from the units of output derived from a given unit of an input. The V calculation combines information about production—the marginal product—with information about satisfaction from that production—the marginal utility.

Value of the marginal product—VMP—the value of the output from each successive unit of a factor input. It is equal to the output price times the factor marginal product. Because of the assumptions of eventually diminishing marginal productivity and of firms being price takers in a perfectly competitive situation, the VMP eventually falls. Given falling VMP the firm will only hire more units of an input if the price of it goes down. This is why the demand for factors slopes downward.

Very long run—the period in which the endowment of natural resources, labor, and capital changes and thus shifts the long-run aggregate supply.

Voluntarily unemployed—those people who neither have nor desire a job. Examples of people who may choose to be voluntarily unemployed include retirees, lottery winners and full-time students.

Wage-price spiral—a situation in which rising prices push workers to demand higher wages to maintain the real value of their incomes, then in turn higher wages push up production costs driving up prices, which leads back to higher wage demands and so on and on . . . the cycle continues with wages chasing prices and prices reflecting higher wages.

Waiting premium—an additional return required to entice people to loan their funds for longer periods of time.

Web of connections—the relationships among the many parts of a general system that weaves them all together into a single system.

World Trade Organization—WTO—the only international body dealing with the rules of trade between nations. The WTO creates the legal rules for international commerce and trade policies through WTO agreements that have three goals: to help trade flow as freely as possible, to achieve further liberalization gradually through negotiation, and to set up an impartial means of settling disputes.

APPENDIX: A LIST OF OBJECTIVES

You have successfully completed a section when you have mastered the objectives listed for that section.

So how do I go about mastering the basics in a manner that I can demonstrate on an exam?

The simple answer is practice, practice, practice; but practice is only effective if it is done effectively.

So how do I practice effectively?

The simplest description of effective practice is to practice for an effective performance. To perform effectively, you must first determine the correct performance (e.g., What is the level of efficiency of a general competitive equilibrium in the terms of an economist?—If you're not sure, ask!). Once you're sure you know the correct performance, you must practice it as you will perform it—which in the case of this course is on paper with no books or notes. In other words, you should be sure you know the correct response to each objective; and when you're sure you do, you should practice each objective by looking at the objective and then writing out your response on a piece of paper without any assistance from books or notes or others. Once you've done this for a set of objectives, go back and identify those you did correctly and those you didn't. Review the latter. Repeat the process later. Continue this process until you can do the objectives all easily in the performance (exam) format. Then when you walk into the exam, you'll know that you have most of it under control. It is truly a performance, like a piano recital: You've practiced it so many times that it feels good to show your audience how well you've mastered the material.

1.0 INTRODUCTION

1.1 GENERAL INTRODUCTION TO OUR STORY

1. Explain how an econosystem resembles an ecosystem.
2. Distinguish the terms "understand" and "learn" as I define those terms. Give an example that represents this distinction.
3. Explain why common definitions are important. Give an example of how communication breaks down when people use the same words in different ways.
4. Expand on the following assertion: Economics is one tool in a social science tool kit. Identify the other tools and describe how one hones one's skills with these tools.
5. Comment on the following statement: Economics is Truth.

1.2 THE SUBJECT OF ECONOMICS

1. Choose a poem or a song or passage from a book or some similar piece. As we develop our economics tool analyze the message of your piece with that tool. Identify the strengths and the weaknesses of that tool.

2. Comment on the following assertion: Economics is about poetry.

3. Identify the fact of the human condition from which the study of economic life begins. Explain.

4. Define opportunity cost. Give an example.

5. Identify the one resource that is inevitably scarce for all individuals. Illustrate how its scarcity confronts each individual with a quandary of choice by giving an example.

6. Critique the following assertion: Money is the great escape from scarcity.

7. Contrast the challenge of choice faced by individuals and that faced by society as a whole.

8. Explain the relationship between scarcity and opportunity cost.

1.3 A PREVIEW OF THE STORY

1. Describe the subject of microeconomics. Identify root word on which the term microeconomics is built.

2. Describe the subject of macroeconomics. Identify root word on which the term macroeconomics is built.

3. Contrast the subject of microeconomics and macroeconomics.

4. Identify what markets do well under the right conditions.

5. Critique the following expression: Moral markets.

1.4 MY METHOD FOR TELLING THIS STORY

1. Define vision—according to Schumpeter.

2. Identify the steps in the process of model building. Describe and explain the importance of each.

3. Identify two sources of problems in a model. Explain each case.

4. Identify the point at which ideology enters the scientific process. Explain the effect of ideology on model building. Respond to the following statement: Ideologically biased theories are useless, so we must only put our trust in theories that are not ideologically tainted.

5. Explain why theories with malleable definitions or assumptions are difficult to refute. Explain why such malleability is a theoretical flaw.

6. Define assumption. Explain why scientists adopt assumptions. Review the benefits and costs of this technique.

7. Explain the distinction between strong and weak assumptions. Describe the relationship among strong assumptions, weak assumptions, and relaxed assumptions. Give an example of relaxing an assumption.

8. Explain the value of starting analysis with strong assumptions and then relaxing them.

9. Identify what the *ceteris paribus* assumption holds constant. Demonstrate how the *ceteris paribus* assumption is used with an example.

10. Explain why maintained assumptions are so significant in a model.

2.0 MODELING INDIVIDUAL CHOICE

2.1 MODELING INDIVIDUAL CHOICE-INTRODUCTION
No objectives for this section

2.2 MODELING INDIVIDUAL CHOICE—OUR ASSUMPTIONS AND DEFINITIONS

1. Identify the motive that we assume drives the choices of all individuals all the time.

2. Define utility, rational economic behavior, consume, and goods and services. Specify the arrangement of these terms as they are used in the model.

3. Define preference ordering. Specify the assumption our model makes about an individual's preference ordering.

4. If I say "You're nuts to want to jump out of an airplane—even with a parachute." Does that make you nuts? Explain in terms of our model.

5. Identify the assumptions of the Robinson Crusoe case, that are ultimately relaxed. Explain what each one does for the model.

2.3 DIMINISHING MARGINAL UTILITY

1. Define margin. Give an example of a margin.

2. Define marginal utility. State the assumption of diminishing marginal utility. Explain this assumption using an example.

3. Explain why we assume perfect divisibility of units.

4. Explain why our theory is often referred to as marginal analysis.

5. Given a schedule showing units of a good or service consumed and the marginal utility derived from each successive unit, calculate the total utility achieved with each successive unit. Given a schedule showing units of a good or service consumed and the total utility achieved with each successive unit, calculate the marginal utility derived from each unit.

6. Given a graph representing the marginal utility derived from consuming a good or service, interpret the pattern represented in that graph. Compare and contrast the patterns in several such graphs that have the same axes.

2.4 CONSTRUCTING A DECISION RULE

1. If there is not scarcity and there are "n" different things to consume where "n" is some large number, identify the decision rule an individual will follow in consuming all "n" things. Explain the rule.

2. Describe a bliss point.

3. Identify the ultimate determinant of how closely our decision rule reflects reality.

4. Explain the purpose of starting out with such an unrealistic decision rule. Describe how the process will unfold from that point.

2.5 RELAXING OUR "NO SCARCITY" ASSUMPTION: EXPANDING OUR DECISION RULE TO REFLECT THIS NEW COMPLEXITY

1. Define optimize. Explain the concept: optimal allocation.

2. Describe how the utility maximizing decision rule changes as we relax the no scarcity assumption. Explain why this new rule is, given our assumptions, the only way one can maximize utility.

3. Explain the concept of a constrained optimization problem. Identify the constrained optimization problem we all face.

2.6 RELAXING OUR "NO PRODUCTION NECESSARY" ASSUMPTION: EXPANDING OUR DECSION RULE TO REFLECT THIS NEW COMPLEXITY

1. Describe society's endowment. Explain the relationship between society's endowment and scarcity.

2. Illustrate the following assertion: a society's endowment is finite, but it is not fixed.

3. Define natural resources and labor. Give examples of each.

4. Define capital. Distinguish between physical and human capital. Give an example of each. Distinguish between production and financial capital.

5. Define process of production.

6. Explain the concept: allocation of a factor.

7. Define technique and technology. Describe the relationship between these concepts.

8. Compare labor intensive and capital intensive techniques. Explain how a choice is made among techniques when technology offers an array of more labor or more capital intensive techniques.

9. Specify the arrangement of these terms as they are used in our model: factors, allocated, process of production, techniques, technology, goods and services.

10. Explain the concepts: scale of production and returns to scale. Contrast these two concepts.

11. Define marginal product. State the assumption of diminishing marginal product. Explain this assumption using an example.

12. Define value from the marginal product—V. Describe the information that is combined in the concept.

13. Given marginal product (MP) schedules for a particular factor used in several production processes and given the marginal utility (MU) schedules for the products of these processes, *ceteris paribus:*

   a) Calculate the value marginal product (V) schedule for each factor allocation.

   b) Explain why V ultimately falls.

   c) Given also a specific constraint on the units of the factor available, identify the allocation that would maximize utility.

14. Identify the general rule for factor allocation given scarcity and assuming a one period time horizon and no risk. Demonstrate that given our assumptions this is the only way to optimize.

15. Explain the statement: One might say that according to economic theory, a good life is a life of good balance.

16. Given a set of V schedules. Identify the optimal allocation for a given resource constraint. Identify how the allocation will change if the constraint changes.

17. Identify and explain what practical applications there are for a model of the decision rule people follow.

2.7 RELAXING OUR "NO FUTURE" ASSUMPTION: ADJUSTING OUR DECISION RULE TO REFLECT THIS NEW COMPLEXITY

1. Describe intertemporal choice. Give an example.

2. Describe the challenge of intertemporal choice.

3. Explain the concept of discounting the future. Give an example. Identify economists' assumption about our attitude toward satisfaction that will be realized in the future.

4. Define discount rate. Describe what the discount rate measures. Comment on the following assertion: The "right" discount rate is 10%.

5. If I promised (and assume I'm trustworthy) two people the same deal, either $100 at 5 pm tomorrow or $100 exactly one year from 5 pm tomorrow, and only one of them accepted, *ceteris paribus,* identify the person with the higher discount rate.

6. If I went to two people and asked to borrow $100 to be paid back a year from now (assume they both know I'm totally trustworthy) and one asked for more interest on that loan, *ceteris paribus,* identify the person with the higher discount rate.

7. Describe how a changing discount rate can affect one's choices. Give an example.

8. Describe how socialization can affect an individual's discount rate.

9. Define present value. Explain how we use this concept in our choice process.

10. Identify the decision rule that takes into account that choices across alternative allocations generate flows of future utilities, but does not reflect risk or uncertainty.

11. Define saving and investing. Identify, *ceteris paribus,* who you would expect to do more saving and investing: Someone with a high discount rate or someone with a low discount rate.

2.8 RELAXING OUR "NO RISK AND UNCERTAINTY" ASSUMPTION: ADJUSTING OUR DECISION RULE TO REFLECT THIS NEW COMPLEXITY

1. Define risk. Explain the impact of risk on decision (choice) making.

2. Describe the process of assigning a probability to a risk. Comment on the following statement: Risk assessment is the same for everyone.

3. Explain the concept of expected present value.

4. Define uncertainty. Distinguish between risk and uncertainty. Explain the impact of uncertainty on your decision (choice) making.

5. Identify something that was once an uncertainty in your thinking, but is now a risk.

6. Identify the decision rule one would follow in a world of scarcity, a future, and risk and uncertainty. Explain.

7. Explain why the word "perceived" is so important in the discussion of risk.

8. Identify the sources of our perceptions. Give examples.

9. Illustrate the way different perceptions lead to different choices among individuals with an example.

10. Using our model, explain the process of choice between two options like going to college and getting a job. Describe how our model explains the demographics of undergraduate students.

11. Using our model, explain how mind-altering drugs can affect one's choices.

12. Describe how perception management can be used as a tool of government policy. Give examples.

13. Describe how perception management can be used as a tool of private enterprise policy. Give examples.

14. Explain how our model applies to advertising.

15. Illustrate with an example how socially developed perceptions of gender roles affect behavior according to our model.

16. Find a life story (e.g., an obituary) that represents a life of social and/or political and/or economic challenges, and use the model to analyze how this person responded to those challenges.

17. Give and explain an example of how our model applies to a public or private use of media.

18. Explain why policy is complicated. Demonstrate, with an example, how complicated policy based on our model can be.

19. Comment on the following assertion: Since our model doesn't give answers, it's really not very useful.

2.9 CONCLUDING OUR ANALYSIS OF INDEPENDENT INDIVIDUAL CHOICE

1. Explain the statement: When Robinson Crusoe decides to produce, it is automatically a decision to consume, and when he decides to invest, it is automatically a decision to save.

2. Identify where Robinson Crusoe's choice coordination system is located. Describe the quality of that coordination system. Critique the following statement: Because he does not have to coordinate his choices with anyone else, Crusoe's decisions always work out perfectly.

3. Identify the issue that really distinguishes the simple, isolated world of Crusoe from the complex world of interdependence in which we actually live. Explain the distinction.

3.0 INTERDEPENDENT CHOICE AND MARKET COORDINATION

3.1 FACTORS THAT GIVE RISE TO COMPLEXITY, INCLUDING THE DIVISION OF LABOR AND THE GAINS FROM TRADE

1. Identify and explain several reasons why we give up the security of total independence for the vulnerability of interdependence.

2. Explain the connection between social complexity and social productivity.

3. Explain the concept: division of labor.

4. Identify and explain the three reasons Adam Smith cites for the increased productivity from the division of labor.

5. Identify a potential problem that the division of labor can generate. Explain with an example.

6. As Adam Smith does, choose an article of clothes you are wearing and make a list of all of the hands that went into producing that article. Be thorough, be imaginative, and be logical in your ordering.

7. Define surplus. Explain why the division of labor gives rise to individuals holding surpluses.

8. Explain why the division of labor gives rise to exchange.

9. Identify the role of a coordination mechanism in a complex society in which there is a division of labor.

10. Define: gains from trade.

11. Demonstrate the benefits of division of labor and exchange with an example of the gains from trade when labor is divided.

12. Explain the concept: absolute advantage.

13. Explain the concept: comparative advantage.

14. Identify the condition that limits the division of labor. Explain with an example.

15. Describe the coordination system in a traditional society. Identify the strengths and weaknesses of such a system.

16. Describe the coordination system in a command economy. Identify the strengths and weaknesses of such a system.

17. Identify the role of markets in a liberal society.

18. Identify the features of a liberal society under ideal conditions that make it such an attractive system.

19. Describe the morality of markets.

20. Describe the relationship between a free market system and justice. Explain.

21. Explain the concept: distributive justice. Describe John Stuart Mill's conception of what this concept means in a liberal society.

22. Explain the concept: commutative justice.

23. Identify the premise of a liberal, free market system.

3.2 THE ROLE OF MONEY IN MARKETS

1. Distinguish between financial and production capital. Identify which one is money. Explain the purpose of each kind of capital.

2. Define barter. Explain the problem with a barter system by using examples.

3. Define general equivalent. Explain why barter gives way to the use of a general equivalent as trade expands and becomes more complex. Identify the good that has been accepted most widely and for the longest time as a general equivalent.

4. Identify three roles of money. Explain each.

5. Identify four characteristics of a general equivalent that would make it a good candidate for money. Explain each.

6. Define commodity money and fiat money. Contrast these two kinds of money. Give examples of each.

3.3 HOW A MARKET WORKS

1. Name the famous book that Adam Smith wrote about economics, and give the year it was first published.

2. Describe how a dynamic feedback system works.

3. Describe the magic of a market system.

4. Draw a fully labeled generic market picture.

5. Identify what the supply line in a market picture represents.

6. Identify what the demand line in a market picture represents.

7. Describe what functional form represents. Give an example.

8. Explain what demand, D, represents. Distinguish between demand and quantity demanded. Critique the following statement: Along a given demand line, demand changes.

9. Given an initial condition of demand on a market picture, show by drawing a new demand line what would happen to the demand line if demanders' attitudes changed and they desired more of this item.

10. Identify what the vertical line within a functional form stands for.

11. Identify where in the D functional form the shift variables are located. Use an example to describe what a change in a shift variable does to the demand line.

12. Explain what supply, S, represents. Distinguish between supply and quantity supplied. Critique the following statement: Along a given supply line, supply changes.

13. Given an initial condition of supply on a market picture, show by drawing a new supply line what would happen to the supply line if suppliers' attitudes changed.

14. Identify where in the S functional form the shift variables are located. Use an example to describe what a change in a shift variable does to the supply line.

15. Draw a market picture that represents an excess supply condition. Show graphically and explain how, under perfectly competitive conditions, the market price will respond to this excess supply condition.

16. Draw a market picture that represents an excess demand condition. Show graphically and explain how, under perfectly competitive conditions, the market price will respond to this excess demand condition.

17. Identify the term used to describe the market condition when there is either an excess supply or an excess demand in the market.

18. Explain why a disequilibrium is not a stable condition in a perfectly competitive market.

19. Given a scenario about a shift in supply or demand, show graphically and explain how the market will adjust after this shift.

20. Identify the signal on which the entire market system depends.

21. Explain the following statement: The market system is a price signaling based system.

22. Describe an administered price system. Give an example. Explain the problem with such a system.

23. Illustrate the concept of rationing by time. Contrast this process with how a market rations items.

3.4 THE GENERAL MARKET SYSTEM

1. Contrast the vulnerabilities of Robinson Crusoe with those of someone living in a market system.

2. Identify the two primary sets of players in our basic model of a complex society. Specify the role of each. Specify the objective of each. Using a circular flow diagram describe and explain the interaction between the two sets of players (show where they interact, what each brings to the interaction, etc.).

3. Comment on this statement: The economic production, exchange, and consumption process begins and ends with individuals.

4. Describe the role of firms in the market system.

5. Identify the two basic kinds of markets. Distinguish these two kinds of markets by describing and contrasting how the market players participate in each.

6. Describe the circular flow of real things.

7. Describe the circular flow of money.

8. Explain the relationship between the circular flow of real things and the circular flow of money.

9. Interpret the assertion: The circular flow of the market system has no beginning and no end.

10. Explain the relationship between General Equilibria and a General Competitive Equilibrium.

11. Describe the relationship between our nice assumptions and General Competitive Equilibrium.

12. Explain why we call the nice assumptions "nice."

13. Identify our two nice assumptions. Explain each, specifying the elements of each.

14. Clarify what equal access to information does and does not mean.

15. Demonstrate that information is not costless, by citing and explaining an example.

16. Identify and explain a violation of the equal access to information assumption.

17. Identify and explain a violation of the equal access to the market assumption.

18. Describe how market power affects the character of the competition. Illustrate with an example.

19. Illustrate market failure with an example.

20. Identify the efficiency and equity consequences of market power and market failure.

21. Explain the concept: Pareto optimality. Identify the person it is named after. Specify the standard for Pareto optimality and explain that standard.

4.0 THE PRODUCT MARKET DEMAND UNDER PERFECT COMPETITION

4.1 INTRODUCTION
No objectives for this section

4.2 PRODUCT DEMAND

1. Using a simple version of our decision rule as a point of departure, demonstrate why a product demand line slopes down.

2. Define: price taker. Explain why all participants in the markets are price takers under perfect competition.

3. Identify what own price elasticity of demand measures.

4. Define: elastic demand. Define: inelastic demand.

5. Contrast elastic and inelastic demand.

6. Give examples of elastic and inelastic demand. Explain.

7. Given two product demand graphs drawn on identical axes, identify which is the more elastic demand.

8. Explain why own price elasticity is such a big deal in the world of policy.

9. Identify and explain a private policy case representing how a firm (other than the McDonalds case cited) might use own price elasticity information.

10. Identify and explain a public policy case (other than the cases cited) representing how a government agency might use own price elasticity information.

11. Show graphically and describe the case of perfectly elastic demand.

12. Show graphically and describe the case of perfectly inelastic demand.

13. Identify which case, perfectly elastic or perfectly inelastic demand, you would wish for if you were going to sell a product—assume *ceteris paribus.* Explain.

14. *Ceteris paribus,* identify which kind of good would exhibit a more inelastic: a necessity or a luxury. Explain. Give and explain an example.

15. Interpret the expression "price is no object" in economic terms.

16. Explain how the number and quality of substitutes affects own price elasticity. Give and explain an example.

17. Explain how the time frame affects own price elasticity. Give and explain an example.

18. Explain how the price of the good relative to a person's wealth and income affects own price elasticity. Given and explain an example.

19. Identify four factors that determine the own price elasticity of a good or service. Explain each. Describe the relationship among these four factors.

20. Write out and explain the equation economists use to represent the measure of own price elasticity.

21. Explain why an absolute value sign is used in the own price elasticity equation.

22. Explain why the equation uses percentage change rather than absolute change. Give an example.

23. Given one of these cases, $\varepsilon > 1$ or $\varepsilon < 1$ or $\varepsilon = 1$, identify and explain the case.

24. Describe the relationship between own price elasticity and total revenue as price changes.

25. Critique the following logic: Assuming fixed costs, if you charge more you make more.

26. Describe the relationship between own price elasticity of demand and advertising.

27. Describe ways in which firms can try to influence the own price elasticity of demand for their product.

28. Identify the own price elasticity of demand that suppliers in a perfectly competitive market face.

29. The supply of drugs in the city has been reduced significantly by a government crackdown, but drug-related crime is up. Explain how that is possible. Does this mean that interdicting drugs is a bad idea? Explain.

30. Critique the following assertion: Interdicting supply is the solution to the nation's drug problem.

31. Identify and explain a case in which simple minded thinking that does not consider own price elasticity Issues can lead to an unintended result.

32. Respond to the following statement: This is one hell of a model. It's loaded with great answers to policy puzzles.

33. Explain the concepts: tax incidence/tax burden.

34. Describe with an example how the own price elasticity of demand can affect the impact of a tax with respect to:
    a) Revenue generation.
    b) Changing market behavior.

4.3 EXPANDING THE DEMAND RELATIONSHIP—IDENTIFYING THE SHIFT VARIABLES

1. Write out the full product demand relationship in functional form including the shift variables.

2. Identify the shift variables in the product demand relationship.

3. Give an example of tastes as a shift variable. Demonstrate graphically how the market will respond in your example.

4. Define: cross price elasticity of demand.

5. Give the equation that measures the cross price elasticity of demand.

6. Define: complements.

7. Describe the relationship between two goods that have a negative cross price elasticity, Give an example.

8. Define: substitutes.

9. Describe the relationship between two goods that have a positive cross price elasticity. Give an example.

10. Describe the relationship between two goods that have a negative cross price elasticity, two goods that have a positive cross price elasticity, and two that have a zero cross price elasticity. Give examples of each case.

11. Describe the connection between cross price elasticity and the concept of a market system as a web of connections.

12. Explain how the market system is like a spider's web.

13. Develop a case (different from the one covered) that demonstrates the importance of cross price elasticity to private policy making. Include internal and external cross price effects.

14. Develop a case (different from the one covered) that demonstrates the importance of cross price elasticity to public policy making. Your case should be designed to highlight the complexity of policy.

15. With cross price elasticity as a reference point, comment on the assertion that when it comes to policy, be it public or private, anyone who says it's simple is either simple minded or thinks your are.

16. Draw and label market graphs for three related goods. Specify the relationships. Show how a change in supply conditions for one of the goods will affect the equilibrium price and quantity exchanged in all three markets. Note: assume that the second and third goods are independent of one another, i.e., set $\varepsilon_{2 \times 3} = 0$. Explain why this assumption simplifies the analysis.

17. Define: normal good.

18. Define: inferior good.

19. Give the equation for income elasticity.

20. Identify the sign of the income elasticity equation when a good is normal, when a good is inferior.

21. Critique the following statement: Some things are inherently inferior goods.

22. Give and explain a personal example of a normal good.

23. Give and explain a personal example of an inferior good.

24. Describe the relationship between individuals' demands for a given good or service and the market demand for that good or service.

25. Given several individual demand lines, construct the market demand line.

26. Comment on the following statement: Market demand movements depend on the net effect of all the individual changes. Identify the sources of such changes. Note whether these are the only determinants of the market level of demand. If not, identify another source of market demand shifts.

27. Describe and show graphically cases of entry and exit on the demand side of the product market.

28. Describe how shifting demographics can cause entry and exit and strongly affect product market demand.

29. Give examples of how public or private policy is affected by demographic changes.

30. Identify another source of product market entry and exit besides demographics.

5.0 PRODUCT MARKET SUPPLY

5.1 PRODUCT SUPPLY

1. Give the title of the principles book Alfred Marshall wrote on economics and the year it was published.

2. Give the title of the principles book David Ricardo wrote on economics and the year it was published. Describe Ricardo's view on the product supply line and what that view implied about the determination of a product's price.

3. Identify the three economists who in the 1870s took issue with Ricardo's view on the determination of a product's price. Explain their view on the determination of a product's price. Identify the state of supply line that underlies their view.

4. Describe the relationship between Marshall's analysis, and those of Ricardo and of Jevons/Menger/Walras.

5. Explain the role of time in Marshall's demarcations of market conditions.

6. Explain the point Marshall is making when he writes: "We might as reasonably dispute whether it is the upper or the under blade of a pair of scissors that cuts a piece of paper, as whether value is governed by utility [(demand)] or cost of production [(supply)]."

7. Draw a generic marginal product curve.

8. Assuming a constant input cost, explain how the marginal cost curve is derived from the marginal product curve.

9. Identify the level of productivity an input has achieved when the marginal cost of the product it is making is at its lowest level.

10. Identify the level of cost a production process has achieved when the marginal productivity of the variable input is at its highest level.

11. Demonstrate that the upward sloping section of the firm's marginal cost curve is its supply line.

12. Describe the costs that go into the cost structure represented by the marginal cost line.

13. Define: normal return. Describe and explain an example other than the one in our story.

14. Describe the condition of a firm that is just covering the costs embodied in the marginal cost curve.

15. Identify the variables that go into a firms cost structure. Explain the relationship between these variables and the shift variables of the firm's supply line.

16. Write out the functional form of a firm's supply relationship. Identify each variable.

17. Cite a case of a change in input costs for a firm and describe how the firm's cost structure and supply line would change as a consequence. Given the supply side of the case, identify the best case for the firm to face in terms of elasticity of demand. Explain with graphs. Your case should be different from that in our story.

18. Cite a case of a change in technology for a firm and describe how the firm's cost structure and supply line would change as a consequence. Given the supply side of the case, identify the best case for the firm to face in terms of elasticity of demand. Explain with graphs. Your case should be different from that in our story.

19. Cite a case of a change in environment of production for a firm and describe how the firm's cost structure and supply line would change as a consequence. Given the supply side of the case, identify the best case for the firm to face in terms of elasticity of demand. Explain with graphs. Your case should be different from that in our story.

20. Describe the relationship between the firms' supplies for a given good or service and the market supply for that good or service.

21. Given several firms' supply lines, construct the market supply line.

22. Comment on the following statement: Market supply movements depend on the net effect of all the firms' changes. Identify the sources of such changes. Note whether these are the only determinants of the market level of supply. If not, identify another source of market supply shifts.

23. Describe and show graphically cases of entry and exit on the supply side of the product market.

24. Represent the relationship of firms and individuals to the market under our nice assumptions, the price takers relationship, graphically.

25. Describe the elasticity of demand faced by a firm in a perfectly competitive market. Explain why it is as you describe.

6.0 REPESENTING THE POWER OF THE INVISIBLE HAND IN THE PRODUCT MARKET

6.1 THE MAGIC OF MARKETS—PRODUCT MARKET EFFICIENCY UNDER OUR NICE ASSUMPTIONS

1. Given data on marginal costs in production compute the average costs.
2. Given data on marginal costs in production compute the total costs.
3. Given data on total costs in production compute the marginal costs.
4. Given data on average costs in production compute the total costs.
5. Describe what the marginal cost and the average cost each represent.
6. Describe the relationship between the margin and the average. Use an example.
7. Comment on the following assertion: When the margin is above the average it pulls the average up. When the margin is below the average it pulls the average down.
8. Comment on the following assertion: When the margin is going up it pulls the average up. When the margin is going down it pulls the average down.
9. Describe and explain the relationship between the marginal cost curve and the average cost curve. Given a MC curve, draw an appropriate AC curve. (Note: With no numbers on the axes, there's one crucial element in consistency.) Given an AC curve, draw an appropriate MC curve. (Note: With no numbers on the axes, there's one crucial element in consistency.)
10. Identify the point along the AC curve at which the MC intersects the AC. Explain the special significance of that point in terms of the cost structure of the firm.
11. Define: total revenue, total cost. Describe, in terms of total revenue and total cost, the condition of a firm when it is: making a profit, suffering a loss, breaking even.
12. Given a generic firm/market picture showing a current market condition and given either the AC or the MC of the generic firm's cost structure, complete the firm's cost structure and:
    a) Identify the demand line of the firm.
    b) Identify the supply line of the firm.
    c) Identify the quantity the firm will produce.
    d) Identify the average cost of production for the quantity the firm will produce.
    e) Identify the total revenue of the firm.
    f) Identify the total revenue of the firm.
    g) Identify whether the firm is making a profit, suffering a loss, or breaking even.
    h) Identify the size of any profit or loss of the firm.
13. Given a generic firm/market picture showing the cost structure of the firm and either the supply or demand line in the market, complete the market picture such that the firm is:
    a) enjoying a profit
    b) suffering a loss
    c) breaking even
14. Explain the following statement: Profit is gravy. All firms want a profit, but no firm needs a profit.
15. Describe how profit functions as a signal under the nice assumptions that give perfect competition.
16. Given a generic firm/market picture in which the initial market conditions and the generic firm's cost structure are given, and in which the firm is initially making a profit, show how the market will respond. Identify the place where the market response will end. (Note: This point must be determined in reference to the generic firms cost structure.) Do the same in the case of an initial loss condition.

17. Explain the following statement: Profit is a powerful yet ephemeral signal.

18. Using appropriate graphs explain how, given our nice assumptions, the market dynamic drives production to the most efficient method.

19. Using appropriate graphs, explain the following assertion: In the dynamic of a perfectly competitive market system success and even simple survival are only possible for the quick and the agile.

6.2 MARKETS, PERFECT COMPETITION, CREATIVITY, AND MATERIAL PROGRESS

1. Describe how the perfectly competitive market encourages creativity. Give examples.

2. Explain the expression "Build a better mousetrap and the world will beat a path to your door" in terms of our model.

3. Describe the role of an entrepreneur in the market system.

4. Describe two ways an entrepreneur can use creativity to "get ahead."

5. Describe the constant challenge facing an entrepreneur in a perfectly competitive market.

6. Explain how a perfectly competitive market system encourages people to constantly be thinking of new products, better versions of old products, or ever more efficient ways of producing products.

7. Describe the power of the "invisible hand."

8. Explain what the market system can and cannot do with respect to efficiency and equity.

7.0 THE FACTOR MARKET

7.1 THE FACTOR MARKET—INTRODUCTION

1. Contrast the roles of individuals and firms in the factor market and in the product market. Give an example of each of these kinds of markets. Identify the kinds of exchanges made in each of these kinds of markets.

2. Describe the relationship between factor markets and individuals' incomes.

3. Describe what an excess supply in a labor market would look like in real human terms.

4. Using an appropriate graph, explain how, given our nice assumptions, a labor market will adjust from an initial excess supply condition.

5. Using an appropriate graph, explain how, given our nice assumptions, a labor market will adjust from an initial excess demand condition.

7.2 FACTOR MARKET SUPPLY

1. Explain why the supply curve for a factor would slope upward.

2. Write the factor supply relationship in functional form. Identify the shift variables in the factor supply relationship.

3. Give examples of cases in which individual labor supply shifts.

4. Identify the sources of market labor supply shifts.

5. Identify reasons why an individual might voluntarily choose to enter or leave the labor market. Give an example of each case.

6. Explain the following statement: If nurses' pay did not include an interest as well as a wage component, there would eventually be no nurses.

7. Describe the conditions that lead one to move around within the labor market.

8. Explain the concept: sunk costs.

9. Describe the role of sunk costs in decision making. Give an example.

10. Describe how labor mobility creates a web of connections among the factor markets.

11. Identify the level of return all participants in the factor markets can expect under our nice assumptions.

7.3 FACTOR MARKET DEMAND

1. Identify the reason firms buy factors.
2. Explain the concept: derived demand. Give an example.
3. Describe the value of the marginal product (VMP)—what it is and how it is calculated.
4. Explain why the demand line for a factor slopes down.
5. Write the factor demand relationship in functional form. Identify the shift variables in the factor demand relationship.
6. Explain how, ceteris paribus, an increase in product demand will affect the derived factor demand. Give an example.
7. Explain how derived demand reflects the concept of a web of connections.
8. Define: input substitution, labor intensive technique, and capital intensive technique. Explain why a firm would switch from a labor intensive technique to a capital intensive technique or vice versa.
9. Explain the concept: elasticity of input substitution. Describe cases of high and low elasticity of input substitution.
10. Describe how factor markets will adjust to changing relative prices of labor and capital. Give examples.

8.0 GENERAL COMPETITIVE EQUILIBRIUM (GCE)

8.1 GENERAL EQUILIBRIUM THEORY

1. Explain the concept: general equilibrium theory.
2. Identify the first person to theoretically analyze general equilibrium theory.
3. Explain the concept: simultaneous system.
4. Identify and describe at least four treads that weave markets into the web of a general system.
5. Identify the givens in general equilibrium theory.
6. Explain why general equilibrium theory is essential for representing economists vision of the market system.
7. Define: partial equilibrium analysis. Contrast the role of partial equilibrium analysis with general equilibrium theory in modern economics.

8.2 GENERAL COMPETITIVE EQUILIBRIUM (GCE)

1. Describe the efficiency of a general competitive equilibrium. Explain.
2. Describe the equity or justice of a general competitive equilibrium. Explain.
3. Explain the statement: If any individual market is still adjusting toward equilibrium, then all markets must still be adjusting. Or, so long as anything is changing, everything is changing.
4. Given that our nice assumptions hold, describe the relationship between the distributive outcome of the market process and the distribution of society's endowments among individuals.
5. Identify and explain the standard by which economists measure the efficiency of any general equilibrium.
6. Explain the concept of equity. Explain why there is no scientific basis for setting a standard of an optimal equity condition. Comment on the following: Equity is/is not an economic issue.
7. Explain Kenneth Arrow's statement that "even under assumptions most favorable to decentralization of decision making, there is an irreducible need for a social or collective choice on distribution." Identify the nature of this social choice.
8. Identify and explain the role of commutative justice in a market system.

9.0 MARKET POWER, MARKET FAILURE, AND GENERAL EQUILIBRIUM

9.1 INTRODUCTION TO MARKET POWER AND MARKET FAILURE

1. Describe the relationship between the concepts: general competitive equilibrium and general equilibria.
2. Identify the unique characteristic of a general competitive equilibrium that distinguishes it from all other general equilibria.

9.2 MARKET POWER

1. Describe and explain the effect of market power on the general system.
2. Describe the benefit of power.
3. Describe the costs of power.
4. Define: monopoly, monopsony. Give examples of each.
5. Identify the source of naturally occurring market power and explain its relationship to commutative justice.
6. Cite and explain examples of naturally occurring market power.
7. Identify and explain two reasons why a natural gift is not always a ticket to a big income.
8. Explain the following statement: A natural gift is an opportunity to exploit an advantage in the market, but to make it work for you, you have to work at developing that gift.
9. Define: economies of scale. Explain how such economies can create natural market power. Give an example.
10. Describe how natural advantages and thus natural market power can erode. Give examples.
11. Explain the concept: artificially created market power. Give examples.
12. Describe the purpose of patents. Explain why a patent is artificially created market power.
13. Define: rent-maintenance activity. Give and explain an example.
14. Define: rent-seeking activity. Give and explain an example.
15. Describe and explain the possible connection between rent-seeking/maintenance activity and contributions to political groups.
16. Explain how socialization connects to markets.
17. Describe how socialization that demarcates expectations by gender or race affects market outcomes. Give examples.
18. Explain how socialized perceptions, your own or those in the market, can constrain your range of choices and effectively limit your access to the market.
19. Identify the difference between how social and political institutions function as potentially powerful constraints on market behavior.
20. *Ceteris paribus,* show and explain how these two markets for comparable jobs would adjust if one of these jobs initially had a higher wage.
21. Describe the consequence of any institutional constraints, social and/or political, that crowded women into a limited set of labor markets. Use graphs to tell your story.
22. Describe the equity and efficiency implications of market power.
23. Explain how controlling access to education can serve as a rent-generating mechanism. Give examples.
24. Describe the costs and benefits of a rent-generating structure like apartheid.
25. Explain how and why non-violent and/or violent resistance to a rent-generating power structure can possibly lead those who hold power to negotiate. Give examples.

9.3 MARKET FAILURE

1. Describe the phenomenon called market failure.
2. Describe a public good. Give an example.
3. Explain why a public park is not a pure public good.
4. Explain why national defense in often cited as a good example of a pure public good.
5. Describe the free rider problem. Explain why it occurs.
6. Explain why public television and public radio suffer from the free rider problem.
7. Explain the role of property rights in a liberal, market society.
8. Describe an externality. Identify the general cause of externalities. Identify the "missing signal," the absence of which allows externalities to occur.
9. Contrast positive and negative externalities. Give an example of each.
10. Explain why pollution is often associated with the concept of negative externality.
11. Demonstrate with an example how an externality can be positive and negative at the same time in the same place.
12. Using an appropriately labeled graph, represent the case of a positive externality. Interpret your graph. Show and explain the difference between the optimal view of activity from a private versus a social perspective.
13. Using an appropriately labeled graph, represent the case of a negative externality. Interpret your graph. Show and explain the difference between the optimal view of activity from a private versus a social perspective.
14. Given an externality graph identify the exact size of the positive or negative externality it represents.
15. Using an appropriate graph, describe the efficiency and equity effects of a negative externality, of a positive externality.
16. Describe a risk externality. Give an example.

10.0 THE MICROECONOMY AND GOVERNMENT

10.1 INTRODUCTION

1. Identify the possible roles for government in the micro market economy.
2. Identify the two principles that underlie the debate about the role of government in the economy.

10.2 GOVERNMENT INTERVENTION IN THE MICROECONOMY—CASES AND ISSUES

1. Describe why government intervention in an externality problem is a real and significant challenge.
2. Identify some key questions that must be addressed relative to the case for government intervention to solve a market power problem.

10.3 GOVERNMENT INTERVENTION AND EFFICIENCY—THE PHILOSOPHICAL DEBATE

1. Comment on the statement: Some governments abrogate their responsibility by having no economic policy.
2. Identify the distinguishing characteristics of a coherent policy.
3. Identify and explain the philosophical questions you must answer for yourself before you decide for yourself what role if any government should play in this complex web we call a microeconomy.
4. Critique the following statement: All economists with their head screwed on tightly know they've got a good model, know how to use it, and basically agree on policy.
5. Explain the concept: *laissez-faire*. Identify its origin.
6. Contrast the policy perspectives of a non-interventionist and an interventionist. Identify and explain the philosophical foundation that underlies each of these positions.

10.4 DISTRIBUTIVE JUSTICE AND THE ROLE OF GOVERNMENT

1. Identify the most fundamental problem of government intervention in the name of equity.
2. Explain why achieving a consensus on a definition of equity is a significant challenge.
3. Explain why, even if a generally acceptable definition of equity is agreed upon, the government still faces the problem of implementing a policy that will realize equity.
4. Describe the objectives and the problems of a rent control policy.
5. Describe the efficiency/equity trade-off.
6. Comment on the following statement: the efficiency/equity trade-off is unavoidable.

11.0 INTRODUCTION TO MACROECONOMICS

11.1 OVERVIEW

1. If the web of connections that makes up the economy is a micro phenomenon, explain why we study the economy at a macro level. Identify and describe a non-economic example of the contrast between micro and macro perspectives and the value of each.
2. Comment on the following statement: microeconomics and macroeconomics are about different things.
3. Describe the relationship between conditions in the microeconomy and conditions in the macroeconomy.
4. Identify and describe the four basic aggregate questions our macroeconomic model is designed to explore.
5. Describe the different perspectives of an interventionist and non-interventionist with respect to macro policy. Identify the source of these different perspectives.

11.2 DEFINING TERMS

1. Define Gross Domestic Product.
2. Define each term and explain the distinction between: Full, sustainable capacity GDP and Actual GDP.
3. Identify the condition at which the microeconomy must be functioning if the macroeconomy is performing at full sustainable capacity GDP.
4. Identify how economists use comparisons of actual GDP to the full GDP. Explain with cases.
5. Cite the conditions that economists define as a recession, as a depression.
6. Explain why we need to be careful when we think of GDP as indicator of the well-being of individuals in a society or as an indicator of general social welfare. Give examples.
7. Explain the following assertion: With any aggregate variable we must be careful to look behind the aggregate number if we want to understand the underlying micro reality. Give examples.
8. Define labor force, voluntarily unemployed. Explain the relationship between the labor force and the voluntarily unemployed.
9. Distinguish employed, unemployed, unemployment rate.
10. Identify and explain the three different kinds of unemployment.
11. Distinguish the three kinds of unemployment by their respective causes.
12. Describe why job search takes time, and how this relates to frictional unemployment. Give an example.
13. Identify and explain the problem that causes structural unemployment. Give an example.
14. Explain the following statement: with frictional and structural unemployment the problem is not a lack of jobs.

15. Explain the following statement: frictional and structural unemployment are both consistent with a dynamic, growing, healthy economy. Identify how each kind of unemployment can be reduced.

16. Explain the concept: the natural rate of unemployment. Identify the relationship between the natural rate and what economists mean by full employment. Explain with an example.

17. Define demand deficient unemployment. Explain why it is referred to as one of the villains in our macro story.

18. Describe the kinds of costs demand deficient unemployment imposes on society. Give examples.

19. Identify how much (roughly) the unemployment rate in the U.S. rose from 1929 to 1933 as the Great Depression took hold of the country.

20. Define inflation, deflation.

21. Distinguish a macroeconomic change in the price level from a microeconomic relative price adjustment.

22. Identify and explain the efficiency and the equity costs that inflation or deflation impose on an economy.

23. Describe hyperinflation and how it affects an economy.

24. Define indexing. Describe how people use indexing to protect themselves from inflation. Give an example. Identify why it's called indexing.

25. Distinguish between nominal and real values. Explain why nominal economic values can mask underlying real changes across time.

26. Explain the following statement: Changes from year to year in nominal GDP may reflect changes in real production (the actual physical output), the price level, or both.

27. Explain why real values are useful for comparisons of economic data over time and nominal values are not.

28. Identify the two methods the government uses to measure the price level.

29. Explain what the CPI is and how it's determined.

30. Distinguish the scope of the CPI and the GDP Deflator.

31. Describe how to take price effects out of nominal values. Given a nominal value and the appropriate price level measure, calculate the real value.

12.0 THE BASIC MACRO MODEL

12.1 INTRODUCING OUR MACRO PICTURE

1. Draw and label our Macro Picture. Identify a point as YF. Given the AD and AS lines you draw, identify the current level of real GDP (Y*) and the current price level (P*).

2. Show cases of an AD shift and interpret what is happening to the price level and real GDP as the line shifts. Do the same for AS.

12.2 AGGREGATE DEMAND

1. Identify what is included in aggregate demand.

2. Define aggregate expenditure. Describe the relationship between aggregate expenditure and aggregate demand.

3. Identify the relationship that the AD line represents. Explain why the AD line slopes down.

4. On an appropriately labeled Macro Picture, show graphically and explain how the AD line will shift if AE increases, if AE decreases.

5. Identify the six components of AE. Explain what each is. Specify the letter used to stand for each of the components and whether these are measured in real or nominal terms.

6. Explain why in the AE equations, some variables are preceded by a plus sign (+) while others are preceded by a minus sign (-).

7. Identify what (G-T) stands for. Specify the condition of the government's budget and the government's net effect of AE when (G-T) > 0, when (G-T) < 0, or when (G-T) = 0.

8. Identify what (X-M) stands for. Specify the condition of trade and the net effect of trade on the AE when (X-M) > 0, when (X-M) < 0, or when (X-M) = 0.

9. On an appropriately labeled Macro Picture, show graphically and explain how a dramatic fall in investment (I) contributed to the Great Depression.

10. On an appropriately labeled Macro Picture, show graphically and explain how a dramatic rise in military spending by the government shifted the economy from high unemployment of the Depression to very low unemployment. *Ceteris paribus,* we would expect this shift in AD to stimulate inflation—explain why it did not do so during World War II.

12.3 AGGREGATE SUPPLY

1. Define: long run. Comment on the following statement: It takes 20 years to reach the long run.

2. Identify the condition of the microeconomy when the economy has reached the long run as we define it.

3. Identify the level of real GDP in the macroeconomy when the long run condition has been reached.

4. On an appropriately labeled Macro Picture, show graphically and explain the position of the LAS.

5. Define: very long run. Identify changes that can occur in the very long run that shift LAS. Give examples. Show how growth in capacity is represented in our Macro Picture.

6. Define: short run. Identify the variables that are constant in the short run.

7. On an appropriately labeled Macro Picture, show graphically and explain the shape of the short run aggregate supply (AS) line. Do this by interpreting movement along the line from segment to segment.

8. Describe the issues surrounding the l segment of our AS line that are central to the larger debates about macro policy. Explain why these issues are so important for this policy debate.

9. Explain what "to heat up" means in the macroeconomy and explain what causes this to occur.

10. Describe what the AS line represents.

11. Identify what is assumed constant along a given AS line.

12. Identify the shift variables with respect to the AS line.

12.4 COMBINING AD, LAS, AND AS

1. On an appropriately labeled Macro Picture, show graphically and explain the case of increasing unemployment due to falling aggregate demand.

2. On an appropriately labeled Macro Picture, show graphically and explain the case of falling unemployment and falling price level as AS shifts down due to falling factor prices.

3. On an appropriately labeled Macro Picture, show graphically and explain the case of increasing unemployment and increasing price level as AS shifts up due to rising factor prices.

4. On an appropriately labeled Macro Picture, show graphically and explain the case of falling unemployment and rising price level due to increasing AD.

5. Define: tight labor market. Describe how such a labor market condition affects the negotiating position of workers. Identify which workers may not enjoy this good negotiating position.

6. Define: wage-price spiral.

7. Describe the dynamic through which a tight labor market might give rise to a wage-price spiral.

8. Explain why workers ask for indexed wages in the face of a wage-price spiral. Describe the effect of such indexing on the spiral.

13.0 Aggregate Demand

13.1 CONSUMPTION

1. Identify the basis on which the average individual determines her level of consumption.
2. Explain the concept of "smoothing out" consumption over time.
3. Define: permanent income. Describe the relationship between permanent income and consumption.
4. Describe personal financial planning.
5. Identify the source of aggregate income in the economy and how we measure it in our model.
6. Explain the "b(P*Y)" in the consumption equation.
7. Define: autonomous consumption. Give examples.
8. Write out and explain the consumption function.
9. Explain how consumer confidence affects the aggregate level of consumption.

13.2 INVESTMENT

1. Identify the market in which the level of investment is determined.
2. Explain why people go to the long term capital market for funds.
3. Describe what the long term capital market does.
4. Define: financial capital. Distinguish financial capital from real, production capital.
5. Explain why financial capital is often referred to as liquidity.
6. Describe the role of financial intermediaries in the capital market. Identify some financial institutions that serve as financial intermediaries.
7. Explain why the market in which financial capital is exchanged for real investments is the *long term* capital market.
8. Draw and label a long term capital market picture. Explain each axis.
9. On an appropriately labeled capital market picture, draw the supply line.
10. Explain why the long term capital supply line slopes up.
11. On an appropriately labeled capital market picture, draw the demand line.
12. Explain why the long term capital demand line slopes down.
13. Explain the role of expectations in the long term capital demand.
14. Define: expected rate of return. Give an example.
15. Explain the following statement: the interest rate is the price of liquidity.
16. Describe the relationship that must exist between the expected rate of return and the interest rate for an investment to make sense. Explain.
17. *Ceteris paribus,* show how a specified shift of either supply or demand in the long term capital market changes the level of investment. Then show in our Macro Picture how this change in investment affects the aggregate economy.
18. Describe how perceptions of risk of default affect interest rates.
19. Describe the relationship between short term interest rates and long term interest rates.
20. Identify the premiums that are added on to the short rate line to establish long rates. Explain each premium.
21. Identify the three factors that determine the level of long term capital supply.
22. *Ceteris paribus,* describe how a specified change in the short rate capital supply and/or inflationary expectations will shift the long term capital supply line.

23. On an appropriately labeled capital market picture, show how entry into a country's capital market will shift the capital supply line.

24. On an appropriately labeled capital market picture, show how exit from a country's capital market will shift the capital supply line.

25. Explain the relationship between domestic wealth accumulation and entry or exit into a nation's capital market. Describe examples.

26. Define: international capital flows.

27. Explain the relationship between international capital flows and entry or exit into a nation's capital market. Describe examples.

28. Explain why international capital flows are often the most volatile source of entry or exit.

29. Explain why international capital flows are playing a bigger and bigger role in the economies of individual nations.

30. Describe the conditions that, *ceteris paribus,* lead to flows of international capital into a country. Give examples.

31. Describe the conditions that, *ceteris paribus,* lead to flows of international capital out of a country. Give examples.

32. Explain the concept of foreign direct investment. Give an example.

33. On appropriately labeled graphs, *ceteris paribus,* show how an international capital flow into a country affects that country's capital market and in turn its macroeconomy.

34. On appropriately labeled graphs, *ceteris paribus,* show how an international capital flow out of a country affects that country's capital market and in turn its macroeconomy.

35. Explain the effect of expectations on capital market demand.

36. On an appropriately labeled graph, *ceteris paribus,* show how increasingly positive expectations shift the capital market demand line. Then explain and show on an appropriately labeled Macro Picture how this change in expectations in the capital market affects the macroeconomy.

37. On an appropriately labeled graph, *ceteris paribus,* show how increasingly negative expectations shift the capital market demand line. Then explain and show on an appropriately labeled Macro Picture how this change in expectations in the capital market affects the macroeconomy.

38. Explain and show graphically how achieving peace in previously a war-torn nation can, *ceteris paribus,* increase investment and improve macroeconomic conditions.

39. Explain and show graphically how the depression of the Great Depression contributed to the depths the U.S. economy sank into.

13.3 THE TRADE BALANCE

1. Explain why international trade exists.

2. Identify the condition that makes analyzing international trade between France and Germany especially easy.

3. Explain why most international trade requires exchange of currencies.

4. Comment on the following statement: I bought a piece of art from Mexico for dollars right here in town, so that international trade did not require any exchange of currency.

5. Identify the market in which nations' currencies are exchanged.

6. Draw and label a euro/dollar foreign exchange market in which the euro is a commodity priced in dollars.

7. Explain what it means for a currency's value to be allowed to "float" in the foreign exchange market.

8. Explain the process that will unfold in a foreign exchange market when a currency is allowed to float, and identify the condition the market will reach through that process.

9. Suppose the demand for dollars by folks holding euros expands. Show what this would look like on an appropriately labeled graph in which dollars are the commodity. Show what this would look like on an appropriately labeled graph in which euros are the commodity.

10. Describe the relationship between the two exchange rates: euros/dollar and dollars/euro.

11. Given the euros/dollar exchange rate, identify the dollars/euro exchange rate.

12. Describe what it means for a currency to get weaker or to get stronger. Give an example.

13. Critique the following assertion: Strong currencies are good and weak currencies are bad.

14. *Ceteris paribus,* using all appropriate graphs (appropriately labeled), show and explain how a shift out in the demand for financial capital in the United States affects U.S. interest rates, and (assuming some of the increased quantity supplied comes from overseas) how this in turn affects the dollar exchange rate, the trade balance, the aggregate demand and the macroeconomy. *Ceteris paribus,* do the same for a case of falling demand for financial capital.

15. *Ceteris paribus,* tell the same stories about the U.S. economy as described in Objective 14, but let the shift in demand for financial capital be in the Japanese capital market.

16. Describe and explain the market forces that, under normal circumstances, would slow down the outward flow of financial capital and ultimately stop it before it became a hemorrhage?

17. Describe a global financial panic. Explain the underlying conditions and kinds of events that can lead to such a panic. Describe an example.

13.4 THE GOVERNMENT'S BUDGET POSITION

1. Identify the conditions that determine the government's budget position.

2. Describe how the U.S. budget is determined.

3. Identify and explain how parties that are not officially part of the budget position determination try to influence the budget process.

4. Explain how unfolding events can dramatically shape budget decisions. Give an example.

14.0 AGGREGATE SUPPLY AND THE MICRO FOUNDATIONS OF MACRO

14.1 SOURCES OF AGGREGATE SUPPLY SHIFTS

1. Identify the source of shifts in the short run aggregate supply line.

2. Give an example of an event that would shift AS. Describe the event and, using an appropriately labeled Macro Picture, show and explain how the event you've described would affect the macroeconomy.

14.2 TRANSISTION TO POLICY

1. Using appropriately labeled Macro Pictures, show and explain two kinds of macro shocks that can lead to unemployment.

2. Identify the micro conditions that ensure that the macroeconomy will move back to full employment.

3. Identify the micro conditions under which the macroeconomy can get stuck in a less than full employment position.

15.0 POLICY: THE PROMISE AND THE PROBLEMS

15.1 BACKGROUND TO POLICY DEBATE, THE MICRO/MACRO CONNECTION

1. Using appropriately labeled Macro Picture and micro picture, show and explain the micro condition that must exist when there is demand deficient unemployment in the macroeconomy.
2. Using appropriately labeled Macro Picture and micro picture, show and explain how under our nice assumptions micro factor market adjustments eliminate macro demand deficient unemployment.
3. Comment on the following assertion: Under our nice assumptions micro adjustments bring the macroeconomy to full employment and everyone is better off.
4. Using appropriately labeled Macro Picture and micro picture, show and explain the micro condition that must exist when there is inflationary pressure in the macro-economy.
5. Using appropriately labeled Macro Picture and micro picture, show and explain how under our nice assumptions micro factor market adjustments eliminate macro inflationary pressure.
6. Explain the following assertion: In the terms of our story, the quality of the invisible hand is analogous to how realistic our nice assumptions are.
7. Describe and explain the possible macro consequences if the nice micro assumptions are strong assumptions.
8. Describe and explain the polar case positions in the debate over government economic policy.

15.2 THE PROMISE AND THE PROBLEMS

1. Describe most economists image of the ideal long run and very long run conditions in the macroeconomy. Identify the micro issue that is not resolved even if this macro ideal is achieved.
2. Describe how most economists envisioned macro shocks until the 1970s. Identify the assumptions that underlay this view.
3. On an appropriately labeled graph, draw the Phillips curve. Explain what it represents.
4. On an appropriately labeled graph, describe and explain the conditions that give rise to a wage-price spiral.
5. On an appropriately labeled graph, describe and explain the conditions that give rise to stagflation.
6. Identify the three basic dimensions of macro policy.
7. Identify the fundamental, philosophical difference of opinion that lies at the heart of the macro policy debate.

16.0 MONETARY POLICY

16.1 THE INSTITUTIONAL CONTEXT

1. Define: monetary policy.
2. Identify the institution that manages monetary policy in most countries.
3. Identify the institution that manages monetary policy in the United States.
4. Describe the institutional position of the Fed in the U.S. government.
5. Describe the appointment process of members of the Fed. Specify the number of members on the Federal Reserve Board and the term length of a member of the Fed and of its Chair.
6. Identify the membership of the Federal Open Market Committee.
7. Distinguish the Fed from the U.S. Treasury Department.

8. Describe how the Treasury Department gets the funds to pay the government's bills if the government's tax revenues are not sufficient to pay those bills.

9. Explain the relationship between the price of a treasury bond and the interest rate received by the owner of that bond.

10. Describe the financial system. Explain the role of financial intermediaries in the financial system.

11. Give an example of a financial intermediary. Explain how financial intermediaries make a return from the business they do, and identify the size of that return if perfect competition prevails.

12. Define: asset, liability, portfolio. Explain the relationship of assets and liabilities in a portfolio.

13. Define: liquid assets. Give and explain an example of a liquid asset. Give and explain an example of an illiquid asset.

14. Define reserves.

15. Explain why financial institutions need to hold some of their assets in a liquid form.

16. Define: full reserves.

17. Explain why a financial institution does not want to hold full reserves.

18. Define: fractional reserve system.

19. Describe the level of reserves a prudent bank would hold in a fractional reserve system.

20. Explain the benefits a fractional reserve system brings to an economy.

21. Identify the down side of a fractional reserve system.

22. Describe how a run on the financial system can get started and how such a run can bring down even the most prudent banks in the system.

23. Explain the purpose of reserve requirements.

24. Identify the tools the Fed uses to try to keep the U.S. financial system responsible.

25. Explain the role of the Federal Deposit Insurance Corporation in maintaining stability in the financial system.

16.2 THE IMPLEMENTATION OF MONETARY POLICY

1. Describe what the Fed does when it engages in open market operations.

2. Explain the relationship between Fed open market operations and the level of reserves in the financial system.

3. Define: excess reserves.

4. Describe how the Fed can create excess reserves in the financial system.

5. Describe the response of banks that find themselves holding excess reserves.

6. Identify the market through which banks exchange reserves. Identify the term (length of time) of the loans made in this market.

7. Identify the term (title) used for the rate paid for reserves in the Federal Funds Market.

8. Identify the Fed Open Market activity that lowers the Fed Funds Rate. Describe the steps in the events that start with Fed Open Market activity and result in a lower Fed Funds Rate.

9. Identify the Fed Open Market activity that raises the Fed Funds Rate. Describe the steps in the events that start with Fed Open Market activity and result in a higher Fed Funds Rate.

10. Describe the relationship between Fed Open Market Operations and the amount of liquidity in the financial system.

11. Describe the Fed's Discount Rate. Identify the most common reason for the Fed changing the Discount Rate.

16.3 POLICY ISSUES—FINANCIAL CRISES

1. Describe the relationship between real values and asset values in a speculative bubble.

2. Explain how a speculative bubble gets started and expands.

3. Explain the source of and the role of speculation in a speculative bubble.

4. Describe how a speculative bubble might burst.

5. Explain how the bursting of a speculative bubble can have affects on the real economy.

6. Describe and explain the role the Fed can play in keeping a bursting speculative bubble from becoming a real economic disaster.

7. Explain the interventionist and the non-interventionist positions with respect to Fed intervention in a financial crisis.

16.4 POLICY ISSUES—AGGREGATE DEMAND MANAGEMENT

1. Describe the relationship between the Fed's Open Market Operations, the Fed Funds Rate, and the long term capital supply line.

2. Using an appropriately labeled graph show the macroeconomy in the less than full employment condition. Show and explain, using all relevant graphs (appropriately labeled), how the Fed can intervene in the economy to stimulate the economy and reduce unemployment. Include every step in the logic from the initial Fed policy to the final employment effect.

3. Identify the leap of faith that a non-interventionist sees in an interventionist attempt to use Fed policy to bring the economy to full employment.

4. Using an appropriately labeled graph show the macroeconomy in the less than full employment condition. Show and explain, using all relevant graphs (appropriately labeled), how a non-interventionist argues that intervention is not necessary to fix a less than full employment problem in the economy.

5. Identify and explain the problems that a non-interventionist claims can be caused by an interventionist monetary policy. Identify and explain the interventionist reply.

6. Explain the problem with the natural rate that makes calibrating any interventionist policy difficult.

7. Explain how it is plausible that two economists could look at the same reported unemployment rate and argue respectively that the economy needs more stimulus and that the economy is already over stimulated.

8. Explain why the shape of the AS line matters in the interventionist versus non-interventionist debate.

9. Describe the role that different assumptions about the structure of the economy play in the interventionist versus non-interventionist debate.

10. Explain why it is virtually impossible to resolve different assumptions about the structure of the economy empirically.

11. Identify the different structural assumptions often made by interventionists versus non-interventionists with respect to the natural rate and the shape of the AS line.

12. Explain why, even if we know the natural rate and the shape of the AS line, interventionist policy would still be very tricky business.

13. Using appropriate graphs describe and explain how, *ceteris paribus*, a Fed intervention to stimulate the economy can, *ceteris paribus*, affect the trade balance and in turn Aggregate Demand and the entire macroeconomy. Include every step in the logic from the initial Fed policy to the final full macro effect.

14. Using appropriate graphs describe and explain how, *ceteris paribus*, a Fed intervention to contract the economy can, *ceteris paribus*, affect the trade balance and in turn Aggregate Demand and the entire macro economy. Include every step in the logic from the initial Fed policy to the final full macro effect.

15. Identify the policy the Fed would pursue to stimulate the economy. Explain how such a policy can in fact lead to a "double stimulus."

16. Describe the danger if the Fed overstimulates the macroeconomy.

17. Explain the problem with imposing a wage-price freeze on a market economy.

18. Describe how the Paul Volcker-led Fed squeezed inflation out of the economy. Using appropriate graphs, explain the process of the policy from the Fed tools used through the markets it affected to its consequences for the macroeconomy.

19. Explain what a gold standard is and why some non-interventionists believe the country should go to a gold standard. Explain the non-interventionist's criticism of a gold standard.

20. Identify the ultimate source of the debate between the interventionists and the non-interventionists. Explain.

17.0 FISCAL POLICY

17.1 THE INSTITUTIONAL CONTEXT

1. Define: fiscal policy.
2. Describe a government fiscal policy that is stimulative.
3. Describe a government fiscal policy that is contractionary.
4. Explain how, *ceteris paribus*, a budget surplus affects the macroeconomy.
5. Explain how, *ceteris paribus*, a budget deficit affects the macroeconomy.
6. Explain the role of Treasury bonds in the government budget process.
7. Explain what a government default is and describe the impact of such a default.
8. Describe the factors that can affect the relationship between a government and the international capital markets.

17.2 THE IMPLEMENTATION OF FISCAL POLICY

1. Show on our Macro Picture how, *ceteris paribus*, a stimulative fiscal policy affects the macroeconomy.
2. Show on our Macro Picture how, *ceteris paribus*, a contractionary fiscal policy affects the macroeconomy.
3. *Ceteris paribus*, identify and explain how the government budget would have to be changed in order to stimulate the economy.
4. *Ceteris paribus*, identify and explain how the government budget would have to be changed in order to contract the economy.
5. Explain and show graphically how a stimulative fiscal policy can generate inflation. Identify what this possibility depends on.
6. Identify where the government gets the funds to finance a deficit.
7. Show graphically and explain the effect of increasing government borrowing in the capital market, noting the effect on the interest rate and the total funds exchanged.
8. Using appropriate graphs describe and explain how, *ceteris paribus*, increasing government borrowing affects private investors' participation in the capital market and the level of private investment.
9. Define the crowding-out effect.
10. Identify the factor that determines the size of the crowding-out effect. Explain.
11. Using appropriate graphs describe and explain how, *ceteris paribus*, government activity in the capital market can affect the supply side of that market.
12. Using appropriate graphs describe and explain how, *ceteris paribus*, government activity in the capital market can affect the exchange rate and the trade balance.
13. Explain how the Fed can monetize the deficit and how that eliminates the problems of crowding out.
14. Explain the dangers of the Fed monetizing the deficit.
15. Using appropriate graphs describe and explain, *ceteris paribus*, the non-interventionist's argument that interventionist fiscal policy is not necessary and is fruitless and distorting.

16. Identify and explain the constitutional amendment that some non-interventionists advocate. Explain the non-interventionist response to this proposed amendment.

17. Explain the interventionists' argument for their position and their case against the non-interventionists' position.

18. Identify and explain the two points about this debate over government economic policy that we must always keep in mind.

19. Identify what interventionists and non-interventionists share in common as they make their cases and explain the source of the differences in their cases.

18.0 TRADE POLICY

18.1 TRADE POLICY TOOLS

1. Explain why global economic analysis is fundamentally different from national economic analysis.

2. Define: open economy macro.

3. Identify the condition that makes trade policy even more complex than monetary or fiscal policy.

4. Explain the statement: Global economic relations are a strategic game among nations.

5. Describe how adopting different domestic policies regarding acceptable production conditions can create advantages or disadvantages in the global market place. Give examples.

6. Describe ways in which a nation can generate a positive trade balance through developing a competitive edge.

7. Describe ways in which a nation can generate a positive trade balance through developing red tape and many regulations.

8. Describe two ways in which a nation can generate a positive trade balance by manipulating the exchange rate for its currency. Explain the limitations and problems with each.

9. Describe how a nation can use a quota as a trade policy tool. Explain the risk of such a policy approach.

10. Describe how a nation can use a tariff as a trade policy tool. Explain the risk of such a policy approach.

11. Explain how a tariff war gets started. Identify who usually wins a tariff war.

18.2 TRADE POLICY ISSUES

1. Identify the period when the first western writings specifically economics and economic policy began to emerge. Explain the events that stimulated this writing and the focal point of these writings.

2. Explain the concept of a zero sum game.

3. Explain the Mercantilist view of how to expand the wealth of a nation.

4. Identify the kinds of policies prescribed by Mercantilism, and explain the logic of these policies.

5. Explain the concept of a positive sum game.

6. Describe the constructive possibilities for liberal society describe by Adam Smith.

7. Explain the following assertion: The promise of a free and open global economy is essentially a generalization of the desirable outcome that we learned about in micro.

8. Identify and explain the problems of a global liberal system.

9. Describe why governments often find Mercantilist policies politically attractive, and why such policies can lead to degenerative global relations.

10. Explain protectionism and briefly describe the political dynamics that lead to such policies.

11. Explain how a trade war can hurt all participants.

12. Paraphrase Keynes' concerns regarding Mercantilist trade wars and his prescription for avoiding the disaster such policies can generate.

13. Describe the challenges facing emerging nations in the global economy. Explain some of the strategies such nations pursue to capture a global market share for their products.

14. Describe the special vulnerability of emerging nations to international capital flows.

15. Describe the role of the IMF in the global economy and how the IMF is sometimes seen by countries in desperate need of assistance.

16. Describe the WTO including: What it is, its objectives, its principles, the case for its existence.

17. Identify and explain an inherent weakness in any multilateral trade organization or agreement, such as the WTO.

18. Explain the benefits and the cost of going to a common currency like the euro.

19.0 CONCLUSION

19.1 SOME HISTORICAL BACKGROUND ON THE INTERVENTIONIST VERSUS NON-INTERVENTIONIST DEBATE

1. Explain Say's Law. Describe how Say's Law relates to the interventionist versus non-interventionist debate.

2. Describe the interventionist *v.* non-interventionist debate between Ricardo and Malthus: Explain Ricardo's assumption, logic, and policy. Describe Malthus' critique of Ricardo's position.

3. Explain the impact of Ricardo's *Principles of Political Economy* on the interventionist *v.* non-interventionist debate in mainstream economic theory. Describe Keynes' response to this impact.

4. Identify where Keynes saw strength and where he believed he saw a flaw in the mainstream, "orthodox" economic theory he inherited. Explain his argument that the theory he inherited only captures a special case that does not exist in reality.

19.2 WHY CAN'T ECONOMISTS RESOLVE THIS DEBATE ONCE AND FOR ALL: THE PROBLEM OF TESTING

1. Explain why there are multiple views of the economic process within neoclassical, mainstream economics and why no one view is able to prevail.

2. Explain why a theoretical model must be operationalized in order for it to be tested.

3. Identify the problems one faces when *theoretical definitions* are transformed into *technical definitions*. Give examples. Explain how this problem contributes to the inability of scientists to falsify models and thus makes it possible for competing models to coexist.

4. Identify the technical criteria for being in the labor force. Cite and explain a problem with these criteria. Identify the technical criteria for being counted as employed. Cite and explain a problem with these criteria. Define *discouraged worker, underemployed*.

5. Identify the four criteria for inclusion in the technical definition of the GDP. Explain the rationale for each.

6. Identify the problem with the GDP technical definition criterion that production must be exchanged for money. Give an example. Explain the concept of an *underground economy*.

7. Identify an exception the government makes to its own criteria for the technical definition of GDP. Explain why the exception is made.

8. Explain what a proxy variable is and why they are used. Describe the problem with using proxies. Give an example.

9. Explain how a model is specified in order for regression analysis to be performed. Explain the importance of the "sign" and "significance" results of a regression analysis.

10. Describe two ways that one can manipulate the specification of the model in order to achieve desired sign and significance results. Explain the terms: cooking the data or data mining.

11. Explain how this ability to manipulate the test contributes to the inability of scientists to falsify models and thus makes it possible for competing models to coexist.

19.3 CONCLUSION

1. Explain why the rationality of individuals serves as the source of both virtue and vice in competition.

2. Given the kind of society you desire (in terms of equity and efficiency), describe what you believe the role of government should be in achieving that society.

INDEX